Globalisation, Company Strategies and Quality of Working Life in Europe

WORK – TECHNOLOGY – ORGANIZATION – SOCIETY

Edited by Wiking Ehlert, György Széll and Heinz Sünker

ARBEIT – TECHNIK – ORGANISATION – SOZIALES

Herausgegeben von Wiking Ehlert, György Széll und Heinz Sünker

Band 25

PETER LANG

Frankfurt am Main · Berlin · Bern · Bruxelles · New York · Oxford · Wien

Francesco Garibaldo
Volker Telljohann
(eds.)

Globalisation, Company Strategies and Quality of Working Life in Europe

PETER LANG
Europäischer Verlag der Wissenschaften

Bibliographic Information published by Die Deutsche Bibliothek
Die Deutsche Bibliothek lists this publication in the Deutsche Nationalbibliografie; detailed bibliographic data is available in the internet at <http://dnb.ddb.de>.

This book has been produced with financial support
of the European Commission,
Directorate General Employment and Social Affairs.

ISSN 0946-8811
ISBN 3-631-52519-2
US-ISBN 0-8204-7300-6

www.peterlang.de

Table of Contents

Foreword

FRANCESCO GARIBALDO
VOLKER TELLJOHANN

This volume assembles the most relevant contributions presented at the European Conference on 'Globalisation, Company Strategies and Quality of Working Life in Europe' which was held from 19th to 21st June 2003 in Bologna.

The opening of the Conference was dedicated to a general introduction to the theme globalisation, company strategies and quality of working life in Europe. The core of the Conference was made up of ten working sessions organised on two tracks: the sectoral dimension and the horizontal or cross-industry dimension. Each one of the sessions was dedicated to sectoral experiences or to specific thematic aspects in the field of the quality of working life. The following part of the Conference regarded a round-table discussion on the challenges for social actors in the process of structural changes.

The Conference speakers represented 10 EU Member States and came from various academic fields, such as the social sciences, economics, labour law, engineering, political sciences, psychology and educational sciences.

From a scientific point of view the main objective of the Conference was to examine, firstly, whether there is a relationship between company strategies and the quality of working life, and if so, how this relationship can be characterised, and, secondly, whether there is empirical evidence to support a distinction between a 'high road' and a 'low road' approach to innovation and competition. In this context a number of questions concerning the impact of globalisation were raised, including its contribution to the worsening or improvement of the quality of working life.

On the basis of the papers presented in the two tracks, two main questions for future research were proposed: First, to examine the diffusion of groupwork, not in the sense of a special organisational redesign instrument but as an exemplar of the transformation of work (high road, post-Fordism and so on), and what this transformation of work means for workers. Second, to examine the conditions which can help enforce a high-road development, that is the regulations and institutional conditions, including

trade union strategies, which help to frame competition and innovation in a different, notably high-road direction.
But the Conference had also a concrete outcome. It regards the setting up of an EU-based network of experts and institutions dealing with work and labour research. After having founded the international network of intermediate institutions dealing with work and labour research (RLDWL – Regional and Local Development of Work and Labour) in 1999 and after having already held three international congresses[1], the objective of the European members of the RLDWL-network was to set up an EU-based section of the network in order to be able to more efficiently coordinate exchanges and cooperation between the EU-based members of the network. Therefore, the final session of the Conference was dedicated to setting up RLDWL Europe. During this session a working programme for RLDWL Europe was adopted which is based on four main issues:

1. *Direct and indirect participation.* In regard to this subject it has been proposed to adopt a research method based on case studies right to find out some empirical evidences at the European level. There is also the intention to involve the candidate countries in this typology of research.

2. *Government and Governance.* The research projects of the European Network may focus on the importance of a clear definition of what falls under the competence of government and under the competence of governance also trough a redefinition of the concept of networking: it should be an opportunity for everybody and not only for few actors endowed with power. A comparison at the European level may be a fit research method.

3. *Learning Organisations.* In a dynamic context it is necessary to develop a common learning framework for all the organisations. The best manner to pursue this aim it could be the analysis of some cases at the European level.

4. *The new role of the trade unions and the employer associations at the national and at the European level.* With regard to this area it was

---

[1] The three international Congresses that have been held by RLDWL are the following:
- Ravello (I), 1999, *The role of intermediate institutions for social stability and democracy*
- Rio de Janeiro, 2000, *Regional and local development of work and labour – the role of intermediate institutions*
- Osnabrück, 2002, *Labour, globalisation and the new economy*

proposed to use some instruments of qualitative research: discussion groups, scenario building and research conferences.

Furthermore, it was decided that the network should foster the

- gathering and dissemination of information on ongoing developments and initiatives in the different countries and sectors;
- exchange of researchers, especially junior researchers to gain a better practical knowledge in other countries;
- development of common research and consulting initiatives.

The Conference as well as this volume were made possible by the financial support of the European Commission, Employment and Social Affairs DG. Furthermore, we wish to thank the Hans-Böckler-Foundation and the European Trade Union Institute which have supported the RLDWL-network from the very beginning.
For putting this book into good shape we are indebted to Claudia Maestrali, Sabine Müller and Alberto Pagliarini from the Institute for Labour Foundation in Bologna.

Bologna, January 2004

Francesco Garibaldo *Volker Telljohann*

Introduction

VOLKER TELLJOHANN

Today, from the point of view of the European Social Model, one of the most important challenges regards how to manage globalisation and, in this context, how to guarantee a policy approach capable of reinforcing economic development as well as employment and social policy. One answer seems to lie in the role of *quality*. Quality is considered one of the key elements in the European Social Model. It links the two basic objectives of competitiveness and cohesion and so quality represents a driving force for both economic development and social inclusion. The mutually reinforcing interaction between economic, employment and social policies is reinforced by the Lisbon Strategy. As quality is considered of crucial importance for competitiveness as well as for cohesion, the goal of moving towards full employment has to be pursued by trying to create not just more jobs but also better ones.

The Nice and Stockholm European Councils have emphasised the importance of quality in work referring in particular to working conditions, health and safety, pay, gender equality, a balance between flexibility and job security, employee involvement and good and flexible work organisation allowing a better reconciliation between working and personal life. The Laeken Summit drew attention to the close links between quality of work and productivity. Thus, in the present context of worldwide competition, Europe needs to focus on the quality of jobs in order to create a competitive advantage in regard to its competitors. As a consequence, one of the challenges of the European debate is to reach a definition of what actually constitutes work and employment quality and of what could be adequate job quality indicators.

In June 2001 the European Commission presented a Communication on employment quality which underlined the role of the European Social Model and the modernisation of social policies in times of rapid social, economic and industrial change with a view to utilising human resource capacities most effectively. As there is evidence that the continuous upgrading of quality in work contributes to improvements in economic performance, productivity and dynamism, the aim has be to incorporate quality in employment and social policies. In December 2001 the Laeken European Summit adopted an initial list of key indicators and contextual indicators.

According to the Communication, *quality of work* is a multi-dimensional concept which includes a) characteristics related to the wider work environment as well as to specific conditions of job performance; b) employee characteristics and the matching of employee characteristics and job requirements; c) job satisfaction.

Quality in work, however, does not merely depend on employment and social policies. In the end, the crucial question concerns the characteristics of company strategies. There is indeed a growing body of empirical evidence that employment levels are strongly depend on company strategies and the forms of work organisation which result from the respective company strategies.

Starting from the early 1990s, the connection between new forms of work organisation, productivity, innovation and employment has earned itself growing recognition in the European Union. Indeed, the aim of connecting work organisation, innovation and employment provides a defining European approach to competitiveness. The documents of the European Commission, such as the EU Green Paper on "Partnership for a New Organisation of Work" underline the role of work organisation for the improvement of competitiveness and the increase in employment levels. At the same time, a better work organisation can also offer a positive contribution to the quality of working life.

As has been shown by various research works there is empirical evidence that the quality of organisational change depends on the chosen innovation trajectory. The different trajectories may indeed have contradictory effects in regard to employment and the quality of working life. While a mere cut in costs and innovative strategies that only regard the process generally determine a decrease in the demand for labour, the latter can instead be increased by creating new products, exploring new sectors and developing new markets. That means that the company's innovation strategy and its work organisation are of crucial importance in order to achieve high performance and competitiveness.

It is evident that a pathway based on the development of new products and markets is closely related to a considerable investment in human resources. Continuous training processes are needed that cannot have limited objectives but must have as their aim a broadly-based qualification of the workforce, which includes social and methodological competencies, and a general knowledge of technology and work organisation. Broad-based training constitutes a prerequisite for working conditions that better meet human desires and needs. Obviously, this kind of qualification puts the worker in a more favourable position on the external job market.

The argument thus goes that the quality of working life depends, amongst other things, on company strategy and its consequent positioning on the market. The basic hypothesis consists of the argument that there exists a dynamic link between company strategies and the quality of working life that can be analysed according to a classificatory scheme that ranges from a minimum configuration associating pure cost-based competition with a very low quality of working life, to a positive configuration associating company strategies based on quality and knowledge with a high quality of working life. That means that, as a general rule, we can distinguish between two kinds of company, that is, the ones pursuing the *high road*, and those pursuing the *low road* towards innovation.

The idea of these two business models is clearly just an abstract notion that should be considered as a mere artifice constructed for heuristic purposes. Indeed, each company, from many points of view, represents a mix of these two ideal-types, but it is in any case possible to identify a prevalent tendency, a guiding value, which also has a political and cultural dimension, which the individual decisions and the specific instrumental rationales are submitted to.

Finally, it is obvious that social partners and their organisations play an important role with regard to the dissemination of models based on job quality. Consequently, the tradition and culture of industrial relations has a major influence on the application of quality-centred models. In order to improve the dissemination there is a growing need to develop partnership and cooperative practices even further.

Objectives

This publication should contribute to the discussion on the need for a social dimension to globalisation and what can be the European model's specific response to the challenges and consequences of globalisation. In particular, this volume focuses on the role of the quality of work as the European strategic response to the challenges deriving from globalised competition. It will be shown how an increase in the quality in work can contribute to increasing productivity, improving living standards and fostering sustainable economic growth.

One important theme of this publication regards the question of whether there is any relationship between company strategy and the quality of working life and, if so, what kind of relationship this actually is.
By presenting and discussing relevant experiences in the field of the quality of working life which have been made in the different Member States and in the different sectors we will attempt to identify good practices and define those characteristics which constitute job and employment quality. The contributions are structured in such a way as to allow us to examine elements of quality of work concerning job characteristics in a more narrow sense, especially including objective and intrinsic characteristics, on the one hand, and the work and wider labour market context, including such topics as gender equality, health and safety, flexibility and security, social dialogue and worker participation, on the other. On these grounds this book tries to contribute to the definition of an analytical framework for the quality of work and the identification of possible standards and indicators. Furthermore, the discussion of these international experiences should contribute to the making of proposals with regard to coherent approaches for incorporating quality in employment and social policies.

What we Have Learnt from our Experiences

FRANCESCO GARIBALDO

Premise

The Institute for Labour Foundation (IpL) was set up in April 1998, that is five years ago, at a time when a long wave of industrial relations conflicts – the 1980s and the beginning of the 1990s – seemed to be coming to an end, paving the way for a different approach to the world of work and the industrial relations system. The Institute was founded as a kind of bet on that possibility, rather a sort of investment aimed at sustaining that opportunity and preventing the risk that this Region, and more generally Italy, should be left out of the challenge that was beginning to open up at European level. It did indeed seem as though something was changing.

Organisational Models

In relation to the organisational models, against a backdrop of the growing awareness of the structural limitations of the Taylor-Ford model, a possible pathway started to take shape for the European Union area that was not merely the slavish translation of the then-triumphant Japanese model and its American versions – so-called *lean production*.
Indeed, in 1997 the Green Book of the Commission was published, entitled *A partnership for a new organisation of work,* which you will find information on in a folder containing a review of recent studies organised by the Commission.
A few years before – during the Clinton Presidency – the Dunlop Commission had been set up, named after its Chairman, a scholar of industrial relations systems, with the ambitious objective of re-thinking the organisational models as well as the industrial relations system in the United States. The Commission started studying the European model – through research conducted with empirical evidence – with particular

attention to German as well as Scandinavian countries; the Commission organised a series of auditions with European experts, which I was invited to as well, where I found an extremely open atmosphere.

In those years some European consortia were being founded, analogous to IpL, called *Work and Technology*; the consortium produced one of the fundamental studies linked to the drafting of the Green Book; within the scope of that project a strategy was devised that juxtaposed a *high road* to competitiveness with a *low road*, which was at the basis of the first IpL programme and later referred to officially by the Commission; the document written by Peter Brödner, Paul Oehlke, Ulrich Pekruhl and myself dates back to 1999; Brödner and Pekruhl will be speaking on the 20th. The activity of the Consortium has continued through the Innoflex programme, which is drawing to a close now, coordinated by Professor Peter Totterdill, who will be speaking on the 20th, and oriented to finding a balance between the quality of working life and corporate efficiency.

As we have by now highlighted in many reports, it can actually be argued that the stereotype generally accepted by the political and institutional European and Italian systems and, for a long time, by nearly all of the international scientific community as regards the general direction being taken by the ongoing changes concerning work and organisations, can be summarised like this:

1. The old Taylor-Ford model of production and its equivalent in bureaucratic work, is believed to be finished or reduced to a marginal position. The "volatile" nature, in other words, unforeseeable and unplanned, of the markets and more in general of the socio-economic context of the working activities indeed require so many sudden changes that it is necessary that there should be an intrinsic organisational flexibility that can only spring from the mobilisation of the creative and flexible potential of human labour. This potential can only be released if the individual's *enterprise* is rewarded, that is, his or her autonomy and responsibility. On this basis, new forms of working cooperation can then be introduced.
2. The new jobs and the new ways of doing the old ones should thus be characterised by a high content and demand for knowledge. This demand cannot be satisfied by the classical sequential pattern "school-work-pension" but requires constant updating. People who are not adequately educated and do not have access to continuous phases of training and updating will be discriminated against and marginalized.

3. Intelligence will subjugate the traditional manual skills that will gradually be absorbed by machine systems driven by sophisticated software, by some "technological slaves" capable of responding to vocal commands or following unplanned behaviour oriented to a functional purpose.
4. Thus, the capacity to manipulate symbols – specifically of a logical-mathematical kind – would become the guiding value behind the new specialised laboratories: the knowledge workers, the ones who will organise and run the working processes and will constitute the new elite, based on merit and not on class or the control of capital.
5. Thus an era would begin based on an objective re-equilibrium of the power relationship between Labour and Capital, because Capital would no longer need a substantially infinitely interchangeable labour force – with the exception of a few "chiefs" or super-specialists – but a diffuse intelligence that would make the working relationship so individualised as to make the old contract and earnings systems obsolete. Thus, the prevalent forms of highly "individualised" Industrial Relations systems would predominate and even the classical instruments of the Industrial Relations system would be superseded – collective contracts, in-company union representation, etc. – by forms of individual bargaining. Indeed, the re-balancing of the power relationship between the individual worker and the company would allow collective representation and collective bargaining to be superseded, made to offset for the pre-existing imbalance of power.
6. The persistent differences between those who work would become an objective measure of the differences of capacity in terms of autonomy, creativity and autonomy.

In this perspective there appeared, as a fundamental risk for the worker's health and safety, to be an information overload that, associated with an evident intensification and extension in the use of time, would have created serious dangers to the mental and physical integrity of the new workers.

In this light one of the fundamental vehicles of innovation for Europe should have become organisational innovation combined with technological innovation[1]. There followed a renewed interest, also political

[1] European Commission, *Partnership for a New Organisation of Work. Green Paper*, European Commission, Brussels, 1997.
http://europa.eu.int/comm/employment_social/soc-dial/social/green_en.htm

and administrative, in the classical socio-technical issues concerning organisational planning[2]:

1. the redundancy of the functions instead of the parts, in other words, from complex organisations with simple jobs to simple organisations with complex jobs;[3]
2. the principle of minimum specification. The planning principle based on the critical minimum specification can be defined as the principle that identifies the minimum set of conditions necessary to create organisational units capable of being self-regulated. The optimum condition is that the affected unit should not require external activities of supervision and control, and that therefore the management function should only have a role of mediation between each unit and the whole.

Form here first a series of Community programmes, projects and indications were born, followed by the European Union, later. This set of measures is oriented towards two basic strands: training and public schemes supporting organisational innovation.

These initiatives have by now got more than a decade of testing behind them, even if with incessant changes in methods and approach; for example, from the anthropocentric systems of production – as models and criteria of organisational planning – to the partnership for a new work organisation more oriented to social dialogue.

What appears to be relevant to our point of view is the fact that this supply policy – more or less intellectually and technically complex and sophisticated – has not had "any takers", excepting the important exceptions linked to the different countries, the different economic sectors, the different strategic market positioning of the companies and, why not, the cultural relationship diversities with the issues of power and work. Taken and valorised as exceptions, there remains the fact, by now documented also in recent reports of the Directorate General of the Commission[4], that this is not the dominant trend.

---

[2] Herbst, B. P. G., *Socio-Technical Design: Strategies in Multidisciplinary Research*, London, Tavistock Publications, 1974.

[3] Dankbaar B., Ditter L., Hertog F., *From complex organisations with simple jobs to simple organisations with complex jobs*, in "Human Relations", vol. 50, no. 5, 1997.

[4] European Commission, Employment and social affairs, unit D3, *New Forms of Work Organisation: The Obstacles to Wider Diffusion. Final Report and Annex (Case Studies)*, Business Decisions Limited, 2002.

Ennals R., *The existing Policy Framework to Promote Modernisation of Work: its Weaknesses*, Kingston, Centre for Working Life Research, 2002.

The underlying culture that has nurtured Taylorism-Fordism is still alive and kicking and is actually experiencing a new lease of life even in sectors where it has never before penetrated – such as a part of intellectual work itself – and is accompanied to new phenomena, as had been expected, of the knowledge overload. All of this is accompanied by a situation of uncertainty and fierce competition, even individual, which derives directly from the mechanisms of labour market deregulation.

What is thus created is an explosive cocktail: a cocktail that combines, from the point of view of labour organisation, the worst of the old system with the worst of the new. How could this have happened? How did the company system manage to come to terms with all the things we had listed in the premise, that is, with the evident limits of Taylorism-Fordism? And what about the unions? And the governments?

It certainly did not escape the notice of the leading actors of the day that a sort of "turbo-capitalism" as it has been called to good effect, was starting to raise its head. This had viewed the fall of the Berlin Wall in 1989 as a green light for the questioning of the juridical, cultural and political fundaments that had characterised the period 1930-1980. From the point of view of the legal culture, the bases of the so-called *Wagner Act* were being questioned, that is to say, the bases of *The National Labor Relations Act*, the law on the national Industrial Relations in the USA dating back to July 1935, which I shall come back to presently. On the cultural and political levels, the right of association itself was being questioned, that is the idea, the cultural basis and the legitimating of the German "social market capitalism", the reformism of the Roosevelt New Deal, the British Labour Party, and so on, that the relationship between the capitalist and the worker is unbalanced from the point of view of power and so the worker, through the right of association, positively re-established the relationship by creating the basis for a fairer society.

Now please allow me a brief historical digression[5]. To earn the right of association this the British union committed itself to a struggle against the 1799 *Combination Acts* which outlawed any possible union/association of

---

Totterdill P., *Developing new forms of work organisation: the role of the main actors*, Nottingham, The Work Institute, 2002.

Brödner P., Latniak E., *Source of Innovation and Competitiveness: National Programmes Supporting the Development of Work Organisation*, IAT, Gelsenkirchen, 2002.

[5] The references I have used are Webb S. and B., The History of Trade Unions, London, Longman & CO, 1911, original version 1894; Cole G. H. D, Attempts at General Union. A Study in British Trade Union History, 1818-1834, Wesport, Connecticut, Hyperion Press, 1979, original version 1939.

unskilled and skilled workers in negotiating their pay and working conditions given that such a union/association could be identified as a *combination in restraint of trade*, a limitation of commercial practice, in short, a monopolistic or oligopolistic market distortion. The struggle reached a conclusive end, at least until now, only in 1875. Indeed, if in 1825 the British parliament acknowledged the workers' right to industrial action, the situation was not resolved as some legal loopholes were devised, until 1875 when a Conservative government, after defeating a liberal Whig government that opposed it doggedly, passed a law substituting the one on the "Masters and Slaves", used to defeat that of 1825, with one called "Employers and Workers"; the two social actors, as we would say today, were conceived of as two equal parties to a private contract and there was the full recognition of collective bargaining, with all its bells and whistles, from picketing to collective action, provided it was peaceable and lawful. Thus, questioning the right to association and the need, even juridical to re-balance the power of the company with a strong collective powers on the part of the workers, questions the fundaments of industrial civilisation built up in the West between the mid-19th century and the end of the Second World War.

Turbo-capitalism and its power to avert the post-war social equilibrium were thus perfectly perceived, at the time when the Institute For Labour was set up, but there prevailed the idea that there would have been a sort of confrontation, to use an expression fashionable then, between the Emilia model and the Anglo-Saxon one, and that Europe would have chosen a variant of the Emilian model, building up an alternative pole to Anglo-Saxon capitalism and to Toyotism, appropriately blended into the *lean production* model.

Why then, between these two alternatives, has the Anglo-Saxon model prevailed unchallenged, at least as far as Southern Europe goes?

Industrial Relations Systems and Labour Law

In relation to the Industrial Relations systems, the Zanussi experience that we presented in October 1998 dates back to those years – with the participation of the company and the unions – and to one of the earliest IpL projects which we pointed to as the path to be followed, even if we suggested it should be extensively reformed, as we stated in a critical analysis of the system, which was asked of us soon afterwards by the very

Zanussi participative system itself. It is worthwhile remembering, seeing that we are living in times when memory is a neglected art, that in those days the Zanussi system was being pointed to by the whole union as an experience worth betting on and that when our study, requested both by the company and by the unions, documented the weaknesses inside the system, in substance the lack of an activity of participated planning that went beyond the mere involvement of the company and the national leaders, there appeared before us a split between those who were thinking of a *democratic reform* of the system and those who were thinking of its authoritative accentuation. Our analysis, which Volker Telljohann will talk to you about in more depth, into the relationship between direct and indirect participation and the need to achieve their equilibrium comes from far afield, from the need to reflect carefully upon the Zanussi experience.
The issue of the EWCs dates back to September 1998, a matter which we, together with the Friedrich Ebert and Hans Böckler Foundations and the CGIL, CISL, UIL of Emilia-Romagna, appraised a pioneering work started up by Volker Telljohann during a dedicated conference, work which is still in progress. It is also since then that the Institute has been studying, also at international congresses, the future of bargaining and the union, while constantly underlining the role of nationwide bargaining, as opposed to the corporate drift, and the central issue of representation. Tomorrow Professor Cella and Dr. Telljohann the day after will be analysing the Italian and European Industrial Relations scenario, while Professor Mariucci and Professor Focareta will be examining the issues of labour rights also in the light of the unmitigated deregulation of the labour market put into effect in these past few months by the present Italian government.
Also belonging to that period is the work of a group of experts, coordinated by Alain Supiot, on the future of the right to work in Europe, a study whose conclusions, issued in June 1998, were presented by us in September 1998 right here in Bologna. One of the members of that work group, Professor Mingione, will be taking the floor tomorrow morning.
I would like to quote the whole conclusion of the first chapter of that report:

> *"We can see a growing diversification within the remunerated labour contracts. An initial classification allows us to distinguish between three categories:*
>
> - *the traditional dependent workers who work on the basis of an employment contract in which subordination is essential;*

- *other contracts that envisage the realisation of a job in exchange for payment;*
- *independent entrepreneurs.*

The second category seems to be called upon to develop further, even if that development cannot yet be quantified. The spread of free collaboration contracts, at times subject to the legislation on social security, at times to labour legislation and at times to commercial law, poses a critical question for the future of labour rights.

The traditional vision has it that labour rights are only applied in those cases in which the worker works under conditions of strict subordination. However, the group of experts agreed with the orientation that reckoned it was worthwhile extending, under some circumstances, this field of application so as to include other types of labour relations. Hence, the prospect is that of a common right to work in which some sectors can instead be adapted to the diversity of the working situations (subordinate labour in the traditional sense; para-subordinate work that is economically dependent). In this perspective, however, it is worthwhile not separating the issues of labour rights from those of social security, two inseparable aspects of employment status. It is possible that the European Union will play an important role in the formulation of the fundamental rules for ensuring basic safeguards to all of the people working under conditions of economic dependence.

Generally speaking, the group of experts believes that it is worthwhile avoiding the persistence of a division between subordinate workers well protected by a labour contract and people who work under other kinds of contract that offer them lesser protection. One of the fundamental historical functions of labour law has indeed been to ensure the conditions for social cohesion. This function cannot continue to be performed if not in the extent to which labour law incorporates its evolution in the forms of contemporary society's labour organisation and does not focus solely upon those created it and who today are undergoing a decline."[6]

---

[6] Supiot A. (edited by), *Il Futuro del lavoro*, Rome, Carocci, 2003, page 37.

Local Development Systems

One of the first actions of the Institute was the publication of the first issue in our series of *working papers*, edited by Ash Amin, on the future of the Emilia model, a study that focused on the critical nodes of the model indicating an escape route, even an institutional one; a route that we felt, as institutional innovation, as fully-fledged participants. From there we had the constant attention of the Institute for Labour Foundation on issues of local development and environmental sustainability, as a strategic chance to valorise work and product innovation. In this perspective, we have taken part in various initiatives aimed at developing product innovation in different sectors, also by means of new organisational models and a different approach to work, from organic agriculture to issues of environmental sustainability. From there came the drafting of our second report on Government and Governance in Emilia-Romagna, currently in press in our series of publications.
So in complete harmony with this we have dealt with the issue of the social quality certification. The Region, specifically speaking the Schools, Vocational Training, University, Work and Equal Opportunities Boards, through a tender of the FSE, has invited a number of Institutes, coordinated by us, to draft a feasibility plan for a social quality certification of the regional enterprises. The studies, the research and the projects in which other Institutes as well as ourselves have been involved over the past few years have led to the drafting of certification project aimed at sustaining a process of comprehensive repositioning of the SME system towards a situation of international excellence. By international excellence we mean, in short, a situation characterised by the concept of developmental social sustainability and, therefore, by the basic elements of the high road to development and competitiveness. The proposal, still undergoing evaluation, has found support among the actors involved, particularly the unions Cisl, Cgil, Uil that have wanted, even through an official declaration, to give their backing to this project.

The Productive Models

At the same time as the inception of the Institute for Labour Foundation, I myself coordinated a study into the networks and the nodes, on behalf of the committee headed by La Forgia, i.e. on the role of ICT in sustaining a

process of organisational, social, cultural and economic renewal of the Region, making no any concessions to those fallacies that have subsequently been called the ideology of the new economy; I can well remember how Sebastiano Brusco constantly reminded me that if there is a network in which there are nodes and the network gains value from the nodes and not vice-versa, meaning that it is the social quality of the processes that counts, then the rest follows. About one year afterwards came the study on the Tetrapak model and the analysis of the new outsourcing models in the framework of the globalisation processes. This double-edged analysis on ICT and on the new outsourcing models helped us to learn about which similar processes were taking place in Europe and the USA, thus creating research links that still persist today. From that analysis our idea of a high road and a low road to competitiveness took further shape; we were indeed able to put forward an organisational platform based on flow-working, the existence of working teams and the analytical articulation of a model of structural flexibility, to be juxtaposed to disarticulated labour relations. The analysis of outsourcing models has allowed us to see the trends emerging in Europe; this has taken place with a collaborative agreement with the Faculty of Sociology of Eichstätt – Professor Greca who will be speaking on Saturday morning – which means the world of Audi and BMW in Bavaria, with the IAO Institute of the Fraunhofer in Stuttgart, and so with the heartland of German motor car production, with the Scandinavian countries and, lastly, with the University of Aachen, in other words one of the German poles of technological excellence, through contacts with Professor Brandt, and his colleague Strina, who will be speaking on the 20th. The analysis performed here initially together with Ducati Motors and Tetrapak, and later on in Piedmont through our collaboration with the Province of Turin – the materials are at your disposal – have allowed us to isolate an hypothesis of industrial and organisational policy on which we have recently held a public meeting in Turin with the Province, and which was one of the hypotheses at the basis of the social quality brand or certifications model that we, together with other Regional institutes, have devised for the Region. From this set of studies and experiences derived our contribution to the three-year regional programme for productive activities.
This complex model of an alternative road to turbo-capitalism, which we are still following today, has found a positive response in a few companies, nearly all of which public ones, which have chosen to share with us a road of organisational re-thinking. Amongst these we wish to mention the Civic

Hospital of Guastalla, the Agac of Reggio Emilia and, only for the part relating to the industrial relations system, the public utilities company Hera. We are, nonetheless, witnessing cases of focal companies and consortia with a strong tradition and regional roots, alert to the positive valorisation of the local system, understood both as the qualification of the relations network with the inter-related companies (sub-suppliers, partners, etc.), and as support to the active participation processes of the workers in company development; we are actively collaborating with some of these. As I have already said these are just islands in the ocean and this is one of the major debating points in the Europe of today. Why is it that what appears to be logical and reasonable, and even seems to be working well, does not find any buyers? Is there a road that leads to extending the exemplary cases, transforming them from cases to be put on display to mainstream ones, that is to say the dominant trend?

The Labour Market

Structural flexibility versus numerical flexibility, stability of work versus temporary, unstable work, etc., there's no need for us to repeat what Professor Gallino has already told us better than anyone else, also in his recent lead article on the newspaper *La Repubblica*; unfortunately, he has been forced to withdraw his participation for family reasons. Our analysis into the weight of the new forms of non-standardised work and its social consequences has found room in the research performed with the Emilia-Romagna Region and with the Catalan region, recorded in a book[7], also at your disposal, but also in the research into young people, including immigrants, held in Reggio Emilia, which Professor Mottura will talk to us about tomorrow, amongst other things. The analysis by Gallino and by Sennet, has found a voice and analytical support in our initiative of Bologna 2000, of which you can find some trace in the materials at your disposal. This reflection has also been fuelled by the analyses performed by Professor Serravalli who will be speaking tomorrow[8]. Serravalli's analysis is especially important as it allows us to see under which conditions we have managed to avoid certain mechanisms of temporary work and the

---

[7] Sbordone F., Castoldi R., *Affittasi lavoratore. Relazioni di lavoro, motivazioni e criticità nell'utilizzo del lavoro interinale. Esperienze in Emilia-Romagna*, Milano, F.Angeli, 2002

[8] Un utile lavoro di riferimento per le nostre considerazioni è Seravalli G., *Sviluppo economico e mercato del lavoro a Reggio Emilia,* Reggio Emilia, 2001

segmentation of the labour market and why, in more general terms, this overturns the standard explanation on unemployment.

Health and Safety

The Health Committee, in collaboration with that of the School, Vocational Training, the University, Labour, Equal Opportunities, has given the Institute for Labour the task of analysing the social and organisational determinants of workplace accidents, which still occur very frequently, and the work-related health problems. This choice, a particularly brave one in this day and age, breaks away from the traditional pattern of an epidemiological-health type, albeit a necessary one, to underscore those aspects that are connected with the original mission of the Institute for Labour: how human labour is utilised. Professor Rebecchi will speak to us tomorrow about the problems connected with the health of the worker, also relating our work here in the Region with the work being performed on the same issue in Turin and with the studies started up in Ravenna and Bologna. In this research strand there emerge with absolute clarity the social costs of the prevalent turbo-capitalist choice made by the private as well as the public companies, including the services companies, both in terms of male and female workers and the company as a whole.

Labour and Gender

Ever since our earliest actions we have dealt with the issues of gender in the workplace through a series of research projects and targeted actions. Amongst these the most important was performed within the Emilia-Romagna Region itself in 1998. It was a research and development action that led some Directorates of the Emilia-Romagna region to test new patterns of work organisation based more on the integration of the skills and cooperation.

The gender issue has also been dealt with over the past few years from the health and safety point of view in the workplace and from a theoretical standpoint (a specific contribution to the issue of health in a gender perspective is contained in the Second Annual Report of the Institute for Labour Foundation on workplace Health and Safety), and the practical one (e.g. through the realisation of a case study at the public transport company in Bologna, called ATC, and more recently at the municipal transport company of Turin[9]) with the aim of formulating proposals and actions to improve the quality of men and women's working life.

Where do we Stand?

Temporary Contracts and Citizenship

Before moving on to our more analytical job of reconstruction, we would like to try to set out the main aspects relating to work in this phase, in the seven dimensions listed above, naturally as we see them, on the basis of our research and our participation in the discussions in Europe and Italy. I would like to use the words of an academic, a colleague with whom we collaborate, Professor Enzo Bartocci, Chairman of the Giacomo Brodolini Foundation. Bartocci writes in his editorial to the September-December 2002 issue of the journal Economia & Lavoro:

> *"The advent of the industrial society between the 19th and 20th centuries, and the social pact of those who fostered it, came about on the basis of an exchange: political and social rights for consensus. It was this exchange that allowed the antagonistic conflict to be overcome and what we could call the conflicting integration of the working classes within capitalistic society as a pluralistic society inside which conflict and confrontation constitute the very conditions of democratic life. The trends that are currently taking shape take us back in time. The political rights – not being formally questioned – are being eroded and are losing significance in the presence of a decline in the social rights given the bi-univocal relationship existing between the two spheres that taken as a whole configure the area of citizenship."*[10]

And he adds:

> *"In other words, a radical modification in the system of legislative and contractual safeguards cannot be justified in protection of the*

---

[9] Cfr. Castoldi R., Sbordone F., *Donne, salute e lavoro. Differenza di genere e salute sui luoghi di lavoro*, in *Lo stato della salute e della sicurezza dei lavoratori in Emilia-Romagna. 2. Rapporto su salute e sicurezza dell'Istituto per il Lavoro*, Milan, F. Angeli, 2002.

[10] Bartocci E., *Relazioni Industriali e società democratica,* in "Economia & Lavoro", A. XXXVI, no. 3, 2002, p.6.

world of work, unless we consider the two faces of the change. On the one hand, what has happened in the productive structure and in the modern forms that economic competition takes on, on the other the new social stratification and the transformations that have come about in the labour relationships, in social demand, in the equilibria present in society and the labour market. The suppression of the corporations between the end of the 18th century and the beginning of the 19th century and the prohibition on setting up forms of representation of interest in the new class that was being born out of industrial production system, to the extent to which it did not take account of the "social question" that this revolution had provoked, was at the basis of the antagonistic conflict that enflamed the more developed countries of western Europe between the second half of the 19th century and the first half of the 20th century. Mutatis mutandis, the introduction of a drastic reduction in the current system of safeguards and guarantees without their adequate reformulation mirroring the problems hic et nunc could promote analogous phenomena."[11]

Lastly:

The most dynamic and aggressive aspects of international capitalism are indeed taking advantage of the exceptional nature of this transition situation in order to highlight their level of freedom and discretion within the market and to reduce the sphere of regulatory intervention and control by the States. The development of policies of a neo-liberal sort produced by globalisation has triggered off a process of growth in the social differences (Krugman, 2003) and is provoking the temporary nature of the equilibria that underlie every societal pact, of every democratic order.(...) Flexibility, understood as a category of policy and as a obligatory model of each choice, is undermining, as previously observed, the action and the role of the large mass organisations that in the industrial societies have constituted the moment of amalgamation and integration of entire social classes, channelling their demand for an institutionally regulated management of the conflict. The crisis of the unions, after that of the political parties, can have more serious consequences in Italy where, unlike the other Western countries, there isn't such a

[11] Ibidem, p. 7.

widespread presence of association expressing a democratic pluralism (...)[12].

It could be argued that the Fondazione Brodolini and the journal belong, just as we do, to the world of the past and thus do not accurately grasp the *unstoppable innovation,* as was the popular slogan a few decades ago; if this was true we are in good company, suffice it to quote Gallino and Supiot not to mention a great American sociologist, Richard Sennett, one of those who has accompanied the key phases in the transformation of work with his analytical intelligence:

> *"It is quite natural for flexibility to generate anxiety: no one knows which risks are worth taking or which paths are worth following. In the last century, many paraphrases have been created to get round the negative implications of the expression "capitalistic system", and we have started talking about the "free enterprise system" or about "private initiative". Today, the term "flexibility" is used in the same way to get round the negative connotations of the concept of capitalism. The argument thus goes that by opposing the rigidity of bureaucracy and reserving greater attention to risk, flexibility allows individuals to have a greater control over their own lives. But actually the new regime substitutes the old forms of control with new ones, rather than limiting itself to abolishing the rules of the past – and these new forms of control are often even more difficult to recognise.*[13]

And he concludes the book by saying:

> *The question "Who is it that needs me?" is a question of personality that is questioned at its very roots in modern capitalism. (...) It could be said that capitalism has always had these characteristics. But not in the same way. The indifference of old capitalism linked to classes was rigidly materialistic: the indifference emanating from flexible capitalism is more personal, because the system itself is characterised in a much less rigid way, and its form is less legible. (...). It is logical to react to the feeling of not being indispensable with a lack of responsiveness. This is as true of the flexible work community as for the markets that submit the middle-aged workers to*

[12] Ibidem, p. 8.

[13] Sennet R., L'uomo flessibile, le conseguenze del nuovo capitalismo sulla vita personale, Milano, Universale Economica Feltrinelli, 2002, pp. 9-10.

downsizing. (...) The Other is missing, and so we end up without relations. The real relationships with others, created by recognising the reciprocal misunderstandings, are then further emptied of meaning by the incomprehensible comunitarianism and by the moral protection, from these clear shared-value declarations, from the "us" group of the puppet communities. (...) But the flexibility celebrated by them does not offer, and cannot offer, any guide to a normal life. The new bosses have refused the careers in the old sense of the word, i.e. the long paths along which we can travel; the stable and lasting lines of behaviour are for them foreign territory.[14]

In short, we must say clearly that it appears to us that the situation is wholly uneven, we are not at all at the stage of the flexibility recommended in the Supiot report and by other scholars, i.e. an individualisation of the means by which to perform work, negotiated collectively, which takes account of the personal specificities, from age to gender, from the options of general life to the specific phases of life, the children, the relatives, the desire to study and re-train, the new methods for doing work, etc.. On the contrary, we are faced with the absolute objectification of work that loses every material content and every subjective determination in order to be infinitely adaptable to the needs of short-term profit and, in any case, invested capital – *casino capitalism*; the one that Gallino, with a effective image calls *disposable work*. In a Region such as this one, and in other very similar ones in Italy as well as Europe, that is characterised by the important presence of manufacturing and services connected to it, and by a very high number of SMEs, smaller rather than medium-sized, this involves different consequences, depending on the economic cycle. In the high cycles it becomes a form of prolonged personnel selection, in the negative ones it allows for widespread temporary work. In all the cases the process of knowledge accumulation specific to a branch of activity, when it is not an actual profession, accelerates the elements of price competition to the disadvantage of others; in short, it triggers off a truly negative cycle, at the system level. At the level of the individual there arise problems of meaning, the social roots, etc. reported by so much recent sociological literature.

---

[14] Ibidem, pp. 146, 147 e 148.

The Power of Coalition

This process is born from the breakage in the equilibrium based on the power of coalition; the fact that this is central is culturally documented, not only by European history but also by American history. The Wagner Act was indeed born from the struggle against business unionism, "*aziendalismo*", as we might say in Italian, because business unionism had led to a situation that can be summarised as follows:

> *"The typical business union in 1920 and 1930 – the "works counsel" or "workers' representation plan", as the management called it – had been established and financed by the management and was limited to the workers of a single productive unit. The employees would periodically elect the representatives from their ranks, who would usually meet the management representatives in monthly conferences to hear the workers' complaints, the operative problems in the workshops and, less frequently, salaries and benefits. The final authority over all the decisions, including the complaints, rested upon the management's shoulders. The management's consent was requested for each modification to the constitutional rules and to the statutes of the organisation. No funds were available for strike action."*[15]

Senator Wagner, and the circle of progressive reformers which he belonged to, was certainly strongly influenced by the Institutional School of Veblen, and Commons and by the Co-operativism of Dewey. Dewey's contribution should be underlined because Wagner's idea comes from there that there are no objective economic laws regulating the relations between the social partners and thus society, including the company, can be reformed because it is elastic and dynamic. From this point of view, Wagner thought that industrial peace and the macroeconomic growth and the social stability were secondary objectives coming after the achievement of social justice through democratic consensus in the workplaces:

> *"For Wagner, the hierarchical workplace, on the vast scale of the mass industry was an 'impersonal heartless machine' in which 'the isolated worker (...) is powerless to defend himself from the occasional mistakes of the company that control him (...) and he has*

[15] Barenberg M., *The political economy of the Wagner Act: Power, Symbol, and Workplace Cooperation*, "Harvard Law Review", Vol. 106, No. 7, May 1993, p. 1.385, note 16.

no chance of getting the management to know what the nature of his problem.' The relationship between entrepreneur and worker in modern industry - 'the most important relation in the life of the worker – has taken the character of the relationship of authority between the sovereign and the subjects or citizens'."[16]

Lastly, in order not to leave any doubts, in 1928 Wagner, addressing the AFL, said:

Cooperation has only three equals. To be equal to the immense complex of modern capital the wage-earner has to be organised before being able to provide cooperation to his employer.[17]

I think I can be allowed to say that this is certainly reformist.
At the time when the Government's decree laws, inspired by the White Book, speak of the individualisation of the labour relationship as an antagonistic movement of liberation from the homogenisation of collective bargaining, then it is worthwhile going back to the origins of this story, taking one step after the other.
When the debate began on the limits of the Fordist-Taylorist experience and until the beginning of the Japanese model, one could reasonably argue that the weight of individualisation of the labour relationship that it contained, together with the formation of a new blend between indirect participation, in short the one guaranteed by the existence of the unions and the contracts, and the direct one, aiming to get personal investment elements in work to emerge, had a dual evolutionary possibility. That is, it could translate into a questioning of the power of coalition that had not only been the basis for the birth of the unions but the birth itself of work on the basis of citizenship and thus its related rights; vice-versa it could translate into a new and more advanced re-dislocation of that power and those rights, re-modulating them upon the demands and the capacities of individuals.
In actual fact, things have not quite gone that was given the fact that the large and medium-sized company, both in industry and in the distribution

---

[16] Ibidem, p. 1422, the citations in inverted commas are of Wagner, selected by Barenberg, and are respectively: 81 Cong. Rec. 2940 (1937) and Speech at the National Conference of Catholic Charities 4 (Oct. 3, 1933) in *The Robert Wagner Papers*, Georgetown University, at 600 SF 103, Folder 28.
[17] Wagner R.F., *Le nuove responsabilità del Lavoro Organizzato*, Discorso alla convenzione della AFL di New York 2, 6 (August 28, 1928) in *The Wagner Papers* at 599 SF 102, Folder 8.

and the advanced tertiary sector, through a highly elaborate and precise segmentation of the labour force, also made possible by a progressive weakening of the union role, have partially been able to compensate for the defects of Taylorism-Fordism, without conceding anything to the reforms that has so often been talked about.
On the contrary, with the publication of the "White Book" a lot of space has been dedicated to the discussion on the supposed potentialities of the individual regulation in the labour relationship. We agree with what has been stated by Cella:

> *"...it can be said that, to a fairly plausible extent, that for the workers, if we leave aside the very special skills and the very favourable market situations, the spread of such kinds of contract would in the medium-long term lead to a drop in the normative safeguards and in the earnings safeguards. (...) In short, the risk is that of pre-disposing an individualised and hyper-flexible regulation not so much for the workers more endowed with subjective resources, as for the weaker workers more exposed to market fluctuations. A nice social long-sightedness, there's no doubt about that! How can one not suspect that such proposals are above all put forward to undermine industrial relations and the capacity of representation of confederate unionism?"*[18]

The mechanisms of labour segmentation
We have already illustrated the mechanism[19] but it is worthwhile presenting it once again; flexibility can be classified as follows:

1. **Numerical.** The company modifies the quantity of human work it uses in order to have the production made and the production to be made coincide. This can be done by acting on the nature of the employment relationship (part-time, temporary work, fixed-term contracts and unstable jobs) so as to dispose of a higher number of workers, when necessary, without changing the stable minimum amount of production that guarantees the equilibrium point at times when the market is slack. In Italy this has been chosen by large-scale distribution. On the other hand, it is possible to act upon working time through overtime, yearly

---

[18] Cella G., *Lo scenario individualista e il sindacato confederale,* in "Lavori. Quaderni di rassegna sindacale", No. 4/2001, pp. 44-45.
[19] Garibaldo F., Sbordone F., Telljohann V., *Forme della divisione del lavoro e delle sue modalità organizzative*, in *Sviluppo, lavoro e competitività in Emilia-Romagna*, Milan, F.Angeli, 2000, pp. 285-321.

working time and the creation or the elimination of working shifts. In Italy this has been the choice made by the metalworking industry.

2. **Functional or internal.** This consists of an action upon the organisational structure and the workers. Essentially this amounts to a transformation of the company organisation and the work based on a diffuse autonomy. It is what is studied in the two NUTEK reports on Sweden and the Disko report on Denmark, by EPOC, etc.. The flexibility originates from a flexible structural capacity deriving from an organisation that is sufficiently elastic to adapt itself to changes. The most mature phase of this strategy is product innovation.
3. **Outsourcing strategies, also known as *sub-supply*.** Thus, here we refer both to the classical ones, driven by reasons of sheer volume and to the new ones of *co-makership*, that is, based on a strategic integration between focal companies and sub-supply companies, whose theoretical statute should be discussed starting with the debate on the division of labour.
4. **Wages incentives.** These can be used to support both I and II.

The flexible factory to which we refer can be represented as follows:

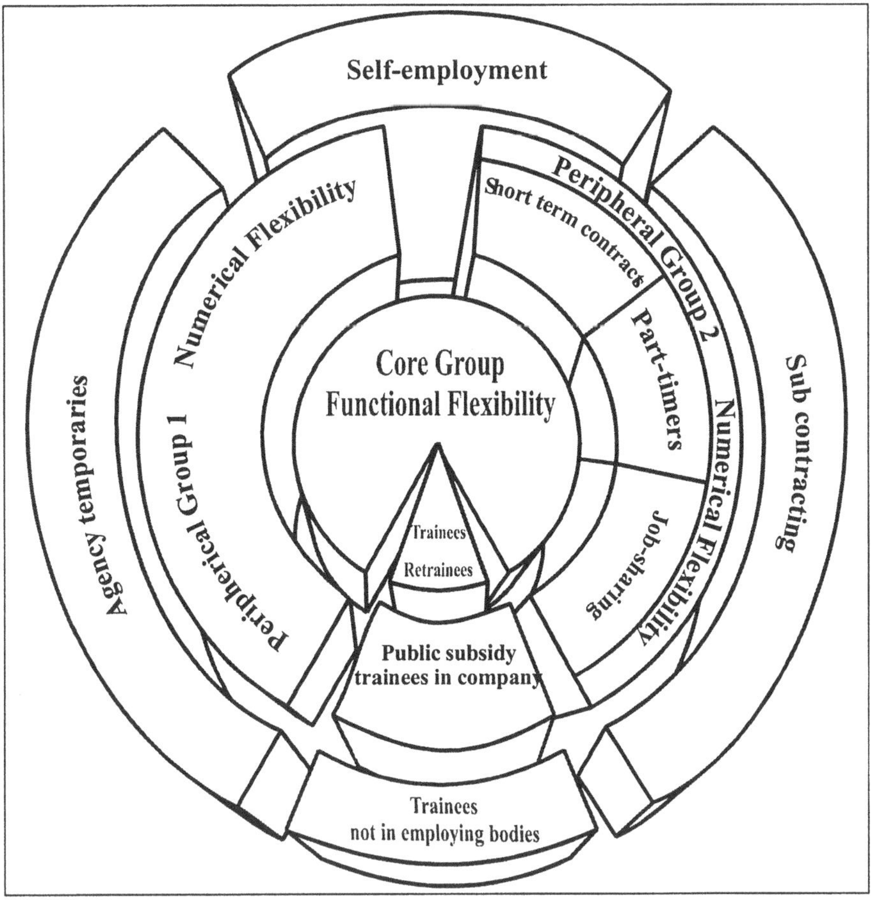

Source: John Atkinson, 1988

Large and medium-sized companies have give risen to the phenomenon of sub-supply that has nothing to do with the third-party manufacturing of the past; indeed, in this new version the work given outside the factory does not only or prevalently regard additional quotas of work, in short a form of classical numerical flexibility, but the separating of whole activities necessary to the completion of the working process – whatever it may be, even that of a hospital, for instance, - and their allocation to another company that has made it into its own productive aim. In this way, various different objectives can be achieved[20]:

1. offloading a part of the investment and warehousing costs onto others;
2. offloading a part of the responsibilities of the employment levels onto others;
3. differentiating the hourly cost, on a par with other factors, between inside and outside, thus taking hold of a higher proportion of the value creation or, in the case of a negative situation, reducing the losses;
4. offloading the *just-in-time* costs onto others: in practice, the sub-supplier must be equipped, even through specific models of work organisation, to absorb all the "variations" that the contractor experiences both in terms of the volumes and principally in terms of the speed of the response in changing the mix – in some cases less than an hour, generally speaking within 4-5 hours;
5. optimising the investments and the working process both for the contractor and for the sub-supplier that specialise by concentrating on well-defined activities;
6. fully exploiting the chance to organise production through "heterogeneous cycles, with parallel tasks, associated by addition." This is a fundamental point as it implies that there can be parallel cycles, functionally connected through a small temporal displacement with the result of reducing enormously all the production times – both those of design and the process *lead times* and the overall *time-to-market*. For economic reasons, rather complex to explain theoretically, in order to fully deploy its advantages this process must put into play the equipment or resources that are mutually used, this pushes, when the prime reason is not merely cost-cutting, towards forms of strategic integration between the sub-suppliers and the contractor companies.

The persistence of neo-Taylorist conditions

The sub-supply practice together with the growing pressure on timescale is pushing a large number of Small and Medium enterprises, besides the industrial micro-companies as well as a large part of the tertiary sector – the whole logistic chain, the high added value specialised services, etc. – and

---

[20] For a review of the literature on this topic see:
Bardi A., *Strategie aziendali e modelli organizzativi, linee di sviluppo e tendenze evolutive nel settore dell'auto*, Working Paper, no. 8, IpL, 2002.

nearly all of the so-called new economy, towards a rediscovery of new Taylorist and Fordist forms with enormous pressure on the use of time of the individuals, classical tools for the technical ones – times and methods, time saturation, etc. – but also new ones, deriving from the growing weight of information technology, which operate on time "condensing" it. The condensation can be measured by a *proxy*: the quantity of information and concepts that are utilised in the time unit by a person who is fuelled by the computerised systems capable of working at a much higher speed than our traditional reading pace.

We thus have the fact[21] that in constrained industrial work, still very much alive, time gets longer - overtime as a normal condition – and is concomitantly condensed - at times through the reduction in the breaks but above all generally through an extension in the working tasks – for example, the certification of the work done or the filling in of evaluation and documentation forms - which, generally speaking, instead of representing a conquest of autonomy and responsibility, as the workplace reforms demanded, have been transformed into a further concentration of time. The flexibility to deal with the unexpected events is realised by the use of temporary staff, overtime, lay-off schemes, etc. and/or with the outsourcing of whole activities.

In unconstrained industrial work, the breaking down of the regulatory working devices negotiated at the time at company level and never transformed into general cogent norms, has led, as for the constrained one, to a lengthening and a condensing of working time. Furthermore, there has, generally speaking, been an intensive exploitation of the non-formal aspects of the working activity, such as *ad hoc* groups or forms of factual peer coordination, which allow for the integration and thus the easier working of the organisations without recognising any of those activities and thus actually determining a progressive decline in the individuals' activities and motivations: Such a process of decay leads to growing *turnover* rates that are managed through new mechanisms of labour market deregulation, as long as they are possible, after which compromises are reached each time the lessons learned from the facts indicates that the system's limit of governability has been exceeded.

In the work of providing health-care – hospitals and hospices in general – and in the schools there is a growing situation of undersizing of staffing levels also deriving from a choice, with unchanged or decreasing resources,

---

[21] All the evaluations that follow are based on our research works, including the third issue of the recently published Report.

of managerial control of a bureaucratic kind that subtracts functional resources for a control that is to a large extent ineffective if not wholly wrong of the service delivered, within a model of efficiency, that refutes those elements of personal autonomy and self-enforced working cooperation that is supposed to be encouraged.
In the tertiary activities, there is generally a labour force segmentation that is increasingly elaborate and rigid, which determines for most people a working condition in which all the potentially negative elements of an activity are accumulated (for example, the case of the *call centres*).
Then there are the new jobs linked to information technology and to the new activities of the culture industry. In these cases, there is pressure on working time that is no less than that of the traditional manufacturing industry. In relation to the issue of autonomy we can see a transition phase that has characteristics that are very similar the ones that at the end of the 19th century and the start of the 20th century concerning rationalised industrial work. As in that case there will be whole activities and sectors where that will be impossible but the pace, the productivity criteria and thus the conditioning of the working activity, if nothing happens to modify it with some counter-trends based on the power to balance the market mechanisms, will be driven by the rationalised companies.

The Working Relationship and Citizenship

The past decade in Italy and in Europe has been characterised by an intense legislative and contractual activity which has seen the deregulation of the labour market. A large range of different types of working relationship have been introduced that cannot be traced back to the traditional full-time and open-ended employment contract. On the side of the companies and their representation associations there has been no mystery about the fact that such policies were born from the need to make available to companies both an incoming and outgoing labour force flexibility; furthermore, in such a way the market would have allocated the resources in a optimal way and there would have been an increase in employment. On the other hand, both inside the union organisations and on the part of the governments that were more overtly sensitive to union claims, it was argued, with a significant contribution from social research, that these new patterns, opportunely controlled and calibrated, would have allowed for a greater individualisation of the working methods with the conquest of greater freedom for the individual, this would have been specifically of great help for some figures, such as women, owing to maternity and the work of care

provision, and young people still going through the phase of alternating between the different experiences of life and work.
In actual fact, what is by now apparent to everyone is that only a small fraction of the workers have used the new labour relations to answer their vital autonomous needs; generally speaking, when that has taken place this has happened for the women in the case of part-time work; it is necessary to remember that even in these cases this has not always happened without paying a price at the level of one's psycho-physical equilibrium, as research from a years ago has shown.[22]
In most cases, what has happened is that the labour market has become progressively segmented, thus determining the creation of an area of male as well as female workers who spend important parts of the lives, if not their whole lives, pursuing one unstable temporary job after another.
In these cases, the pathogenetic effects are both direct and indirect; indirect because often these people are in such a condition of negotiating weakness as to be submitted to any working condition without complaint; direct because the constant uncertainty and the competition that accompanies it have deleterious effects on the individuals but also on the quality of the working environment.
It is necessary to take a step back. Indeed, I have just stated that the rights to citizenship that have marked the "short century", which Hobsbawm speaks of, are born from the power of coalition constructed upon the working identity, which today sounds like an insult to the new standard version of modernity, condensed into a single idea. Let's pause for a moment to reflect on this passage.
It should be enough to re-read what Marshall wrote (that is, Thomas Humphrey Marshall, the sociologist) on two aspects: the birth of the rights to civil citizenship for the working classes and the ideals of the other Marshall (Alfred, the economist) to make each man into a *gentleman*, that is, to be admitted to taking part in the social fabric, the culture, the quality of life. On the first aspect, in 1949 he underlined the fact that:
"*There is, therefore, an important difference between fully-fledged collective bargaining, through which the economic forces try to achieve an equilibrium in a free market, and the use of civil collective rights to state the fundamental claims to the elements of social justice. So the acceptance of collective bargaining has not only been a natural enlargement of the*

[22] *Il Tempo Spezzato: orario di lavoro e tempo soggettivo*, Roma, Ediesse, 1993.

civil rights; it has meant the passage of an important process from the political sphere to the civil one of citizenship."[23]

Moreover, this is the Prof. Cella's reading as well at a seminar of the Italian Association of Sociology[24]. In short, only through collective bargaining and the conquest of the right to perform it was there a shift, as a civil right, from being servants to workers.

In regard to the statement of the other Marshall, several times he goes back to the fact that, as Maranini observes *"The second thing that the statement that "a gentleman has to be made of every man" means is that under the conditions of capitalistic labour organisation the worker cannot be a 'gentleman'"*[25]. He cannot be so, T. H. Marshall said, because working life quantitatively and qualitatively subordinates him, so if it is degraded it drags the rest down with it. Collective bargaining allowed for a change in the conditions of work and thus contributed to the broadening of citizenship.

A lot of time has gone by but another great sociologist writing today - Richard Sennet – presents us with the problem once again, no longer arranged in the same way as Marshall, a life absorbed by a job, but already in the one our reformists think to, a life broken up into many jobs, and this does not seem to have basically shifted the problem: people cannot be citizens in Alfred Marshall's sense if work is not a principle of self-realisation, part of one's own individuality and vehicle to participate in the tasks of society. On the other hand, what do the economists Amartya Sen and the philosopher Martha Nussbaum speak to us about when they speak of the concept of capacity? In other words, the need for all the human beings to be given the chance to actually develop their specific human potential, in the way they wish to. Aristotle called them virtues, today we speak of capacities, Marshall thought of the gentleman and Marx of our "generic nature"; but the issue is always the same: you cannot divide human beings into two parts: one, for which one expects the mobilisation of one's own resources and creative capacities, entrusted to the market *per se*, and based on the conception of purely utilitarian human beings; the other, in which we are conscious citizens and dedicated to the common good.

Such an approach positively translated into our daily work, is a real reference and not only a declared one, if we move within the humus of

---

[23] Marshall T. H., *Cittadinanza e classe sociale*, UTET, Turin, 1976, p. 36.

[24] Cella G.P., *Lavoro, lavori, cittadinanza* in "Parolechiave", no. 14/15, 1997, pp.35-48.

[25] Maranini P., *Introduzione* in Marshall T. H., op. cit., p. XIII.

action research, that is, humus that allows both the male and the female workers to be co-participants and co-designers in each hypothesis of transformation. For these reasons we have drafted the operative protocols that we call *discussion groups* and *research conferences*, which we try to stick to in each organisational action. For the same reason, we are acquiring the capacity to utilise the techniques for the *construction of the scenarios*, also thanks to our collaboration with Professor Rasmussen, who will be speaking the day after tomorrow; a collaboration tested during the Europe-India collaboration project which we took part in together.

Breaking the Equilibrium

The hypothesis I am putting forward, then, very briefly, is that the potential we saw at the time Institute was being founded and that led the Commission to draft the Green Book on the new forms of labour organisation, have floundered upon two stumbling blocks: a) the breaking of the equilibrium between capital and labour which started around the mid-19th century in England, and then gradually consolidated through the Wagner Act in the United States, the growth of the union movement in continental Europe and then in the world – see the birth of the ILO – and reinforced by the competition between the two economic *blocs* – social and ideological, until 1989 and based on the power of coalition of the union and the legitimating also institutional in no longer considering work as a good like any other; b) the breakdown in the relationship between social rights in the productive sphere and political and social rights as citizens.
The breakdown comes about both for the innovative and re-organisational processes on the side of Capital but also for the prevailing of neo-liberal policies, also in Europe, both in the national States and at the level of the Commission, that strengthen, indeed stimulate, practical behaviour opposed to the philosophy indicated by the search for the high road and the new forms of work organisation based on workers' individual and collective autonomy, their creativity and intelligence, etc..
Besides, it is enough to take a look at Italy. I do not wish to launch myself into a full-blown analysis, which is beyond the scope of this talk, but rather I will stick to our task; in short, the research we have performed in the car sector, the textiles sector, the industrial structure of this region, in the analysis of some national sectors, etc.. Everything we have investigated, often together with all the social actors. What has emerged? Something

simple and straightforward. If I support the maxim of work deregulation, if I make available infinite numerical flexibility, if I cut research funds, if by propagating as a source of rationality all the short-term behaviours that maximise profits, if (...) etc, then what will the overall effect on the economic and social level be? On the economic level, it can be said, as has already been stated (A. Singh, 1997):

> *"The growing availability of undervalued work allows companies to compensate for their organisational and managerial limits, to put off the demolition of obsolete facilities and to undertake destructive forms of price-based competition. The absence of wage control means that backward companies from the technological and managerial point of view can survive, and this contributes to stopping the more advanced companies expanding their own market shares. (...) More in general, the growing availability of underrated work, together with the high levels of unemployment, create an environment in which entrepreneurial activity exhausts itself in the cutting of wages, worsening the conditions of the employed workers, as well as the exploitation of under-paid labour." When it appears, this tendency generates other social consequences: a segmentation or rather a polarisation of the labour force, as "the demand for labour is contained, only skilled workers will find a job, even when the companies could not be specifically in need of those skills. (...) Thus, all other things being equal, a weak demand for labour for a long period contributes to fuelling the evident increase in the inequalities between skilled workers and unskilled workers that have emerged over the past two decades".*

On the social level, it can be added to what has already been said by many others that you will be hearing about in the next few days on the effects for the individuals, the fact that the realistic perception, by the individuals, particularly the young, of the public schizophrenia between professed ideology and actual behaviour, determines growing elements of escape from industrial work and health care - meaning with this most of public work, privileging congruous activities with the intermittent and disaggregated character of the working activity. Then the consequences on health and safety are imaginable, and Professor Rebecchi will speak to you about them. The union organisations, furthermore, have been trapped in the dogged defence of their own role; this has meant the extreme difficulty in repositioning themselves both in the direction of direct and democratic

representation of all the figures of work - both stable and unstable - , and in the reorganisation, here and there, whether or not initiated by new forms of organisation on the industry basis unifying traditional unions that no longer have serious limits justifying their existence. The most recent challenge that summarises the two problems is how to perform their own role of representation and negotiating in the presence of new forms of *outsourcing* and the construction of enterprise networks. It is not our task to teach "the cat how to climb up the tree" but simply to be aware of the effects of this situation on a European scale: the dramatic decline, with a few exceptions, amongst which Italy, in the rate of unionisation in Europe, the difficult realisation of a balance between direct and indirect participation through the recovery of direct managerial modalities of the relationship with the individual workers, both male and female, with a progressive reduction in the bargaining area, a mechanism that reinforces the circuit of inefficacy of the union action on matters of great import for the individuals besides the capacity to balance the unilateral power of the company on sensitive matters for all the workers, besides in general the right to fair and equitable treatment. On top of this is the difficulty in being present in the enterprise network with complex policies with the risk of determining negative circuits, even in these cases, which are self-enhanced, between inefficacy, unfairness of treatment, and thus a reduction both in representation and representativeness. Nor does the idea of a unionisation oriented to the services to the individual rather than to the organisation of a power of balancing appear to be a balancing congruous to this situation.
In short, thinking to the realisation of what we thought at the birth of the Institute means making an about-turn. Obviously, this does not depend on ourselves, nor do have we any particular right to suggest panaceas or general political hypotheses or government schemes; we can keep to our specific field and ask ourselves whether, in the present situation, we can still play a role that is not merely that of performing studies and research and, if so, which role can we play?
Before trying to answer this question it is worthwhile making a digression on the policies of Commission that have accompanied the idea of spreading the hypotheses of the Green Book and, more generally, the policies of dissemination of the Union based on two powerful ideas: the network and the exemplary cases, also known as the "best practices".
It is not hard to grasp the ambiguous content of the former concept and the one explicitly based on the idea of a perfect market that supports the latter.

The concept of network is in itself ambiguous given that it can represent two opposing models. The first one, still prevalent today, is the one accompanied by the qualification of the so-called *bottom-up* approach juxtaposed to the *top-down* approach; according to this doctrine the networks between subjects that come to an agreement from the bottom, before an offer of support from the Union, should be the irresistibly diffused mechanism, but in reality it is quite evident that the idea of equality of opportunities that ideologically justifies that model is completely unreal. Indeed, who accesses an opportunity "from the bottom" is only the person who is strong, or because he or she is part of a lobby supporting him or her, or because he or she disposes of the knowledge resources of the mechanisms and the existence itself of that opportunity.
A paradoxical situation thus arises: the public resources that should support the weak confirm the role of the powerful; and this is the most diffuse situation in the various programmes of the Union with few and relative exceptions, the ones that, not by chance, have assigned a specific role as mentors to the intermediate institutions and to civil society, or those that are mediated by the local governments have, when they have done so, explicitly constrained the procedures and given room to the intermediate institutions and civil society.
Then the theory of the *best practices* does not have empirical confirmation, in fact, in the few cases in which there have been some checks there is an evident incapacity of the *best* to set a trend, unless the *best* is not already a trendsetter, in which case there is rampant dissemination.
Then, if the policies of the Union must not merely accompany the "natural trends" but, on the contrary, overcome the resistance, interrupt the negative cycles, open up new unexplored roads, then in the first place it is not only necessary to offer opportunities but also to build together some proposals with those who agree with it, make then operative and reward them systematically with general accompanying policies that select those trends as the ones to be sustained. Exactly the opposite to what is actually happening right now.

A Working Hypothesis

In the first place, we have to reconfirm our mission, albeit knowing that we are not working on the dominant trend, of providing support to everyone who wants to "have a go". By now these are exceptions, mainly in the

public area or among the public utilities companies, with a strong union tradition, but always existing. We think that both on the union side and the managerial side more courage could be used in daring to criticise, as some have already done, the evident limits of the sycophantic culture of "managerialism as a universal science"; a culture that, after the speculative bubble, should make room for a rethinking of the management criteria of the public bodies that are better balanced at the level of specific tasks, the operative rules necessary in that context, an effective project participation of both the male and the female workers. This is what we are trying to do also at European level by proposing a network of hospitals that is explicitly dedicated to developing projects heading in this direction.
In a specific context such as that of Emilia-Romagna, we then think that policies such as those should accompany the social quality certification if they are properly supported, even in their evident nature as a counterpoint to the national policies, something completely legitimate in the context of the new constitutional charter, then spaces would open up which, albeit at risk of being discarded, would certainly be broader. Such spaces could open up only before an evident assumption of the project by the union organisations, which already appears to be the case, and by company associations which, in the design phase, have declared their assent.
Furthermore, if the general hypothesis that I am putting forward has some fundament then it is a question of contributing to breaking down those structural constraints that prevent a new course in labour policy. By contributing to re-reading the reality of the ongoing processes with those who wish to move in this direction, beyond any ideological stance, and thus elaborating frameworks of reference for the actors, all the actors, is neither an straightforward nor a useless task. In this framework the educational policies, that Lombardi will speak to us about tomorrow, are very important.
Let's take a look at two concrete cases that we are already working on: *outsourcing* and the enterprise networks, on the one hand, and the specialised industrial profiles, on the other.
Our work, in some ways pioneering in nature and thus being valorised at European level, on the sub-supply networks, provides the union organisations and the companies with a general framework of reference in relation to which conflict can be re-modulated. Indeed, from the empirical evidence alternative possibilities emerge for solutions, and around such possibilities there can be a new specific framework of industrial relations. Like the attempt to operatively redefine a framework of relations between

the companies, the institutional and territorial context allows the local actors to redefine the system of governance.
The work we are starting now on the "low-tech" companies, that is, the traditional manufacturing – the textiles, most of the mechanical industry – attempts to outline a pathway for the transformation of this sector so that it can maintain an important role over the coming decades. This has a technological and a strategic management dimension, but also an organisational and working nature that, once elaborated, can provide a contribution, in the same direction as indicated earlier. For this reason we are working towards the creation of a broad coalition of actors around this European research project, by means of the creation of a *National Reference Group* (NRG), i.e. a national group of reference, which should contribute to emphatically stating the strategic importance of traditional manufacturing in relation to the innovation and growth processes of the traditional sectors as well as the advanced ones, in other words, with a high technological content. We would like this coalition, which we would like them to take part in, besides the world of research, the public actor, the social partners and the managers, to contribute to opening up a new era for national and European industrial policy.
The same applies to our commitment, within a specific project, and in the process of being defined with some new ones on the direction of environmental sustainability and the organic food productions.
Therefore, the search for a multi-dimensional framework of reference, in a European perspective, to the emerging problems of regional and national society, is not merely a way to seek refuge in research, in the desperate attempt to invent a role for oneself, but the possible form today for dealing with the same issue, unless we do not resign ourselves, on the one hand, to the neo-authoritarian drift that necessarily marginalizes any organised form of struggle against the socially unacceptable repercussions of the domination of neo-liberal culture and practice; on the other, to a practice of rationalisation and accompaniment of a tendency that can only be abhorred by anyone who shared the experience of the birth of the Institute, for the very reasons that motivated its inception.
Lastly, workers' health and safety; this is an immense field to work in, and which we want to work in.
In order to take these issues forward with greater determination also at the European level we have decided to set up, at the end of this congress, a European branch of the International Network of Intermediate Institutions

dealing with labour issues. On the role and the prospects of this network the co-chairman of the network, Prof. Széll, will be talking to us on the 20th .

References

Bardi A., *Strategie aziendali e modelli organizzativi, linee di sviluppo e tendenze evolutive nel settore dell'auto*, Working Paper, no. 8, IpL, 2002.

Barenberg M., *The political economy of the Wagner Act: Power, Symbol, and Workplace Cooperation*, in "Harvard Law Review", Vol. 106, no. 7, May 1993.

Bartocci E., *Relazioni industriali e società democratica*, in "Economia & Lavoro", A. XXXVI, no. 3, 2002, p.6.

Brödner P., Latniak E., *Source of Innovation and Competitiveness: National Programmes supporting the development of work organisation,* IAT, Gelsenkirchen, 2002.

Business Decisions Limited, European Commission, Employment and social affairs, unit D3, *New Forms of Work Organisation: The Obstacles to Wider Diffusion. Final Report and Annex (Case Studies)*, 2002.

Castoldi R., Sbordone F., *Donne, salute e lavoro. Differenza di genere e salute sui luoghi di lavoro*, in *Lo stato della salute e della sicurezza dei lavoratori in Emilia-Romagna. 2° Rapporto su salute e sicurezza dell'Istituto per il Lavoro*, Milano, F. Angeli, 2002.

Cella G.P., *Lavoro, lavori, cittadinanza* in "Parolechiave", n. 14/15, 1997, pp. 35-48.

Cella G.P., *Lo scenario individualista e il sindacato confederale,* in "Lavori. Quaderni di rassegna sindacale", no. 4(2001), pp. 44-45.

Cole G. H. D, *Attempts at General Union – A Study in British Trade Union History, 1818–1834*, Wesport, Connecticut Hyperion Press, 1979.

Dankbaar B., Ditter L., Hertog F., *From complex organisations with simple jobs to simple organisations with complex jobs*, in "Human Relations", Vol. 50, no. 5, 1997.

Ennals R., *The existing Policy Framework to Promote Modernisation of Work: its Weaknesses*, Kingston, Centre for Working Life Research, 2002.

European Commission, *Partnership for a New Organisation of Work. Green Paper*, European Commission, Brussels, 1997
http://europa.eu.int/comm/employment_social/social/social/green_en.htm

Garibaldo F., Sbordone F., Telljohann V., *Forme della divisione del lavoro e delle sue modalità organizzative*, in *Sviluppo, lavoro e competitività in Emilia-Romagna. 1° Rapporto Annuale dell'Istituto per il Lavoro*, Milano, F.Angeli, 2000, pp. 285-321.

Herbst B.P.G., *Socio-Technical Design: Strategies in Multi - Disciplinary Research,* London, Tavistock Publications, 1974.

Marshall T. H., *Cittadinanza e classe sociale*, Turin, UTET, 1976.

Sbordone F., Castoldi R., *Affittasi lavoratore. Relazioni di lavoro, motivazioni e criticità nell'utilizzo del lavoro interinale. Esperienze in Emilia-Romagna*, Milan, F.Angeli, 2002.

Sennet R., *L'uomo flessibile, le conseguenze del nuovo capitalismo sulla vita personale*, Milano, Universale Economica Feltrinelli, 2002.

Seravalli G., *Sviluppo economico e mercato del lavoro a Reggio Emilia,* Reggio Emilia, Camera del Lavoro, 2002.

Supiot A. (edited by), *Il Futuro del lavoro*, Carocci, Rome, 2003, pag. 37

Webb S. e B., *The History of Trade Unionism,* London, Longman, 1911.

Il Tempo Spezzato: orario di lavoro e tempo soggettivo, Rome, Ediesse, 1993.

Totterdill P., *Developing new forms of work organisation: the role of the main actors*, Nottingham, The Work Institute, 2002.

Wagner R.F., *The new responsibilities of Organised Labour*, Speech at the AFL convention in New York 2, 6 (August 28, 1928) in *The Wagner Papers* at 599 SF 102, Folder 8.

Innovation Strategies, Work Organisation and Competitiveness. Experiences in EU Member States

PETER BRÖDNER, ERICH LATNIAK

Introduction: Scope and Method of the Study

By organising a Conference on "New Forms of Work Organisation", the Danish EU Presidency has brought back this topic back to the European agenda again after five years of silence since the Green Paper on "Partnership for a New Organisation of Work" has been published in 1997 (EC 1997). In the context of this conference, the authors have been asked by the European Commission to prepare a study on national programmes supporting new forms of work organisation the main results of which are reported here.

Although activities promoting new forms of work organisation on the European level have been rather poor, activities on the national level have continued to exist at least in some member states. This overall picture is in sharp contrast, however, to the fact that a number of strategic agreements recently being approved by the European Council are strongly dependent on the development of new forms of work organisation. First of all, work organisation issues are linked to the European Employment Strategy established in the "Luxembourg process" in 1997, where at least two of the "four pillars" are rooted in new forms of work organisation: "employability" and "adaptability". Second, on the Lisbon Summit, Europe has been announced to become more productive and the leading knowledge-based society in the world. Clearly, this high pretension can only be turned into reality, if the dynamics of knowledge creation and knowledge transformation into practice is, among other things, widely rooted in new forms of work organisation providing wide scopes for acting and learning. Finally, the improvement of quality of work annunciated at

the Nizza Summit again has a broad development of new forms of work organisation as a precondition. New forms of work organisation, thus, are highly relevant for achieving such strategic objectives.
In this perspective, the study identifies and evaluates essential outcomes from national programmes supporting the development of work organisation and to derive recommendations for future initiatives. The focus is on the recent state of national programmes supporting the development and dissemination of new forms of work organisation rather than project activities funded from other sources (like e.g. ADAPT or EQUAL) or regional initiatives. The description of relevant programmes in the EU member states concentrates on work organisation issues such as the development and implementation of direct participation schemes (e.g. continuous improvement teams), group work, concurrent engineering teams, mobile work, project teams or learning organisations based on work design. The report is based on existing publications as well as on a questioning of distinguished experts in the field.

Relevance for Economic Performance: Work Organisation Matters

Many factors affect the economic performance of an enterprise, its capacity to flexibly react to market demands, and its ability to improve productivity and competitiveness. On the macroeconomic level, enterprise performance largely depends on national framework conditions and institutional settings, as the "rules of the game", such as taxes, market regulations, industrial relations or the growth, availability and quality of human, technological and financial resources. These basic conditions for economic acting may vary among regions or states, but within a region or state they set a common framework for all economic actors alike.
In times of economic turbulence, an enterprise's economic performance then even more depends on its own way of doing business, however, in particular on its business strategy, its work organisation, and the way it develops human and technological resources. As in boat racing, competitiveness is not so much a question of how the winds are blowing, but rather how one is setting one's sails. Accordingly, human resources are seen as a main source of competitive advantage in a dynamic business environment. It could be demonstrated by research that organisations must cope not only with efficiency, quality and flexibility demands, but also with the more frequent and rapid implementation of new processes and products or services largely depending on human skills and knowledge

(Alasoini/Halme 1998, Andreasen et al. 1996, EC 1998, IMF 2001). This has also been the background for the EU Green Paper on work organisation (EC 1997; for impact and social partners' responses see EIRObserver 1999).

There is a growing body of empirical evidence for the crucial role of an enterprise's innovation strategy and its work organisation to achieve high performance, innovation capacity, and competitiveness. On one hand this evidence is based on a great number of case studies elaborating the differences in strategy and work organisation between flexible, high performance competitors and those being less successful, and it draws on data from broad surveys investigating the relative performance in major parts of the economy in some member states (Finland, Sweden, Germany).

Findings from a Swedish survey based on a sample of 2000 operating units (representing approx. one third of all operating units with more than 50 employees in Sweden) can be summarised as follows: 25% of all operating units in the sample had a flexible organisation with decentralised responsibilities. They were most common in the finance and trade sectors, followed by the manufacturing industry, while traditional work organisation was still widespread in the construction and communication sectors. Considering the effects for performance and competitiveness, the results are very clear: flexible organisations were more productive (+20-60%), showed a much lower rate of personnel turnover (-21%), and a lower rate of absence due to illness (-24%) than traditionally organised operational units. Moreover, flexible organisations were much more effective in using computer technology to reduce lead times as well as delivery times than traditional organisations (NUTEK 1996). The significance for competitiveness has been confirmed by a second study covering operational units with more than 20 employees: "Strategies that focus on decentralising work organisation and on human resource development are positively associated with productivity and growth." Moreover, the learning schemes identified had a positive relationship with the enterprises' levels of productivity and profit (ITPS 2001).

Basically the same picture shows up again from the findings of a Finnish survey within the framework of the National Workplace Development Programme based on 1384 interviews with management representatives in the private sector. It too investigated into the economic effects of "functionally flexible enterprises" as compared to traditional ones. Functional flexibility in this study was defined by the two properties that employees have many opportunities to influence decision-making and that there are many elements of continuous learning in work (all other forms of

work being called traditional). A regression analysis of several factors revealed that flexibility had by far the highest effect on productivity and that productivity of flexible enterprises was 50% higher than that of traditional firms. Flexible enterprises also paid roughly 30% higher wages than traditional ones (Antila/Ylöstalo 1999).
Similar results can also be reported from a German process innovation survey in the investment goods industry based on data from more than1300 enterprises. Various new forms of work organisation contributing to build flexible enterprises clearly have positive effects not only on productivity (even more so, if implemented all together; see fig.1). Moreover, these new forms of work organisation also positively affect quality and lead times of products (Lay et al. 1996).
The Europe-wide EPOC survey ("Employee Participation in Organisational Change") covering more than 6000 firms in EU member states again basically confirms these findings: 68% of the firms having implemented, for instance, semi-autonomous groups as a corner stone for flexible organisations could realise cost reductions. Throughput times could be reduced in 87% of these firms, 98% improved their products and services, and 85% increased sales (EPOC Research Team 1998).
Despite the empirical evidence for economic superiority of new forms of work organisation (at least in those markets that demand for flexible organisations) and despite high rhetoric efforts in promoting the benefits of flexible organisations, their real dissemination still is rather low in most European countries. They are on the advance, but progress is slow. The vast majority of firms obviously miss the opportunities to broadly develop and use their human resources in terms of skills and competencies and, thus, to fully exploit the potentials of flexible organisations for their economic performance and competitiveness.
The big exception is the Nordic countries as the Flexible Enterprise Survey has revealed. It was carried out as part of the so-called NORDFLEX project that included Denmark, Finland, Norway and Sweden. There are some differences in the methodology, questionnaire design and samples, but it is still possible to compare some of the results. The share of private sector operating units with 50 employees or more, where employees work in teams, is 74% for Finland, 75% for Denmark, 69% for Norway and 91% for Sweden. If we examine only operating units where more than 50% of employees work in teams, the corresponding figures are 30% for Finland, 10% for Denmark, 58% for Sweden (the data for Norway not being available; NUTEK 1999).

Fig.1: Productivity effects of different new organisational conceptions
(Lay et al. 1996)

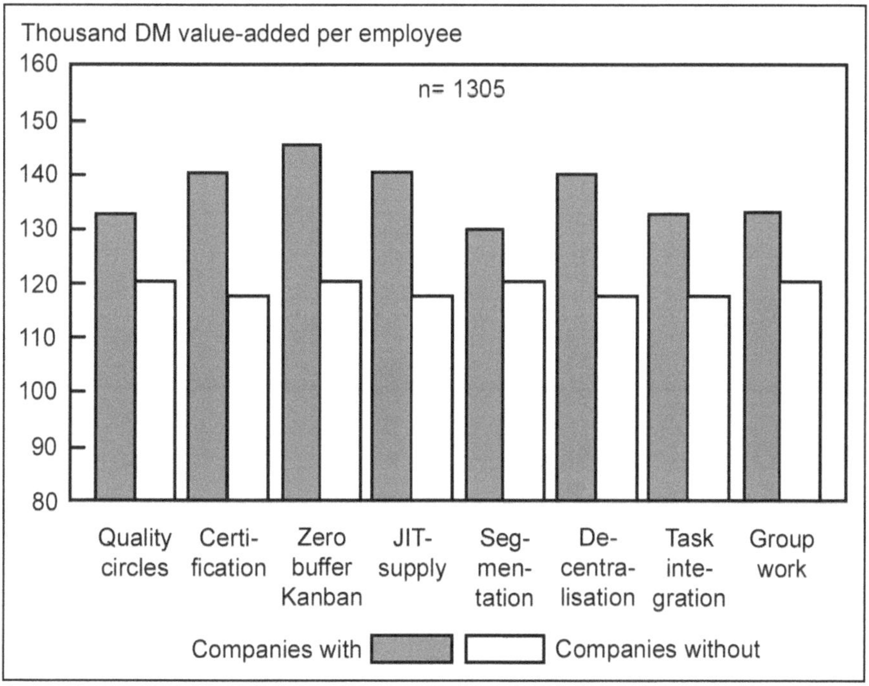

In contrast, EPOC data show the dissemination of group work in different degrees of employees' influence on decision-making in all EU member states (see fig. 2). Regarding the lack of data, this can serve as a rather strong indicator for what has been called above a flexible organisation. So far, the EPOC survey is unique in covering all EU member states; for more detailed insight, it is necessary to look at existing country surveys.

A recent survey in Germany questioning a representative sample of employees for the whole economy demonstrates the spreading of different forms of group work over time during the period 1993-1998 (Nordhause-Janz & Pekruhl 2000). The study found out that in the German economy (production and services) the dissemination of all forms of group work increased from 6.9% to 12.9% of workplaces with an estimated average increase of +1% per year. But the degree of the most advanced type of semi-autonomous group work as the strategically relevant form for flexible organisations remained on a much lower level (1998: 3.2%; see fig. 3).

Fig. 2: Dissemination of different forms of group work in EU member states
(EPOC Research Team 1998)

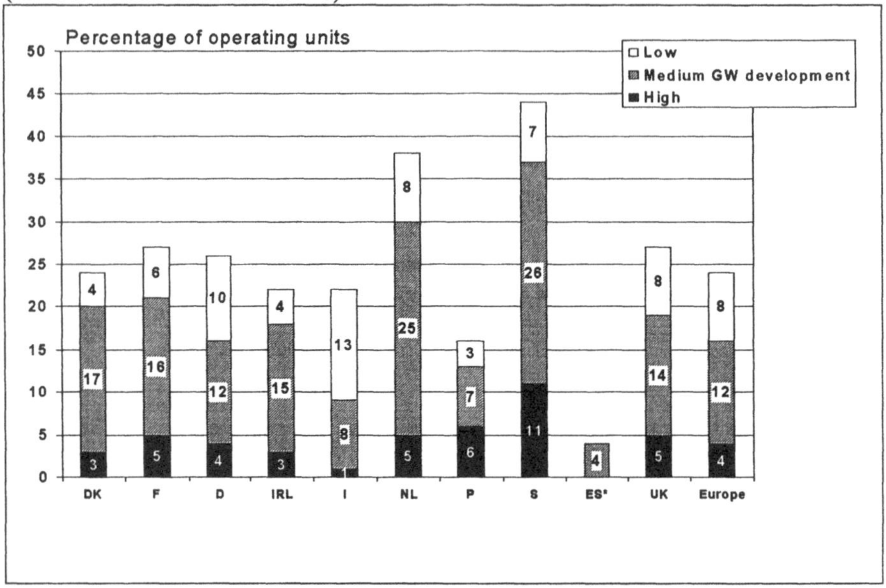

Fig. 3: Dissemination of group work in Germany 1993/1998
(Nordhause-Janz & Pekruhl 2000: 49)

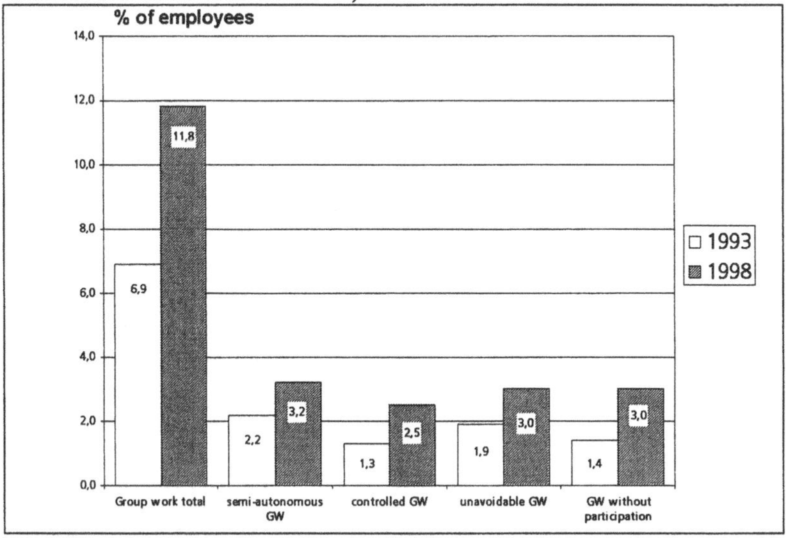

The simple distinction between flexible forms of work organisation based on higher degrees of autonomy and traditional, heteronomous work structures as applied in most surveys is not sufficient. As the European Work & Technology Consortium has worked out as one of its major findings (based on a great number of case studies in different sectors and countries), new forms of work organisation appear in two completely different settings that must be differentiated according to the enterprise's innovation strategy (Work & Technology Consortium 1997 and 1998, Brödner et al. 1998).

The so-called "low road" strategy of innovation, on one hand, solely seeks to cut costs (to decrease the denominator in the productivity formula) in order to become more flexible and efficient. Accordingly, the focus of process innovation is on numerical flexibility and cost cutting, on reducing headcounts ("downsizing"), on outsourcing of non-core businesses, and on IT-driven "business process reengineering", without changing basic conditions of operation, however. The "high road" strategy, on the other hand, primarily aims at expanding business by widely developing and comprehensively using its human resources, learning and innovation capacities (i.e. by increasing the numerator in the productivity formula without neglecting potentials in effort reduction, though). Accordingly, here the focus is on new business opportunities, on exploring demands for new products and services, on developing individual and collective competences, and, therefore on high autonomy and ample learning opportunities in work processes for knowledge creation and appropriation, thus creating improved basic conditions of operation (cf. Brödner et al. 1998, Di Martino 2001).

The difficulty to discriminate between these two strategies (and simultaneously the reason why it has been overlooked for long time) is that both strategies partially make use of the same new forms of work organisation, in particular decentralisation and group work, although to a different degree and producing different effects. It is, therefore, not sufficient to only look at new forms of work organisation, but also to uncover the innovation strategy behind as well as the way they are implemented and the effects they produce. Regarding these differences, the empirical data from the German process innovation survey, in particular the low dissemination of semi-autonomous group work and different degrees of operational decentralisation, indicate that the "high road" strategy is much less widespread than the "low road" strategy (cf. fig. 3 above, Brödner/Latniak 2002). Obviously, „cutting the buck is much easier than expanding the bang" (Hamel/Prahalad 1994).

The distinction between "low road" and "high road" strategies of innovation is also strongly related to OECD's differentiation between numerical and functional flexibility.

Numerical flexibility solely adapts the quantity of labour input to fluctuating demand, while functional flexibility "usually involves high skill levels and collaborative approaches to work and depends on high-quality labour inputs" (OECD 1995, chapter 6: 5). The majority of enterprises follow the "low road", though, implementing numerical flexibility by building core competences supported by a peripheral work force that can easily be hired and dismissed. Exactly this rather short-sighted personnel adjustment practice deprives them of the capacity to broadly develop skills and competences needed for functional flexibility as well as for knowledge creation and appropriation on the "high road".

This mirrors the fact that radical changes in organisational structures are obviously difficult to achieve and that there is strong resistance against new forms of work organisation. The shift from traditional work organisation or from cost-centred "low road" to expansive, competence-centred "high road" strategies of innovation is tantamount to a deep cultural change, of course, and requires high long term efforts in collective learning with sufficient human resources. The dominance of traditional work organisation and "low road" strategies lets us fear, though, that the necessary resources may have been consumed or weakened to an extent that hinders enterprises to master the strategic turn.

Moreover, it has to be realised that the socio-technical perspective as theoretical conception lying behind the promotion of flexible new forms of work organisation with high degrees of autonomy, wide scope of action, and diverse opportunities for learning suggested that these work structures would without further conditions contribute to higher quality of working life. Detailed analysis of new forms of work organisation has disappointed these expectations, though. In group work situations, in particular those with highly qualified workers, high autonomy, and much learning opportunity like e.g. in high performance teams or in project teams, we often find high degrees of work-related stress putting the workers' mental health at risk. This rather surprising empirical fact requires theoretical reflection to the effect that structural properties of work do not per se create high quality of work and that, in contrast, in a resource-centred perspective, human and social resources needed in work can only be defined in relation to the real action requirements in the working situation. Autonomy, for instance, in this sense is not a resource as such, but only in its sound relationship to other working conditions and requirements like time limits or material supply; otherwise it will produce stress.

In a resource-centred perspective, it is therefore necessary to investigate the relationships between given requirements and available resources for work and to bring them into a reasonable balance by means of work design. Only then it will be possible to create socially "sustainable work systems" that do not consume or wear out human and social resources (causing various stress symptoms), but rather maintain and re-create them within the processes of work (Brödner 2002, Docherty et al. 2002).

National Programmes and their Impact

National programmes supporting the development of work organisation are rather unevenly distributed among EU member states. While e.g. Finland, Denmark or Germany have implemented more than one national programme with efforts to promote work organisation in different areas, other member states, in particular Austria, Belgium, France, Greece, Italy, Luxembourg, The Netherlands and Spain, seemingly have no national activities of this kind, although there might be some regional or project-based efforts with public funding like ADAPT or EQUAL. Comparing new national initiatives with programme activities in the early 1990ies, it seems that efforts even have been reduced in terms of number and volumes of programmes (Latniak 1995).

When evaluating the national programmes identified, an important relational aspect has to be regarded. That is the relation of the programme's volume to the size of the economy (as e.g. measured in terms of GDP). If we, for instance, compare the efforts of promoting new forms of work organisation in Finland with those in Germany, we have to consider that the German economy is ca 15.3 times the size of the Finnish economy. This means that Finland, actually spending some 8.5 million e for its three programmes supporting the development of new forms of work organisation, would fictively spend 130 million e if it had the size of the German economy, where the real efforts amount to ca. 40 million e only. Hence, Germany takes less than one third of the Finnish efforts to support the development of new forms of work organisation. This result is even more emphasised, if we consider the more or less supportive industrial relations in both countries. While the social partners in Finland are very active in raising awareness for and the promoting of new forms of work organisation as a vehicle for improved competitiveness and quality of working life, in Germany they are rather reluctant or indifferent in general, although they participated in the design of the programmes. Similar comparisons can be made with Sweden where the fictive support would sum up to 137 million e.

There obviously is a large slope between Northern and Southern EU member states with respect to the implementation and impact of national programmes supporting the development of new forms of work organisation. This points, however, together with the slow progress in dissemination of new forms of work organisations, to a widening gap between Europe's agreed strategic objectives for further socio-economic development on one hand and its real capacities to achieve those objectives on the other.

Denmark

National Programme "Funds for the Promotion of Better Working Lives and Increased Growth" by the Ministry of Labour:

- *Objectives*: To improve employees' working conditions, to improve enterprises' competitiveness and, in general, to further growth.
- *Key activities*: The core activities are focused on improving employees' working conditions, on reducing the risk of health and qualification-

related exclusion from the labour market and also on improving enterprises' flexibility and development opportunities through a redistribution of job tasks. Training and measures to promote co-operation can also be carried out (if desired with the assistance of a consultant).

- *Target group*: SMEs with less than 250 employees in all sectors of the economy.
- *Volume*: 14 million e with 1500 applications and 228 projects approved during the years 1995 to 1999 (the last projects being terminated in 2001).

National Programme "Action Plan against Monotonous Repetitive Work" by the Ministry of Labour and Work Environment Council:

- *Objective*: To halve the extent of unhealthy monotonous repetitive work before the year 2000.
- *Key activities*: Support of all kinds of research, development, exchange of experience, information and consultation activities at company and industry level to reduce monotonous repetitive work through new forms of work organisation such as rotation arrangements, job extension and job enrichment, or group work and limiting monotonous repetitive work by collective bargaining.
- *Target group*: Industrial enterprises.
- *Volume*: 27 million e for 172 projects in companies and for research and diffusion activities since 1993. Additionally the health and safety system has initiated a large number of activities.

Both programmes and their activities have experienced considerable public awareness and found general support by the social partners. Beside publications, many conferences, seminars, company demonstration meetings have been arranged country-wide and regionally. To a higher degree than before, work organisation issues and their effects on productivity, flexibility and attractivity for workers have been discussed in companies, thus contributing to a general positive attitude towards work change activities. In the case of the Funding of Better Working Lives and Increased Growth Programme, assistance from consultants was included in many projects with positive effects for the progress of projects as well as for the diffusion of knowledge.

Both programmes have also been officially evaluated. In the case of the Funding of Better Working Lives and Increased Growth Programme, evaluation shows that the majority of the projects have played a positive

role for the development of the participating enterprises and that there is reality behind the principles of win-win development possibilities. Often, improvements at workplaces occur at the same time as improvements in the enterprises' profitability pointing to the fact that enterprises very often have unutilised resources.
In the case of the Action Plan against Monotonous Repetitive Work, the evaluation shows that the overall aim to halve monotonous repetitive work has not been reached; only for ca. one fourth of the employees monotonous repetitive work has been reduced, partly by means of job rotation and partly by slowing down work pace or introducing piecework ceilings. There are considerable differences between industries, though, where for instance in the food, beverages and tobacco industries monotonous repetitive work has been cut down by almost 40% by means of automation and changes in work organisation.
According to the EPOC survey, Denmark features a relatively high diffusion of group work as one significant new form of work organisation.

Finland

National Programme "Finnish Work Place Development Programme" by the Ministry of Labour:

- *Objective*: To promote effectiveness and quality of working life by innovation-supporting modes of operation and employee skills at Finnish workplaces. This also includes raising the level of employability, developing the ability to cope with work requirements and reinforcing workplace development expertise in Finland.
- *Key activities*: The key activities are focused on 'research-supported development' projects (eventually assisted by consultants), in particular to achieve changes in the mode of operation at workplaces (e.g. introducing team work, learning opportunities, innovative use of ICT), to disseminate knowledge on workplace development, and to strengthen the workplace development infrastructure in Finland. The programme classifies every funded project by its primary and secondary aims. Programme statistics covering the years 2000-02 and some 150 projects show that 'promoting teamwork, group work or cells' has been an aim in 40% of the projects and 'development of organization structures' in 13%. In addition, many other projects may have touched work organizational issues (e.g. those with the aim to 'develop work processes'). One may say that work organization development is a major issue in the programme.
- *Target group*: All sectors of the economy are addressed by the programme. The share of manufacturing and construction of all project

funding is 45% (especially metalworking industry), the share of private service industries 20% and the share of local authorities 30% (especially welfare and health care services).

- *Volume*: 37 million e with 520 projects (ca. 80% of which are development projects) during the years 1996 to 2002. The second phase of the programme continuous up to 2003.

The Finnish Workplace Development Programme has a considerable positive impact on changes of work organisation in Finland, in particular with respect to changes in productivity, quality, work operations and social relations at workplaces. More than 1.000 operating units have so far been funded. An overall programme evaluation is in the making.

As the annual Finnish Working Life Barometer of the Finnish Ministry of Labour has revealed (on the basis of computer aided telephone interview data from more than 1,000 wage and salary earners being representative for all Finnish wage and salary earners), some 80% of the respondents said by November 2001 that employees worked in groups (teams, cells or project groups) 'mostly' or 'partly'. The share of those who said 'mostly' has increased in manufacturing from 34% to 44% from 1995 to 2001 and in private services from 22% to 30%. Corresponding figures from the local authority and central government sectors are also available (concerning the year 2001 cf. the annual report Ylöstalo 2002).

Similarly, the Quality of Work Life Survey by the Statistics Finland (based on face-to-face interviews with 2.979 wage and salary earners) states that in 1997 74% of the respondents said that teamwork is applied at their workplace (Lehto/Sutela 1999). Moreover, the University of Tampere carried out in 2000 a mail survey with 1.775 responses of Finnish wage and salary earners; here the corresponding figure was 81% (Blom et al. 2001; further findings on dissemination of new forms of work organisation can be found in Antila/Ylöstalo 1999 and NUTEK 1999 (cf. chapter 2)).

Some of the reports also point to qualitative problems in working life that are presently being discussed in Finland. This discussion is going on in terms of problems of short-term employment contracts, job insecurity, harassment and exhaustion at work. The programme, however, starts with the assumption that problems like these are not individual and separate problems but basically derive from poor management and poor organization of work not considering sustainability issues.

National Programme "Well-Being at Work Programme" by the Ministries of Labour (coordination), Social Affairs and Health, Education, and Trade and Industry:

- *Objectives*: To improve the quality of life, to promote the working capacity and well-being at work of the Finnish workforce, and to help people stay in the labour market for longer.
- *Key activities*: Providing information and promoting good practices on well-being at work, utilising research results and commissioning new research, supporting projects which promote well-being at work, and monitoring legislation. Development projects emphasize management practices such as on-the-job learning, flexible working time arrangements and methods that successfully reconcile companies′ requirements with employees′ individual needs. Many projects include management training connected with feedback from employees and intermediates to the operations and targets of the work community. Funds are given to the projects for employing external experts (researchers, trainers and consultants).
- *Target group*: The programme covers all sectors of the economy (with following shares of funding: municipal sector 31%, private service industries 20%, parishes, associations and foundations 27 %, government sector 8 %, manufacturing 6 %, farmers and entrepreneurs 8 %).
- Volume: 5,5 million e for about 180 projects (out of altogether 538 applications) during the years 2000 to 2003.

The Well-Being at Work Programme has funded more than 250 operating units. It has gained great positive publicity. Both the project team and for example social partners and research institutions have organised a lot of seminars and conferences concerning well-being at work. In this situation, an active and initiating information campaign is focused on describing the factors promoting well-being and the economic effects of well-being at work as well as on spreading good practices and utilising research findings. The Barometer of Maintenance of Work Ability (MWA barometer) of the Ministry of Social Affairs and Health and of the Finnish Institute of Occupational Health collects information on the prevalence, resources, content, implementation and benefits of MWA activities. Information is collected by telephone interviews. The sample of workplaces represents the entire working population in the private and public sectors. The study shows that over 90 % of operating units with more than two employees have organised some kinds of MWA activities and that, additionally, a multitude of various MWA activities has been started. Moreover, more than one third of the workplaces reported that the MWA activities had increased at their workplaces during the past 12 months (concerning the year 2001 cf. the annual report Peltomäki 2002).

National Programme "Finnish National Productivity Programme" launched by the Economic Council led by the Prime Minister:

- *Objectives*: Main objectives are to increase the functionality of workplace communities, to speed-up productivity improvement in companies and other types of organisations, to promote Finland's competitive edge in international markets, and to raise the employment rate and level of income.
- *Key activities*: Prioritised activities concentrate on improving and utilising the competence of employees at various stages of the career by developing work organisation and workplace culture, on developing suitable methods and practices for improving the productivity of SMEs in the industrial and service sectors, and on launching development projects related to the application of productivity know-how.
- *Target group*: The programme does not finance the development of individual workplaces, but the companies interested in boosting their productivity can apply methods and practices already developed or seek to participate in projects and receive support from researchers or consultants.
- *Volume*: The programme follows earlier initiatives and operates during the years 2000 to 2003 with 11 practical research projects approved in 2000.

Germany

National Programme "Innovative Development of Work – The Future of Work" by the Ministry of Education and Research, managed by the Work Design and Services project management agency:

- *Objectives*: The framework conception aims at developing competence for the future by promoting and expanding the development opportunities of individuals and companies, so that they can shape the processes of change occurring in the working world in an active and human-oriented manner, and thus contribute to economic success and employment. The main objectives are to develop and test integral and sustainable solutions for company and work organisation balancing between human-oriented work structures, business success and employment, to develop approaches and strategies that give working people opportunities for orientation, qualification and development, to provide impulses for the realisation of equal opportunities in the working world, and to support the extensive application of knowledge for work and company organisation and to intensify interdisciplinary cooperation.

- *Key activities* are the identification and balancing of successful changes in work design and company organisation, the effects of demographic change on future work, and the prevention of health and safety at work on the basis of new forms of work organisation
- *Target group*: Funding is provided for collaborative projects and addresses companies (in all sectors of the economy), research institutes, associations, and consultants covering up to 50% of total research and development efforts of a project.
- *Volume*: 30 million e per annum.

National Programme "Production Technologies" by the Ministry of Education and Research, managed by the Production Technologies project management agency:

- *Objectives*: To increase competitiveness of industrial enterprises for sustainable development and to improve their capacity for change.
- *Key activities* are market orientation and strategic product planning (strategic business planning, new perspectives for product innovation such as sustainability, use of software, miniaturisation, integration of services, fast engineering and knowledge management); technologies and production equipment (innovative production devices, flexibly configurable machines and production systems, reduction of value chains); new forms of cooperation between firms (management of enterprise networks, building regional networks, use of new ICT for business processes); humans and learning enterprises (educating workers for future production systems, new methods for work design, organising learning enterprises and human-centred design of production systems).

  At least parts of the first and in total the fourth bundle of key activities are directed to support new forms of work organisation, while the other activities rather promote the development and use of production technologies. The programme thus complements in parts the Future of Work Programme for the industrial sectors that account for ca. 30% of GDP and still plays a major role in the German economy.
- *Target group*: Industrial companies and research institutes in collaborative projects, especially with SMEs. Funding covers up to 50% of total research and development efforts of a project.
- *Volume*: 62 million e per year for total programme; 10 million e per year for activities related to work organisation issues. The programme was launched in 1999 and is designed as a "learning programme" with

undefined end. Approx. 120 partners working on work organisation issues are funded in the first phase.

Germany has a long tradition in national programmes supporting the development of new forms of work organisation since the launch of the Humanisation of Working Life Programme in 1974 and the Manufacturing Technology Programme in 1980. Although the social partners have been involved from the beginning in designing the programmes, in evaluating proposals and even in participating in projects, the impact of the programmes in terms of general awareness of underlying problems, of understanding the contribution of new forms of work organisation to competitiveness, and with respect to their dissemination is relatively restrained (cf. fig. 2). Traditional management practices according to the Taylor model of enterprises still prevail.
Over the years, there have been high efforts to spread and share the growing body of knowledge about the rationale of new forms of work organisation, the ways how they can be implemented, and the effects they have on economic performance and quality of working life. However, despite strong empirical evidence for the economic benefits and despite some public support for organisational development, persistent implementation of new forms of work organisation is restricted to only a small minority of enterprises. As compared to Sweden or Finland, the impact on the dissemination of new forms of work organisation is less.
Moreover, in case of the Humanisation of Working Life programme and its successors (namely Future of Work), programme activities experienced a decline in the 1990ies (after a rapid rise in the beginning and a long consolidation phase in the 1980ies). This is also mirrored in the programme's funding volumes that have steadily been reduced during the 1990ies from a level of 50 to 30 million g. Their relative extent is now approximately one fourth of that in Sweden or Finland only (for details of the programmes' history and the background of the German labour process development see Fricke 2002, Oehlke 2001).
In recent years and particularly in the Production Technology programme efforts in transfer activities on both programme and project level have been enlarged. Besides of conferences, round tables and workshops, many projects have installed industrial working groups with partners not being funded and distribute progress newsletters over the Internet.

Ireland

Under the social partnership agreement "Programme for Prosperity and Fairness" the government-sponsored agency "National Centre for Partnership and Performance (NCPP)" has been established working with the Department of An Taoiseach:

- *Objectives*: The Centre is committed to reconfiguring and refocusing enterprise-level partnership in a manner that invigorates the societal momentum in favour of this concept and also repositions it at the centre of public policy process in accordance with the pursuit of key national strategic priorities. This involves repositioning partnership around issues relating to higher organisational performance, sustaining competitive advantage, modernising public services and promoting working arrangements that are flexible and responsive to changing employment and social priorities.
- *Key activities*: The Centre is involved in supporting and encouraging organisations to address organisational change through partnership-style arrangements, in particular with the following activities: Learning by Monitoring Project – Local Area Government and Health Sector; Training for Trainers Programme – Developing a Competency Framework; Guidelines for Partnership in the Workplace; Guidelines on Financial Participation.
  The achievement of these national strategic priorities is dependent on organisations and individuals across the public and private sector embracing and supporting ongoing change and innovation. Accordingly, projects are focused on development and improvement within organisations – however the NCPP is not a consultancy body. Development occurs through a mixture of research and dissemination, project management, training and a limited amount of direct strategic facilitation.
- *Target groups* are all companies in the private sector, semi-state commercial organisations, and public sector bodies and government departments.
- *Volume*: Funding is through direct government budget (and externally funded projects). NCPP was launched in March 2002; 4 major funded projects are underway so far.

In quantitative terms, new forms of work organisation are already relatively widespread in Ireland. In a survey of 1997 by University College Dublin, delegative forms of participation, for instance, organised around team structures was found in 42% of Irish organisations, while temporary groups

such as project teams or task forces were found in 36% of enterprises. These levels of incidence of new work practices diminish, of course, if the depth and scope for change are taken into account (cf. fig.2, EPOC Research Team 1998, Geary 1999).
In qualitative terms, there are high levels of public awareness around partnership at a national level, although the awareness and understanding of enterprise partnership is less developed. Further work is required to firmly establish the case for partnership – both for employers, employees and unions.
Since March NCPP has already produced joint union/employer guidelines on partnership and NCPP is currently working with the social partners to investigate financial participation. The programme of NCPP is well supported across the social partners. Initial conference activities have been very well attended.
Initial work with the consultancy community has been largely positive – though for some the Centre may be seen as threatening.

Portugal

National Programme "Integrated Programme for Innovation Support (PROINOV)" managed by PROINOV project management agency under the Ministry of Council Presidency:

- *Objectives*: The general objective is to strengthen the competitiveness of the Portuguese economy on the basis of an integrated policy for supporting innovation being compatible with the creation of more and better jobs and the preservation of the country 's social and regional cohesion. Competitiveness, employment and social cohesion are considered to form a strategic core triangle. In particular, the Integrated Programme aims at promoting entrepreneurship and innovation to meet new global and European challenges; enhancing education and training; improving general conditions for innovation; strengthening the innovation system in Portugal.
- *Key activities*: Promoting quality as well as organisational and technology innovation, in particular by disseminating the use of international quality standards and methodologies as levers for adopting and adapting innovative solutions relevant to technology, organisation, management, training, safety and environmental protection, by developing a programme for disseminating new organisational solutions in companies, by giving priority to technological and organisational innovation when granting investment incentives, by promoting an innovation-driven culture through disseminating the results of innovation

projects and organising demonstration events on the role of technological and organisational innovation in improving productivity and daily life of citizens in the workplace, education, transport, housing.
Programme activities include research, development, transfer, and consultancy.

- *Target group*: All sectors of the economy.
- *Volume*: The programme uses European Regional Development Funds directing and bundling them towards PROINOV objectives; period of operation is 2002 to 2006. In starting phase ca 50 applications are being evaluated.

Politically, the newly started Integrated Programme for Innovation Support in Portugal acknowledges the significance of organisational innovation as critical factor to cope with productivity problems and competitiveness. The programme has not been evaluated so far (since it has just started).
There are very few studies on the issue of dissemination of new forms of work organisation in Portugal (covering the late 1980ies and early 1990ies). There are also no specific post graduation courses that could stimulate such studies. There are only two research centres that cover the field: SOCIUS (Research Centre on Sociology of Economy and Organisations, at the Technical University of Lisbon, ISEG-UTL) and IET (Research Centre of Entrepreneurial and Work Innovation, at the New University of Lisbon, FCT-UNL). Consultancy business is not prepared to support such projects, despite the fact that there are several industrial and service companies that are adopting and experimenting new forms of work organisation.
All in all, work organisation is a theme that interests public administration and social partners, but so far there have been very few projects financed on this thematic, however. Most of studies done are supported by the Ministry of Labour or at the European Commission level (e.g. through the Framework Programmes, EFILWC in Dublin (cf. EPOC Research Team 1998) or DG Employment and Social Affairs).

Sweden

National Programme "Sustainable Work Systems and Health" by the Ministry of Industry, managed by the Swedish Agency for Innovation Systems (VINNOVA):

- *Objectives* are to support national societal sustainable growth through initiating and maintaining organisational and individual sustainability, to conduct R & D projects testing new work systems which initiate and maintain organisational and individual sustainability, to establish the 'state of the art' concerning sustainable work systems, to generate 'actionable knowledge' as the basis for government and business policy decisions, and to create a platform for broad experimentation in working life.

- *Key activities*: The programme is basically oriented to improving current practice in Swedish working life on a project basis. Thereby it underlines the importance of generating 'actionable knowledge', knowledge that will help practitioners to solve the problems they are facing. The projects are usually cross-disciplinary and involve close co-operation between the actors involved, be they researchers, consultants or practitioners from both management and personnel and their unions. Thus they involve action research, action learning and the generation of 'actionable knowledge'. Key activities in this context are the design of sustainable work systems, the integration of the design of jobs with the design of the organisation, leadership in sustainable systems, the design of management and feedback systems in sustainable systems, not least requiring balancing/integrating the needs and interest of different constituencies, the design of learning and communication systems, and the development of models and methods for the development of sustainable work systems.
  Projects cover knowledge, facts, models, methods, tools, educational materials and examples from which people may learn and include elements of research, development and learning and may be conducted by appropriate groupings of consultants, practitioners from management or staff/unions, and researchers.
- *Target group*: All sectors of the economy.
- *Volume*: The start-up phases of the programme establishing the state-of-the-art and conducting a number of shorter test projects, had a budget of ca 2.2 million e a year (with 20 projects exploring the state-of-the-art and 15 test projects since 1999). The coming five years may be expected to have an annual budget of ca 16.7 million e. The expected period of operation is 1999 to 2006.

So far, more than 50 partners have been funded within the Sustainable Work Systems and Health Programme (although not all of them are formal contractors to VINNOVA); this number will rapidly grow in the next years. Since the programme is still in its first phases, it has not yet been evaluated. The first editions of the state-of-the-art reports from the programme (in

Swedish only) are out of print, however, and reprinting is under consideration.

The Swedish public is well aware of the issues of work intensity, long sickness absence (> one year), early sickness retirement, burnout, chronic tiredness, exhaustion, or depression:

- Members of VINNOVA and NIWL have been involved in producing government white papers on the extent of the problems related to work intensity and the need for development efforts (two examples are the report from the Sahlin group (SOU 2001) and the Action Plan for Improved Health in Working Life (SOU 2002)).
- The central union organisations have written policy papers based on the reports mentioned above emphasising the need to prioritise leadership and participation issues (Hållbar utveckling (Sustainable development), Stockholm: LO, TCO & SACO, 2002).
- Several national seminars have been conducted by the Swedish Council for Work Life Research, the NIWL and the central union organisations.
- International seminars have been held (on the basis of Docherty et al. 2002) at the Academy of Management (USA 2000), the European Academy of Management (Barcelona 2001, Stockholm, 2002), the Work Intensification conference (Paris 2002) and the Complexity and Organisations conference (USA, 2002)

The diffusion of new forms of work organisation being developed and spread in the context of previous programmes, in particular the Swedish Working Life Fund Programme with its 23.000 development projects, appears to be far more advanced than in other European countries (cf. chapter 2, especially fig.2 above, EPOC Research Team 1998, NUTEK 1996 and 1999, ITPS 2001). This clearly indicates a high degree of public awareness of the significance of work organisation for economic and social progress and of the commitment of the social partners.

United Kingdom

National Programme "The Partnership at Work Fund" by the Department of Trade and Industry:

- Objectives: The Partnership Fund is designed to develop a new approach to employment relations, based on partnership at work underpinned by a legal framework of minimum, decent standards.
- Key activities: The Fund aims to improve relationships between employers, employees and their representatives in order to secure

performance improvements in the workplace, by supporting projects which: implement a culture change towards partnership; address business issues facing the organisation; implement schemes to enhance work-life balance and disseminate best practice in partnership.

- Target group: Funding is available to companies, business intermediaries including employer federations, trade unions and other employee representatives, trade associations, Business Links, Learning and Skills Councils (or equivalents), public sector bodies and charities are all eligible to apply. Bids can come from an individual workplace submitting a project between the employer (or their representatives) and employees (or their representatives); a trade union working with the employer, the employees, a Business Link or LSC (or equivalent) working with a business or organisation. There is no set number or combination of partners. The Fund is available to organisations in England, Scotland and Wales.
- Volume: The Prime Minister launched the Partnership at Work Fund in 1999. The initial £5m funding, which has now been distributed with the first four calls was made available over four years. An additional injection of £9m is available over next 2 years.

Support is available for up to 50% of total eligible costs of individual projects, up to a limit of £50,000 support per project.

160 successful projects are currently receiving funding under the Partnership at Work Fund. There were 33 successful bidders in the first round of the scheme, 40 in the second, 37 in the third and 49 in the fourth. Quantitative data on the dissemination of new forms of work organisation are not available (except EPOC data, cf. fig.2). Warwick University is currently conducting an independent evaluation on the Partnership Fund. The results of this survey will be published soon.

The Role of Social Partners

While focusing on the dissemination of new forms of work organisation, it is evident that industrial relations and the social partners' organisations play a crucial role in this respect in the EU member states. Three aspects shall briefly illustrate their importance.

First, on a workplace level, according to the varying regulations or collective agreements, there is an involvement of employee representatives (unions representatives or works councils) in organisational change processes. As the EIROnline issue on "The involvement of employees and collective bargaining in company restructuring" (2001) states, representational employee participation occurs over various aspects of enterprise restructuring, with major variations. While in most countries there predominantly is an information and consultation of employee representatives, there are specific co-determination rights in processes of organisational change in Germany: e.g. there are quite far reaching co-determination rights of the works councils in the enterprises based on the regulations of the Works Constitution Act. This covers information, consultation and co-determination on various structural issues as are change of production facilities, introduction of new equipment, new production systems, production processes, or work organisation, closures, mergers, or collective redundancies.

Experiences of change processes repeatedly demonstrated that the information and consultation of the employees play a crucial role for the success of the change process. Attitudes towards the change process – based on experiences of those involved – and the way how conflicts are resolved must be taken into account when thinking about the role of social partners and employees representatives on a enterprise level. This clearly leads to a new long term management perspective of building a trust based and co-operative enterprise culture. "Creating a culture of partnership takes time" as the latest EC programme report stated (EC 2000: 15). For a dissemination of new organisational structures and practices, information and the attitudes, activities, and experiences of employees and their representatives are important for scale, scope, and economic success of the change process. In this sense, the UK and Irish activities for building partnership address a core issue which is a prerequisite for successful organisational change processes in the enterprises.

Secondly, changes of organisational structures normally lead to new tasks to be performed by the employees. Apart from co-determination rights or information and consultation practices – which directly involve the employees and their representatives –, in many cases the wage and remuneration systems as well as working time regulations or personnel development schemes are closely linked to tasks and task descriptions. Accordingly, these systems must be adapted to the new structural determinants especially if profit sharing and different types of bonuses are discussed. As many of the wage systems are based on social partners' collective agreements on different levels, these organisations become involved in these changes. As there is a kind of tradition of excluding bargaining of wages from these programmes, there is still a need to "backing up" change processes by social partners in a certain way.

Thirdly, the social partners' organisations are important for raising the awareness on certain aspects and on the importance of organisational change. By distributing information on methods and effects of the organisational restructuring among members and in public, by supporting these change processes in different ways (offering tools etc), and by influencing public policy (i.e. by supporting programmes like those we investigated) and accompanying public discussion, they can provide an active role to a development of a sustainable and 'high road' oriented development of organisational structures in their countries.

Keeping in mind that enterprises themselves have to decide whether to change organisational structures or to join the programmes, there is a danger of "preaching to the saved": Only enterprises which are already aware of these problems will often take the chance to become active or to join the programme activities while at the same time a large part of the enterprises seems to keep existing structures and practices. As long as we can identify a limited dissemination of these practices in many European countries (cf. chapter 2), there is a need to intensify the promotion of organisational change practices, especially in the SME sector.

It is fairly evident that the tradition of industrial relations and their prevalent character (co-operative vs. adversarial) has a major influence on the existence and the shaping of the programmes in each country. Furthermore, the experiences e.g. of the "lean production" debate led to some sceptical view on co-operative restructuring efforts inside the unions (e.g. the "lean and mean" discussion in the Netherlands and Sweden) while at the same time, there is still an ongoing emphasis towards deregulation of industrial relations. Nevertheless, the continuing challenge of Europe's industry needs to be managed by joint activities of the social partners – without neglecting different legitimation, orientation, and interests. But there is a need to further develop partnership and co-operative practices, and in this respect these national programmes can be seen as a kind of learning environment. The re-orientation of the social partners' attitudes can be seen e.g. in Finland where the adversarial industrial relations of the 1980's changed towards a more co-operative structure. In Portugal, there is some indication for a beginning change related to states' programmes.

Accordingly, at least three different levels of activity and support of the social partners for the programmes in question can be discriminated.

First, as in most cases, the social partners' organisations are represented in the design and development periods of the programmes. There are representatives and experts joining the programme development in advisory boards or councils in which the policy activities are advised and discussed. This is the case in Denmark, in Finland, in Germany, in Ireland, in Portugal, and in Sweden. E.g., the Irish National Centre for Partnership and Performance (NCPP) which has been established under the social partnership agreement "Programme for Prosperity and Fairness" e.g. is working with the Department of An Taoiseach and it has a 16 member council: 4 employers representatives, 4 Union representatives, 4 government representatives, and 4 independent members. For the UK Partnership Fund, no information on a co-operative board or council is reported. A specific point in Sweden is that the unions and employers' organisations are members of the boards of the operating agencies (NIWL, VINOVA), as well.

Secondly, focusing on the operative level of programme management, the activities of the social partners are less widespread. According to our results, in the Danish Action Plan e.g., the social partners have been active in the project steering group and the work environment councils participated in the local steering groups of the enterprise projects. In some of the programmes, as are e.g. in Germany or in Sweden, there are expert boards or programme management groups joining the selection of projects or following the ongoing projects. In Portugal, the social partners were involved in these operational activities, too. Compared to the programme development level, we can say that there is a limited participation of the social partners on the operational level.

Thirdly, social partners' activities on a project level are fairly exceptional. For Sweden, it is reported that direct participation of employees is the regular case in the projects while a representative participation is performed according to the enterprise tradition and practice. Only for programmes in two countries, we could find activities of the social partners' organisations on the enterprise level.

- In the German programmes, there are a few projects carried out by unions or union related organisations. On the one hand, they are directed towards the development and dissemination of adapted information and tools for works council members e.g. On the other hand, there is a project of the service sector union (VER.DI) investigating into the options to work structuring in call centres (i.e. a research oriented project). Furthermore, in the enterprise projects of the German programmes, representatives of management and works councils must be involved.

- In Ireland, we could identify an active role of the social partners on a project level as well. For example, both ICTU and IBEC nominated individuals to work on the "Working Together for Change and Modern Workplace – Guidance for the Unionised Commercial Sector" project.

Conclusion: Recommendations for Further Initiatives

In this final section of the report a number of recommendations for further initiatives are derived from the balance and evaluation of the material gathered above. They focus on implementation and dissemination issues and are grouped according to the main actors involved: enterprises, social partners and policy makers. Future initiatives promoting the development of new forms of work organisation must consider and reflect on general trends that recently have been investigated, in particular the polarisation of work structures, the innovation strategies, and the new dimensions of work-related stress.

Initiatives on the Level of Enterprises

(1) Considering the unbroken trends towards customer orientation and integration of production and services as well as towards networking of organisations (e.g. virtual enterprises), it still is rather unknown territory, which effects these new management strategies really have on work organisation, in particular on working tasks and working conditions. Although there exist a number of case studies covering these issues, an overall picture is still missing so far. Therefore, comprehensive investigations are needed to identify new roles and working tasks, new competencies and qualifications needed, the working conditions and work loads in this context, since the different acting perspectives and practices of producing things and of communicating with customers or partner organisations are eventually coming into conflict. Especially, knowledge is missing about how the independently operating units can develop the necessary social relationships like trust or shared know how needed for cohesion.

(2) With broad dissemination of new management strategies such as customer orientation, decentralisation, or collaboration in enterprise networks and new working tasks and working conditions, a gap between the new working requirements and existing organisational cultures will open up. Consequently, this will give rise to the need for cultural change and collective learning processes as well as for the development of appropriate procedures to master these change processes.

(3) The alarming differences in performance, quality of work, and employment between "low road" and "high road" strategies of innovation need to be reflected on a broad basis. According to the data presented, the vast majority of enterprises either working in traditional tracks of division of labour and hierarchical command and control or just following the mainstream "low road" of innovation, under-utilises its resources and still operates below its potential. Many enterprises, thus, act counter to their own interests of exploiting business opportunities and of making profits. Even worse: They frequently deprive themselves of the human resources and the capacity to radically change their work organisation to pave the way to the "high road". Since they thus fail to build the business processes and the human resources for the "high road" strategy as a necessary entrepreneurial basis, Europe as a whole will fail to achieve its strategic objectives for employment and for building an advanced and productive knowledge-based society. Reflecting on the conditions for implementing the "high road" strategy, further recommendations have to be regarded.

(4) The working situation for (mainly intellectual) workers with high qualifications, broad scope for action and learning in high performance teams is rather unknown terrain, in particular with respect to work-related stress. In the past, the paramount focus of work analysis and design has been on functionally divided shop floor work and routine office work that, of course, formed the vast majority of work places. While the share of highly qualified work in flexible decentralised, more autonomous groups and project teams is rapidly increasing, more and more workers are experiencing all kinds of high work load and multiple stress reactions such as states of exhaustion, depressions, or burnout syndromes. As signalled by these growing numbers of cases with work-related mental stress reactions, it becomes necessary to shift the focus of work analysis and design to these new kinds of working situations. This appears even more indicated as the stress reactions, beside the individual workers' health risks, causes rapidly

growing costs on the level of the enterprise as well as on the level of the society (Gabriel/Liimatainen 2000). This also requires, that, based on the theoretical perspective of a resource-centred analysis, new methods for identifying, analysing, and evaluating the specific resources needed for work in relation to given requirements are being developed and tested. With respect to work design and the implementation of "sustainable work systems", it is further necessary to explore the conditions under which these resources can regenerate and develop rather than being consumed in work processes Brödner 2002, Docherty et al. 2002).

(5) Under the same resource-centred perspective, a diversity of approaches to constrain and to cope with high time pressures and work loads already being tried out in some advanced enterprises should be tested more systematically. Enterprises with large numbers of highly demanding work places causing mental stress should be encouraged to experiment with new forms of sustainable work systems. In order to develop best management practices in this respect, they should be supported to explore appropriate opportunities and conditions for a good balance of requirements and resources in work processes such that the personal and social resources can regenerate and develop.

(6) Considering ageing work forces throughout Europe, initiatives for organising work-related continuous learning processes are needed. The implementation of life-long learning strategies primarily is a matter of long term development of human resources in enterprises and highly depends on new forms of work organisation that offer sufficient learning opportunities. Reflecting on own practices and learning then are an integral part of work tasks contributing to continuous improvement of working processes, and most learning occurs during work. Offline training efforts may complement and support such work-related learning if appropriately designed. Best practice demonstrators in this perspective should be developed (Brödner/Klaßen-Kluger 1998, EWON 2001).

Initiatives on the Level of Social Partners and Policy Makers

(7) Regarding Europe's pretentious strategic objectives on one hand and realising the poor and unbalanced state of dissemination of new forms of work organisation – with public awareness as well as managerial and unionist interest rather shrinking than expanding – on the other, it appears necessary to define a coherent European strategy for the development and dissemination of new forms of work organisation. Such a strategy is

currently missing as the real development of process innovations in Europe is "project-driven rather than strategy-driven" and " since the publication of the Green Paper there have been no new measures designed to build capacity or to animate workplace change" (Ennals et al. 2001: 271). The strategy has to clearly distinguish between macro and micro level perspectives and activities, but has, at the same time, to safeguard that both are mutually adjusted and complement each other. Efforts of re-regulating framework conditions (such as working time, social security, education and training) under the perspectives of "flexicurity" and "sustainability" as prerequisites for human resources development must be linked to and combined with the promotion of new forms of work organisation serving as vehicles to improved economic performance, competitiveness, employment and growth. Unless the combination of these perspectives is successfully implemented, the agreed strategic efforts to increase employment and to build an advanced and productive knowledge-based society are bound to fail.

(8) The great relevance the development of new forms of work organisation has for both quality of working life and for productivity and growth is, contrary to pressing empirical evidence, still widely underestimated (if not even denied) throughout Europe. Hence, there is a great risk that the EU fails to build cornerstones needed for erecting the four pillars of its Employment Strategy. Consequently, urgent initiatives are needed to raise public awareness for the underlying work organisation issues and their impact on growth and human resources development (in particular in the southern EU member states). Such initiatives fostering the broad implementation of "high road" strategies for creating wealth and quality of work should be integrated into the benchmarking procedures of the European Employment Strategy. To this end, annual National Action Plans (NAPs) should contain clear statements on the dissemination of new forms of work organisation and on the impact they have on economic performance and employment based on regular surveys. These results provide indispensable complementary information to national efforts in de- and re-regulating framework conditions (and they may dissolve neo-liberal myths about economic development). The Finnish practices in connection with their National Programmes can serve as a model for this.
(9) As the High Level Expert Group on economic and social impacts of industrial change (headed by Peer Gyllenhammar) has already recommended in 1998, a forum for industrial change processes (beyond EIRO activities) should be further developed (High Level Expert Group

1998). Its objective should be to create and exchange more information and knowledge on industrial change processes with special emphasis on work organisation, innovation and employment. Such activities may also support the efforts of raising awareness for the problems and effects of implementing sustainable work systems on the "high road". In particular, much more reflection should be given to the slope between Northern and Southern countries in the implementation of new forms of work organisation. Meanwhile the European Monitoring Centre on Change (EMCC at the European Foundation) has been established that may serve as a nucleus for such activities the intensity and impact of which should be increased, however.

(10) The social partners have great responsibility in raising awareness of both managers and highly skilled (intellectual) workers for the health risks of demanding flexible work in high performance teams and, accordingly, for the development and broad implementation of sustainable work systems. They on their turn are challenged to explore new working time regulations that allow for flexible limitations of working requirements on one hand and enables enterprises to create work processes in which personal and social resources can be regenerated and developed on the other.

(11) As much as new forms of work organisation serve as a vehicle to comprehensively develop and use human resources, as much they also create risks for (mental) health and well-being. According to the resource-centred perspective on work, health can only be safeguarded, if conditions of work allow for regeneration of the resources used in work. Complementary to the efforts of analysis, design and evaluation of work that have to be taken at enterprise and work process level, initiatives for re-regulation of framework conditions on the societal level are needed, since health damages produced by high work loads (in particular in flexible high performance teams with much autonomy) cause high costs for the social security systems. In particular, this re-regulation efforts (e.g. sabbaticals, or learning leaves) should focus on social security issues with specific consideration of flexibility needs of organisations ("flexicurity") and on issues of consumption and regeneration of individual and social resources ("sustainability").

References

Alasoini, T.; Halme, P. (Eds.), 1999: *Learning Organisations, Learning Society*, NWDP Yearbook 1999, Helsinki: Ministry of Labour

Andreasen, L.E.; Coriat, B.; Hertog, J.F. den; Kaplinski, R. (Eds.), 1995: *Europe's Next Step: Organisational Innovation, Competition and Employment*, Ilford: Frank Cass

Antila, J.; Ylöstalo, P., 1999: *Functional Flexibility and Workplace Success in Finland*, Helsinki: Ministry of Labour

Blom, R.; Melin, H.; Pyöriä, P., 2001: *Tietotyö ja työelämän muutos: palkkatyön arki tietoyhteiskunnassa*, Helsinki: Gaudeamus

Brödner, P., 2002: *Flexibilität, Arbeitsbelastung und nachhaltige Arbeitsgestaltung*, in: Brödner, P.; Knuth, M. (Hg.): *Nachhaltige Arbeitsgestaltung. Trendreports zur Entwicklung und Nutzung von Humanressourcen*, München: Hampp, 489-541

Brödner, P.; Garibaldo, F.; Oehlke, P.; Pekruhl, U., 1998: *Work Organisation and Employment. The Crucial Role of Innovation Strategies*, Projektbericht 1998-05, Gelsenkirchen: IAT

Brödner, P.; Knuth, M. (Hg.), 2002: *Nachhaltige Arbeitsgestaltung. Trendreports zur Entwicklung und Nutzung von Humanressourcen*, München: Hampp

Brödner, P.; Klaßen-Kluger, L., 1998: *Zukunft der Arbeit und älter werdende Arbeitnehmer*, in: Bosch, G. (Hg.): *Zukunft der Erwerbsarbeit. Strategien für Arbeit und Umwelt*, Frankfurt/M: Campus

Brödner, P.; Latniak, E., 2002: *Will They Ever Take the „High Road"? Recent Findings on Organisational Changes in German Industry*, in: Smeds, R. (Ed.): *Continuous Innovation in Business Processes and Networks*, Proceedings of the 4th Int. CINet Conference, Espoo: Helsinki University of Technology, 119-130

Di Martino, V., 2001: *The High Road to Teleworking*, Geneva: International Labour Organization

Docherty, P.; Forslin, J.; Shani, R. (Eds.), 2002: *Creating Sustainable Work Systems: Emerging Perspectives and Practice*, London: Routledge

EIRObserver 1999: *A new organisation of work: The EU Green Paper and national developments, Complementary Supplement*, EIROnline 2/99

EIROnline 2001: *The Involvement of Employees and Collective Bargaining in Company Restructuring. A Comparative Study*, EIROnline 7/01

Ennals, R.; Totterdill, P.; Ford, C., 2001: *The Work Research Foundation. A national coalition for working life and organizational competence*, Concepts and Transformation 6:3, 259-273

EPOC Research Team, 1998: *New Forms of Work Organisation. Can Europe realise its potential?* Dublin: European Foundation

European Commission (Ed.), 1997: *Green Paper on Partnership for a New Organisation of Work*, Com(97) 128, Brussels: CEC

European Commission (Ed.), 1998: *Modernising the Organisation of Work – a Positive Approach to Change*, Kom(98) 592, Brussels: CEC

European Commission (Ed.), 2000: *Government Support Programmes for New Forms of Work Organisation*, Brussels: European Commission

EWON (Ed.), 2001: *Integration of the Ageing Work Force*, Brussels: European Commission

Gabriel, P.; Liimatainen, M.-R. (Ed.), 2000: *Mental Health in the Workplace*, Geneva: International Labour Organization

Geary, J.F., 1999: *The New Workplace: Change at Work in Ireland*, Int. J. of Human Resource Management 10: 5, 870-890

Hamel, G.; Prahalad, C. K., 1994: *Competing for the Future*, Boston (MA): Harvard Business School Press

High Level Expert Group 1998: *Strategy for Industrial Change*, final report to DG Employment and Social Affairs, Brussels: EC

IMF (Ed.) 2001: *Enterprise Restructuring and Work Organisation*, Research Paper, Geneva: IMF

ITPS (Ed.), 2001: *Enterprises in Transition. Learning Strategies for Increased Competitiveness*, Östersund: ITPS

Latniak, E., 1995: *Public Schemes Promoting Active Involvement of Employees in Innovation*, Luxembourg: SPRINT/EIMS

Lay, G.; Dreher, C.; Kinkel, S., 1996: *Neue Produktionskonzepte leisten einen Beitrag zur Sicherung des Standorts Deutschland*, ISI-Produktionsinnovationserhebung Nr. 1, Karlsruhe: FhG-ISI

Lehto, A.-M.; Sutela, H., 1999: *Efficient, More Efficient, Exhausted: Findings of Finnish Quality of Work Life Surveys 1977-1997*, Helsinki: Statistics Finland

Nordhause-Janz, J.; Pekruhl, U., 2000: *Managementmoden oder Zukunftskonzepte? Zur Entwicklung von Arbeitsstrukturen und von Gruppenarbeit in Deutschland*, in: dieselben (Hg.): *Arbeiten in neuen Strukturen? Partizipation, Kooperation, Autonomie und Gruppenarbeit in Deutschland*, München: Hampp

Nutek (Ed.), 1999: *Flexibility Matters – Flexible Enterprises in the Nordic Countries*, Stockholm: Nutek

Nutek (Ed.), 1996: *Towards Flexible Organisations*, Stockholm: Nutek

NWDP: *Progress of the Finnish National Workplace Development Programme. Interim report of the managemant group to the Economic Council*, Helsinki: Ministry of Labour

OECD 1995: *Technology, Productivity and Job Creation, in particular Part 6: Technology and the Changing Nature of Jobs: Organisational Change and Human Resources*, Paris: OECD

Oehlke, P., 2001: *The Development of Labor Process Policies in the Federal Republic of Germany*, Concepts and Transformation 6:2, 109-140

Peltomäki, P., 2002: *Tyky-barometri: työkykyä ylläpitävä ja edistävä toiminta työpaikoilla vuonna 2001*, Helsinki: Finnish Institute of Occupational Health

Work & Technology Consortium (Ed.), 1997: *A Medium Term Plan for Collaborative Action at the European Level, Final Report*, Vol. V Case Studies, Brussels: European Commission

Work & Technology Consortium (Ed.), 1998: *Work Organisation, Competitiveness, Employment. The European Approach*, Brussels; European Commission

Ylöstalo, P., 2002: *Työolobarometri lokakuu 2001*, Helsinki: Ministry of Labour.

Globalisation, Enterprise Restructuring and the Role of Pacts for Employment and Competitiveness

VOLKER TELLJOHANN

The Background

The *Post-Fordist production model* at company level was developed as a result of fundamental corporate restructuring processes which are characterised by the introduction of new information technologies, new forms of work organisation, transnational mergers and acquisitions, changes in company organisation as a result of in- and outsourcing processes as well as the introduction of shareholder-value orientation as the dominant form of corporate governance. These developments had a major impact on the development of industrial relations, and in particular on interest representation, participation and collective bargaining. One of the most important changes regards the general tendency towards decentralisation of industrial relations. Analysing the development of collective bargaining systems one can observe this tendency very cleary.

Collective bargaining systems in Western European countries have been undergoing profound changes in recent years. In nearly all these countries we can observe a tendency towards a decentralisation of collective bargaining. We can find it in countries which traditionally are characterised by a high level of centralisation of collective bargaining like Germany with its predominant model of industry-wide collective agreements as well as in countries with multilevel collective bargaining systems like Italy. The tendency of decentralisation can be considered as the beginning of a fundamental paradigm shift in collective bargaining.

Since the eighties one can observe a growing shift in the power relations between capital and labour. Management, in fact, has various possibilities to undermine or change existing labour regulation. The threat to move production or to shift investments to countries with lower labour costs may force works councils and trade unions to accept concessions with regard to statutory or collectively agreed standards. Especially within transnational enterprises local management itself is exposed to growing pressure from central management. Benchmarking processes are aimed at increasing competition between the various production sites. As a result issues like labour productivity, labour costs, flexibilisation of working time and new forms of work organisation have become part of such benchmarking processes. Finally, the shareholder-value orientation results in short-term oriented strategies and the elimination of those parts of the enterprises which are not able to meet the profit targets (Bieling/Schulten 2001).

Pacts for Employment and Competitiveness

Growing concern, at all levels, with the development of the European Union's social dimension, has greatly boosted research and analysis of trends characterising relations between the various parties (Governments, trade unions, enterprises), called upon to provide answers regarding the system's competitiveness and its social cohesion.

Consequently, over the past few years, the European Union's efforts to combat unemployment have been notably intensified, and pressure has also increased on Member States to take effective measures in this sense. At the same time, a number of solutions are also being put forward to help achieve this objective. They essentially take the shape of the promotion and intensification of social dialogue on EU and national level. In order to optimise the management of this demanding phase of change, the preferred approach is to get the parties involved and encourage relations with them rather than simply resorting to market forces, or to the uncertain outcomes of conflict situations. Such is the scope of the changes (technological, organisational, managerial) and the challenges presented by market globalisation.

The need to understand what is going on in the field of industrial relations has therefore drawn much attention to the *Pacts for Employment and Competitiveness (PEC)* that have been set up in numerous enterprises in the EU in recent years. Indeed, it is apparent that the challenges of global economy and the resulting decisions made by the European Union on the subject have put the social parties in a position where they are forced to address these various issues in a cohesive manner. This approach derives from the awareness that answers must be found. Answers that, on the one hand, give economic parties all the tools they need to compete on the European and world markets while, on the other, guaranteeing the maintenance and development of the social dimension that is supposed to be one of the European Union's outstanding features, especially on an employment front where it still lags behind other nations. Sisson et al. (1999) define PECs indeed as mutual agreements between enterprise or company management and works councils. The contents of the agreements regard both, the strengthening of competitiveness of the company and the safeguarding of the company's employment situation. On the one hand, works councils agree on measures aimed at cutting costs, expanding flexibility and increasing labour productivity, on the other, management promises to renounce dismissals.

The very characteristics of the PEC have turned it into the instrument that under certain conditions best interprets this need, partly and above all to avoid (or control) conflict situations that would certainly not bring any advantages on the competitiveness front, and are unlikely to help on the employment front, either. Following on from the study of development of this form of relationship between social parties is the need to analyse its tangible applications in the individual Member States and in various sectors. The electricity industry has been one of the first sectors to be analysed in different Member States from a comparative viewpoint. The research project investigated the contents of ten PECs in the electricity industry in five EU Member States (United Kingdom, Ireland, Germany, France, Italy).

In the following, the main results of this comparative analysis of the PECs in the electricity sector will be presented.[1]

The Case of the Energy Sector

The EU policy of liberalisation has also covered the energy sector: directive 96/62 gave liberalisation of the sector the go-ahead and ordered all Member States to break with the monopoly reigning in energy, and to accurately lay down the methods and deadlines for this liberalisation process. Similar policies, all tending towards liberalisation of the remaining monopolies and towards the construction of a European market in the true

[1] For a more detailed presentation of the results of the research project which was promoted and coordinated by the European Foundation for the Improvement of Living and Working Conditions see Telljohann, V., 2001, Pacts for Employment and Competitiveness in the Electricity Sector, Transfer Volume 7 4/2001, 636-649

sense of the word, have been applied to other sectors featuring a strong public presence, such as transport.
The importance and central nature of such public enterprises has meant that all the actors have had proceed with caution in such arenas, partly in consideration of the high levels of employment that have traditionally developed within public monopolies. On the other hand, the need to avoid generalised conflicts in such strategic sectors, especially in such delicate situations, has often made it more opportune to involve union forces in the restructuring processes. It is, therefore, particularly interesting to conduct an in-depth analysis of a sector having all these features in order to see how relations between the parties have developed, what results have been achieved, and at what cost.

The Nature of PECs

The European Union Energy Sector Directive no. 96/62 laid down that Member States were to start up a market liberalisation process obliging energy suppliers to face the need to manage the changeover from a near-monopoly to an internationally competitive enterprise. In the energy sector, PECs are thus the consequence of a process aimed at assessing the competitiveness of individual companies which adopt adequate strategies to face the changing scenario of competition. With regard to the above, the only exception is the British examples, where the privatisation process started at an earlier date compared to the other analysed companies within the framework of nationally-established reforms.
In general, negotiations which later lead to the signing of PECs are begun following a management initiative, based on their need to foster restructuring processes. In fact, in most cases, management will start negotiations after having already drafted concrete proposals and requests. The strategies for managing market liberalisation are aimed, amongst others, at cost-reduction, production diversification and a greater awareness of customer requirements. Within this framework, increasing flexibility in all shapes and forms is considered essential, especially as concerns working time, labour contracts and pay rises. As regards the reduction in working time there is a case that can perhaps be considered unique in Europe, in which a Government has actually taken a stance (albeit indirect) in the context of PEC negotiations: this is the case of France, where the former French Government tried to encourage companies to adopt the instrument of working time cuts in order to safeguard or increase job levels.

When it comes to the restructuring process, in nearly every case management aims to implement broadly accepted solutions. The choice of a consensus-oriented approach can probably be put down to the sensitive nature of the sector. The attempt to achieve general consensus encourages management to involve workers' representatives, thereby legitimising the measures to be implemented with a view to fostering business competitiveness.

Hence, the examined PECs are not characterised by unilateral concessions made by employees and their representatives, but by real 'swaps' aimed at generating mutual benefits. The cases analysed show that workers' representatives succeed in achieving the management's commitment to

- limit the number of redundancies, sometimes also together with job assurances for the future;
- adopt working time reductions;
- implement or extend forms of direct participation.

In exchange, workers' representatives are willing to accept measures able to contribute to an increase in labour productivity, including such as:

- flexibilisation of working time, work organisation and pay rises;
- labour mobility;
- reduction in labour costs.

It must be stressed, however, that issues such as vocational training and employability are hardly at all mentioned in the analysed PECs. In general, such measures are linked to sustaining strategies fostering internal mobility.

Overall, negotiations are characterised by the willingness to organise general consensus, and, as a consequence, the parties involved try to identify mutual benefits. Hence, the negotiation processes are not normally flanked by strikes and other forms of conflict. In some of the most advanced situations, PECs have undoubtedly contributed to redefining the business culture based on a widely accepted long-term vision and ethical principles, thereby starting up a corporate governance strategy that also takes into consideration stakeholder interests.

As far as the mutual benefits are concerned, this aspect is definitely less developed in the cases observed in the United Kingdom. There it may be safer to talk of unilateral approaches with some openings offered by management. The management of the privatisation process of British companies is indeed aimed at assuring productivity rather than social harmony.

But also with regard to the cases analysed in the other four countries it has to be stressed that in general the exchange cannot be considered equivalent. On the one hand, there are clear defined concessions with regard to items

like remuneration and working time which have a concrete impact on organisational and economical aspects of living and working conditions, on the other hand, employees achieve in exchange less tangible and secure guarantees and rights.
We may conclude that the contents and processes of PEC, as well as the role of the actors, vary according to the peculiarities of the national industrial relation systems and their specific traditions of collective bargaining. In the specific case of the electricity industry we can also argue that the PECs are strongly characterised by sectoral influences. This is due to the specific nature of the electricity industry, on the one hand, and to the changing framework conditions which derive from the EU directive, on the other.

Ambiguities and Inconsistencies – a New Role for the Social Partners?

Enterprise restructuring and the deregulation of employment conditions through cost reductions, increased efficiency and the application of short-term performance criteria, represent a widely diffused approach to the reduction of labour costs as a response to global competition. Although in many cases works councils are confronted with a declining negotiation power and, as a consequence, are forced to make concessions in order to maintain employment levels this does not necessarily mean a weakening of their institutional position. On the contrary, the involvement in cooperative crisis management may even result in a consolidation of their institutional role. That means that works councils find themselves between participation and cost cutting.
Furthermore, PECs are not always able to provide employees with absolute certainties. Businesses are evidently subject to market liberalisation processes and therefore to international level competition. It can happen that, even after short periods of time, PECs are sometimes unable to guarantee the business' ability to adapt to the new competitive and constantly changing framework and it is therefore necessary to redefine the contents of the PECs.
Although PECs are generally a source of legitimisation for both workers' representatives and management, re-adjustments requesting further concessions will negatively affect the credibility of the involved parties and may lead to a legitimisation crisis.
The most obvious question at this point is whether the management's choices regarding the restructuring process should always be considered

suitable and timely. As was shown by some of the cases considered above, the ability to forecast and anticipate market liberalisation processes, and therefore the choice of a more pro-active strategy, considerably extends the action range and the chance of choosing an aggressive approach for dealing with the restructuring requirements, characterised by innovation, diversification, quality improvement and not just cost reduction.

From the point of view of the workers' representatives, it is of utmost importance to be able to interpret and assess management projects. Considering that management chooses participation as a means for legitimising the restructuring project, workers' representatives have to decide what stance to take. A strategy that just contrasts management projects appears to be an unrealistic approach as it is neither an alternative nor does it respond to employee expectations (Sisson and Artiles 2000). Indeed, almost all the cases analysed reveal a pragmatic rather than an ideological approach.

Although it may appear reasonable to accept participation, the question again concerns how it should take place: a mainly formal participation within a pre-set management project or real participation within an ongoing process. There is thus the opportunity of taking on a reactive and defensive role aimed at damage limitation or trying to participate on the grounds of alternative proposals. In the latter case, the approach towards restructuring means the management has to provide exhaustive information in good time. As to the workers' representatives they need a specific kind of knowledge that can ensure their autonomy in the phase of project design. This strategy, which requires management to give up its traditional prerogatives, will contribute to creating mutual trust and to guaranteeing the credibility of all the parties concerned. Up to now, however, there seems to be little evidence of a strategy characterised by a proactive role by worker representatives.

However, sharing the project and therefore the need for strong motivation during the implementation phase does not just depend on the quality of worker representative participation, as the direct participation of employees is equally important, as several of the analysed cases have shown. These findings confirm the numerous research studies that have underlined the importance of employee participation in ensuring the use of their knowledge, know-how and creativity, as these qualities are essential for the effective implementation of organisational innovations (Garibaldo, Sbordone and Telljohann 2000: 318).

At the beginning of the nineties the transformation towards a new Post-Fordist production model was regarded as an opportunity to overcome

Tayloristic forms of work organisation by the introduction of more employee-oriented forms of work organisation based on more democratic forms of direct employee participation. New forms of work organisation based on a stronger involvement of employees were expected to improve working conditions as well as the competitive position of the company, creating thereby a win-win situation and supporting the integration of labour in company strategies. According to Dörre (2001) these expectations, however, have often been disappointed. Bieling and Schulten (2001, 22) reach similar conclusions: "Although there has been some innovative examples of new work organisation, the prevailing trend so far seems to be that external economic pressure coming from fierce competition and shareholder-value orientation create a significant barrier to more substantial changes in work organisation and sometimes have even promoted a Re-Taylorisation of work." Thus, the increases in labour productivity strived for in PECs in general are meant to be gained by intensifying work processes rather than by improving work organisation. Thus, it cannot be excluded that PECs may contribute to a deterioration of working conditions.

Finally, it is worth emphasising that PECs represent an important aspect of the overall tendency towards the decentralisation of collective bargaining. It should, however, also be borne in mind that the vigour of the decentralisation trends varies depending on the national context and the respective traditions in the field of industrial relations. Within the framework of the cases analysed, France and the United Kingdom probably represent the two extreme poles. In any case, the results of the decentralisation processes are ambivalent: the analysed cases show that decentralisation can either promote new achievements, simply contribute to improving some of the regulations of collective agreements, or they can even have harmful consequences.

Evidently, as far as PECs are concerned, contradictions may arise between the choices made by works councils, on the one hand, and the regulations set in the collective agreements signed by the trade unions, on the other. This phenomenon of micro-corporatism usually arises when a defensive approach is adopted. Some of the most dramatic examples are given by the enterprises of the ex-DDR. Although collective agreements already provide for a differentiation between the Eastern and Western Länder with regard to the level of standards, PECs are characterised by a level that is even lower than the collective agreements set for the Eastern Länder, which is *per se* generally considered relatively low.

There is, then, the risk that the collective agreement may lose its role of establishing minimum standards for all the workers of the same branch. This issue is probably more difficult to overcome in two tier representation systems where workers' representatives have greater autonomy with regard to external trade union organisations, rather than in one tier systems where there is a higher degree of integration between works councils and trade unions.

Bieling and Schulten (2001) confirm that there is the problem that PECs in several cases openly contravene labour laws or norms laid down in collective agreements and, more in general, that they contribute to an increasing pressure to change existing labour regulation in order to give more regulatory competence to the company level. Indeed, most of the EU Member States have experienced a process of *organised decentralisation* according to which many provisions of existing labour law or collective agreements have been opened for a more flexible implementation at company level (Traxler et al. 2001).

In general, there seems to be an inherent tendency in PECs to contribute to segmentation and the creation of hierarchies within the labour market. As to the management of redundancies, on the one hand, solidarity solutions are devised within the enterprise – for example the reduction in working hours for the whole workforce which even accepts pay reductions in return for job assurances ; on the other, when it comes to reducing the workforce, the first strategy is to resort to in-sourcing, thereby leaving an even weaker labour market segment to face the problem. Also with regard to pay, PECs on the one hand contribute to a differentiated treatment of the existing workforce, and the new recruits, on the other.

To conclude, it may be said that in the examined countries, PECs generally contribute to changing industrial relations, from the point of view of both procedures and contents. The most significant tendencies regard the decentralisation of bargaining, the introduction of new forms of direct and indirect participation and the flexibilisation of working hours as well as work organisation. Although the changing process in industrial relations might be desirable under certain circumstances, there is also a number of related risks not only concerning the segmentation of the labour market, the undermining of collective agreements and the adoption of a flexible approach exclusively benefiting the company, but up to a certain extent, also a tendency to introduce new forms of participation.

A number of issues regarding participation need to be answered to avoid the failure of the new experiences. The relationship between participation and bargaining needs to be clarified, as does the relationship between direct and indirect participation. Unless respective responsibilities and the links between the various levels of responsibility are made clear, the new experiences risk failing. The introduction of new forms of participation needs to be supported by training initiatives, as participation not based on the competence of the involved parties will necessarily remain formal and will not reach the level of a real exchange.

At policy-making level an important aspect regards benchmarking and the dissemination of the best practices (Sisson and Artiles 2000). It is hoped that an enhanced knowledge base will allow for the definition of a clearer and more reliable picture with regard to the dissemination and contents of PECs. The dissemination of best practices obviously depends on the presence of a context favourable to social dialogue. Such a context is essential towards ensuring not only the negotiation but also the implementation of the PECs. From this viewpoint, European-level initiatives regarding the European company statute, the extension of the right to information and consultation and the consolidation of EWC rights are essential.

Lastly, this survey has confirmed the fact that the employability issue has little voice in the PECs. As also stated by Sisson and Artiles (2000), this can be accounted for by the fact that businesses do not invest in measures oriented at improving employability unless they can be sure of drawing some advantages. So it is up to policy-makers to support appropriate means for encouraging investments in training and employability.

As it has been shown, PECs are neither a form of mere concession bargaining, nor a form of equivalent exchange. The fact, that from the employees' point of view PECs have a basically *defensive character* and that they do not represent an equivalent exchange indicates that they are to a certain extent expression of a shift in power relations between capital and labour.

In most cases, indeed, PECs seem to represent a way of socio-economic restructuring which tends to favour a world-market oriented, cost-cutting competition strategy. If on the one hand the involvement of works councils and trade union organisations may contribute to a strengthening of their institutional role in the framework of company-level industrial relations, on the other, there is the risk to rely exclusively on formal or procedural participation which might result in a weakening of autonomously defined interests on the part of trade unions. According to Bieling and Schulten (2001) the adaptation to the pressures of restructuring are often accompanied by political self-restraint on the side of works councils and trade unions.

The Impact of PECs on the German Industrial Relations System

In 1999/2000 the German Institute for Economic and Social Sciences (WSI) carried out a works council survey which was addressed to interest representatives in companies with more than 20 workers (Seifert 2002). The findings of the survey which are based on 1,390 assessable questionnaires suggest that PECs have contributed to a paradigm shift in German collective bargaining and corporate policy.

The German collective bargaining system is characterised by industry-wide agreements that apply either nationwide or throughout a region. The most important aspects which are regulated by the agreements signed by trade union organisations and employers' associations regard wage rates, working conditions and working hours. The collective agreements lay down standards which apply throughout their scope of application. These standards are guaranteed irrespective of the economic performance of an individual company.

Recent developments, however, show that in the German collective bargaining system decentralised levels are gaining in power. Through opening clauses collective agreements have begun to leave more room for flexible arrangements at company level. In this way management and works councils have the possibility to agree on deviations from collective bargaining standards and negotiate company-specific solutions with regard to topics like pay and working time. Nevertheless, company level actors have to take into account the limits specified by collective agreements. Collective bargaining guidelines make it possible that parameters of pay and working time which are central to employment and competitiveness can vary within a company-level agreement. The possibility to agree on deviations that undercut standards laid down in collective agreements is linked to certain preconditions most of which relate to a poor economic situation of the company.

According to the results of the works council survey about 30 % of the companies with a works council have signed agreements on safeguarding employment. Compared with the 1997/98 works council survey the share of companies with a PEC rose by six percentage points. That means that there is an increasing tendency to sign PECs; a tendency which is particularly strong in enterprises with more than 1,000 employees where we have a share of 46 % against 12 % in companies with 20 to 50 employees.

In general the PECs are based on company alliances between the local management and the works council which sometimes is supported by local trade unions. The objective of PECs consists in integrating labour into the company strategies which are aimed at an improvement of competitiveness of the enterprise or single production units.
The majority of these PECs contain commitments to renounce business-related dismissals for a certain period of time. Such promises, however, do not role out the possibility to reduce employment levels by utilising early retirement schemes or staff turnover.
It has to be underlined that the economic situation of the enterprises with PECs reveals substantial differences. Taking the company's order book situation and the profit as indicators for the economic situation of the companies only in a minority of cases the economic situation of the enterprise is judged to be critical. That means that PECs are not only to be found in enterprises which are in difficulty but they are signed by both, prosperous and struggling companies. As a consequence, PECs are losing their exceptional nature and are becoming a regulatory instrument at company level.
There are, however, differences with regard to the contents of PECs which are related to the different economic situations of the analysed companies. That means, that the different problems are reflected in some way in the contents of the agreements. In companies which are not in a economically difficult situation PECs are not a reaction to an acute economic threat to the company. In these cases the agreements in general lay down an extension of working times and plant utilisation times as well as measures regarding the modernisation of work organisation and training activities. In companies with a poor economic position agreements more frequently regard monetary adjustments, cuts in overtime hours and reductions in working time in order to safeguard employment.
The above described developments show that the at company level a paradigm shift in company-level strategies regarding flexibility is taking place. By utilising PECs as a new instrument of regulation there are new options available at company level and, as a consequence, internal flexibility is becoming more important and, to a certain extent, is replacing external forms of adjustment.
The growing importance of PECs confirms the tendency of increasing decentralisation of collective bargaining within the German industrial relations system. Standards defined by industry-wide collective agreements become more and more guidelines for company specific solutions. Thus the former nature of collective agreements is in a process of transformation;

they are becoming more flexible but still succeed in maintaining a guiding function.

Restructuring Processes and the Role of European Works Councils (EWC)

Forms of Involvement of EWCs in Restructuring Processes

As employees of transnational enterprises are particularly exposed to the risk of restructuring processes which in many cases include lay offs or shifts of production at transnational level EWCs see it as an important challenge to get effectively involved in such restructuring processes. According to Kerckhofs and Triangle (2003, 124) "between 1999 and 2001, one third of companies with an EWC underwent a transnational merger or acquisition". In general these kind of restructuring processes have an impact on employment as well as on working conditions.

Although the rights of EWCs are formally limited to information and consultation in recent years there have been several cases of a more far reaching involvement of these European bodies of interest representation. The timely involvement of EWCs in restructuring processes is of course an indicator for the quality of industrial relations, but it is, however, not sufficient to guarantee an effective and positive role of the EWC within restructuring processes. It is equally important to precisely define the concept of consultation. Besides the timeliness it is necessary to guarantee the possibility for EWCs to develop alternative proposals to the projects presented by the management.

Furthermore, for a successful involvement of EWCs it is indispensable that they decide on their coordinating role in regard to both, the development of an autonomous strategy and the actions to be carried out in order to reach the commonly agreed objectives.

With regard to Pacts for Employment and Competitiveness it is obvious that, at least in theory, the added value of an effective involvement of bodies of interest representation at European level consists in the possibility of overcoming the limits of local responses which are often characterised by a logic of competition between the different production sites. At European level, on the contrary, EWCs have the possibility to try to develop a commonly agreed European-wide response to management strategies.

Since the end of the nineties there have been various cases of involvement of EWCs in transnational restructuring processes which were successful to a different degree. In his overview report Carley (2001) lists four cases (Danone, Deutsche Bank, Ford, GM) in which EWCs had a negotiating function in the framework of company restructuring processes and two other cases (Vivendi, SLdE) in which EWCs had a strongly influential factor with regard to company globalisation and expansion strategies.
Besides there have been other cases as for example Electrolux in which the EWCs were involved in restructuring processes but without having had a role of negotiation. In 1997 the top management of the multinational Electrolux announced to the European Works Council a lack of Group plant competitiveness compared to general international standards in the sector. The management argued that the lack of competitiveness is a hindrance – in a sector characterised by major production over-capacity, stagnation of main markets, falling prices, tendency of the consumer to look at the low end of product ranges, entry of new non-EU producers – to the consolidation of production and employment at Group level. Consequently, it announced its intention to carry on with a group restructuring process involving the closure of numerous industrial plants and major employment cuts. The Electrolux management pointed out to the EWC that even if the actual size of the job cuts had been accurately defined (25 production units and 50 warehouses, totalling 12,000 fewer workers), it had not yet been decided which plants to close and where. The management declared to the EWC members that Electrolux intended to close down the less competitive plants and to concentrate production and investments in the others. The EWC members were thus urged to table national debates in the various countries in order to increase the efficiency and the competitiveness of their own plants. As a matter of fact, a sort of European-wide 'auction' was started which indeed caused major internal competition between the countries, during which each plant sought to prove it had achieved a certain standard of efficiency and productivity such that the group's benchmarks of competitiveness was assured. As a result on that occasion there were major disagreements between the national representatives of the EWC, evidently and predictably committed to defending the individual positions.
From the point of view of the delegates the involvement of the EWC in the restructuring process has highlighted some gaps.
Although, the management informed and consulted the EWC on a regular basis with regard to the planned measures of restructuring the EWC did not succeed in influencing management decisions. The main shortcomings

were probably the insufficient internal cohesion of the EWC and the lack of coordination between the EWC and the external trade union organisations, especially the European Metalworkers' Federation. In this case the involvement of the EWC represented, therefore, a mere formal act (Piazza/Telljohann 1999).
In other cases EWCs succeeded in encroaching in the field of negotiations, sometimes at the management's initiative, but sometimes also at the EWC's initiative. The most innovatory example is the agreement signed between the Ford EWC and central management on the separation of the producer of car components, Ford Visteon (Klebe/Roth 2000). The agreement, which applies to Visteon plants in Germany, UK and France, ensures that employees transferred to the new company still enjoy their previous existing rights. In this agreement Ford also commits to provide sourcing to the new company.
In the case of the Deutsche Bank in 1999 a joint position on job security was signed in which the group committed itself to arrangements which went considerably beyond those in the EU Directive (Carley 2001). In 2000 an agreement was signed between the management of GM and the European Employee Forum (EEF) on the consequences of the alliance with Fiat. In this case the EWC succeeded in obtaining the following rights:

- continuous and timely information about developments in the alliance;
- the alliance must not lead to workforce reductions, plant closures or the worsening of working conditions;
- existing collective bargaining agreements must continue in force;
- workers subject to transfer should have the right to remain and return;
- current national or EU-wide representation bodies and unions should be recognised in any new enterprises that may be formed.

In 2001 another important framework agreement on restructuring initiatives was signed between EEF and management. In this agreement management committed itself to avoid forced redundancies in relation to the planned restructuring initiatives and to maintain the vehicle production in Luton (UK). This agreement is probably one of the most important ones signed at European level as it "...provides for a concrete set of rules to be applied in specific circumstances; and a framework for lower-level action". (Carley 2001, 53).

Conclusions

The above mentioned cases show that in several cases EWCs succeeded in going beyond information and consultation procedures. In most of these cases trade unions are successful in using EWCs to generate common positions and to achieve concessions from management in safeguarding jobs, working practices and conditions. In this context Ford and GM have to be considered the most relevant cases. In these and the other cases (Danone, Deutsche Bank) the agreements signed at European level deal with both, company development factors and employee-side factors. Especially the cases of Ford and GM have shown that the room for manoeuvre and for really influencing decisions is much bigger at a higher level as at local level works councils are mostly confronted with implementation discussions only. Furthermore, these cases show that EWCs are not necessarily vehicles for international labour regime competition (Hancké 2000).

In the case of Electrolux, on the contrary, management succeeded in involving the EWC in a strategy based on competition between the various plants in the countries represented by the EWC. The EWC was not able to develop a European-wide common strategy and, as a consequence, local interests prevailed within the groups internal strategy of competition. In the face of pressure made by central management the EWC members did not make full use of the mechanisms provided for in the EWC-agreement and they did not succeed in developing an adequate co-operation with the European Metalworkers' Federation.

Especially at European level it seems indispensable that there is a close cooperation between EWCs and European trade union federations when facing the necessity to develop a European-wide strategy in response to transnational restructuring processes (Telljohann 2003, 43). According to Rehfeldt (2004) "EWCs by themselves will always have great difficulties when they try to define the common interests of the workforces in different European plants and in different economic situations. Union intervention will always be necessary in order to facilitate a compromise between different interests and different strategic approaches".

The cases of Ford and General Motors show that it is possible for trade union organisations and EWCs to develop European-wide strategies able to counterbalance management's restructuring plans. Nevertheless, one has to be aware that these experiences represent not generalisable best practice cases. As it has been shown, in order to conclude similar agreements it is necessary to guarantee, first of all, a close co-operation between EWCs and trade union organisations. Furthermore, the co-operation between EWCs and national works councils as well as between European and natioanl trade union organisations is also of utmost importance for the success of a European-wide strategy of coordination and bargaining.

References

Bieling, H.J., Schulten, T. (2001) 'Competitive Restructuring and Industrial Relations within the European Union: Corporatist Involvement and Beyond?' *WSI Discussion Paper No. 99*, Düsseldorf.

Carley, M. (2001) *Bargaining at European level? Joint texts negotiated by European Works Councils,* Dublin: European Foundation for the Improvement of Living and Working Conditions.

Dörre, K. (2001) ‚Gibt es ein nachfordistisches Produktionsmodell?' in Candaias, M., Deppe, F. (eds.), *Ein neuer Kapitalismus?,* Hamburg: VSA, 83-107.

EIRO European Industrial Relations Observatory (1997) *Collective bargaining on employment in Europe. Comparative supplement,* Dublin: European Foundation for the Improvement of Living and Working Condition.

European Commission DG Employment and Social Affairs (1999) *European social dialogue bulletin, Annual report.*

European Commission (1997) *White paper* on *growth competitiveness and employment*, Luxembourg: Office for Official Publications of the European communities.

European Commission (2000) *Communication to the European Council and Parliament on recent progress and perspectives related to the implementation of the internal electricity market,* Luxembourg: Office for Official Publications of the European communities.

European Commission (1997a) 'Green Paper on Partnership for a new organisation of work' in *Bulletin of the European Union , supplement* 97, Luxembourg: Office for Official Publications of the European communities.

European Commission (2000a) *Industrial Relations in Europe,* Luxembourg: Office for Official Publications of the European communities.

European Commission (1998) *Managing change. Final report of the high level group on economic and social implications of industrial change,* Luxembourg: Office for Official Publications of the European communities.

European Foundation for the Improvement of Living and Working Conditions (1997) *New forms of work organization: Can Europe realise its potential? Results of a survey of direct employee participation in Europe*, Luxembourg: Office for Official Publications of the European communities.

European Foundation for the Improvement of Living and Working Conditions (1999) 'Employment trough flexibility: Squaring the circle?' *Findings from the EPOC Survey* , Luxembourg: Office for Official Publications of the European communities.

Fajertag, G., Pochet, P. (2000) 'A new era for social pacts in Europe' in Fajertag, G., Pochet, P., (eds.) *Social Pacts in Europe New Dynamics,* Brussels: ETUI.

Ferner, A. and Hyman, R. (Eds.) (1998) *Changing Industrial Relations in Europe,* Oxford: Blackwell.

Flaei Cisl (2000) 'Il sistema elettrico alla ricerca della sua identità' (The electric system in search of its identity), *Conference proceedings*, Rome.

Garibaldo, F., Sbordone, F. and Telljohann, V. (2000) 'Forme della divisione del lavoro e i processi di cambiamento del lavoro e delle sue modalità organizzative' in *Primo Rapporto dell'Istituto per il Lavoro. Sviluppo, Lavoro e Competitività in Emilia Romagna*, Milano: Angeli.

Hancké, B. (2000) 'European Works Councils and Industrial Restructuring in the European Motor Industry' in *European Journal of Industrial Relations,* Vol. 6, No. 1, 35-60.

Hassel, A. (1998) 'Soziale Pakte in Europa', *Gewerkschaftliche Monatshefte*, Vol. 49, No. 10.

Kerckhofs, P., Triangle, L. (2003) 'EWC developments in 2002' in Gabaglio, E., Hoffmann, R., (eds.) *European Trade Union Yearbook 2002,* Brussels ETUI, 105-126.

Klebe, T., Roth, S. (2000) 'Die Gewerkschaften auf dem Weg zu einer internationalen Strategie? Am Beispiel der Automobilindustrie' in *Arbeitsrecht im Betrieb,* 12, 749-759.

Marginson, P., Sisson , K. (1996) 'European collective bargaining: a virtual Prospect?' *ETUI Discussion Paper, DWP 96.091 (E)*, Brussels: ETUI.

Piazza, L., Telljohann, V. (1999) 'Investigating Participation at Zanussi: Final report', *IpL Research Report*, Bologna.

Rehfeldt, U. (2004) ‚European Works Councils and International Restructuring: A Perspective for European Collective Bargaining?' in Charron, E., Steward, P. (eds.) *Work and Employment Relations in the Automobile Industry*, London: Palgrave MacMillan.

Rosdücher, J. (1997) *Arbeitsplatzsicherheit durch Tarifvertrag*, Munich and Mering: Rainer Hampp Verlag.

Schulten, T. (1999) 'Auf dem Weg in die Abwärtsspirale? Tarifpolitik unter den Bedingungen der Europäischen Währungsunion', in Schulten, T., Bispinck, R., (eds.) *Tarifpolitik unter dem Euro,* Hamburg: VSA-Verlag.

Seifert, H. (2002) *Pacts on Employment and Competitiveness. A paradigm shift in German collective bargaining and corporate policy?* Paper presented to the 26th Annual Conference German Studies Association, October 4-6, 2002, San Diego, California.

Sisson, K. and Artiles, A. M. (2000) *Handling restructuring. Collective agreements dealing with employment and competitiveness,* Dublin: European Foundation for the Improvement of Living and Working Conditions.

Sisson, K., Freyssinet, J., Krieger, H., O' Kelly, K., Schnabel, C., Seifert, H. (1999) *Pacts for employment and competitiveness: concepts and issues,* Luxembourg: Office for Official Publications of the European Communities.

Spineux, A., Francq, B., Leonard, E., Barre, Ph., Leloup, X., Walthery, P., Gilot, M. (1998) *Annual Report on Social Concertation and Collective Bargaining, Third part: The development of agreements relevant to employment and labour market policies*, Louvain: Institut des Sciences du Travail.

Streeck, W. (1998) 'The Internationalisation of Industrial Relations in Europe: Prospects and Problems', in *Politics and Society*, Vol. 26, No. 4.

Telljohann, V. (2001) 'Collective bargaining under the conditions of EMU and the crisis of the Social Pact in Italy', in Schulten, T., Bispinck, R., (eds.) *Collective bargaining under the Euro. Experiences from the European metal industry*, Brussels: ETUI.

Telljohann, V. (2001) 'Pacts for Employment and Competitiveness in the Electricity Sector', in *Transfer*, Vol. 7, No. 4, 636-649.

Telljohann, V. (2003) 'Regolazione sociale a livello transnazionale: un nuovo modello di azione sindacale?' in *Economia & Lavoro* Vol. 37, No. 1, 29-46.

Traxler, F. (1997) 'The logic of social pacts', in Fajertag G., Pochet, P. (eds.) *Social Pacts in Europe,* Brussels: ETUI.

Traxler, F., Blaschke, S., Kittel, B. (2001) *National Labour Relations in Internationalized Markets,* Oxford: University Press.

Zagelmeyer, S. (2000) *Collective Bargaining on Employment in the European Union in Norway,* European Foundation for the Improvement of Living and Working Conditions, Luxembourg: Office for Official Publications of the European Communities.

The Paradoxes of Subjectivization of Work

RAINER ZOLL

In a first approach it is relatively easy to describe the subjectivization of work by answering the question: how do these workers work? They work too much. They work long working hours; instead of seven to eight hours they work ten to twelve and sometimes even more. And not only that, in the same time they work in a very intensive way. Sometimes they take work home and continue to work at home. Their way to work is a transgression of limits, limits of time and sometimes limits of space. They are blurring old and seemingly well established boundaries. Therefore we speak also of "entgrenzter Arbeit", of working without limits. This type of work is "ambiguous" because on one hand there are for the workers "chances of enlarged margins" in the execution of tasks, on the other hand "dangers of self-regulated overcharge of work". (Sauer 2001b, p.38)

In the world of work, many scientists observe the spreading of this new form of work which is in reality very old, but new is the quantitative diffusion. It is old because we know this way of working from scientists, artists, managers, independent workers and so on. What is new is the quantitative diffusion of this type of work, its spreading to other spheres of employment. It began with the computer-people, then it spread to the IT-workers in general and now to many other white collars workers and even some blue collar workers.. It is described as subjectivization of work, working without end ("Arbeit ohne Ende"), super-intensification of work; these workers are also called "Arbeitskraftunternehmer" (entrepreneurs of their own workforce). Very often they are "burnt out" at 45. These mainly highly qualified workers have fun doing their work, they realize themselves in work, get responsibility, get margins of disposition to act relatively freely.

The question is: Why do these workers work so much and so hard? It is clear: they identify with their work – and their main reason for doing this is their desire to realize themselves in work. They want to get a deep inner gratification in their work – as young people say, they want to get fun in their work – and they get it. Of course we must differentiate, state subjective differences – as always. There are many of them who have mainly this motivation to work without limits. But there are some of them who are work addicts, that is their drug is working, in other words: they are workaholics (cf. Heide 2002). Others simply fear for the security of their job; they see their colleagues working like that, working without limits, so they do the same in order not to be the first to be fired. But it can also be that they feel it necessary to give this working performance because they fear not to be recognised as good workers. So there is one main reason , the desire for self-realization. But there are others and they are manifold and often there is a mix of reasons.

But why does this phenomenon occur now and not before? I can give some empirical evidence on this which does not answer directly the question but which gives some hints on the possible development. 15 years ago a research group under my direction made an empirical research on "work orientations of young people". We discovered an important socio-cultural change. In the core of this change there was – and is – a deep felt desire for self-realization. Young people want to realize themselves in their live, they do not want to wait for happiness in some uncertain beyond or another – perhaps socialist – society as their fathers or grandfathers did, they live now and they want gratification now. That is a big change in the time orientation. It is a switch from future oriented expectations to expectations oriented to the present. As work is an important part of life, they looked for self-realization in work. But the desire for self-realization found at that time an outlet in work only when the places offered had creative aspects or implied social caring. And these places were few, could only satisfy few young men and women. To give some examples of the work they looked for: all professions with artistic aspects like photographers, actors, journalists and so on; or jobs with creative sides in technical work like R+D-engineers. And on the other side professions like nurses, social workers and professions caring for old and sick persons. Note that we have since that time an minority of male nurses and men caring for old people.

The majority of young people who did not see a chance of getting a workplace where they could realize themselves in work turned their wishes of self-realization to activities outside work, very often making music or similar things. These young people had in average 24 years of age when we interviewed them 15 years ago.

When we looked now for some people who work without end because we wanted to interview some persons who could be considered to be prototypes, examples of subjectivization of work, we did not ask for a certain age. We asked for certain qualities, we looked for, above all, people working without time limits. The astonishing thing was that we found people exactly of that generation we had interviewed 15 years ago: which means persons, mainly male, now 39 to 40 years of age.

Here some details on Paul who is one of these persons interviewed. He is group leader of a small team of seven IT-workers, information-specialists as they are called, who elaborate software for controlling and caring for a production process. He says he works 50 hours a week but it is probably more, even given that he has an arrangement which permits him to stay two afternoons with his young children. But very often after these afternoons he returns to his office what he is not obliged to do at all. Sometimes late in the evening his superior passes and tells him – not taking it very seriously - that legally he is not allowed to work more then 10 hours a day. He identifies totally with his work, likes it, has fun doing it. Work takes an enormous place in his life. He even separated from his wife over conflicts they had about his attitude towards working. He became team leader after only 4 years of employment in the firm where he works. He thinks that workers councils and trade unions are valid institutions - only he does not need them and does not care for them. But his attitude towards the software he is producing is characterized by a relationship of caring. The language he uses for describing this relationship is one of nurses or caring people in general. The only bridges to society in general are his friends whom he meets once or twice a week in the evening and his young daughters because he is preoccupied by their future.

The phenomenon of these people is a big problem for trade unions, for civil society and for society in general. That raises the questions how the concerned individuals react, how trade unions face these problems and if new protective arrangements are possible. The questions which must be studied in future arise from that: Do this very active individuals, who could be called the elite of workers in knowledge society, interest themselves only for their work – as is to be feared – or do they care for the society, act as citizens ? Where are they located in civil society?

And turning to the personal side: It is evident that this way to work implies dangers, dangers above all for the health of the concerned workers. In many countries we observe already that the danger is above all that these workers are burnt out at 45 to 50 years of age. Because of its diffusion the burn-out-syndrome has already become a very accepted word. The burning out takes many different forms (cf. Färber 2001). The symptoms are augmented by economic insecurity. The consequences of this insecurity is well described by Richard Sennett in his book “The corrosion of character” (1998).

Furthermore we have to do with a vicious circle: The burning out augments the insecurity, and insecurity augments the danger of burning out. The question is if the concerned workers do not feel this danger in their younger years. Do they feel any need for protection – collective or legal – or do they go to the burn-out-syndrome unprepared and unprotected?
These dangers can be understood better when they are described as paradoxes. The paradoxes of subjectivization of work exist on many levels: 0n the individual level; for the trade unions for the civil society, for the political society and on the level of everyday's life. Here I will only deal with the two first ones.

The Paradox of Subjectivization of Work for the Individual

Since long many workers strive for self-realization in work. But until now only few groups of very specialized workers were given the chance to find this kind of fulfilment.. So for example artists who partly were independent workers, partly worked in employee-situations but where they needed (and mostly got) a certain degree of freedom and autonomy in order to achieve the creation of a work of art. So they could realize themselves in their work, self-realization was an element of their job. A similar argumentation is valid for many scientists. And of course one can observe excessive work loads in both of these professions.
With the subjectivization of work the phenomenon of working in an excessive way spreads to other groups of workers, first IT-workers but now also other professions. Contrary to the artists and scientists where the employment-relationship is very often less oppressive, where domination is – and must be – less marked, these new workers – doing now subjectivized work – had formerly work situations where the capital-labour-relationship showed itself clearly as domination in orders given by the superiors in the hierarchy of plants and offices. But for these people now this work situation changes and tends to be more similar to that of artists and scientists. What was formerly described as exploitation (we don't discuss the word here, we use it in order to be short and comprehensible) now becomes, with these new workers, self-exploitation. Formerly workers did their work mostly because they needed the wages for their living; in some cases they choose a certain work because it interested them more then others. Now this minority of new workers do their work because they want to do it, because it interests them much more then other types of work and

even more then many other things in life. In other words: implicitly they want the self-exploitation.

They work so much more then in a "normal" work-situation that there can be no doubt about the difference: They want this work situation, it gives them a lot of satisfaction. Contrary to many managers who often work in a similar excessive way these new workers do not have a financial interest in the results of their work. Their interest in the economic success of their work is indirect – they could not continue to do this if it was not successful – but in general they do not have a financial participation in their work. And if in some cases they have, this is not decisive for their work motivation.

The paradox of the work situation of these individuals lies also in the circumstance that by their excessive working they undermine the basis, the foundation of their working activity, their health, their physical and psychic well-being. The unlimited self-exploitation has negative consequences for them in future (cf. Fergen/Pickshaus 2001). They risk to live the burn-out-syndrome and more; cases of cardiac infarction, heart problems, collapse of hearing and so on could be some of the consequences – since they are reported for professions where excessive work loads are known to exist: scientists and managers. The "new" workers in general are not aware of the risks of their intensive (and extensive) work life. Or they minimize them, as an interviewee, a prototypical case, puts it: "I know I will not become old, perhaps 69, but I will work until 69!"

Reformulating the paradox: if these "new" workers get on one hand freedom and autonomy in their work, on the other hand they hand this freedom over to an internalised instance in them which drives them to work in an excessive way which is resembling to forced work. One could say if the "new" workers do not feel the un-freedom, the bondage, the constraints, if they are happy with it, why worry? First because they expose themselves to dangers for their health – and of course when they are "burnt out", they regret their work excesses; second because some constraints are nevertheless very visible because these workers are very often directly exposed to the market what means that they simply do not want to see the dangers and the market pressures as constraints; third the freedom and autonomy in work can also be understood as a new indirect, soft but powerful way of domination; fourth because these "new" workers concentrate so much on their work that very often they are not capable of participating in activities in the civil and political society.

In other words, the new management strategy certainly gives a relative freedom and autonomy to the workers concerned but in the same time this

strategy enables management to use hitherto unused capacities of the human being. As the quoted interviewee says, he needs in his work all his experience, also the experience he made in his life outside work, in his married life and the following separation of his wife. Gorz and others call this the grip, the seizure of the whole person. So while, on the one hand, autonomy, share of responsibility and relative freedom in work is without any doubt a progress for these workers, on the other hand they do not take in consideration the reverse side of the medal.
Freedom, autonomy – and the seizure of the whole person: a paradox.

The Paradox of Subjectivization of Work for Trade Unions

Years ago trade unions above all in Europe developed a discourse on a better shaping of the contents and the forms of work. This discourse started – as known – with a critique of Taylorism and Fordism. The well described work situation of a blue collar worker on the assembly line served as a negative foil in order to outline norms and principles which should govern better work situations. These principles are a greater autonomy, that is above all greater margins of disposition in the execution of the work tasks, more responsibility for the result of the work, a greater influence on the conditions of work and of course a richer content of work.
For examples for these demands for better work we can refer us first to the famous conference of the Istituto Gramsci on "Science e organizzazione del lavoro" (Editori Riuniti, Rome 1973) where Giuseppe Bianchi and Pietro Merli Brandini defined "Autonomy" in the following way: "that the content, the structure and the organisation of tasks must be so that the individuals and the groups, who have to execute these tasks, have the possibility to programme, govern and control their own work and its results (prestazioni)." (ibd. p.417) The authors speak expressis verbis of the psychologic request of the workers for "self-realization and individual growth what is of fundamental importance for promoting their work motivation." (ibd.) They repeat the critique of taylorism: "Routine and repetitive work tend to oppress the individuals who are forced to live in situations without stimulus." They draw the consequence: "Human beings need for self-realization a variety of experiences." (ibd.) And they underline the demands: "Participation of the individual in the decisions regarding his work." (ibd.) "A greater degree of responsibility and of freedom in the execution of the tasks to fulfil." (ibd. p. 418)

As a second example we can refer to texts of the German Metalworkers Trade Union IG Metall of the 1970ties where they define as principles for good work exactly the same ideas: more freedom in the execution of tasks, more autonomy and a richer work content. I quoted these examples in order to show that the demands of workers and their representatives really were autonomy in work, freedom in the sense of margins of disposition and a share of responsibility, in short now old trade union demands.
The novelty of the present situation is that a certain stratum of workers – mostly highly qualified white collar workers but not only – receives all this from the management in the framework of a new management strategy without that they had to fight for it – with or without the trade unions; there was no trade union intervention whatsoever. They receive all this because management sees in it the advantages for itself: above all the dedication of the workers to their work. Neither workers not managers see any link to the old trade union demands. More: these workers in general do not recognise any need of adhering to trade unions or participating in activities of workers' councils or similar institutions; they are not hostile but distant and neutral. "I don't need them!" These institutions are just strange for them.
So, not only that trade unions have great difficulties to organise these workers but in future, as the number of these workers tends to grow, they will have a lot of difficulties to augment the percentage of organised workers, even more, the percentage will probably decrease. Anyway, it is already decreasing now. And this despite of the fact that these workers got what trade unions ask for since decades. The structure of these paradoxes repeats itself on the levels of civil society, political society and in everyday's life.

In the framework of the general movement of reregularition the phenomenon of subjectivization of work is an important change in the employer-employee-relationship: the normal worker, pure manpower, is replaced by the individual worker (P.Rosanvallon 2001, E.Senghaas-Knobloch 2001), what could have strong negative consequences for the protective function of collective bargaining. Obviously these changes are part of the general tendency of reregulation menacing essential parts of social compromise in highly industrialized capitalist countries. Now this concerns social compromise as a whole – as described by Robert Castel in the perspective of social policy: The core of social compromise was that workers had acquired as countervailing power a social propriety, a social capital which consists "in a certain amount of rights and social services that are guaranteed by the state" (2001a). These "rights, guarantees and

protective measures help (the workers) to deal with the most important social risks"; now they are menaced "by the collapse of a whole structure, by the passage to a quite different regime of work organisation in a society totally dominated by the market." (ibid.)
The system of collective bargaining is a vital part of social compromise which is now equally menaced by reregulation, especially by the penetration of the market in the direct sphere of production. The menace comes from two sides; one is the <precarization> of employment, the substitution of secure jobs by precarious ones; this side is not treated here because this is already done in a number of researches and analytical texts. The other side is the substitution of normal manpower by the individual worker as it happens in a new wave of rationalisation (M.Lallement 2001, W.Glißmann 2000). This process includes a further differentiation of the labour force (s. R.Castel, D.Sauer, M.Lallement, all 2001) and the individualization of work and work organisation (the same and P.Veltz 2001, J.L.Laville 2001, Glißmann 2000). Alongside with this we find several by this time well known dynamics of transgressing established frontiers, above all those of working time; <working without end> is in some European languages already a familiar slogan. (the same and A.Gorz 2001b, E.Senghaas-Knobloch 2001)
The process of subjectivization of work and of individualization of the employer-employee-relationship must be regarded in two perspectives, one of management and one of the workers: For the management these processes are a new form of rationalisation. The sphere of production is directly exposed to the market (s. Glißmann, Gorz b, Sauer, Senghaas-Knobloch, M.Moldaschl 1998), the single worker is induced to take over traditional functions of management. That means that management has less charges of work and responsibility but that workers take over this part of work and responsibility. This is only possible with a much greater freedom of manoeuvre for these workers; they get more autonomous. Partly this transfer corresponds to old trade union and worker demands but in this form their realization is in the same time part of a rationalization process and leaves trade unions without power. At least for the moment.
Largely discussed is the thesis that workers become entrepreneurs of their own manpower (Voss, Pongratz; resuming: Gorz 2001b). In the same time the individual worker is urged to use abilities and talents which he employed beforehand in a quasi private mode prudently in order to deal in a for him more convenient way with work and in order to protect him; but now the work organisation claims the systematic use of all these abilities and talents (Sauer, Gorz b). It is a seizure of "the whole person and the

whole life of the worker" (Gorz 2001a, 12) because these abilities and talents are acquired in the lifelong experience of the worker, very often in the everyday's life outside work. Furthermore the worker as individual is made responsible in a quite extensive measure and sense for his work, much more then beforehand which is a non expected but until now accepted charge for him (Lallement, Senghaas-Knobloch).

All this implies that these workers are often realizing themselves in the work process, that they have fun doing their work. This means also that they get certain chances of development, of self-realization in work. These chances can be used to a certain degree when the character of the special production demands – in order to favour creativity – to concede some freedom because without this innovation and creativity are not possible. Particularly in the realm of information techniques these chances seduce workers to enter the vicious circle of <working without end>, a vicious circle similar to those known in dependency, in addiction (s. Glißmann, Glißmann/Peters). – Newer observations state that the whole process now touches not only white collar workers but also blue collar.

The consequences of this process for workers are often disastrous : the continuous self-controlled overstrain and the continuous stress lead finally to the burn-out-syndrome, to being forced to quit the job (s. R.Sennett 1998). The direct confrontation of the single worker with the market, the self-organisation of workers used as means of controlling work (Sauer), the entering of vicious circle processes, the market-induced stronger competition of workers, all that leads to overstrain. The subjects transgress themselves the protective frontiers raised by collective bargaining, they just do not care for these frontiers what leaves trade unions and workers councils or shop stewards relatively helpless. The traditional guarantees of the personal security of workers are menaced (Castel, Veltz)

In this situation there seems to exist only a classical black-and-white-alternative: Either the whole system of collective bargaining – in view also of other attacks – has the tendency to break down or new protective measures are found and enforced, workers acquire new forms of "social propriety" (Castel 2001b). The precondition for this is that workers have at least some impulses of resisting the overstrain and communicate with others on the subject.

The possibilities seen by the cited authors are quite diverse: Dieter Sauer notes that such impulses come from the life-world outside the working places in which the whole process penetrates more and more (Sauer, R.Reich 2001). This is confirmed by the example of Paul where the future of his daughters induces him to be preoccupied by the future of society. -

Eva Senghaas-Knobloch hopes that protective measure can be deduced from the definition of the work role, the professional role which should imply guarantees (2001, 183ff). Here we must note that Paul – even if he is conscious of the necessity of permanent training- does not enter really in this discussion because he does not look for guarantees; but he is worried by the vagueness of the definition of his professional role. Anyway, these workers have an interest in permanent training. It is a work related question where they feel concerned. - Wilfried Glißmann pleas for enlightenment of the concerned workers, enlightenment about the nature of involvement in the vicious circles of these processes (2001). - André Gorz states that the "production of self" is more and more used as a resource by the management side but he thinks that the "production of self" can emancipate itself from the appropriation tendencies and set itself its own aims (2001b, 66). - Pierre Rosanvallon writes that "when the problems of subordination in the plants refer more and more to the recognition of the particularity of individuals then the way of human rights in work must be developed." (2001, 32) - Which way or which ways can be followed depends largely on the reaction of the subjects, of the workers.

A research on this topic should be open for the discovering of possible old and new forms of access to citizenship, but also the lack of any kind of commitment. This question appears to us as being of utmost importance. If in a knowledge based society, the most active workers, who are also probably intellectually an outstanding part of the workers, refrain from any sort of commitment, do not take part in any form of citizenship activity, interest themselves only for their work, then this is threatening not only the substance of democracy but also the social cohesion of society. (Zoll 2000, p.123ff)

We have empirical hints that these often very individualistic workers are nonetheless capable of acts of solidarity - so that social cohesion does not seem to be totally at stake for the moment – but how does this all fit together and above all, how could this complex cluster of often very divers if not contrary orientations evolve in future. The conscious, voluntary part of governance should take these social patterns into account.

References

Bianchi, Giuseppe; **Merli Brandini,** Pietro 1973, *Lavoro umano e processo produttivo*, in **Istituto Gramsci**, *Scienza e organizzazione del lavoro*, vol. II, Editori Riuniti, Rome, p.411-439

Bolognani, Mario; **Fuggetta**, Alfonso; **Garibaldo**, Francesco, 2002, *Le fabbriche invisibili. Struttura, sapere e conflitto nella produzione del software in Italia*, Rome, Meta Edizioni.

Castel, Robert, 2001a, *Die neue soziale Frage*, Vortrag am Institut für Sozialforschung, Frankfurt/M, in

Frankfurter Rundschau, 4.9.2001, p.22

Castel, Robert; Haroche, Claudine, 2001b, *Propriété privée, propriété sociale, propriété de soi – Entretiens sur la construction de l'individu moderne*, Paris, Fayard

Cella, Gian Primo, 2001, *Lo scenario individualista e il sindacato confederal*', *Quaderni rassegna sindacale*, II/4, 43-50.

Garibaldo, Francesco, **Sbordone**, Francesca, **Telljohann**, Volker, 2000, '*Forme della divisione del lavoro e i processi di cambiamento del lavoro e delle sue modalità organizzative*' in Istituto per il Lavoro (eds.) *Sviluppo, Lavoro e Competitività in Emilia Romagna. Primo Rapporto Annuale dell'Istituto per il Lavoro*, Milan, Angeli, 285-321.

Glißmann, Wilfried, 2000, *Ökonomisierung der «Ressource Ich» - Die Instrumentalisierung des Denkens in der neuen Arbeitsorganisation*, in «Denkanstösse – IG Metaller in der IBM, Mai 2000, Frankfurt/M

Glißmann, Wilfried; **Peters**, Klaus, 2001, *Mehr Druck durch mehr Freiheit*, Hamburg VSA

Gorz, André; Vincent, Jean-Marie, 2001a, *Dialogue, in Variations No.1*, Paris, Syllepse

Gorz, André, 2001b, *La personne devient une entreprise*, in *Revue du MAUSS*, No.18, p. 61-66, Paris, La Découverte

Heide, Holger (ed.), 2002, *Massenphänomen Ar beitssucht*, Atlantik Verlag Bremen

Lallement, Michel, 2001, *Daedalus laborans*, in *Revue du MAUSS*, No.18, p.29-49, ibid.

Laville, Jean-Louis, 2001, *Travail, la nouvelle question politique*, in *Revue du MAUSS*, No.18, p.79-91, ibid.

Martens, Helmut; **Peter**, Gerd; **Wolf**, Frieder O. (ed.);2ßß1, *Zwischen Selbstbestimmung und Selbstausbeutung*, Campus Verlag, Frankfurt/New York

Moldaschl, Manfred, 1998, *Internalisierung des Marktes – Neue Unternehmensstrategien und qualifizierte Angestellte*, in: *SOFI/IfS/ISF/INIFES (Hg.): Jahrbuch Sozialwissenschaftliche Technikberichterstattung* 1997. Berlin, p. 197- 250

Pickshaus, Klaus; **Schmitthenner**, Horst; **Urban**, Hans-Jürgen (ed.) 2001, *Arbeiten ohne Ende*, VSA-Verlag, Hamburg

Provasi, Giancarlo, 2002, '*La società della conoscenza e il futuro del lavoro'*, *L'impresa al plurale – Quaderni della partecipazione*, 9, 15-28.

Reich, Robert 2001, cited by Alain Caillé, in *Présentation, Revue du MAUSS,* No.18, p.7, ibid.

Rosanvallon, Pierre, 2001, *Intérêt général et représentativité, in Revue de la Cfdt*, No. 37-38, p.31-35, Paris

Sauer, Dieter, 2001a, *Konfrontation mit dem Markt – Zur neuen « Unmittelbarkeit » moderner Arbeit, Empirische Befunde und theoretische Überlegungen,* Vortrag an der Universität Bremen, 29.11.2001

Sauer, Dieter; 2001b, *Unternehmensreorganisation und Entgrenzung von Arbeit – Thesen zum Umbruch*, in *Martens* et al.

Senghaas-Knobloch, Eva, 2001, *Neue Organisationskonzepte und das Problem entgrenzter Arbeit – Zum Konzept der Arbeitsrolle als Schutzmantel*, in Senghaas-Knobloch, Eva, *Macht, Kooperation und Subjektivität in betrieblichen Veränderungsprozessen*, Münster, Hamburg, London, Berlin, LIT, p.171-194

Sennett, Richard, 1998, *The Corrosion of Character*, New York, W.W. Norton

Veltz, Pierre, 2001, *La nouvelle révolution industrielle*, in *Revue du MAUSS*, No.18, p.67-70

Voss, G.; **Pongratz**, H.J. 2000, *Vom Arbeitnehmer zum Arbeitskraftunternehmer. Zur Entgrenzung der Ware Arbeitskraft*; in

Minssen, H. (Hg.), *Begrenzte Entgrenzungen. Wandlungen von Organisation und Arbeit*, Berlin

Zoll, Rainer 2000, *Was ist Solidarität heute?* Frankfurt/M, Suhrkamp, *La solidarietà – Egualianza e differenza*, Bologna 2003, Il Mulino

Strategies for Organisational Change and the Role of Participation

KEVIN P O'KELLY

Introduction

The future of the European Social Model and, in particular, the issues around how to find an acceptable compromise between business demands for greater competitiveness, improved quality, increased productivity and workplace flexibility and the social rights and responsibilities business has to employees and the wider community, is an important and active debate in Europe. To compete in ever increasing global markets should European enterprises follow the American way of corporate governance or should Europeans continue to develop their own distinct approach to work, to involvement and to the employment relationship?

The right of workers to be informed and consulted on key decision that will affect their workplace and their jobs and to participate in these decisions has been a basic principle of European Social Policy. While these employee rights are enshrined in the European Charter of Fundamental Rights (Article 27), soon to be incorporated into the new Constitutional Treaty thus conferring the status of primary law on them, are they under threat, or being 'side-lined' in the pursuit of greater profits and increased return on investment?

Within the EU the rights of employees or their representatives is recognised in a number of ways, for example, through legislation dating back to the 1970s - on collective redundancies[1], transfer of

[1] Directive 75/129/EEC – now Directive 98/59/EC

undertakings[2] and on occupational health and safety[3]. More recently the principal was extended through the European Works Council directive[4], the information and consultation framework directive[5] and the directive on employee information, consultation and participation in European companies (SEs)[6]. With the transposition of these Directives into national laws and with their implementation, in a practical way in many EU enterprises, it would appear that worker rights are secure and sit on the solid foundation of EU Social Policy.

Apart from the legislative approach, the EU also provides employee representatives, working together with employer representatives, the opportunity to influence sectoral policies at the EU-level through twenty-seven EU Sectoral Social Dialogue Committees and to determine, again with employer representatives, EU legislation on social issues, under Article 138 of the Amsterdam Treaty. These levels of social dialogue underpin the principal of information and consultation rights for European workers.

Four Approaches

At the enterprise level four different but complementary approaches to employee involvement are found across the EU:

Representative participation, can take many forms and is an approach used in most EU Member States, from the co-determination systems in Germany, enterprise-level works councils in the Netherlands, Comité d'entreprise in France to employee board-level representatives in Ireland or Greece. With regard to works councils or enterprise committees, these usually serve two complementary roles: a) as fora which management can use to communicate to the employee representatives and, through them, to the wider workforce, the financial, economic, employment, product, marketing situation and other relevant information on the performance of the enterprise,

[2] Directive 77/187/EEC – now Directive 2001/23/EC
[3] Directive 89/391/EEC
[4] Directive 94/45/EC
[5] Directive 2002/14/EC
[6] Directive 2001/86/EC

thus creating greater awareness of the business strategy, improving understanding of each other's concerns and building trust; and b) as fora for consultation and, when possible, for securing agreement, in a non-adversarial way, to proposed workplace changes, the introduction of new technologics, ncw forms of work organisation and other forms of re-structuring. For trade unions and other employee representatives, works councils provide a mechanism for the receipt of useful information, to convey employee concerns to management and as a means of influencing the implementation of company policy.

As a basis for the transmission of information and the consultation of employees, the concept of works councils has been extended to transnational companies operating within the European Economic Area, for issues of a European nature. Less that 800 European works councils have been set up, out of close to 2,000 covered by the EU Directive but, on the whole, these provide an important source of information for the workforce and employee representatives on key business performance indicators and a tool for management to consult with these representatives on any issues which it considers are important to the performance of the company, the maintenance of employment and the challenges of the market. European works councils also help both sides to understand the difficulties of operating in different countries and ensure that workers in subsidiaries have an opportunity to be informed on and committed to corporate policies.

Representative participation can also be at the highest level within an enterprise, either on the board of directors (in a unitary board system) or on the supervisory board (in a dual-board system). This form of representation provides employees and their representatives with the opportunity to be part of the policy formation process and to influence key decision-making of the future strategies and direction of the company. This is a form of employee involvement that has found favour in many Member States, in different forms and to varying degrees. It is of increased interest at the EU-level as it is recognised as a possible form of participation in enterprises registering under European company legislation (SEs).

Since the mid/late-1980s, direct participation has been growing in importance as a management strategy to increase productivity and greater flexibility in enterprise as well as to improve. The European Foundation, in its EPOC Project defined 'direct participation as:

> *Opportunities which management provide, or initiatives to which they lend their support, at workplace level, for consultation with and/or delegation of responsibilities and authority for decision-making to their subordinates either as individuals or as groups of employees, relating to the immediate work task, work organisation and/or working conditions.*[7]

The objective is to involve employees directly, both individually and as work groups, in issues which affect their day-to-day work by introducing procedures

a) to consult them, for example, through regular performance review meetings, suggestion schemes, attitude surveys or at regular team meetings (i.e. quality circles); or b) to allow individual workers to make key decisions on how to perform and control their own work by delegating such issues as scheduling of work, quality of the product or service, dealing with 'internal' and 'external' customers, time keeping or working conditions. A work team might also be delegated control over these issues for its members, in addition the team may also make decisions on internal allocation of work, job rotation or the introduction of improvements to the work process.[8]

---

[7] *Conceptualising Direct Participation in Organisational Change – The EPOC Project* Office of Official Publications of the European Communities, Luxembourg (1994) ISBN 92-826-8773-2 (EF/94/23). For the EPOC survey of 6,000 European workplaces the definition was refined in *Direct Participation and the Modernisation of Work Organisation* K Sisson, Office of Official Publications of the European Communities, Luxembourg (2000) ISBN 92-897-0018-1 (EF/00/29), as: *Consultative participation*: whereby management encourages employees to make their views known on work-related matters, but retains the right to take action or not; *Delegative participation*: whereby management gives employees increased discretion and responsibility to organise and do their jobs without reference back.

[8] *Useful but Unused – Group Work in Europe* Office of Official Publications of the European Communities, Luxembourg (1994) ISBN 92-828-5568-6 (EF/98/59)

Financial participation, either through profit sharing schemes or employee share ownership arrangements, has become a popular, if controversial, form of employee involvement in recent years. It not only provides employees with an input into the decision-making process as shareholders, but can also allow them to share in the financial success of their companies. European Foundation research and other studies have shown that the implementation of successful financial participation schemes can improve the links between the employees and the enterprise, resulting in industrial peace, improved productivity, the smooth introduction of flexibility in the organisation of work and, consequently, greater competitiveness.
The studies established that firms with other employee involvement arrangements, such as representation through works councils, joint works committees, or some similar form of arrangement, and/or direct participation, are more likely to also have forms of financial participation and for these to be more successful - each works better than if it is a 'stand alone' arrangement. Indeed, a strong, positive relationship was found between financial participation arrangements which are open to all employees and team-based work organisation and the evidence points to an increase in productivity when employee share ownership is combined with other forms of employee participation in decision-making.
With regard to the levels of internal communications, firms with share ownership schemes and with profit sharing arrangements for the whole workforce are more likely to communicate information on the company's strategic plans and on the economic and finance situation to their employees. Furthermore, the Foundation's research found no evidence to show that forms of financial participation weaken or undermine the representative role of trade unions or works councils within an enterprise.[9]
The final form of employee involvement in enterprises is through collective bargaining. Collective bargaining is based on an adversarial, 'win-lose', approach and, while many issues in the

[9] *Employee Share Ownership and Profit-Sharing in the European Union*, A Pendleton et al, European Foundation for the Improvement of Living and Working Conditions, Dublin, (2001)

employment relationship will always fall within the ambit of collective negotiations - for example, remuneration - management decisions that may have a direct impact on jobs and the organisation of work are, very often, included. This results in limiting the scope of workers to reacting to management decisions after they have been made, often resulting in workplace conflict, lose of trust and, in extreme cases, strikes.

There are indication, however, that collective bargaining is been re-invented by management and employee representatives to deal with re-structuring and to find mutually acceptable solutions to balancing between the need for greater flexibility within the enterprise and the concerns of the workforce for job security. With the growing market challenges presented by globalisation, intensification of competition and privatisation of State owned enterprises collective agreement which address the challenges of competitiveness and employment are growing as a mechanism for greater employee input into developing business strategies to meet these challenges.

Again this topic has been the subject of European Foundation research by examining collective agreements which strive to balance competitiveness with job creation and job protection. It is suggested in the findings of this research that these agreements differ from traditional contracts and regulations. As most initiatives, which aim to include employees in the process of change, particularly at the company level, represent a serious attempt to use a co-operative partnership approach, these collective agreements try to combine three major business elements: competitiveness, employment and partnership.[10]

Two Papers

This session addressed how we, in Europe, can introduce organisational change and what contribution can employee participation have in this process. Two papers were presented which

---

[10] *Handling Restructuring – Collective Agreements on Employment and Competitiveness* K Sisson et al, Office for Official Publications of the European Communities, Luxembourg, ISBN 92-897-0030-0, (EF/00/73).

are relevant to this debate. First Prof. Dr Ulrich Pekruhl, University of Applied Sciences, Solothurn, Switzerland, reporting on a study project to determine what is meant by employee participation and the overlap of its different components - economic, democratic and social perspectives.
The paper argues that, while in the past these three perspectives were looked on as a whole, which, in the past, has caused confusion, contradictions, false hopes and fears by trying to 'square the circle'. In fact, it stresses that the considerable overlap between the three perspectives should be examined to establish the common and the different interests of those involved in workplace participation.
The second paper, by Erich Latniak, Institut Arbeit und Technik, Gelsenkirchen, Germany, (in collaboration with Anja Gerlmaier), reported on an ongoing research project which is studying the changing role of participation in the design of work. The paper set out the basic ideas on employee participation in work design and what should be the result of such involvement – improvement of working conditions, greater commitment to work, finding solutions to design problems, contribute to increased productivity and greater flexibility, etc.
Using a telecommunications sector project on a joint approach to product development as an example, the paper outlined the limits of participation, the indirect forms of control and the skill demands. The project identified contradictory demands such as a shift towards an 'internalisation of markets' and control by context variables and given sets of objectives.
The two papers asked searching questions about the nature of employee participation in Europe today. They highlight the difficulties of introducing effective employee participation which can have a meaningful impact on organisational change. By doing so, they make a useful contribution to the debate on new forms of work organisation, employee involvement, the direction of the European Social Model and how these contribute to the Luxembourg Employment Strategy and the commitment at the Lisbon European Council to recognise the close links and inter-dependence of EU policies on economic growth, employment creation and social cohesion.

Contested Terrain: Employee Participation in Companies

ULRICH PEKRUHL

Introduction: Three Anecdotes and the Problem

Some time ago I took part in an event at which a Director General of the EU Commission presented a Green Paper on the subject of work organisation, which was prepared in his directorate, to representatives of the German employers' associations. The central point of this Green Paper is the statement that *participation* by employees in the planning and structuring of their work could bring about a lasting improvement in the competitiveness of European enterprises. It was therefore necessary to think how such forms of participation could be encouraged. As a complete surprise – complete surprise? – these proposals encountered powerful polemic objections among the representatives present: the State/the EU should please keep right out of this matter, the employers would continue to make decisions for their businesses! In view of the intensity of the arguments presented, one might get the impression that the Green Paper was not promoting a strengthening of the economic power of the companies, but the "expropriation of the expropriators".

In a video produced by Werner Fricke, employee participation in different forms of group work is presented through certain business examples. I like to show this video to my students, as the opportunities, but also certain risks, of this form of participation are explained very clearly here. However, I see questioning looks on the students' faces when I tell them the title of the film: "The other half of democracy". Does the rule of "one man, one vote" apply in the companies shown, or are there general elections? Of course not. Is there any election at all? Yes, for the position of group spokesperson, though this election is confirmed – or not – by the management.

In a research project on behalf of the Hans-Böckler-Stiftung (Bundemann-Jansen/Pekruhl 1992) the aim was to determine the relationship between company and union co-determination ["Mitbestimmung"] on the one hand

and new management concepts on the other. The subject of the research was the Bertelsmann Group, which was one of the first German companies to introduce numerous instruments for employee participation and claimed a "participative corporate culture". Although not expressed so clearly, the participating unions were hoping above all that the project would make it clear that the company's offers were not "true" participation, but only "social techniques" (Breisig 1990), with the aid of which the employees could be exploited more efficiently and, moreover, would be diverted from "true" participation, namely institutionalised co-determination.

These three anecdotes lead directly to the subject of this paper and at the same time give initial indications of its practical relevance: the mixing of different levels when we talk about *employee participation.* Some fear democracy, others desire it, when the issue is in fact increased efficiency and a third group want to show that these forms of increasing efficiency are "pseudo-democratic" and a diversion from true democracy.

This mixing of levels is also to be found in many publications on this subject; an entire research tradition is concerned with the phenomenon of "organisational democracy". An example of this is Weber (1999), who uses a wealth of material to discuss and emphasise in his article "Organisational Democracy" that this is almost impossible to find, although there is so much talk of participation in enterprises. This is attributed to the fact that "information and human relations management techniques – such as hearings – (...) can be rated as pseudo-democratic from the point of view of democracy theory, in so far as those affected are excluded from rights of joint decision-making" (272). Weber also summarises the position of many labour researchers that "co-operation that can be revoked by superiors in the hierarchy at any time, also constitutes a form of pseudo-democracy, although this may serve temporarily as a pre-form of organisational democracy" (op. cit.). If this co-operation is taken further and, say, takes on the form of semi-autonomous working groups, this can be seen as "direct democracy". Which brings us back to the video mentioned above, and to the widespread hope that models of industrial participation in themselves encourage democracy. "... the development of the technical and organisational productive forces implies a trend that encourages rather than discourages civil rights" (Müller-Jentsch 1994). To be able to determine the stage that an enterprise has reached on its path to a democratically organised business, it is then possible e.g. to define and measure degrees of employee participation: (1) no participation, (2) information, (3) consultation, (4) co-operation, (5) joint decision-making, (6) self-determination (IDE 1981 according to Weber 1999, 272). What all these

approaches have in common is that the democratic yardstick is being used to measure something that cannot be measured by it, i.e. gradations of democracy are being determined in a system which was never designed for democratisation. More on this below.
This linking of models of efficiency improvement through participation-oriented forms of work organisation with democratic claims has its origin in the early days of the socio-technical movement in Scandinavia at the beginning of the 60s. At that time the principles of socio-technical structuring of working systems developed (above all) in the empirical studies of the Tavistock Institute (with its strong emphasis on the participation aspect) were being introduced to a series of Norwegian companies (Thorsrud 1984). These socio-technical experiments were promoted by the state and the participating companies were supported in their plans by academics. At the same time these academics had a high socio-political commitment and saw the opportunity to use the participatory elements of the Socio-technical system structure as a cornerstone of "industrial democracy". The other cornerstones were: worker control of the corporate management by selected representatives and nationalisation of the means of production (op. cit. 339). This effort was further encouraged by a societal climate which was inclined to take a positive view of trade union claims for democratic influence in the companies. "Workplace democracy" was to be introduced into companies.
The fact that the linking of labour structure and democratisation was due above all to the specific political situation is evident from consideration of the contrary example to Scandinavia: in the USA the implementation of the findings of the human relations school (here too, strong elements of worker participation can be found) in many companies was not least an explicit weapon *against* a democratisation of the companies. The employees were to be involved in the industrial processes ("Involvement") and so to give up all ideas of democracy or even trade union influence. The introduction of "Human Resource Management" (as the operational interpretation of the Human Relations ideas) in American companies (Muller 1999) was linked in not a few cases with the explicit aim of making the company "union-free". To characterise the Human Relations movement, Volpert (1975) describes a caricature showing a factory shop with a poster: "Despite wage robbery and harassment – I love you. The Boss." The attitude to HRM – particularly in its European adaptation – has changed fundamentally (Ochsenbein/Pekruhl 2003); but HRM is still in that conflict field between democratisation, humanisation and economic efficiency, which is the subject of this paper.

So if employee participation (in the structuring of their work) can be both encouraging and hostile to democracy, it can be assumed that employee participation and democracy are by no means two sides of the coin, but two separate concepts – both of which can sail under the flag of "Participation", as the participation of employees plays an important role in some way. Before I go into this in more detail and discuss the consequences from this angle, however, I want to point to a third level, which also tends to get mixed with the other two.

The issue is the humanisation perspective. For example Weber (1999) sees the "promotion of targets motivated by humanism" as a basis for organisational *democracy* and with the description of these humanistic targets also mixes the concepts of "humanisation of working life" with those of "co-determination in the workplace" (270). A similar uncertainty thus permeates a large part of the debates on the German QWL programme. Sometimes the talk is of democratisation, sometimes of humanisation, so implicitly treating these two as equivalents takes place in claims for work pointing in an entirely different direction.

In the following I should like to argue that the three levels mentioned should initially be kept distinct both analytically and politically, that each of the three concepts be discussed in its individual rationality, in order then to check the possible connections and contradictions that exist in industrial reality, and what that means for the development of democracy, humane work and economic efficiency.

Economics, Democracy and Humanisation

The consideration of employee participation deals with three different concepts each with entirely different internal logic and equally different underlying contexts, namely economic, political and ethical (Figure 1). In all three cases employee participation is an important means of reaching the objective, but also for very different objectives with equally different implications for participation in practice.

Figure 1

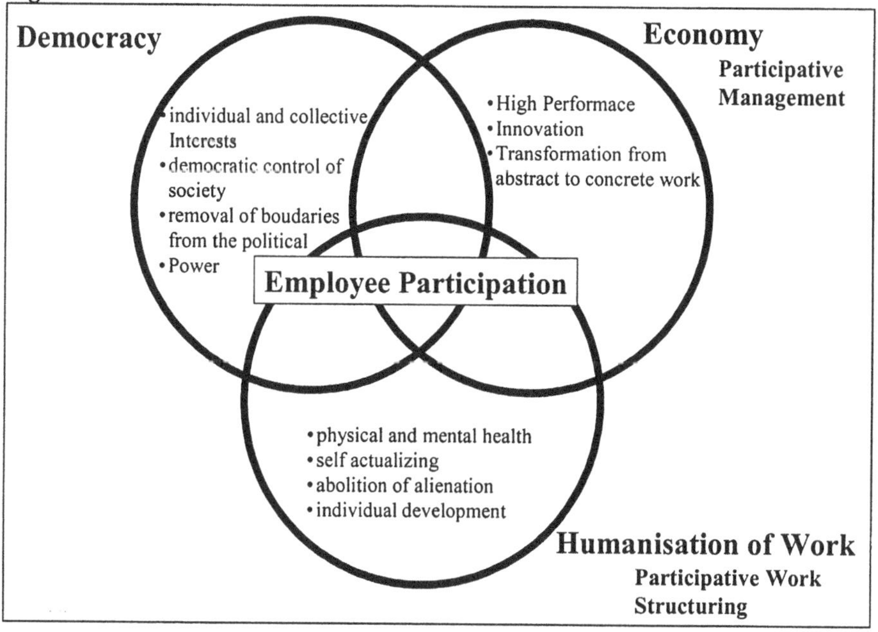

Participative Management

From the *economic* perspective the central issues are efficiency of service provision, strength of innovation, expansion of market potential, economic survival in enterprises or in service-providing organisations in general. In view of the fact that in a global economy means of production and technical know-how are increasingly becoming more universally available, the attention not only of industrial efficiency experts but also of product developers and marketing specialists is focusing increasingly on a resource which is (still and relatively) exclusively tied to a limited economic area: the human workforce (Ochsenbein/Pekruhl 2003). In addition there are enormous increases in demands on flexibility (in all its dimensions) of enterprises and we are finding that the capacity for adaptation and rapid decision-making are more natural to people than machines and programs. After all, like products and services, production processes are becoming increasingly knowledge-intensive. This knowledge can be written down and thus transferred virtually at will, but first of all this knowledge has to be generated by people. It is then largely linked to the ability of the employees, that is to the ability actually to transform that knowledge into increased productivity or innovation on the basis of a wide variety of

learning experiences (Pekruhl 2001). The importance of Human Resources for the competitiveness of the enterprise is thus growing dramatically.
The management of an enterprise is thus faced with two old questions but with a new urgency. Firstly, how can the qualifications of the employees be combined optimally with the technical and organisational structures of the business and, secondly, how are employees motivated to make their available qualifications actually available to the enterprise and with sufficient intensity and sustainability? The second question addresses the so-called transformation problem, which plays a central role in the labour process debate (Smith 1994): how can an enterprise succeed in transforming abstract work, the capacity for work acquired on the labour market, into concrete work, that is into real individual work performance?
As far as is known, these two questions were first raised systematically – "scientifically" - by Frederick Winslow Taylor (1993), who saw the solution to the transformation problem in the enterprise making itself largely independent of the knowledge and intention of the employees, by structuring work as simply as possible and specifying it in the greatest possible detail. These simple tasks can then be monitored precisely and their execution by the employees is directed by performance-related pay. These principles have made a triumphal entry not only into the world of production but also in the services sector – and that triumph is not yet ended.
However, since the nineteen thirties calls from the USA have been loud, accompanied in the 1950s by ones from the Tavistock Institute, which analysed the principles of Taylor's concept and were able to show that in a taylorist work organisation neither the capacity for work of the workforce nor its potential motivation would be used optimally. The well-known Hawthorne experiments led to the establishment of the above-mentioned human relations movement[1], which indicated that people work with more motivation, i.e. achieve higher performance, if they feel themselves accepted and valued in the workplace and the work itself has a recognisable value for them. Consultation, participation, involvement – *participation* – are important factors, to generate the desired intrinsic motivation (produced by the content of the work) and a sense of acceptance.
The name Tavistock stands for the development of the socio-technical system structure (STS) also mentioned above. The STS approach primarily attaches an entirely new ranking to the qualification of the workforce.

[1] The fact that this development was rather more complex is ignored here for the sake of brevity.

Qualification here is not a residual quantity derived from a given technology and fixed organisational structures, but instead is a central element which in turn should have effects on the structuring of technology and organisation. With this the trend towards de-qualified labour is reversed, in that technology and organisation are structured in such a way that the highest possible qualification of the workers can be used efficiently. So while Human Relations is concerned primarily with the quantitative utilisation of the labour capacity, STS sets out to make the qualitative potentials of the human worker as comprehensively useful as possible for the production process. This also puts an end to Taylor's "service by instruction", as comprehensive use of the employees' qualifications gives them far-reaching rights of intervention in the planning and execution of their work. So here *participation* stands for the use of qualifications.

The STS approach also shows that the participation of all the players concerned in the *structuring* of the socio-technical system enhances its quality and increases its acceptance by the players – an indication which was taken up and further developed by various concepts of organisation development (OD): participation by the players is one of the central premises of OD (Sydow 1985, Cummings/Markus 1979).

Neither the human relations school nor STS and OD had a significant influence on the reality in by far the majority of companies in Europe or the USA until the end of the 1970s. This changed – slowly – with the pressure of competition outlined above and the growing relevance of human labour for competitive success. Numerous "new management concepts" or "new production concepts" made an appearance, which were intended to take account of this development. Whether Lean Production, Total Quality Management, Fractal Factory, Business Process Reengineering or Knowledge Management, these concepts, which replaced each other and penetrate each other, which were reflected in countless sub-concepts, all have one thing in common: the fundamental principles of the human relations and the STS approach play a central role[2], *all these new management concepts are based on a more or less far-reaching participation by employees in the planning and structuring of their work.*

To distinguish the political and ethically based approaches to participation I suggest that we use the term *participative management* here and define it as follows: "Participative management systematically uses and encourages the

---

[2] But without always a direct reference to the previous work and concepts of STS or human relations.

abilities and the motivation of employees to continuously optimise the development of goods and services. This is done through participation in decisions on structures and processes in work and production" (Pekruhl 2001, 5).

Participative Work Structuring

The demand for a *humanisation* of work is derived from an *ethical* view of the commercial enterprise. Business ethics reject the imperative of the economic and – standing in the tradition of the Enlightenment – ask about the morality in the enterprise. Categories such as justice, human dignity, accountability, solidarity or sustainability are the *leitmotifs* for this approach and at the same time act as a standard for commercial conduct. The realisation of ethical behaviour in business results

- either through the intermediary of the societal value system
- or through self-commitment of individual enterprises or entrepreneurs
- or through statutory or wage agreement regulations.

This can be illustrated through the example of humane work:
On the level of *societal values*, for example, it is taken for granted in European companies that no child labour is being used (but for the sake of caution this is still regulated by law). European enterprises which allow children to work for them in their Asian or African subsidiaries are reproached by society (and thus through consumer power also economically) – if they are found out.
A good example of the *self-commitment* of an enterprise is the Bertelsmann group (Bundemann-Jansen/Pekruhl 1992, Mohn 1985). Building on the conviction of the Group patriarchs, that an enterprise must basically also accept its social responsibility, different measures for humanisation of work are being implemented, for example in the area of occupational health. Public programmes (e.g. the German programme for humanisation of working life or the EU Commission's Corporate Social Responsibility Initiative) begin mainly at this level and endeavour to promote the self-commitment of enterprises.
Finally there are the *statutory regulations*, which specify the minimum standards for humane work (maximum working hours, exposure limits etc.) and *collective wage agreements*, in which the working conditions may also play a role.
So what should be understood here by humane work? Firstly, humane work means freedom from physical and mental injury, the work should be feasible for the workers, and directly and for a foreseeable time be (largely)

free of damage and cause no serious impairment to health (Hacker/Richter 1980 according to Ulich 1991, 118). In addition, however, it is also related to the personality of the workers, their personal development targets, which should be encouraged – or at least not hampered – by the work, their wish for self-determination, which does not have to be abandoned at the factory gate and their goal of self-realisation, which Maslow (1981) defines as follows: "A man must be what he can be" (74). After all, the issue is also to reduce alienation from work in production processes with a high division of work, that is to change that condition in which a person "only feels at home in himself away from work and in work feels remote from himself", as Marx describes it in one of his early works (MEGA I/2, 368)[3].

Two examples of a practically-based operationalisation of the concept of "humane work" will be dealt with in more detail later:

- The concept of expanded scope for action is a need concept, in which the claims of the employees to humane work are derived from the basis of action regulation theory.
- Behind the second approach is an industrial science understanding of which aspects of the work put stress on the physical and mental health of those employed, and which aspects represent resources for the maintenance or restoration of health. The tool for this is the "Salutogenetische Subjektive Arbeitsanalyse" (SALSA) of Riman/Udris.

The basis of the *"expanded scope for action"* concept is the action regulation theory, which creates a hierarchic ranking of regulation requirements and – to put it very briefly – assumes that the workers who come closest to doing justice to human needs are those who open up a broad scope for action. So the central factor is the completeness of the actions, which includes the planning, implementation and monitoring of the consequences. In this Ulich (1991) distinguishes two dimensions of human scope for action: firstly the horizontal dimension of the scope for activity and secondly the vertical dimension of the scope for decision-making and monitoring. A taylorist organisation of labour means a narrowing of the decision options while increasing the division of labour and thus a reduction in the scope for action. The concept of expanded scope for action represented an important theoretical framework for the humanisation discussion in Germany and was used above all as a reason for the positive

[3] In "Deutsche Ideologie" he discloses his personal ideas of humane work in a society which allows him "to do this today, that tomorrow, to go hunting in the morning, fishing in the afternoon, rearing animals in the evening, to criticise after food, because I want to, without ever becoming a hunter, fisherman, shepherd or critic" (MEW 3, 33). An early attempt on the subject of job rotation.

effects of semi-autonomous group work on the work situation of the employees. Job rotation and job enlargement in the semi-autonomous working group bring about an expansion in the scope for activity of the employees. Using planned rotation of tasks and expansion of activities (on the same level of qualification) monotony and one-sided stress are reduced at the same time. An expansion of the scope for decision-making and monitoring is only possible, however, through job enrichment. And that job enrichment primarily means nothing other than *participation* in the planning and structuring of one's own work.

The concept of "*Salutogenetischen Subjektiven Arbeitsanalyse*" (SALSA) of Riman and Udris (1997) asks about the health risks and resources in work. The concept assumes that the work not only includes factors which lead to health problems, but that features of activity also exist which serve to maintain and restore the health of workers. The starting points for SALSA are models of systems and action theory, in which health is interpreted positively and thus means more than the absence of sickness.

This described balance depends on the extent to which certain personnel, organisational and social resources are available in the labour process. The personnel resources include individual dispositions, in which workers see themselves as a match for their work situation and see that as meaningful and capable of being influenced. Organisational resources allow a person to come to terms with the demands of the work and to master the associated stresses. These are "all work conditions, industrial institutions and aids which can make it easier for a person to come to terms with the demands of the work and to master, tolerate or avoid stresses" (op. cit., 283) The social resources include above all recognition and support by supervisors and colleagues and a positive social climate. For our context it should be remembered that in addition to the "traditional" demands for a work structure which is acceptable from the point of view of health, other aspects, which are related to the content of the work itself, play a role: Possibilities for *participation* in work have a positive effect on the workers' health situation.

This operationalisation of humane work through the concept of the scope for action and the Salutogenetischen approach shows that in a humane labour structure, participation plays a central role. I summarise the relevant concepts in the term *participative work structuring.*

Co-determination ['Mitbestimmung']

Finally there is also the *political* view of employee participation. The issue here is *democracy,* that is attested rights of the individual to express his will in a democratically legitimate process. The issue is power and influence, the application of interests on the majority principle. An entirely controversial discussion here is the question whether democracy has anything to do with the economic enterprise or the economic sphere as a whole. The economic liberal's answer to this question is clear (No!, for anyone who is still in doubt). But critical academics question the point of "organisational democracy". According to Habermas "a modern, market-led economic system cannot be switched at random from money to administrative power and democratic development of an informed opinion (...), without a threat to its capacity to perform" (Habermas 1990, 27 cited by Frerichs 1995, 409). Frerichs, who in his article is aiming towards a foundation in democracy theory for approaches to participation, summarises the counter-position of Beck and Negt/Kluge as follows: "On the other hand Beck and Negt/Kluge stress the need, because of the importance and the risks of the technical-economic development, to open up such questions to public discussion, to use the skills of non-professional social players for structuring and to lower the traditional barriers between economics and politics in favour of new political forms" (Frerichs 1995, 414). A "removal of boundaries from the political" (Beck) and its extension to the economy are thus the counter-argument to Habermas and liberal political approaches.

Only: this "removal of boundaries from the political" in the field of economics is a social science suggestion rather than social reality. Even if there are also initial small signs of a corresponding development. Although in the initiatives of the EU Commission on corporate social responsibility briefly mentioned above, the main focus is on the (ethically and morally founded) discourse, it is hinted between the lines that such a discourse can certainly relate to democratically legitimised processes. These indications will most certainly ensure that the CSR Green Paper meets the same fate as the Green Paper on work organisation mentioned at the beginning.

But if we do not focus primarily on the exchange between a political system on the one hand and the economic system on the other, but consider the political *in the* economic, the perspective changes: the issue then is the "democratic underlay of representative political systems by new forms of openness and participation at the *points of origin* of the political" (Frerichs 1995, 417, Herv. U.P.). In this Frerichs posits that "the participation of the workers in the structuring of industrial production (...) tends to involve the discourse on the "what" and "how" of production" (op. cit.). So is there a link between participative management and democracy? In Frerichs' statement the decisive words are "tends to": how can these tendencies be encouraged, who does so with what power resources and who tries to prevent these tendencies? This brings us to the question of micropolitics in industry, which under the conditions of participative management offers opportunities for co-determination (see below) by the workers on production. The specialist skills for structuring of work processes can be used as a source of power for influence by labour and interest groups" (op. cit., 419). I will return to this context at the end of this article.

There are, however, also those democratic elements which are firmly anchored in German companies, namely corporate co-determination through the Co-determination Law and industrial co-determination through the Works Council Constitutions Act. The one form of co-determination guarantees employee representatives influence on the supervisory boards of large enterprises, the other form guarantees consultation on company decisions which have direct or indirect effects on the employee's workplace. Frequently in this connection the issue is "indirect participation", as the workers are not included in the decision processes directly, but through the intermediary of the interest representations who are democratically elected by them.

The idea of "co-determination in the workplace" which from the mid-1970s was increasingly discussed in the trade unions and politically propagated – unsuccessfully – was intended to close this gap in participation (or rather: gap in democracy). Co-determination in the workplace means that the individual employee can jointly determine aspects affecting his immediate work. Jointly determine! It is important to emphasise that, as the great similarities between participative management and co-determination in the workplace (about which more below) cease at precisely this point: whereas in the one case participation is granted by the management and can equally be limited again, in the other case it is a question of agreed, legal rights. So I think it is important, where the political aspects of participation are concerned, always to talk of *co-determination* in order to make the effects on the corporate power structure clear.

Squaring the Circles?

Three types of employee participation, three founding relations, which at first sight have almost nothing in common: here economic efficiency, there the ethical demands on commerce and finally the demand for democratic influence on the economic process. But then we look again at the practice of participation in companies and a miracle happens: squaring the circles succeeds: the practical implementation of participation seems to merge seamlessly, all approaches merge in a large concept of "employee participation" (Figure 2).

Looking first at those aspects of participation which immediately affect the work:

- Employees who have a wide scope for action and who are therefore satisfied with their work, work with greater motivation and feel more committed to the aims of the company: humane work increases the productivity and commitment of employees and at the same time the wide scope for action means that the employees are permitted a direct influence on the structuring of their immediate work – precisely what "co-determination in the workplace" demands.
- The comprehensive use of human qualifications in the work process is associated with the dismissal of the taylorist division of labour, the employees are asked for their ideas and these are incorporated in production and innovation; the work becomes challenging and interesting and thus more humane; at least a first step in the direction in which workers can also be quite at home in work.
- The fundamental requirement for humane workplaces with freedom from physical and mental injury corresponds to the economic reasons for reducing the sickness levels in the companies (in order to reduce labour costs, but also because highly qualified employees cannot readily be replaced). The demand for lasting freedom from injuries at work is increasingly also being taken up for economic reasons, as some companies understand that the inexpensive early retirement of many workers causes a great and almost irreplaceable loss of potential experience.
- Finally participative, humane, healthy workplaces are attractive workplaces. In the "war for talents" the companies with the best chance of survival are those that can use not only attractive remuneration but also attractive workplaces to attract and retain the brightest employees.

Figure 2

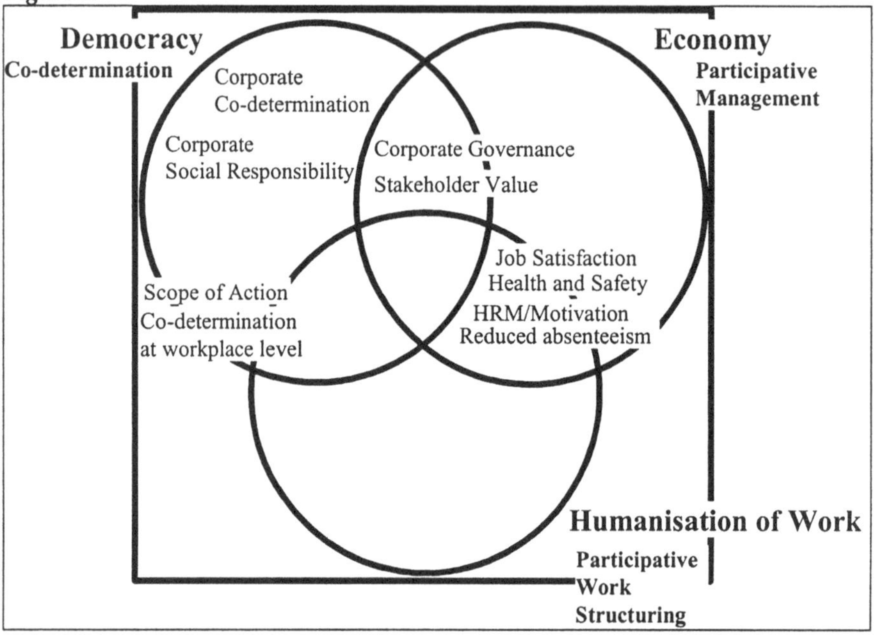

And at least at the level of operational work – both in production and in the services sector – it seems that there is a form of work organisation which particularly encourages the synergies described above between democracy, humanisation and economics: group work. Job rotation, job enlargement and job enrichment can be realised in a working group which is responsible for a coherent demanding task. At the same time the knowledge and skills of the group members are used to optimum economic effect, the flexibility of the organisation is increased by decentralisation of decisions and the group workers are motivated to apply themselves in their task. "Workplace democracy" is sometimes spelt "semi-autonomous working group".

But the example of group work shows the fragility of this synergy most clearly. This will become clear at the latest after a closer look at how group work is realised in concrete terms. The span begins with those forms of group work in which car assembly workers standing next to each other on the assembly line deputise for each other (and are responsible for that mutual deputising) and meet together regularly to further optimise their strictly specified manipulations. The last is after all one step away from classic taylorism. This variant of group work, which is also known as toyotism after the Japanese car manufacturer (Benders/Huijgen/Pekruhl

2000, Fröhlich/Pekruhl 1996) then has to put up with reproaches from all those who are concerned primarily with humanisation or democracy, that it is not "proper" group work; Jürgens (1993) and other labour researchers suggest that this form of work organisation should be called "team work" instead of "group work"[4]. Here, as described above, the democratic yardstick is used to measure a form of work organisation that was never designed for democracy. Mr Toyoda's concern is to offer the market innovative, cheap and reliable products. And for that "his" form of group work is – perhaps[5] – the most suitable.

If on the other side of the span of the group work concepts we look at the semi-autonomous work groups and recall the classic definition of Gulowsen[6], it will be clear that this relates to a different society, a society in which the power of the entrepreneur or the capitalist and his managers is restricted in favour of a direct democracy in industry. Here it is very evident that differing ideologies and different interests collide; on the one side there is the private control of the means of production, on the other side the call for societal control of the economy.

Less obvious, and perhaps rather in the form of fears than of actual threats to the democratic or economic position, this contrast is also evident at other points in the structuring of group work in companies. A good example of this is the election of group spokesperson. From the democratic point of view this is a further touchstone for the quality of the work group. From the economic point of view such an election can make good sense, as it encourages commitment in the group members, increases mutual understanding and thus improves the functioning of the group. Nevertheless, I know of no industrial regulation in which the group is permitted to make the final decision on its spokesperson; although there is an election, in the end the management decides. The latter almost always confirms the election, but is not willing to give up its right of direction. From the point of view of humanisation, the jury is still out regarding whether the election of group spokesperson promotes or detracts from the

---

[4] which is not particularly successfully as the word "team" has considerably more positive connotations than "group"

[5] There are very serious arguments that the Toyota form of group work is sub-optimal from purely economic perspectives and that forms of group work which focus on a more comprehensive use of employees, may be more successful overall. (Sandberg 1995).

[6] According to Gulowsen (1971) the semi-autonomous groups can influence establishment of the objectives of their employment at a higher system level owing to their membership of the system: the issues here are the qualitative features of the objective (incl. choice of product) as well as the quantitative features.

quality of the workplace. Although such an election clearly increases the scope for action (Ulich), on the other hand it is quite possible that negative effects of group work such as group pressure, exclusions etc. can be better regulated with a traditional supervisor than with an elected group spokesperson as an equal among equals (Fröhlich 1983). Democracy in the workplace thus does not inevitably mean humane work.

Finally if we consider in how few enterprises the employees have the opportunity even to organise just their own work (or that of the group) largely independently and on their own responsibility[7], the unavoidable impression is that in many corporate managements power political fears are forcing economic rationality into the background. This brings us back to the labour process debate, in which the "Braverman wing" maintained exactly that: out of (justified) fear of loss of control, the management would continue to back taylorist concepts. Burawoy and his adherents on the other hand pointed out that direct control by taylorist mechanisms is replaced by the far more efficient control of the "hearts and minds" of the employees, which would be generated by involvement in the corporate decisions. I fully endorse this second position, but: how many managers have read Burawoy? Although those acting need not by any means always be aware of these power political fears, deeply-rooted cultural values and attitudes may be involved, which are not surveyed and which come to the surface almost as reflexes in relevant situations. This would finally explain the example outlined at the beginning, that of the polemical rejection of the EU Green Paper on work organisation.

With regard to health promotion too, the position is not quite as simple as outlined above. In times of high unemployment, the fear of losing one's job may have at least as great an effect on reducing the sickness rate as a programme of industrial health promotion. Once the sick workers have finally worked themselves into the ground, they can easily be replaced by the "reserves" on the labour market. This sounds highly cynical and will not directly influence the thinking of corporate managements in any way in this form. But in fact it looks as if the economic pressure to establish a company health promotion programme is low if the official sickness rate is below 4%.

The combination of common ground and contradictions also permeates the other sections of the circle in Figure 2; we will cover them briefly. It has frequently been shown that the German model of *industrial co-*

[7] According to an investigation by Pekruhl (2001) this is fewer than 2% of all employees in German enterprises; cf. also Wengel et al. (2002).

determination clearly enhances the quality of *corporate governance*, and is one of the reasons for the international success of the German economy. Nevertheless all co-determination options[8] must without exception be asserted by workers, their associations and party political partners *against* the enterprises and their associations which are unable or unwilling to agree to *co-determination* for reasons of principle.

In the *stakeholder value* approach – by contrast with the shareholder value approach - not only the interests of the capital-providers are considered, but also those of the managers, workers, customers or citizens, i.e. all those who are affected in any way by the corporate policy (Pekruhl 2003). The stakeholder approach is an economic concept and is based on the assumption that failure to consider the interests of stakeholders will lower public acceptance of the enterprise and could thus have a negative effect on product sales. From the ethical point of view the corporate social responsibility approach requires the enterprise to take account of exactly these stakeholder interests. So far, so good, but, if the economic imperatives for the stakeholder value approach become weak and the interests of the stakeholders touch sensibly on those of the shareholders, the common ground is at an end. And if the CSR approach then also comes to talk of "regulation", the communication between the two sides is broken off completely.

So does the term *employee participation* only express the unachievable wish that in the enterprise things may be combined which actually do not belong together and also cannot come together? Then once again the baby would be thrown out with the bath water, as practical overlaps between the concepts actually exist and cannot be ignored. But the same goes for the contradictions.

Implications for Action Research to Look at Efficiency, Humanity and Democracy

So what does this mean for the large community of those action researchers[9] who do not want to give up squaring circles, who therefore adopt the economic, political and humane perspectives at the same time – although perhaps with differing weightings – who want to change reality in

[8] cf. the present debate on co-determination in EU-wide enterprises

[9] Action research should be understood here in the broadest sense as research which intervenes in changing reality at enterprise level and does not merely record the existing position.

this sense and who see an approach to such change in the described segment quantities of the three perspectives? I see three implications, which I should like to explain briefly in conclusion:

- abandoning false hopes and fears;
- investigating, promoting and linking practically *all* perspectives of participation;
- moderating in the "contested terrain".

Abandoning False Hopes and Fears

I have already commented on the false hopes and fears. I have quoted the hope of many labour researchers that democracy in the workplace would be installed virtually by itself, if the enterprises organised the work of their employees "reasonably", namely in such a way that optimum use could be made of their knowledge and skills. But precisely this hope is also a fear of the management. The latter may perhaps not primarily be afraid of democracy in the directly political sense, but due to the fact that at shop floor level something is becoming independent over which it would really want to retain the fullest possible control. Enlightenment is needed for both sides: neither does participative management have anything to do with democracy nor need the management fear loss of control. Participative management is not a democratic institution, quite simply because the "rights" of the employees are not rights, because they are neither documented nor claimable, but rather represent obligations to participate in enhancing the efficiency in the enterprise using knowledge, ability and willingness. On the other hand it should be made clear to the company management that participative management does not result in loss of control, but only replaces direct control by indirect control, i.e. a form of control that is generated via culturally anchored values, agreements, responsibility and intrinsic motivation to work. The fact that the fears among the management are also anchored culturally, and are thus correspondingly difficult to overcome, is something I have already shown above.

Similarly the implementation of participative management concepts does not lead automatically to more humane working conditions, although many pre-conditions for humane work become better. And that exactly is where we have to start:

Investigating, promoting and linking practically all perspectives of participation

Once the levels are distinguished analytically and politically, the possible synergies may be addressed and used in a non-ideological way: the areas in which interests actually coincide can be examined to see how all three aspects of participation can be validated as far as possible; the areas in which interests are different or contradictory are defined and made the subject of negotiation, labour- and micro-policy (see the third implication).

One task of the action researcher in this context is to reveal participation-related ideologies as such. "A common feature of ideologies is the claim that one's own benefit is only a (necessary) side-effect of the orientation on the common good. It is generally also claimed that other interests which conflict with one's own are not the actual or 'objective' interests of those subjects" (Volpert 1994, 125). In this connection it is quite appropriate to reflect self-critically on our own role. Have we not also been guilty in many cases of selling *employee participation* as an ideology, as a concept that does justice to all? To encourage participative concepts in companies, we have convinced management of their economic benefit, and we have brought unions, works councils and staff onto our side with reference to the democratisation and humanisation potential of participative management concepts. And all too often we have kept quiet about the potential lines of conflict so as not to encourage existing scepticism even further. But conflicts have not infrequently overtaken us.

A further task for action researchers, in a time in which the economic imperative is controlling societal reality with distinctly more dominance than ever before, is to set normative signs: humanisation is not "only" a welcome side effect if participative management is realised in a far-reaching variant, but a challenge which should be given equal status with the target of efficiency improvement. The same applies to the democratisation of working life: it is not sufficient to expand the participation options of the employees through appeals to the economic good sense of the enterprise. It is also necessary to advocate it, to open up the economic sphere in the Becksch sense to democratic discourse and a dimension of that discourse is the possibility of co-determination by workers in their workplaces.

That also means that humanisation research and democracy research, humanisation policy and policy for expansion of democratic rights cannot be linked with the economic perspectives from the outset, but should first develop their arguments for themselves, which can then be examined for congruence in industrial reality.

The interfaces between the different aspects of participation are "contested terrain" and thus arenas of micropolitics in which different interests collide. I have already mentioned above that participation affects the political balance of power in the company in a specific way: influence on the structuring of production for economic motives – participative management – potentially increases the power resources of the employees and the representatives of their interests. "Requests by management to use participation as a vehicle in order to increase the motivation and acceptance of the employees and to use their knowledge unilaterally to improve effectiveness, can be transformed into political effects if the employees and the representatives of their interests recognise the dominance aspect of this process and on their side transform the greater level of autonomy of action acquired through participation into negotiation and exchange processes (Frerichs 1995, 420). Micropolitics becomes labour politics if conflicts of interest are not dealt with silently day by day, but instead are made the subject of discussions and negotiations. For the action researcher the task is to encourage this transformation of micropolitics to labour politics and to introduce "all-party" expertise into the labour political processes, to disclose one's own ethical and political positions and to moderate the process from the same all-party position.

With such moderation it will be possible to distinguish between the disputed and undisputed fields of *employee participation,* to ensure sustained consensus in the industrial concretisation of the common ground and at the same time to ensure that the differences of interest are negotiated openly and fairly in the sense that the consensual part is not threatened.

References

Benders, J., F. Huijgen, U. Pekruhl (2000), *Gruppenarbeit in Europa – Ein Überblick*; in: WSI-Mitteilungen 6/2000

Breisig, T. (1990), *Betriebliche Sozialtechniken. Handbuch für Betriebsrat und Personalwesen*, Neuwied/Ffm

Bundesmann-Jansen, J., U. Pekruhl (1992), *Der Medienkonzern Bertelsmann. Neues Management und gewerkschaftliche Betriebspolitik.* HBS Forschung Bd.7, Köln

Burawoy, M. (1979), *Manufacturing Consent: Changes in the Labor Process under Monopoly Capitalism*

Frerichs, J. (1995), *Zum Begriff des Politischen in den industriellen Beziehungen*; in: Arbeit 4/95

Fröhlich, D. (1983), *Machtprobleme in teilautonomen Arbeitsgruppen*, in: Neidhard, F. (Hg.): *Gruppensoziologie. Perspektiven und Materialien*, Sonderheft der KzfSS, Köln

Fröhlich, D., U. Pekruhl (1996), *Direct Participation and organisational change. Fashionable but misunderstood? An analysis of recent research in Europe, Japan and the USA*, Dublin/Luxembourg

Gulowsen, J. (1971), *Selvstyrte Arbeidgrupper*, Oslo

Habermas, J. (1990), *Strukturwandel der Öffentlichkeit*, Ffm

Hacker, W., P. Richter (1980), *Psychische Fehlbeanspruchung: Pychische Ermüdung, Monotonie, Sättigung und Stress*; in: W. Hacker (Hg.): *Spezielle Arbeits- und Ingenieurspsychologie in Einzeldarstellungen*, Berlin

Jürgens, U. (1993), *Mythos und Realität von Lean Production in Japan – eine kritische Auseinandersetzung mit den Ergebnissen der MIT-Studie*; in: *Fortschrittliche Betriebsführung/Industrial Engineering* 42/1

Maslow, A.H. (1981), *Motivation und Persönlichkeit*, Reinbek

MEW 3 (1969), *Marx Engels Werke Bd. 3* (Deutsche Ideologie), Berlin 1969

MEGA I/2 (1982), *Karl Marx/Friedrich Engels, Gesamtausgabe, Erste Abteilung, Band 2* (Ökonomisch-Philosophische Manuskripte), Berlin 1982

Mohn, R. (1985), *Zur Standortbestimmung von Unternehmen in einer modernen Gesellschaft*, Gütersloh

Muller, M. (1999), *Enthusiastic embrace or critical reception? The German HRM debate*; in: Journal of Management Studies 36:4, July 1999

Müller-Jentsch, W. (1994), *Über Produktivkräfte und Bürgerrechte; in: Soziale Welt*, Sonderband 9: Umbrüche gesellschaftlicher Arbeit

Ochsenbein, G., U. Pekruhl (2003), *Strategisches Human Resource Management*; in: G. Ochsenbein, U. Pekruhl (Hg.): *Erfolgsfaktor HRM*, Zürich, fortlaufend

Pekruhl, U. (2001), *Partizipatives Management – Konzepte und Kulturen*, München und Mering

Riman, M., I. Udris (1997), *Subjektive Arbeitsanalyse: Der Fragebogen SALSA*; in O. Strohm, E. Ulich (Hg.): *Unternehmen arbeitspsychologisch bewerten*, Zürich

Sandberg, A. (1995), *The Uddevalla experience in perspective*; in: A. Sandberg (ed.): *Enriching production*, Aldershot

Smith, V. (1994), *Braverman's legacy: The labour process tradition at 20*; in: *Work And Occupations*, Vol. 21, No. 4, Nov. 94

Sydow, J. (1985), *Der soziotechnische Ansatz der Arbeits- und Organisationsgestaltung: Darstellung*, Kritik, Weiterentwicklung, Ffm u.a.

Taylor, F.W. (1993), *The principles of Scientific Management* (Orig. 1911), Routledge

Thorsrud, E. (1984), *The Scandinavian model: strategies of organizational democratization in Norway*; in: B. Wilper, A. Sorge (eds) (1984): *International Perspectives on Organizational Democracy*

Ulich, E. (1991), *Arbeitspsychologie*, Zürich

Volpert, W. (1975), *Die Lohnarbeitswissenschaft und die Psychologie der Arbeitstätigkeit*; in: Großkurth, P., W.

Volpert: *Lohnarbeitspsychologie. Berufliche Sozialisation: Emanzipation zur Anpassung*, Ffm

Volpert, W. (1994), *Interessenbindung und Verantwortung bei der Mitwirkung an Gestaltungsprozessen*; in: L.v. Rosenstiel u.a. (Hg): *Handbuch der angewandten Psychologie*, Landsberg/Lech

Weber, W.G. (1999), *Organisationale Demokratie – Anregungen für innovative Arbeitsformen jenseits blosser Partizipation?* in: *Zeitschrift für Arbeitswissenschaft* 4/99

Wengel, J., G. Lay, U. Pekruhl, S. Maloca (2002), *Verbreitung innovativer Arbeitsgestaltung. Stand und Dynamik des Einsatzes im internationalen Vergleich*, München und Mering

New Forms of Work Organisations, Direct and Indirect Worker Participation. Evidence from the Netherlands

MICHIEL DRUCKER, JAN KEES LOOISE

Introduction

The connection between the introduction of new forms of work organisation and direct and indirect participation is often mentioned in literature (management as well as more scientific). The main idea is that new organisational forms, e.g. in the form of delayering, the introduction of teamwork, new forms of leadership, etc, will stimulate the interest in and use of direct participation and at the same time decrease the interest in and use of indirect participation. The argument is that as a result of actual organisational change employees will be able to participate more directly in daily decision making in their department (direct participation) and therefore have less need for indirect forms of participation like shops stewards or works councils. Examples of this way of thinking can be found with American management gurus and consultants (like Moss Kanter, 1989; Peters 1992) and with their Dutch counterparts (likeGoodijk, 1993, 1995; Wissema et al, 1995; Homan, 1995). But also more scientific oriented authors seem to be attracted by this kind of thoughts (like for instance Marchington & Parker, 1990; Marchington et al 1995; Looise et al, 1996).
However, until now no empirical data exist with respect to the (supposed) connection between new forms of work organisation and the functioning of direct and indirect participation. In this contribution we try to research this connection for the Netherlands. In this contribution, we will establish to what extent these developments have had an impact on the position of the Dutch works council. Our main data come from a recent survey (Van het Kaar and Looise, 1999; Looise & Drucker, 2003), a replica of the last

major survey of works councils in 1985 (Looise and De Lange, 1987)[1]. The survey consisted of separate questionnaires to both the managing director and a works council member (in most cases the chairman of the works council). Beside questions about a large range of issues with respect to the position and influence of Dutch works councils, also questions were asked about the policy with respect to and the existence of new organisational forms and about the amount of direct participation. In this paper we will present the findings on these subjects and explore possible links between them. The quantitative data from the survey has been complemented with qualitative data from a number of extensive case studies within different parts of the large Dutch retail company Ahold. Within this company serious attempts were made to link new organisational forms with new forms of direct and indirect participation (Drucker, 2003).

The paper starts with a brief introduction of the ideas with respect to the connection between the introduction of new forms of work organisation and direct and indirect participation (section 2). To show that these ideas are not just theory, but sometimes are realised in practice, we add to this section a brief description of the development within one of the parts of our the case study, Albert Heijn. In the next sections we present our survey evidence with respect to the existence and backgrounds of new organisational forms (section 3), the connection with direct participation (section 4) and with the position of the works council (section 5) and the connection between direct participation and the works council (section 6). At the end, we summarise and conclude our findings in section 7.

---

[1] Compared to the survey of 1985, the response rates of the latest survey were rather low: 12 per cent(N=407) for the works council survey and 14 per cent (N=475) for the management survey. In 1985 the response rate was 47 per cent for both works councillors and managing directors. The main explanation for the low response rate is the `research tiredness' with works councils and organisations last years, which can also be seen with comparable surveys last years especially regardingin the functioning of works councils.

The (assumed) Connection between Organisational Change, Direct and Indirect Participation

As has been said, in management as well as more scientific literature, we find the idea that organisational change will lead to changes in the interest in and use of forms of participation
An in the Netherlands often used model for organisational change or development is that of Bolwijn and Kumpe (1994)[2]. In this (dynamic contingency) model Bolwijn and Kumpe state that as a result of changes in three key variables, namely markets, competition and technology, four phases in the development of companies can be distinguished: the efficient firm, the quality firm, the flexible firm and the innovative firm. Connected to each phase, they describe the organisational characteristics of the different firms. While the efficient or bureaucratic firm is featured by specialisation and hierarchy, in the quality firm elements of communication and co-operation are needed to get the necessary amount of quality. The organisational characteristics of the flexible firm are integration and decentralisation, while in the innovative firm participation and democratisation are the most important. In fact, Bolwijn and Kumpe state that in the development of companies throughout the four phases the accent is on structural and cultural change alternately. See for an overview of the model figure 1 (without the last row).

[2] Comparable approaches and or models can be found with Lammers (1993), who makes a distinction between the traditional organisation, the classical bureaucracy and the flexible bureaucracy, and with Buelens (1998), who makes a distinction between first-, second- and third-generation organisations.

Figure 1. Development of firms and forms of participation

	Market requirements	*Performance criteria*	*Firm (ideal type)*	*Firm characteristics*	*Forms of participation*
1960	price	efficiency	Efficient Firm	specialisation and hierarchisation	trade unions, works councils
1970	price, quality	efficiency + quality	Quality Firm	communication and co-operation	job consultation, quality circles
1980	price, quality, product line	efficiency + quality + flexibility	Flexible Firm	integration and decentralisation	autonomous teams, teamwork
1990	price, quality, product line, uniqueness	efficiency + quality + flexibility + innovative ability	Innovative Firm	participation and democratisation	integral participation, financial participation

Looise et al (1996) have tried to make a connection between the organisational development as has been sketched in the model of Bolwijn and Kumpe and the development of forms of participation. Based on a historical analyses of the development of participation in the Netherlands, they concluded that the 1950s and 1960s, the period of the efficient or bureaucratic firm in the model, participation took place mainly in the form of (formal) arrangements with unions and (starting in this period) works councils. During the 1970s, the period of the quality firm, you could see the rise of (informal) participation at shop floor level in the form of job consultation and quality circles. However, these forms were only meant for the exchange of information. The employees who participated in it were given no decision rights. That situation changed in the 1980s when in a growing number of companies a spread of autonomous task groups and teams with their own specific duties and rights could be observed. And now at the end of the 1990s and the beginning of the 2000s we witness in a number of (leading) companies' experiments with new integral forms of employee participation. Integral participation refers to a set of different participation practices that are mutually linked, including such forms as works councils, job consultation, teams and financial participation. If we place these developments in the same scheme of Bolwijn and Kumpe we come to the last row of figure 1.

It should be noted however that phase-models are based on ideal-types, which are often inconsistent. In most cases these phase-models they use dramatic shifts and sharp contrasts (for example flexible as opposed to mass production, or democratic as opposed to bureaucratic policy), while it is more realistic to speak of tendencies which combine continuity and change (cf. Vos & Buitelaar 1996). Another weak point in the model of Bolwijn and Kumpe is the deterministic character. According to this model all high-volume manufacturing companies have to go through the described development and it is not possible to skip a phase. In our view it must be possible that some companies stay in the efficiency or quality phase while others move to the flexibility or innovation phase. Another critical remark regards the fact that they only look at the 'key variables' market, competition and technology and not at societal developments. If we look at the development of participation it is clear that societal influences like socio-cultural (labour market, educational level, national culture, etc.) and political-institutional factors (laws, system of industrial relations, etc.) play a decisive role. Finally, there is only scarce empirical material with which proposed—or, more often, prescribed—developments can be confirmed or falsified.

Case Study Ahold/Albert Heijn

Before we start with the presentation of our empirical evidence, we like to present a case study with respect to the (assumed) connection between the introduction of new organisational forms, direct and indirect participation. The case is about a large retailing concern in the Netherlands, (Royal) Ahold and its main daughter company in the Netherlands Albert Heijn. Ahold operates 3500 stores in 17 countries with annualised sales approaching 35 billion USD. The total number of employees is about 300.000 (figures 1999). In the Netherlands Ahold owns six store chains with over 1700 outlets and over 70.000 employees, of which Albert Heijn with about 600 stores and 45.000 employees is the largest.
In the beginning of the 1990's Ahold decided to shift its organisational structure from a 'column-organisation' (with separate activities like production, distribution, sales in different daughter companies) to a 'process-organisation' (with integration of some of these activities within new designed daughter companies and outsourcement of other daughter companies). For Albert Heijn, a supermarket chain, this meant a tight integration with the distribution company, by an ordering system in which stores can order on a day-to-day basis, thus minimising stocks. At the same time, after local experimentation in 1992, the principle of self-steering (the

delegation of responsibilities for operational tasks) was gradually introduced throughout the company. Integration between former daughters and decentralisation within subsidiaries were two separate yet linked developments, as the day-to-day ordering system depends on the ability of employees in the stores to maintain and plan stock in direct contact with the distribution company. The perception of market demands by management was an important cause in the transition toward a new organisation. Albert Heijn aims at a qualitatively higher segment of the market. The quality of service is seen as a crucial part of this. Self-steering was introduced with the motto 'more service with fewer costs'. Equally important was the unpredictability of the customer, which made flexible stock maintenance necessary.

The introduction of self-steering has taken several years. The guiding principle of this introduction has been the freedom of store managers to design their own version of self-steering, leading to a wide array of initiatives, some exemplary, some largely ceremonial. The works council was in the beginning not involved in the introduction of self-steering, shut out by management and sometimes even by employees. Over the years the works council pushed hard for consultation on the matter, emphasising the need for company-wide rules for self-steering, more opportunities for off-the-job training and a decoupling the efforts to raise quality and lower costs. The introduction of self-determination raised two problems for the functioning of the works council. The distance of the works council to its consistuency had always been large, due to the size and structure of the organisation (one works council for six hundred stores spread over the entire country), the character of the workforce (a majority of young part-time workers) and the lack of a union tradition. According to the works council, self-steering made the distance even bigger, because many of the employees saw the works council as a possible impediment to their own self-steering. A second problem was not due to self-steering as such but as part of a larger company philosophy. Not only systems would have to change, but people as well. At the same time top-management decided that these changes would not follow a fixed path, but that the end goal was not clear. This meant that the works council could not anticipate decisions by management and was ill equipped to check these decisions—in the words of the works council, top management had moved upon the 'highway' while the works council was left on a 'graded road'.

The solution the works council worked out for these problems was the split up of its (partly non-existing) role into two parts. The first part is the continuation of indirect participation via the works council, but focused at so-called strategic issues. The second part is the introduction of direct participation, in fact the institutionalisation of the newly introduced right of self-steering for employees at operational level. This frees the works councils from everyday concerns, so that they can concentrate on headlines. The decision to split up the role of the works council was seen as a consequence of the organisational developments within the companies: the integration of activities of different daughter companies and the decentralisation of decision-making to the workplace level. Bu taking this decision the works council regained recognition and support from management. To gap the distance from the works council to the employees so-called 'sounding board groups' were installed consisting of employees, staff members and works council members. These groups give both works council and management information about problems at the work place, thereby creating the possibility of a policy which is more relevant to the needs and wants of the employees. The sounding board groups now function as a linking pin between direct participation and the strategic works council. The changes are supplemented by training programmes, for managers as well as workers.

The case of Ahold/Albert Heijn shows us that there can be a connection between the introduction of new organisational forms (as a reaction to changes in the market environment) and direct and indirect participation. A shift in factors of competition (from price to quality and flexibility) led to a shift from a product to a process organisation and the introduction of self-steering at shop floor level. In connection with this there have been changes in (form and amount) of direct participation and in the (formal) position and role of the works council. However, these changes were not an automatic development but were deliberate decisions taken by as well management as works council. Also the implementation of these changes is not yet finished: all by all the change of perceptions and policies will take almost a decade.

The Existence of New Forms of Work Organisation

According to the model of Bolwijn & Kumpe most companies must be now in the flexibility or even in the innovation phase, with organisational forms that can be characterised as communication and co-operation and integration and decentralisation. However, it is difficult to find evidence for this in empirical data. In our survey we have asked for the incidence of a number of specific forms of new organisational forms. The results show that there is no form of new work organisation that exists in all companies. The most common form seems to be multifunctional teams, which seem to be present in about three quarter of all companies, followed by unit management, intense co-operation with others, delayering and task groups[3], which are claimed to be present in about half of the companies (see table 1). Only telework stays far behind these other forms.

Table 1. Existence of new organisational forms

Unit management	60%
Task groups	43%
Multi-functional teams	72%
Telework	10%

It is often assumed that industry is the leading sector in the introduction of new organisational forms. However this assumption has not been confirmed by the results of our survey: unit-management and task-groups are more frequent in the commercial service sector and the non-profit sector. Multifunctional teams are evenly distributed over all sectors and a bit more frequent in the commercial service sector. If there is such a thing as a leading sector, it is not industry, but the commercial service and non-profit sectors. The distribution of new organisational forms among sectors is shown in table 2.

[3] Task groups or self-steering teams can be seen as a form of organisational change as well as a form of direct participation (see also section 4). However, in the context of our survey task groups are primarily seen as form of organisational change.

Table 2. Distribution new organisational forms to sector and size

	Unit management	Task groups	Multi-functional teams
Sector:			
Industry	49%	39%	74%
Commercial services	75%	48%	82%
Non profit*	64%	48%	75%
Governmental	51%	37%	76%
Remainder	52%	43%	76%
Size:			
<100	45%	38%	58%
100-200	54%	47%	78%
200-500	69%	38%	85%
>500	80%	56%	93%

* *Mainly health care*

New organisational forms are unevenly distributed over organisations of different size (see also table 2). The bigger the organisation, the bigger the chance that it will have new organisational forms, although the relationship is not linear in the case of task groups. This result was to be expected, as the delegation of responsibilities and competencies in smaller companies is more likely to evolve in an informal manner. This explanation is partly supported by the fact that half of the smaller companies (with less than a 100 employees) stated that their organisation consists of informal teams, against 22 percent of the big organisations (with more than 500 employees).

In models like that of Bolwijn and Kumpe a direct connection is made between the introduction of new forms of work organisation and external influences like the intensity and the development of competition. Also in our case of Ahold/Albert Heijn we saw such a connection. However, with respect to the intensity of competition this connection can only be partially found (i.e. for some organisational forms). It was also expected that organisations that competed on quality, choice or uniqueness—as opposed to price—would be more likely to have new organisational forms. We therefore distinguished between organisations that put price over other factors of competition and organisations which put quality, choice or uniqueness over price. Factors of competition seem to weakly predict the incidence of unit management and multifunctional teams. Overall, the incidence of new organisational forms correlates weakly to external factors, mostly in the case of unit-management and multifunctional teams, while the incidence of task groups does not seem to be influenced at all by external factors (see table 3).

Table 3. Connection between competition and new organisational forms

	Task groups	Unit management	Multi-functional teams
Intensity of competition	-	.135**	
Development of competition	.184***		.115*
Factors of competition	.159**	.172**	

*Cramers V, sig. *p<0,05 ** p< 0,01 *** p<0,001*

It was also expected that the incidence of new organisational forms would be more frequent in organisations with decentralised policy; the essence of new organisational forms is, in theory at least, the decentralisation of responsibilities and competencies. We have looked at the de/centralisation in six policy fields: general policy, commercial or market policy, financial-economic policy, technology policy, organisational policy and personnel policy. There were differences between the different new organisational forms with regards to the related policy fields and the strength of the relations. Surprisingly no correlations could be found between task groups and decentralised policies. Unit-management was correlated to decentralisation of especially commercial and personnel policies and multifunctional teams with decentralisation of commercial, technological, organisational and personnel policies. From this we can conclude that unit-management and multi-functional teams seem to be relatively strong related to decentralisation of (parts of) the companies policies, but that task groups seem to be isolated from that polices.

Table 4. New organisational forms and decentralisation of policies

	General	Commercial Financial Technology	Organisational	Personnel
Task groups				
Unit management	.303***	.249***	.191***	
Multi-funct. teams	.179***	.145**	.240***	.106*

Cramers V, sig. *p<0,05 ** p< 0,01 *** p<0,001

At the same time, new organisational forms are more prevalent in organisations in which management sees personnel management as modern (as opposed to traditional) and in which participation is an important part of the personnel policy of the company (table 5). Table 5 shows a high correlation between at the one hand a form of modern personnel management and attention to participation in personnel management and at the other the incidence of new organisational forms like task groups, unit management and multifunctional teams. According to this figures we can conclude that new organisational forms are in the first place a tool of personnel management and only after that a tool for organisational (decentralisation) and economic (increasing competition) reasons.

Table 5. New organisational forms and personnel management

	task groups	unit management	multi-functional teams
Modern personnel management	.205***	.189***	.221***
Active participation policy	.233***	.232***	.137*

Cramers V, sig. *p<0,05 ** p< 0,01 *** p<0,001

Direct Participation and Organisational Change

Direct participation has a rather long tradition in the Netherlands. In the 1960's and 1970's already a number of experiments took place with (the extension of) direct participation in companies like the Post-, Cheque and Girodienst, Philips, the Bamshoeve, Centraal Beheer (Looise, 1975). Direct participation in the Netherlands mostly has the form of `werkoverleg' (job- or work consultation), meaning the regular meetings of the employees working in the same department with their boss to discuss the matters regarding the work and the working conditions. The incidence of work consultation has grown rather fast. According to research of the Ministry of Social Affairs and Labour the average incidence has grown from 21% of all work organisations with over 10 employees in 1979, to 29% in 1985 and 41% in 1992 (Ministry of Social Affairs, 1987, 1993). Based on data from several sources, Looise et al (1998) come to an estimation of about 70% of all work organisations in Netherlands with over 10 employees that have work consultation. In line with the growing incidence also the range of subjects and the amount of participation via work consultation seem to have expanded. Not only subjects with respect to the organisation of the work are dealt with, but also subjects in the field of personnel management

(like the training and education, selection of new personnel) and the company policy in general. With respect to the amount of participation, not only information is given, but attention is also given to the opinion of the employees (two-way communication). Other forms of direct participation besides work consultation in the Netherlands are quality circles and individual participation, but these exist on a (far) smaller scale.
In our survey we asked for the existence of three forms of direct participation (besides forms of indirect participation): individual participation, work consultation and quality circles. Table 6 gives an overview of the results.

Table 6. The existence of (direct) participation

Individual participation	61%
Work consultation	96%
Quality circles	41%
Works council*	(100)%
Union representation	14%
Board representation	14%

**All organisations that participated in the survey had a works council; the average works council density in the Netherlands is about 82%.*

Table 6 shows that the existence of direct participation is far higher than that of indirect participation, the works council excluded. In our survey we asked managers to score the different forms of participation in terms of their relative importance. After the works council, which scored first, work consultation scored second and individual participation and quality circles third (ex aequo), followed by union representation and board representation. Our outcomes are partly in accordance with the findings from the EPOC-survey (European Foundation, 1997). According to this survey 90% of Dutch workplaces has a form of direct participation. Spread over the different forms of direct participation EPOC found in 77% of the workplaces individual consultation and in 61% of the workplaces group consultation (there were no questions about quality circles). The figure of 77% of individual consultation is somewhat higher than our 67% (as the EPOC-survey is based upon opinions of managers, we can best compare with our management outcome), but this can be explained by the difference between the terms consultation (used by EPOC) and participation (used in our survey). With respect to *individual delegation*, which is stronger than consultation, EPOC comes to a score of 59%. The outcome of 61% of group consultation is much lower than our 97% of work consultation (and also than our 82% from the works councils). This difference is difficult to explain. There might be some influence from the difference in company/workplace-size (in EPOC starting form 25 employees and in our case 50 employees), but this cannot explain the whole difference[4]. On the other hand EPOC found that in 48% of all workplaces according to management there is *group delegation*, which is also stronger than group consultation[5].

If we look at connections between direct participation and organisational characteristics, such as industrial sector and organisation size, no significant correlation can be found. However, table 7 shows that there are some differences in the use of direct participation between sectors and – to a lesser extend – organisations of different size. This is especially the case with quality circles, which are most frequent in industry and the non-profit sector and in larger organisations. Individual participation is most frequent non-profit, commercial services and government and in middle-large organisations (between 200 and 500 employees).

Table 7. Direct participation related to sector and size

	Individual participation	Work consultation	Quality circles
Sector:			
Industry	59%	98%	54%
Commercial services	63%	95%	39%
Non-profit	64%	98%	50%
Government	63%	96%	33%
Remainder	53%	90%	47%
Size			
<100	59%	98%	35%
100-200	63%	93%	51%
200-500	71%	97%	50%
>500	58%	98%	51%

The EPOC study found more direct links between personnel composition and direct participation: organisations with more highly qualified personnel were more likely to have forms of direct participation. We have looked if we could find the same evidence, and also if the qualification requirements

[4] In an article about the Dutch part of the EPOC-survey (Huijgen & Benders, 1998) the authors themselves say that they were surprised by this unexpected low figure for group consultation and that they don't have an explanation for it.

[5] This should lead to the implausible conclusion that in almost 80% of the cases with group consultation (including those in temporary groups) in the Netherlands there is group delegation. As this is not the case we must assume that the initial figure for group consultation must be higher.

of personnel are linked to the relative importance of the different forms of participation vis-à-vis each other. We found that direct participation and job consultation do not seem to be affected by the qualification requirements and that only quality circles are more likely to exist in organisations with a relative high number of operational personnel. Also, a shortage of personnel seems to be related to the incidence of direct participation. Although these links are weak, and although the variation can be partially explained by the predominance of personnel categories in itself, these findings do seem to indicate that participation might be a part of broader personnel management, and may be linked to labour market concerns.

In the EPOC-study no relationship could be found between the amount of direct participation (incidence and intensity) and the intensity of competition. The same goes for our survey: no connection can be found between as well the intensity as the development of competition and direct participation. More important than economical reasons, like the amount and development of competition, seems to be the intention of management: especially quality circles and individual participation were more frequent in organisations of which management finds the promotion of direct participation an important aspect of personnel management. The correlation between forms of direct participation and participation can be compared with those between new organisational forms and participation policy. If we do so, it is interesting to note that the correlations between task groups, unit management, multifunctional teams and quality circles and participation policy are all in the same line (strong correlation), while those between individual participation and work consultation are much weaker. This leads to the odd conclusion that the organisation policy with respect to participation does not affect the existence of direct participation so much as it does with new organisational forms. One explanation for this seemingly anomaly can be that some forms of direct participation – like especially work consultation but to a lesser extend also individual participation – have become such a common part of company culture in the Netherlands, that there is hardly a connection with any kind of policy at all.

Table 8. Direct participation and participation policy

	Individual participation	**Work consultation**	**Quality circles**
Participation policy	.144*	.185*	.213***

Cramers V, sig. *p<0,05 ** p< 0,01 *** p<0,001

Given the fact that we found a rather strong connection between company policy with respect to participation and new forms of work organisation and only a partial connection between the same company policy and direct participation, we might wonder about the connection between new organisational forms and forms of direct participation. Is direct participation more likely in organisations with new organisational forms? The results are not unambiguous (see table 8). A direct connection between new organisational forms on the one hand and job consultation and individual participation on the other cannot be found. We should note however that 97% of the organisations had group consultation. Only in the case of quality circles we see a (weak) link between organisational development and direct participation. Quality circles were more frequent in organisations with new organisational forms, individual participation and group consultation were not.

Table 8. New Organisational Forms and Direct Participation

	Individual participation	Work consultation	Quality circles
Task groups		.106*	.107*
Unit management			.210***
Multi-functional teams			.154***

*Cramers V, sig. *p<0,05 ** p< 0,01 *** p<0,001*

Preliminary conclusion is that the introduction of new organisational forms not automatically leads to more general forms of direct participation like individual participation and work consultation This finding seems to be in line with the Ahold/Albert Heijn case: the introduction of organisational change did not automatically lead to more direct participation. Only after the initiative of the works council management decided to stimulate direct participation.

Works Councils and New Forms of Work Organisation

The Dutch works council was first mandated by law in 1950. Before that date co-determination had the form of voluntarily founded *bedrijfskernen (company cores)*. The first bedrijfskern was founded in 1878, the second in

1883. They were inspired by 'enlightened' or paternalistic entrepreneurship. In the period between the two world wars similar institutions were introduced in most large companies and in government agencies. The rise of representative participation on organisation level coincided with the expansion of large scale manufacturing and bureaucratic administration. The first law on works councils in 1950 was inspired by the new wave of human relations. The works council was meant to foster harmony and co-operation to balance the growing distance between employer and employee. The bedrijfskern and the works council were, for management at least, a means to communicate with personnel in a complex organisation with many layers (Looise, 1989).

Since 1950 the number of works councils has steadily grown. Recent figures (Oeij & Stoppelenburg, 1998) show that in 1997 works councils existed in 82% of all Dutch work organisations with 35 or more employees. For the companies and other organisations with over 200 employees and for the companies and other organisations with between 50 and 200 employees these figures were 95% and 84% respectively. In total there are about 13.000 works councils in the Netherlands, with a membership that varies from 5 (in companies with 50 to 100 employees) to 25 (in companies with over 7.000 employees). But not only in quantitative but also especially in qualitative terms the works councils hold a rather strong position. Thanks to successive extensions of the Law on Works Councils the Dutch works council now has rights with respect to: assemble during work time, be (regularly) informed with respect to all matters regarding the company, to give advice with respect to a large number of economic and organisational matters, to veto proposals of the employer with respect to arrangements on social and personnel matters, to take initiatives with respect to all matters related to the company, to make an official appeal in case the aforementioned rights of advice and of veto are not respected or ignored.

Based on these legal rights Dutch works councils seem to have a reasonable influence position in the decision making process within the organisation, especially on social and organisational topics but also on general matters. However regarding commercial, financial and technical issues the influence position of the works councils seems to be very low. Table 9 gives an overview of the perceived influence of works councils with respect to several policy areas by both managers and works council members themselves. Table 9 shows that there are some, but no so large, differences in the opinions of management and works councils themselves about the influence position of the works council. The largest differences can be seen with respect to the area of personnel policy: it is interesting to note that quite a number of more managers than works councils (12%) say that works councils have a large influence on personnel affairs. This means that whether works councils underestimate their influence on this area or managers overestimate the influence of the works council.

Table 9. Perceived influence of works councils on six fields of company policy

Policy fields	Man (n=460)			WC's (n=391)		
	low	reas.	large	low	reas.	large
General	45%	49%	6%	46%	47%	7%
Commercial	89%	11%	-	84%	15%	-
Finance	80%	20%	-	82%	17%	1%
Technology	84%	14%	1%	78%	20%	2%
Organisational	15%	65%	19%	25%	56%	18%
Personnel	8%	52%	39%	17%	55%	27%

If we look at correlation between the works council influence and other factors, we can only find few connections with organisational characteristics. There is a weak connection between works council influence and economic sector: works councils in the non-profit sector have more influence on the general/strategic issues and works councils in governmental organisations on organisational issues, while works councils in industry have less influence on these matters. The same can be seen between works council influence and the incidence of board representation within the company: in companies with a worker director works councils have more influence on general/strategic issues and on financial issues. Another weak connection can be found with the works council composition: works councils with more than average personnel from higher ranks have more influence on technical and personnel issues. A stronger connection can be found with the amount of internationalisation of companies: the more international the company the less influence (especially on general issues) the works council has (Looise & Drucker, 2002, 2003). However, the strongest connection between works council influence can be found with the role and attitude of both (top)management and constituency[6]. In those cases were (top)management has an open and participative style of managing and a positive attitude towards the works

[6] This has also be found in the 1985-survey, Looise & De Lange, 1988.

council, the works council has the most influence. Table 10 gives an overview of correlations between the influence of the works council on a number of fields and the importance is given to participation as a company policy.

Table 10. Works council influence and participation policy

	General	**Financial**	**Organisational**	**Personnel**
Participation policy	.142*	.122*	.157***	.165***

*Cramers V, sig. *p<0,05 ** p< 0,01 *** p<0,001*

In the last decade several Dutch authors have claimed that organisational developments will affect the position of works council profoundly. The works council is, after all, directed primarily to consult with top-management, on behalf of the employees. With a shift of competencies and responsibilities toward and within the workplace, it is likely that the works councils will (have to) play their roles in a different manner. Others even expect that the role of the works council will diminish or – on longer term – even will come to an end. However, if we look at the results of our survey, we see little evidence for this. According to the opinions of both management and works councils there is little (negative) effect from the introduction of new organisational forms on the position of the works council (see table 11). The introduction of task groups, unit-management and multifunctional teams are all related to a *larger* influence of the works council. This is especially the case with the influence on the personnel policy and the general/strategic policy of the company. All three forms of new organisational forms are related to a larger influence of the works council on personnel policy, the introduction of task groups and unit management are related to a larger influence of the works council on the general/strategic policy and the introduction of multifunctional teams to a larger influence on the organisational policy. his might be explained by the fact that changes in personnel policy are the traditional field of works councils. The introduction of unit-management is also linked to a bigger influence of the works council on commercial policy.

Table 11. New organisational forms and the influence of the works council

	General	.Organisational	Personnel
Task groups	.140*	.161*	
Unit management	.159**	.125*	.152**
Multi-functional teams		.138*	.190**

*Cramers V, sig. *p<0,05 ** p< 0,01 *** p<0,001*

It should be noted that table 11 reflects the influence of works councils as reported by management. The works councils themselves did not report a rise in influence organisations where new organisational forms are introduced. It is, however, likely that works councils were actively involved in the introduction of new organisational forms and that this resulted in more influence.
Besides looking for correlations between new organisational forms and the influence of works council, we also asked the opinion from both management and works councils with respect to the possible effects of new organisational forms on the position and tasks of the works council. Table 12 shows that neither management nor works councils think that there are large effects. Both parties see little effect from the introduction of new organisational forms on the position of the works council. If there is some negative effect on the position of the works council, management sees this only as a result of unit management and of task groups, while works councils see as much negative as positive effects.

Table 12. Effects of new organisational forms on the position and tasks of the works council

	Man (n= 442-459)				WC (n= 383-389)			
	None	Weak.	Strong	NE	None	Weak	Strong	NE
Unit management	47	10	5	38	38	5	5	53
Task groups	44	7	2	47	30	1	3	66
Telework	18	1	2	78	19	1	1	78

NE= non existent

The Connection between Direct and Indirect Participation

Historically in the Netherlands there is a weak connection between direct and indirect participation. Both forms of participation have their own different backgrounds. Though the works council, as has been described in section 5, also has its origin in management initiative, this initiative later on

has been taken over by government and unions. The unions changed their negative attitude towards the – at that time still very weak – works councils in the second half of the sixties when they realised that they had been able to raise a growing popularity with of the employees. From that moment on unions fought for a further strengthening of the legal position of the works council. The decisive role with respect to direct participation has always been and staid with management. Attempts from union side to make formal arrangements about e.g. work consultation in collective agreements or even legal regulations have always been blocked by management and employers associations. Only in the Law on the works council we can find some formal arrangements on this point. The first is that, in case management has the intention to implement a system of direct participation in the company (like e.g. work consultation), it is subject to the works councils' right of veto on social issues. The second is an obligation for works councils to support `work consultation and the delegation of decision-making, with the aim to involve as many employees as possible in the arrangement of the work within their own department'.
In practice, up to now, works councils in the Netherlands have not been very active on these rights or obligations. Our survey shows that direct participation or work consultation is not within the ten issues that are most frequently dealt with by works councils. It's on the eleventh place behind subjects like reorganisations, changes in the organisation structure, safety and health, working time arrangements, mergers, reward issues, education and training, appraisal, investments, etc. Only about one fifth of all works councils dealt with the subject of direct participation during the period 1997-1998. Also the contacts between works councils and direct participation doesn't seem to be very strong. Overall the contact of works council(members) and their constituency seem rather weak: only about 10% of the works councils say that they get regular impulses from the employees, about 40% say that this happens only in special cases and about 50% say they don't get any impulse form the employees. In the past several attempts have been made to come to a regular contact between works councils and work consultations, for instance via the appointment of representatives of each department with work consultation in the works council, via fixed contact persons or via the exchange of minutes. Last years these attempts seem have decreased: the number of works councils with contact persons in each department has gone back from 44% in 1885 to 32% in 1998.
The question here is whether the position of the works council is influenced by the existence of direct participation and reverse, whether the works

council's policy influences the existence of direct participation. With respect to the first question table 14 gives an overview of the answers of both management and works councils. The figures show that between one quarter and one third of management thinks that there is a shift in the position of works council as a result of different forms of direct participation and one fifth of the works councils thinks the same. Management sees the largest shift in the position of the works council as a result of work consultation, followed by individual participation. Works councils on their turn see the largest shift as a result of direct participation, followed by work consultation.

Table 14. Shift in position of the works council as an effect of direct participation

	Man (n= 432-439)			WC (n= 365-371)		
	No	Some	NE	No	Some	NE
Individual participation	57%	26%	17%	57%	20%	33%
Work consultation	56%	37%	7%	63%	19%	18%
Quality circles	39%	27%	34%	36%	16%	48%

NE=non existent

However, it is not quite clear what the shift will mean in terms of weakening or strengthening of the position of the works council. As we saw in the last section, in the case of the introduction of new organisational forms the position of the works council (initially) seems to be more strengthened than weakened. So the same can happen with the introduction of forms of direct participation. If we look at the case study of Ahold and Albert Heijn, we see a repositioning of the role of the works council from a broad area of sometimes less important tasks towards a more focused position on the general/strategic policy area. It is difficult to say whether this must be seen as a strengthening or weakening of the position of the works council. It is in no way an attempt to abolish the work council. In our survey we could not find any move in this direction at all.

As far as the link between direct and indirect participation is concerned, no conclusive evidence in the United States can be found regarding the role of human resource management in the decline of unions (Fröhlich & Pekruhl, 1996). The EPOC research-team also found no links between direct participation and managerial attitude toward unions or works councils. Employee representatives were often positive about direct participation and often were 'agents of change', pushing for 'real' participation. It must be noted that through searching for links between organisational forms and direct and indirect participation, the emphasis is put on managerial needs and strategies. The extent to which management wants to deal with unions (Vos & Buitelaar, 1996) and works councils (Looise & De Lange, 1987) helps to determine the success of these forms of participation. On the other hand, unions and works councils are also autonomous and independent (although the works council is less so) organisations. Also, the motives of managers when choosing for particular forms of indirect participation have never been only determined by the organisation form: the bedrijfskern was often introduced as a means to pre-empt unionism. And direct participation in the nineteen seventies was mainly introduced to deal with labour unrest and demotivation (Looise, 1976). Even human resource management, which claims primacy of strategy in personnel management, also is often inspired by socio-political and labour market considerations (cf. Beer *et al.* 1984).

Summary and Conclusions

The aim of this paper was to check the widespread idea from especially popular management literature that in most organisations nowadays new organisational forms have come to existence – mainly because of more intense competition - which on their turn have resulted in a strengthening of direct participation and a weakening of indirect participation. Our research,based on the data from a large national survey into the position of works councils in the Netherlands supplemented with information form a case study with the large Dutch retail company Ahold/Albert Heijn, leads to the following conclusions.

With respect to the existence of new organisational forms, forms like unit management, task groups were found in about 40 to 60 % of all organisations and multifunctional teams even in 76% of all organisations, which means that they are rather broad spread. New organisational forms are most common in the commercial service and non-profit sector and in large organisations and less in industry and smaller companies. Only a weak link could be found between (some) new organisational forms and the intensification of competition and the decentralisation of (parts of) company policy. However, a much stronger link appeared to exist between the incidence of all new organisational forms and the existence modern personnel management and the accent that is given to participation in personnel management. This leads us to the conclusion that new organisational forms in the first place must be seen as a tool of personnel management (change of culture, see also the case of Ahold/Albert Heijn) and only after that as a tool for economic (increasing competition) and organisational (decentralisation) reasons. In practice, of course, several reasons can be connected.

The existence of direct participation is quite high in the Netherlands (see also EPOC, 1997). Our survey shows that almost all organisations have work consultation and about 60% and 50% forms of individual participation and quality circles respectively. Individual participation is most frequent in the non-profit, commercial services and government sectors and in middle-large organisations (between 200 and 500 employees), while quality circles are most frequent in industry and the non-profit sector and in larger organisations. Just like the EPOC-study we could not find a relationship between direct participation (incidence and intensity) and competition (intensity and development). Again, more important than economical reasons like the amount and development of competition is the accent management gives to participation in personnel management. Though, this is especially the case with quality circles and only to a lesser extends with individual participation. Obviously, if management say that they see participation as an important aspect of personnel policy, they seem to mean in the first place new forms of work organisation and not the more traditional forms of direct participation, like individual participation and work consultation. This brings us to the question what management really means if they say that they want to stimulate direct participation (e.g. in exchange of indirect participation). Our impression is that management – deliberately or not – confuses new organisational forms and direct participation. Or with other words: management seems to like new forms of work organisation, though without more regular and institutionalised forms of direct participation.

Works councils have a long tradition in the Netherlands and are heavily institutionalised. They exist in about 85% of all organisations with over 50 employees. Bases on their legal rights they have a large influence on personnel matters, a considerable influence on general and organisational issues and a weak influence on financial, commercial and technical aspects. There is a weak correlation between works council influence and economical sector, the existence of board representation and works council composition. Compared to that there is a stronger connection between works council influence and the amount of internationalisation of the firm. The strongest connection however could be found with the attitude of (top)management towards the works council and also the accent is given to participation in personnel management: if both are positive the works council has more influence on most areas of company policy. The introduction of new organisational forms up to now does not lead to a weakening of the position of the works council, but to a slight strengthening. Main explanation for this result is that the works council gets involved in the organisational change, which initially leads to a strengthening of its position. Asked to their opinions most management and works councils themselves believe that there will not be important changes in the position of the works council as an effect of new organisational forms.

Direct participation has hardly any links with the works council. The works council seems to neither encourage nor discourage direct participation, though some works councils say they stimulate direct participation but in practice this seems to be mainly ritual. And direct participation has not yet consequences for the position of the works council, though a considerable part of management and works councils think that this will be the case on the long run. However, as long as there is no connection between direct participation and other aspects of company policy – which means that up to now there is hardly a deliberate policy with respect to the use of direct participation – there is little chance for effects on the position of the works council.Only the danger exists that works councils are mislead by management who say they want to stimulate direct participation (and meaning new organisational forms without expanding direct participation) and therefore ask works councils to limit their rights. If management refuses to really stimulate direct participation – and there are signs that this is happening: the case of Ahold/Albert Heijn can be an example of this development – the works council should stick to its existing position.

The links between organisational change (as a result of growing competition), direct and indirect participation, which are often posited in the literature, cannot be confirmed by our data. Developments with respect to the introduction of new organisational forms, which take place in a majority of all organisations, are primarily driven by management choice to change the organisational culture and the personnel management. Up to now, they have hardly any effect on both direct as indirect participation. Also the assumed shift in the position of indirect participation as a result of growing direct participation could not be found. Up to now there is hardly any connection between direct and indirect participation al all. This finding seems to be in accordance with the situation in other European countries (European Foundation, 1997). This implies a large challenge for institutions like works councils and trade unions to arrange such connections.

References

Beer, M. & B. Spector & D. Lawrence & Q. Mills & R.E. Walton (1984) *Managing Human Assets*. New York: The Free Press.

Bolwijn, P.T. & T. Kumpe (1990), Manufacturing in the 1990's--Productivity, Flexibility and Innovation. *Long Range Planning*, Vol.23, No 4, pp 44-57.

Buelens, M. "De taakstelling van de organisatie-theorie: het intellectuele verdriet en de pedagogische troost", *M&O*, *Tijdschrift voor Management en Organisatie*, Vol. 51(1), pp. 17-37.

Drucker, M. (2003*), Organisatievernieuwing en medezeggenschap. Dissertation University of Twente*. Enschede: Twente University Press.

European Foundation (1997) *New Forms of Work Organisation: Can Europe Realise its Potential? (EPOC-study).* Dublin: European Foundation for the Improvement of Working and Living Conditions.

Fröhlich, D. & U. Pekruhl (1996), *Direct Participation and Organisational Change. Fashionable but Misunderstood? An Analysis of Recent Research in Europe, Japan and the USA*. Dublin: European Foundation for the Improvement of Living and Working Conditions.

Goodijk, R. (1993), *Op weg naar een strategische ondernemingsraad.* Assen: Van Gorcum.

Goodijk, R. (1995), *Ondernemingsraad en Strategische Besluitvorming.* Assen: Van Gorcum.

Homan, Th. H. (1995) Medezeggenschap in gedecentraliseerde organisaties, *Holland Management Review*, nr. 41.

Huijgen, F. & J. Benders (1998) "Het vallende kwartje; directe participatie in Nederland en Europa", *Tijdschrift voor Arbeidsvraagstukken*, vol. 14, nr. 2, pp. 113-127, p. 121.

Kaar, R. van het & J.C. Looise (1999), De volwassen OR. Groei en grenzen van de Nederlandse ondernemingsraad. Resultaten van het grote OR-onderzoek. Samsom, Alphen aan den Rijn. [The mature works council. Results of the national survey].

Lammers, C.J. (1993), *Organiseren van Bovenaf en van Onderop*. Utrecht: Het Spectrum.

Looise, J.C. (1976), *De Proef op de Som: Een Evaluatie met Experimenten met Medezeggenschap in Nederland*. Utrecht: Stichting Wetenschappelijk Onderzoek Vakcentrales.

Looise, J.C. & F.G.M. de Lange (1987), *Ondernemingsraden, Bestuurders en Besluitvorming*. Nijmegen: ITS.

Looise, J.C. (1989) *Werknemersvertegenwoordiging op de Tweesprong. Vakbeweging en vertegenwoordigend overleg in veranderende arbeidsverhoudingen*. Alphen aan de Rijn: Samsom.

Looise, J.C. & J. de Leede & M. van Beusekom (1996), *De Ondernemingsraad van de Toekomst. De Toekomst van de Ondernemingsraad*. Amsterdam: Welboom.

Looise, J.C., J. de Jong & M. Thunnissen (1998), Organisatievernieuwing en directe werknemersparticipatie. Een tweede leven voor het werkoverleg? *M&O, Tijdschrift voor Management en Organisatie*, Vol 52(6), p. 9-28.

Looise J.C., M. Drucker & J. de Leede (2001), Is there a future for employee representation? In: R. Markey et al (eds), *Models of employee participation in a changing global environment*, Aldershot: Ashgate.

Looise, J.C. & M. Drucker (2002), Employee participation in multinational enterprises: the effects of globalisation on Dutch works councils, *Employee Relations*, Vol24 (1,2), p. 29-52.

Looise, J.C. & M. Drucker (2003), Dutch works councils in times of transition: the effects of changes in society. Organisations and work on works councils, *Economic and Industrial Democracy*, Vol. 24(3), p. 379-409.

Loontechnische Dienst (1987) *Werkoverleg en Werkstructurering in Nederland in 1985*. Den Haag: Ministerie van Sociale Zaken en Werkgelegenheid.

Loontechnische Dienst (1993) *Werkoverleg in het Nederlandse Bedrijfsleven in 1992*. Den Haag: Ministerie van Sociale Zaken en Werkgelegenheid.

Marchington, M & P. Parker (1990), *Changing Patterns of Employee Relations*, Hemel Hempstead: Harvester.

Marchinton, M., A. Wilkinson, P. Ackers & J. Goodman (1993), The influence of managerial relations on waves of employee involvement, *British Journal of Industrial Relations*, Vol. 31, No 4, p. 553-576.

Moss Kanter, R. (1995), *When giants learn to dance*. New York: Simon & Schuster.

Oeij, P.R.A. and P.A. Stoppelenburg (1998) *Naleving van de Wet op de Ondernemingsraden:, Stand van zaken 1997*.Den Haag: SZW/Vuga.

Peters T (1992), *Liberation management*. California: Exel

Vos, P. en W. Buitelaar (1996), *Arbeidsorganisatie en arbeidsverhoudingen in beweging*. Welboom, Amsterdam. [Work organisation and employment relations on the move]

Wissema, J.G. & M.G. Bouts & B. Rutgers (1995) *Contouren van Medezeggenschap op Maat*. Den Haag: Vuga.

Challenges of Work Design. The Changing Role of Direct Participation

ERICH LATNIAK, ANJA GERLMAIER

Preliminary Remarks

The following paper is presenting ideas and interpretations on changes, which can be observed in production and service companies in Germany. It is part of an ongoing effort to understand change processes in organisation and work de-sign. Our intention is to reflect and to partly readjust the conceptual framework of work sciences (work psychology, work sociology or industrial sociology, organi-sation sciences) in this area in order to contribute to a vision of what can be 'good work' in the future.

The initial reason to do so is that the basic orientation of work design has be-come arguable. During the early 1990's, in Germany there was a strong trend towards work oriented design efforts, e.g. semi-autonomous group work. Organ-isational change processes in these years often emphasised participatory ap-proaches, empowerment, or involvement of the workforce thus shifting away from tayloristic structures towards decentralisation and group work. These so called "new production concepts" (Kern & Schumann 1983) seemed to promise an improvement of the working conditions by enabling a broader use of the in-dividual competencies and by providing the opportunity to extend skills and in-fluence, on the one hand. On the other hand, the productivity and companies' flexibility to react to customers' demands should increase at the same time.

There was a widespread public attention on these aspects. Companies as well as unions emphasised the strategic importance of this kind of change in these years. But the diffusion of the "new production concepts" in Germany turned out to be fairly reluctant as empirical investigations could demonstrate since the mid 1990's (Kleinschmidt & Pekruhl 1994; Nordhause-Janz & Pekruhl 2000). It became evident that there was a large gap between conceptual debate and industrial reality.

The situation today is even more contradictory. While human centred work forms like semi-autonomous group work are still rare, the dissolution of central com-pany units and the reduction of hierarchies are fairly widespread (Latniak et al. 2002). In Germany, the decentralisation on a company level has continued, ob-viously. But the impression is that declining growth rates and market problems have led to a shift of strategy in many companies. The new orientation has obvi-ously altered the organisational change processes initiated before. Cost cutting, concentration of tasks, intensification of work, and lay-offs may better character-ise what has happened in recent years. Due to this shift, the hopes of the early 1990's could not be fulfilled: The notion of "rationalisation by humanisation" has been partly misleading, as it has been recently stated (Salm & Kötter 2003: 138).

Due to this situation, more emphasis on empirical research is necessary. The ob-jective is to better understand what is going on in the companies and how 'good work' can be designed in the future. The prerequisite for this effort is to provide a realistic perspective for participatory approaches in work design. We would like to emphasise that there is no single trend determining the future of work even if e.g. there is an ongoing shift towards service work in Germany. But maybe there is a different - indirect or market oriented - type of control emerg-ing in the companies (Lehndorff 2003). There seems to be a growing direct im-pact of market pressure on the employees, which is no longer filtered by organ-isational measures. As a second aspect, employees tend to improve the work design by themselves while it is not guaranteed that all resources needed to fulfil their tasks were provided. If this impression were true, there is a need to reframe the risks and chances of participatory design approaches and participative work structures because there is no clear evidence that participation and growing autonomy would further lead to improved working conditions.

As you may have noticed, this paper is very much referring to German scientific discussion and empirical background. Based on that, it will provide some sketches of a likely picture of future work. It is an invitation to all those concerned and interested to further share experiences and research results in order to read-just the frame of reference in work design. In this sense, this is 'work in progress' directed towards the generation of research hypothesis.

In the following section, we will emphasise the 'traditional' reasons for participa-tory approaches and the anti-tayloristic notion related. The reasons given are valid still but the question today is to reflect the organisational background ex-plicitly in order to avoid unintended consequences. We will then provide some conceptual ideas on the "new logic" of control, which seems to emerge pres-ently. Three concepts describing the results of this control strategy – "delimitation of work", "unconfined jobs", and an increasing intensity of work (emphasised with the German term 'Subjektivierung') – will then be introduced. A description of the work situation of product development teams may illustrate this. After em-phasising some conceptual limits of participation under the circumstances men-tioned, we will finally introduce a research project promoting an adapted ap-proach to understand the work situation and trying to find out more about limits and chances of participation.

Participation – Present View on Work Design

Participation of employees in work design is an accepted standard of work sci-ence and ergonomics in Germany (Luczak et al. 1989). Apart from 'substantial' aspects and objectives (like reducing stress, strain, exposure to unhealthy condi-tions etc.), participation is a kind of 'procedural' aspect referring to individuals as experts of their jobs thus emphasising their competencies and flexibility. In this sense, participative work design and related organisational forms would foster the following aspects:

- The improvement of working conditions and a healthy work environment: It is unlikely that someone would develop inconvenient and unhealthy working conditions for himself.
- The generation of commitment and work satisfaction: If employees contribute to work design, it is 'their own' work system which they create; it is likely that it will be designed to fit to their needs and that the employees would be proud of it;
- The solution of certain design problems: If it is true that there are increasingly complex production and service processes, no external designer is able to identify all the details and problems probably emerging; accordingly, the work design is necessarily limited. Only those people involved in the processes are able to identify all the important aspects and take them into account. Participation is a way to cope with these 'hidden' aspects of work, e.g. tacit knowledge. Employees-in-charge are those to introduce necessary resources in order to solve customer's problems.
- Productivity improvement and the ability of the companies to cope with turbulent conditions: Given work structures designed in a participatory process, it is likely that employees are able to work smarter because they tend to have more information on previous and following process steps

and they know very well about what can be done in their unit or group. They should be able to better and faster cope with unforeseen situations.

Following Pruijt (2003: 73 ff.), we can emphasise the anti-tayloristic notion in par-ticipatory approaches, which can be described by four aspects:

- Participatory approaches tend to foster measures like job enrichment instead of a single task performed monotonously; in this sense, the focus of work design is shifting from the individual workplace to a group task which is covering several process steps including different types of work (plan-ning, execution etc.). This should enable a change of tasks for the em-ployees.
- Participatory approaches foster an integration of design and execution: According to tayloristic principles, design is the scientific task of an expert who knows about the best solution while the execution is the working task of the employee. A key-stone of tayloristic approaches is the separation of both aspects. In advanced forms of semi-autonomous group work, plan-ning is an integrated element of the group task.
- They – at least implicitly – focus on human skills and commitment (cf. above): In order to perform different tasks, it is evidently necessary to extend individual competencies and to learn how to cope with design and planning.
- There is a focus on autonomy and co-determination: If there is a need to increasingly involve employees due to a turbulent market situation, their in-fluence and impact – i.e. their ability to control zones of functional insecu-rity (Crozier & Friedberg 1979) – will be crucial.

These principles can still be helpful, and if they were applied in a certain envi-ronment, it is likely that working conditions can be improved. But the question is: Are these elements of participation still sufficient? Do they guarantee the objec-tives intended? Are they valid in every working environment in order to lead to an improvement of work and productivity?

Challenge: Is there a "New Logic of Control" Emerging?

In this section, we will describe our impression of what seems to be the strategic perspective of the ongoing changes in the companies in order to introduce a frame of reference in which participatory approaches can be applied. We would like to emphasise that apart from cost cutting and the need to become increasingly effective, the 'internalisation of markets' is one of the basic organ-isational changes in many companies at present.

The introduction of market related control practices seems to have an important impact on the working conditions. Internalising of market into the company means a complete shift of the way control structures of production and service processes are designed. In former times, the emphasis was to keep out market turbulences from production areas in order to realise economies of scale. Mar-keting and sales departments filtered the volatile and unstable impacts of cus-tomers' wishes. The transformation of external purchase orders into internal pro-duction orders has led to an integration of the planning and logistic needs of the production units concerned. A production oriented rationalisation strategy be-came viable this way – with the side effect of a slower market response.

Today, due to changing market situation, many companies try to become 'leaner' and closer to the market. There is not only a competition on prices but on delivering customised products at the time the customer needs. Companies need to faster react on customers' wishes. Customers' wishes are the structuring determinant for the production schedule. There are no more filters left over. Fur-thermore, this type of production is much more vulnerable due to the fact that – as an effect of lean production efforts - there are few buffers left over. (Brödner & Forslin 2002: 20) So, we can say that a highly developed customer orientation within a market strategy directed towards a customising of products and ser-vices has led to a situation 'that the cold winds of the market immediately blow into the production building'. Production units are increasingly confronted with customers' demands directly.

The effect on working conditions is quite obvious: The work can't be completely planned due to the immediate reactions on customers' needs; there is a grow-ing need to manage external contacts and argue with customers; concerning the working times; improvisation is increasingly necessary instead of planning. This may cause extended internal communication. Finally, work is finished when the orders of the present day are done. And finally, all this needs to be managed in the frame of a short budget and high expectations on profitability.

Our impression is that these changes go along with a kind of market-oriented decentralisation of formerly hierarchic company structures. (Sauer 2000, Latniak et al. 2002) The responsibility for profitability is now delegated to decentralised units, e.g. profit centres. And, as a side effect of the strategy described, com-pany's management is able to execute increasing pressure on these units by menacing with the competition of external alternatives. It doesn't matter whether this is a real alternative or not if it is clearly stated that production (or service delivery) could be transferred to an external unit. The threat of a 'make or buy' decision is crucial for this strategy. The market pressure is executed in a direct manner – but it is obviously structured and transformed by the top-management.
Due to the increasing complexity of the processes, companies are no more fos-tering a direct 'face-to-face' control structure. Instead, they tend to execute a process control via context variables. They were set by management following the objective to guarantee a positive financial result. E.g. this can be reached by financial objectives given, i.e. by standardised budget and control of se-lected objectives. Processes are less structured in detail, accordingly. It is left over to the employees to further manage success. They are allowed to apply a given budget while management doesn't need to take care of the details.
We see this as one of the driving forces for the difficulties work science, presently, because the outcome of these market related control processes is contradictory (Moldaschl & Sauer 2000). The employees increasingly tend to act similarly to en-trepreneurs: They have to extend effectiveness and profitability of their unit. They can do so due to an increasing "semi-"autonomy (i.e. granted by management) and extended responsibility for budget and for the work process. They are al-lowed to – and need to – design and improve the work process themselves, the need for improvisation seems to grow. The framework for employees' action is set by customers' demands and by a decreasing influence and impact of management on details of the work process while at the same time, financial control-ling and standardisation of processes are gaining importance.

Resulting Conditions of Work

Even if the description is over-emphasised and ideal-type, it may help us to inte-grate several effects of the changes ongoing and of their impact on working conditions in a research perspective. Following the argument above, there are at least three selected topics in the present scientific discussion, which can illus-trate the outcome of the strategic changes mentioned. This is the German de-bate on a 'delimitation of work' ('Entgrenzung von Arbeit'), the French research on 'unconfined jobs', and the – again: German - discussion on 'Subjektivierung', which we will briefly sketch now.

1. The discussion on a 'delimitation of work' (this is a first and tentative translation of the German expression "Entgrenzung von Arbeit") is focusing on a loss of insti-tutionalised and regulatory limits of work as a consequence of the changes dis-cussed above (cf. Döhl et al. 2000, Sauer 2002, Wolf & Mayer-Ahuja 2002). Sev-eral facets of delimitation are covered.
   - If tasks can't be designed completely, the set of competencies and de-mands, which employees need to fulfil, can't be completely defined, as well. Furthermore, the ability to cope with different and unforeseen situa-tions (cf. below: 'unconfined jobs') has much to do with attitudes and creativity. (cf. below: 'Subjektivität'). In this sense, work organisation tends to become increasingly informal.
   - There is a change in working times. Working time is increasingly extended or shortened according to the situation of the company, and it is less regu-lated at many workplaces. People tend to work until their task is fulfilled and all orders are finished in time. Exponents of this position (cf. loc.cit.) highlight the "erosion" of the standard working time regulation.
   - Accordingly, the borderline between work and 'non-work' is beginning to shift. This includes time aspects as well as location aspects (changing or mobile workplaces in the service sector e.g.). The readjusting of the 'work-life-balance' is necessary if people tend to adapt their individual life pref-erences according to extended and unforeseen needs of work.
   - There seems to be a shift concerning the contractual basis of work. The no-tion is that there would be a small group of highly qualified 'core' employ-ees with unlimited work contracts while there is a

growing number of peo-ple working on precarious contracts (limited contracts, supplementary workers from agencies etc.).

The basic idea of 'delimitation' is that companies are increasingly focusing on efficient and effective use of human resources in order to gain flexibility and re-duce costs. Furthermore, in order to solve the problems emerging in this type of work, it is necessary to apply formerly unapplied resources: In this sense, private time is used as an organisational buffer. A maximum of individual flexibility is re-quired from the employees. These tendencies are not really new, but there seems to be an increasing amount of employees touched. Following the sceptic view on this position mentioned by Bosch (2000), it is quite evident that the trends mentioned are not the, or even the only way work is structured. Many work-places are not met by all or at least some of these changes. But from our view, a set of problems is emphasised which is closely related to the market-oriented control aspect we discussed. Furthermore, the effects on the existing regulatory standards of working time and on the contractual background are emphasised.

2. In some way similar to the 'delimitation' aspect, there is a different strand of French research on 'unconfined jobs'. The increasing difficulty to design and de-scribe workplaces and the resulting increase of work intensity is its starting point. The interesting aspect is that two concepts are additionally introduced to work design, "work prescription" and "work confinement":
   - "Work prescription is defined as a prescription of any formal and informal requirements bearing on the job regardless of their source. A salesperson receives prescriptions from the management but also from the clients: the relations are different in each case but the salesperson has to take ac-count of both. …
   - Work confinement is the ability of work designers to determine the work content and environment. … Unconfined jobs are jobs where work design defines only a sub-part of the work environment." (Hatchuel 2002: 45)

With the help of these definitions, the problem of limited pre-definition of tasks can be well described even if tasks become increasingly context dependent. Furthermore, it may help to discuss the different aspects of autonomy. (cf. Hatchuel, loc.cit.)

3. The third notion is the German debate on "Subjektivierung" (Moldaschl 2002a: 20, with sceptic view: Volpert 2002), which is highlighting the need to broadly apply individual skills and competencies to solve the

problems in delivering ser-vices or products. It is strongly emphasising the aspect of individual resources, competencies, and attitudes. The crucial point is that in a tayloristic environment work design was directed towards defining a "one best way", which was the re-sult of a set of analyses and motion studies e.g. Every (trained) person should be able to do it, apart from individual differences – work design in this sense is fairly abstract and "objective". The notion "Subjektivierung" (which can hardly be translated, it approx. means to transform something into a subjective mode) emphasises the growing importance of situational and individual competencies to cope with the work. Here, the keywords are work experience, tacit knowl-edge, creativity, improvisation, individual initiative, informal co-operation and networking. All the elements have been necessary to fulfil job task before, but the present change is indicating that these elements become crucial for com-pany success as well as for individual development. These elements are neces-sary for a successful improvisation as mentioned.

A second emphasis of "Subjektivierung" is on the increasing importance of self-control and self-regulation at the workplace instead of bureaucratic control mechanisms. It is quite evident that traditional hierarchic and bureaucratic con-trol and report structures don't fit to the needs of this type of work, and further-more, they would cause motivational and cultural irritation. The more the suc-cess of a work system is based on attitudes, motivation, willingness of the em-ployees to contribute, to participate actively in structuring work and to solve emerging problems, the less traditional forms of control can be applied. At this point, thirdly, the companies' demands obviously meet individual preferences and wishes to increase individual flexibility. People obviously enjoy to have more influence and autonomy, but there is no direct trade-off between flexibility and time autonomy (cf. Glißman & Peters 2001).
In order to illustrate these concepts by a 'real' work situation, we will briefly de-scribe the work prescriptions in development teams in telecommunications companies which we recently analysed. (Latniak & Schmidt-Dilcher 2000, 61 ff.)
Development teams in telecommunication companies are crucial for the gen-eration of economic success and employment esp. in the new business areas of the sector (mobile). The productivity and creativity of these teams and their abil-ity to fruitfully co-operate with related support functions and with sales is a pre-requisite for the success of the companies. A close and

effective co-operation is necessary in launching periods of new products, particularly. Close co-operation even with external suppliers and customers must be managed.

As "nobody is sure of nothing in this business" (interview statement), the task of product development is a collective one, and everybody involved has to contribute by co-operating with the other team members. The product development units have a 'focal' role for the whole process chain because they are generating, structuring, and controlling development and introduction of ser-vices until they run in a standardised way.

The technical aspect of the task is challenging. Most products rely on a compli-cated use of the infrastructure and they have to cope with a large volume of transactions. If a competitor will launch a certain service, most other competitors will have to follow, or as an interview partner stated: "You don't have the option to launch nothing." So, product development teams have a complex task to fulfil: they have to continuously develop easy-to-use services which are man-ageable for the telecommunications company and they have to be being faster than their competitors.

The development tasks are performed by highly skilled technical staff. But we would like to emphasise that it is much more than a mere technical qualification what is required for a productive work in a development team. Generic skills (communication and interaction) and a certain business related mindset are necessary. For the management of development teams, there was a strong emphasis on a 'consultant type' of skills which is increasingly required, i.e. social networking and communication. This type of skills is necessary to manage teams or groups consisting of different types of experts. The challenge for management is that no single person is able to control the whole development process in all details. There is a need for a non-directive leadership style and to provide the best information and communication atmosphere in the teams to enable their creativity.

Looking at the skills requirements, the complexity of the task is requiring experi-enced specialists. The experience is closely related to a 'learning at work' and to the time of being involved in the development groups. A continuous updating of individual knowledge and skills is urgently necessary for this group of employees. This is causing troubles because if the time for development tasks is short and the high pressure on these teams will last, there will be few time left over for further skills development. A second skills aspect was the "different business mindset" (interview statement). By this notion, it is emphasised that the technical special-ists must have an integrated view on their tasks. It is not sufficient to have a smart technical solution, but the solution must be robust, easy to be used, and it must guarantee economic success at comparatively low costs. A third skills aspect was a strong emphasis on the co-operation and interaction aspect for these groups. We were told that especially young and high performance technical people had problems in co-operating with other team members. The experience was that many of the younger people are not really prepared to productively work in a team. But this mode of working is inevitable because none of the tech-nical specialists can solve all the problems alone. There is a need for interaction supported by management.

The work of the development teams is characterised by a high pressure of time and short budgets which often leads to extremely long individual working hours for those involved. Secondly, there is an uncertainty of success of the new ser-vices – even if the service is technically viable, the competition may cause that the financial results could be limited. Thirdly, due to the continuous need to launch services, the frequency of projects is fairly high. This is the reason why the staff is under an ongoing demand for creativity and productiveness. These three factors indicate that there is a danger of burnout as an effect of the continuous requirements to these groups. The team members are highly involved, they need to continuously upgrade their skills, and they need to closely co-operate.

Figure 1: Work Prescription of Development Teams in the Telecommunications Sector

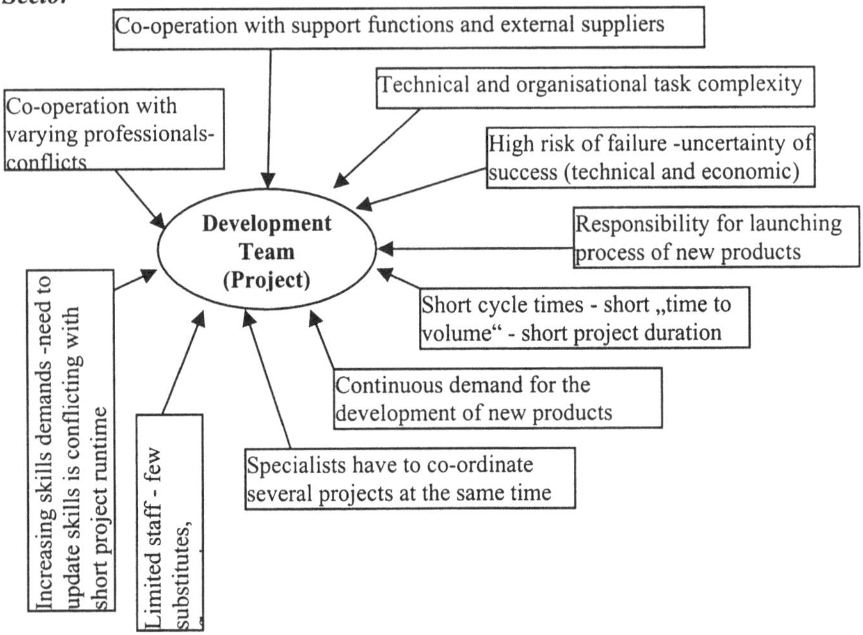

Conceptual Limits of Participation Become Visible

As immediately visible, the work situation of development teams has a very lim-ited similarity to tayloristic structures. A comparison of the different situations will emphasise the limits of the participation concept for the new framework.

In a tayloristic, bureaucratic, or traditional hierarchic company environment, participation of the employees in work and work design is directed towards

- a gathering and joint dissemination of information on work practices in general;
- an extended self-control of work resources as an effect of the reduction of a 'command and control' mode (job control);
- a generation of "meaning" and commitment; participation is always closely related with a reflexive element of design and production processes, i.e. with collective learning about what has been performed before.

So, we can say that in this case, the driving force of participation is the idea to extend the options for employees, to enlarge their scope for action, and their autonomy. If successful, the outcome is a greater degree of autonomy, and a reduction of the traditional command-control-logic by providing an active role to the employees. The vision is to reach a work design with a complete (cogni-tive) control on planning and execution ("vollständige Handlungskontrolle" in terms of the action regulation theory) by those who perform the task. Concern-ing health and stress aspects, there is a trade-off between reduced coercion and control on the one hand and a relief of the stress and strain on the other.

The strategic link to introduce participation has been the heterogeneity of work processes and the involvement of the employees. Heterogeneity can only be managed by the employees-in-charge themselves while work design has reached its limits, here. So, the benefit of participation for the company would be to gain flexibility, to improve process control, and to foster commitment of the employees while there is a loss of direct control and a limited knowledge about the ongoing production and service processes.

Now, comparing this view of participation with the situation of the development project team demonstrates that the extended use of participation would lead to a completely different outcome. There is no bureaucratic or hierarchic com-mand-and-control mode which needs to be changed. Control by the man-agement tends to be executed with a strong emphasis on negotiation and management by objectives, providing sufficient information and furthermore, it is the project manager's task to organise most (substantial) resources needed. Employees are continuously highly involved, and their commitment is more or less a necessary prerequisite for their job. Due to their qualification and scarce-ness on the labour market, the employees of the development team are – at least partly – in a position in which they are able to negotiate their working con-ditions. There autonomy is relatively high.

But at the same time, they have to cope with aspects of 'delimitation' and 'over-'involvement: There is no external protection against extended working time and intensification of work. Along with the emerging forms of indirect con-trol, the question is: Who protects employees from unregulated self-exploitation - in the present situation and in the long run? One of our interview partners, a manager, had to admit, that his influence on these people is limited. They would start to work in a project, being active there for half a year, and then they realise that their social environment has completely vanished meanwhile.

In this sense, the trade-off between an increase of autonomy on the one hand and flexibility, time autonomy, and a reduction of stress and strain is no more valid in every case. The employees of the development team are in danger of burnout while being highly committed. An extension of any participatory aspect would not lead to an improvement of their situation. So, participation in this type of environment obviously is no more a driver for employees' individual auton-omy, power and skills development.

Based on these reflections, we can now emphasise some deficits of the existing participatory approaches:

First, there is a strong backing of these ideas in production work and tayloristic structures. The intention of participatory approaches was and still is to overcome restrictions and effects of tayloristic work structures, as are e.g. monotony and repetitive work. There is a focus on upgrading production work. Most of the ideas mentioned were developed in a production environment emphasising a certain market situation and product type. There was much less emphasis on service work and e.g. on tasks performed by knowledge workers. Due to the changing conditions and company strategies, we see a need to differently emphasise preconditions and the setting of work in order to better adapt these concepts to the new situation. (cf. Pruijt 2003)

Though there was a strong conceptual emphasis on group work in work sciences especially in Germany, the development of analytical support and design tools was directed towards individual work places for a long time. Even the research based on the 'Handlungsregulationstheorie' (action regulation theory) has been widely neglecting co-operative aspects quite long (until Weber 1997). Accord-ingly, problems emerging as an effect of co-operation could only be identified as a factor of stress or strain at the individual workplace and not as a social or co-operative aspect. A tool based support of analysing, designing, or develop-ing co-operative structures in a participatory way is still limited.

As a third aspect, there was a bias on the impact of working conditions and ex-posure ('bedingungsbezogene Analysen') while the coping strategies of the in-dividuals were more or less neglected. In the framework of the 'Handlungsregu-lationstheorie', emotion and experience tend to be underestimated. We see a lack of research concerning extended motivation and commitment of certain employees leading to unhealthy consequences in the long run. (Brödner et al. 2003) The extension of working times according to the companies' needs, the lacking ability to reduce stress, the extended self-exploitation – this could be an outcome of a situation in which highly motivated and highly committed em-ployees are quite

satisfied and motivated, while they are deliberately and volun-tarily performing unhealthy behaviour. As far as we can see, the effects of this kind of 'over-involvement' need to be further investigated.
If it is true that the work situation determines what is a useful way to improve the working conditions, participation must be re-interpreted and applied in a differ-ent manner accordingly. The basic question now is: How should work be de-signed in order to enable employees to do their jobs until retirement and to fur-ther develop their competencies and skills? And what is the role of a participa-tory approach in this context?

Research Project "Sustainability in Project Type Work"

Since the end of 2002, we are about to do a research project which is focusing on the work situation of highly qualified staff in IT or software development pro-ject teams. If the assumption is correct that working conditions like those de-scribed above will further disseminate, then project type work could serve as a prototype for research into problems and difficulties for future work. By investigat-ing into the working conditions, company background, and tasks or problems to be solved, we want to find out more about the individual, organisational, and social resources used by the employees to solve their tasks. (Moldaschl 2002b) It is of primary interest to identify relevant resources of the employees and whether they can be regenerated or further developed. In this sense, the individual re-sources contribute significantly to the project's success.
The investigation is based on case studies in several different companies focus-ing on typical work processes with high skills requirements and a high degree of exposure for the employees. In the empirical studies, our task is to identify con-tradicting demands, rules, resources in project teams first. We want to find out more about buffers and resources used to cope with changing challenges. Based on these findings, we want to develop adapted rules and methods to support work design in this field.
The project is trying to partly provide answers to the problems and questions dis-cussed above. We try to cope with these difficulties by applying an integrated approach which is characterised by the following elements:

- The intention is to foster a saluto-genetic approach (Antonovsky 1997, 1987). It is directed towards a work design that enables employees to keep a healthy balance of demands, exposures, resources, and individual coping. The objective is that people should remain healthy in their working environment.

- This is not only limited to present situation; it is necessary to keep employ-ees healthy and motivated until their retirement. With the notion of "sus-tainable work" (Docherty et al 2002), we want to emphasise that there is a need for a working environment which is providing a frame for healthy, productive, and interesting work for a whole lifetime. The further develop-ment of skills and competencies ('life long learning')and a balance be-tween experience and new aspects is an aspect to be considered. In this respect, work-life-balance is an issue of primary interest, too.
- Taking serious what we just said about the contradictory situation and con-tradictory requirements to employees (Glaser & Büssing 1996, Moldaschl 1991), it is evidently necessary to apply a "relational view" in the analysis: rules, requirements, exposure, and resources need to be analysed and evaluated in relation to the tasks in the projects in question - in an inte-grated manner. (Gerlmaier 2002, Moldaschl 2002b)
- According to the latter aspect, we see an increasing need to take back-ground conditions of the companies (market situation, mergers & acquisi-tions, outsourcing) into account.

We will use a mix of different methods, as are e.g. group interviews on tasks and requirements, observations of the work processes, and surveys with some stan-dardised instruments.

The intention of the project is to identify options for the design of project type work processes which will support a 'sustainable' use of peoples' resources. The work design should enable a regeneration and a further development of the re-sources in use, especially of those identified as being important for the work process or preferred by the employees. The critical aspect is whether – and how – this can be introduced and anchored in the companies' practices in a way that it will be applicable in the future. With this effort, we would like to contribute to answering a set of important research questions:

1. Do company structures really change in the way we described it? Is "de-limitation" and "Subjektivierung" a core trend in German (and European) industry with a severe impact on regulations (time, contracts)? Do com-panies apply the "market-oriented control"? What is really going on em-pirically?
2. What are the conceptual relations and differences between autonomy, granted or semi-autonomy, and participation? Should we further apply

participation in the way we are used to or is it necessary to modify the concept?
3. If there is a new type of work gaining importance: What are adapted criteria for the evaluation and the design of work? How should we define 'social sustainability' and – among that – the role of participation?
4. What can we do in order to take intended and unintended effects of the design approaches into account? In this sense, how can we execute this reflexive type of research?

The overall objective should be to develop and design patterns of work forms, working conditions, and regulating institutions which help to enable a sustain-able use of the individual workforce as well as "good work" and a "good life". This should contribute to a successful and prospering economy based on the sus-tainable availability of high level skills and competencies.

References

Antonovsky, A., 1987: *Health Promoting Factors at Work: The Sense of Coherence*, in: Kalimo, R.; El-Batavi, M. A.; Cooper, C. L. (Hrsg.): *Psychosocial Factors at Work and their Relation to Health*, Geneva: World Health Organisation.

Antonovski, A., 1997: *Salutogenese. Zur Entmystifizierung der Gesundheit* dgvt-Verlag Tübingen (deutsch von A. Franke).

Brödner, P. & Gerlmaier, A., Latniak, E., Voss-Dahm, D. , 2003 (forthcoming): *Projektarbeit und Nachhaltigkeit -Intensität als Preis für mehr Autonomie?* In: Moldaschl, M. (Ed.): *Nachhaltigkeit von Arbeit und Rationalisierung* (Arbeitstitel). München & Mehring: Hampp.

Brödner, P. & Forslin, J., 2002: *O tempora, o mores! Work intensity – why again an issue?* In: Docherty et al., 15–26.

Brödner, P., 2002: *Flexibilität, Arbeitsbelastung und nachhaltige Arbeitsgestaltung.* In: Brödner, P. & Knuth, M. (Hrsg.): *Nachhaltige Arbeitsgestaltung. Trendreportes zur Entwicklung und Nutzung von Humanressourcen. Bilanzierung innovativer Arbeitsgestaltung Teil 3.* München usw.: Hampp, 489–542.

Brödner, P., 2001: *Macht Arbeit wieder krank? Flexibilität und nachhaltige Gestaltung von Arbeit.* Gelsenkirchen: IAT.

Bosch, G., 2000: *Entgrenzung der Erwerbsarbeit – Lösen sich die Grenzen zwischen Erwerbs- und Nichterwerbsarbeit auf?* In: Minssen, H. (Hrsg.): *Begrenzte Entgrenzungen. Wandel von Organisation und Arbeit.* Berlin: Edition Sigma, 249–268.

Crozier, M. & Friedberg, E., 1979 Macht und Organisation : die Zwänge kollektiven Handelns. Königstein/Ts. : Athenäum.

Docherty, P. , Forslin, J. & A.B. (Rami) Shani, 2002 (Hrsg.): *Creating Sustainable Work Systems. Emerging Perspectives and Practice.* London/New York: Routledge.

Döhl, V., N. Kratzer & D. Sauer, 2000: *Krise der NormalArbeit(s) Politik Entgrenzung von Arbeit – neue Anforderungen an die Arbeitspolitik.* In: WSI-Mitteilungen 1/2000, 5–17.

Gerlmaier, A., 2002: *Neue Selbstständigkeit in der Informationsgesellschaft. Ein Vergleich von An-forderungen und individuellen Ressourcenpotentialen bei autonom-flexiblen und arbeitsteiligen Arbeitsformen im IT-Bereich.* Dissertation. Universität Dortmund. Mai 2002.

Glaser, J. & A. Büssing, 1996: *Widersprüchliche Anforderungen in der Arbeitstätigkeit, Zusatzauf-wand und psychischer Streß. Konzepte und Überprüfung eines Vermittlungsmodells.* In: *Zeitschrift für Arbeits- und Organisationspsychologie* 1996 , 40 (N.F. 14): 87–91.

Glißmann, W. & Peters, K., 2001: *Mehr Druck durch mehr Freiheit. Die neue Autonomie in der Arbeit und ihre paradoxen Folgen*, Hamburg: VSA.

Hatchuel, A., 2002: *Sources of intensity in work organisations.* In: Docherty et al 2002, 40–51.

Kern, H. & Schumann, M., 1983: *Das Ende der Arbeitsteilung? : Rationalisierung in der industriellen Produktion: Bestandsaufnahme,* Trendbestimmung, 3. Aufl., München : Beck, 1986.

Kleinschmidt, M. & Pekruhl, U., 1994: *Kooperation, Partizipation und Autonomie: Gruppenarbeit in deutschen Betrieben.* In: Arbeit 3 (1994), 150-172.

Kötter, W., 2002: *Projektarbeit – (k)ein Thema für die Arbeitspsychologie?* In: Moldaschl, M. (Hrsg.): Neue Arbeit – Neue Wissenschaft von der Arbeit? Festschrift zum 60. Geburtstag von Walter Volpert. Heidelberg: Kröning, 399–416.

Latniak, E. & Schmidt-Dilcher, J., 2000: *Employment and Skills in growing business areas of the telecommunication service sector.* Gelsenkirchen: IAT. (reprint 2001 by UNI-Europe Telecom-munications, Nyon)

Latniak, E. & Kinkel, S., Lay, G., 2002: *Dezentralisierung in der deutschen Investitionsgüterindustrie: Verbreitung und Effekte ausgewählter organisatorischer Elemente.* In: Arbeit 11: 143-160.

Lehndorff, St., 2003: *The long good-bye? Tarifvertragliche Arbeitszeitregulierung und gesellschaft-licher Arbeitszeitstandard.* In: *Industrielle Beziehungen 10*, S. 273-295

Luczak, H. et al 1989: *Arbeitswissenschaft: Kerndefinition - Gegenstandskatalog - Forschungsge-biete ; Bericht an den Vorstand der Gesellschaft für Arbeitswissenschaft und die Stiftung Volkswagenwerk.* 3. Aufl. Eschborn [u.a.] : RKW-Verl. [u.a.].

Moldaschl, M., 2002a: *Subjektivierung – Eine neue Stufe in der Entwicklung der Arbeitswissen-schaften?* In: M. Moldaschl: *Subjektivierung von Arbeit.* München/Mehring: Hampp, 23–52.

Moldaschl, M., 2002b: *A resource-centered perspective.* In: Docherty et al., 52–64.

Moldaschl, M., 2001a: *Herrschaft durch Autonomie – Dezentralisierung und widersprüchliche Arbeitsanforderungen*, in: Lutz, B. (Hg.): Entwicklungsperspektiven von Arbeit, Berlin: Akademie Verlag, 132–164.

Moldaschl, M., 2001b: *From team ideology to sustainable work systems.* In: Concepts and Trans-formations 6:2 (2001), 173–194.

Moldaschl, M., 2001c: *Die Produktion der Organisation. Reorganisation und Ressourcenkonflikte am Beispiel Gruppenarbeit.*, München/Mehring: Hampp Verlag.

Moldaschl, M. & Sauer, D., 2000. *Internalisierung des Marktes – zur neuen Dialektik von Koopera-tion und Herrschaft.* In: H. Minssen (Hrsg.): *Begrenzte Entgrenzungen.* Berlin: edition sigma, 205–224.

Moldaschl, M., 1991: *Widersprüchliche Arbeitsanforderungen – Psychische Belastung und doppelte Realität in der Produktion.* Mitteilungen des SFB 333, No. 3. München, 3–50

Nordhause-Janz, J. & Pekruhl, U. (Eds.) 2000: *Arbeiten in neuen Strukturen?: Partizipation, Kooperation, Autonomie und Gruppenarbeit in Deutschland.* München & Mehring: Hampp.

Pruijt, H., 2003: Teams *between Neo-Taylorism and Anti-Taylorism.* In: *Economic and Industrial Democracy* Vol 24 (1), 77-101.

Salm, R. & Kötter, W., 2003: *Gruppenarbit – ein verbrauchtes Leitbild "guter Arbeit"?* In: Peters, J. Schmitthenner, H. (Eds.): *Gute Arbeit ... Menschengerechte Arbeitsgestaltung als Gewerk-schaftliche Zukunftsaufgabe.* Hamburg: VSA. 123-139.

Sauer, D., 2002: *Unternehmensorganisation und Entgrenzung von Arbeit – Thesen zum Umbruch.* In: Sauer, D. (Hrsg.): *Dienst-Leistungs-Arbeit. Kundenorientierung und Leistung in tertiären Organisationen.* München: ISF, 27–38.

Udris, I. & Frese, M., 1999: *Belastung und Beanspruchung.* In: Hoyos & Frei (Hrsg.): *Arbeits- und Or-ganisationspsychologie. Ein Lehrbuch.* Weinheim: Beltz, 429–445.

Ulich, E., 1994: *Arbeitspsychologie*. Zürich: Vdf.

Vieth, P., 1995: *Kontrollierte Autonomie*. Heidelberg: Asanger.

Volpert, W., 2002: *Psychologie der frei flottierenden Arbeistkraft*. In: Moldaschl, M. & Voß, G.G. (Hg.) *Subjektivierung von Arbeit*. München/Mehring: Hampp, 261–279.

Weber, W.G., 1997: *Analyse von Gruppenarbeit. Kollektive Handlungsregulation in soziotechni-schen Systemen*. Bern usw. Hans Huber.

Weber, W.G., Lauche, K. & Verbeck, A., 1999: *Gemeinsame Vergegenständlichungen und kooperatives Handeln in multifunktionalen Entwicklungsteams*. In: Sachse & Specker, 219–251.

Wolf, H. & Mayer-Ahuja, N., 2002: *„Grenzen der Entgrenzung von Arbeit" – Perspektiven der Arbeitsforschung*. In: SOFI Mitteilungen Nr. 30, 197–205.

Call Centres in Europe: Recommendations for the Union?

GIOVANNA ALTIERI

In recent years there has been a trend of exponential growth in European call centres, although different countries vary in the phases of this development[1]

Call centres have become a global phenomenon permeating all production sectors. In fact, direct customer-related activities have increased sharply. Companies attempt to humanise relations with their clientele through customer care, conducting market research and offering new services online. There are even new emergent 'creative' call centres that operate in design, publishing, advertising and public relations sectors, where some companies assign part of the work to specialists in contact with the staff by telephone or e-mail. In the last few years the PA have been setting up call centres to improve service provision. At first, call centres consisted of a switchboard and operators that answered incoming calls but successively the evolution in technologies transformed the operators from 'switchboard operators' to 'high added value employees' and the call centre structures 'from cost centres' to 'profit centres'[2].

Call centres might seem to be a world apart, quite distinct from the 'production universe' as it has its own specific technology: devices to distribute calls so that the user on hold is directed onto the first free operator, operating systems incorporating worker performance indicators, headsets, etc.. Even the language and internal communication are quite unique. The customers are classified by numerical codes, calls coming into the centres are termed as 'inbound', whereas those from the centre to the

[1] According to DATAMONITOR, growth over the next three years will be at 12 percent[1] and for 2002 it is envisaged that 1.3% of the European workforce, equivalent to nearly 2 million people, will be working in call centres. See, Datamonitor "Call centres in EMEA", 2000

[2] see. www.idg.it

outside are termed as 'outbound'. In this 'New Economy' environment, technical English terms have become common in all languages, for instance the Italianised version of 'log in' is 'loggarsi'.
Nevertheless, call centres are faced with age-old production problems: labour force shortages, poor worker motivation, high turnover and latent dissatisfaction.
The world of call centres is a heterogeneous one. In fact the call centres vary according to activities carried out, size, place within the production cycle and market, quality of the industrial relations. So that we can identify a variety of typologies of call centres, with different models for work organisation and flexibility use which have an affect on working conditions. Beside, there are also some features which recur in a lot of call centres also located in different countries[3].
This picture result from a comparative study of call centres in a group of European countries , analysing the various organisation models, work arrangements and their impact on working conditions with the final aim to collect elements to assess grounds for union intervention in this type of structure.

Typologies

We have identified five main typologies of call centres.

1. *in-house*; these are call centres within large companies, with a specialised "mission". They substantially cover the customer care service for the company. This model also includes call centres which are separate branches of the company and can in some cases act as virtual call centres. The work in these structures is exclusively referred to the company. They can be either public or private. Usually the workers have some opportunities for promotion within other sectors of the company, although the study has shown that even here career prospects are in reality somewhat rare. In every case working conditions are

[3] This cases study was conducted inside the IST programme project TOSCA (Social Observation Table of Call centres, co-ordinated by ETUC, and involving 8 different countries around Europe (Belgium, Bulgaria, France, Germany, England, Ireland, Italy, Spain). See http://www-it.fmi.uni-sofia.bg/TOSCA/. The IRES Italian team (composed by G. Altieri C. Oteri, S.Leonardi,) has been the responsible for the cases study report. It is disposable an Italian version of the work: G. Altieri (a cura di) Lavorare nei call centres: un'analisi europea. Collana IRES, Ediesse, Roma, 2002

relatively superior by comparison with other typologies and therefore there is a lower turnover, also because of the existence of trade unions. Trade union access is undoubtedly facilitated by traditional, pre-existing union culture in the company. Nevertheless, trade unions still have problems in coming face-to-face with the workforce as contractual conditions for call centre agents are often different from those applied to workers in other company divisions.

2. *Large call centres in outsourcing.* These are involved in a great variety of activities, they are often partly owned by large companies in the telecommunications, computer or banking sectors. They are often set up to deal with the internal requirements of the parent companies, but they then diversify and open up to the market. Working conditions vary a great deal depending on the type of work and the country in which the call centre is located. There is much use of flexibility in these call centres, both in terms of skills and contracts. This is due to its exposure to variations in the market. The trade unions are rarely present here, despite their being some differences in this respect between the countries studied. This situation stems from the 'newness' of these structures, the young labour force on temporary contracts which leads to relatively high turnover.

3. small call centres in outsourcing. These carry out work for private and public clients across a variety of sectors. Often they have no more than two or three clients at the same time. Here we can find two quite different situations; A) on the one hand there are specialised call centres, for example so-called creative call centres. Here the working conditions and the type of work lead to quite high levels of satisfaction among the workforce. There are also cases of workers who have been promoted into client companies; B) at the other extreme are workers in small call centres where low-profit activities carried out. This is a way for the contractor companies to offload costs and temporal flexibility onto the small call centre which in turn produces negative effects on the workforce. It is striking that even in a new economy sector, tertiarisation often produces the same critical effects on the workforce as those reported in manufacturing.
   Here trade unions are practically non-existent in both situations described, but while in the more specialised call centres there tends to be a degree of paternalism and an informal style of management which does not set great store by status differences in the working hierarchy, in

the more market-influenced situation there is an attitude of "disposability" with regard to the workforce.

4. *'social' call centres*. These are both public and social private structures. They offer medical, social welfare and emergency services so require specialised professionals, such as psychologists, social workers, lawyers, doctors and nurses. The workers are usually very motivated and they regard working in such call centres as a meaningful professional experience. In fact there are many voluntary workers. The fact of not being exposed to "market forces" also has an impact on working conditions, even if in some cases productivity is low. Stress seems to be caused in this case more by the content of the work than how the work is organised. Despite poor pay, motivation and work experience opportunities mean that the turnover is relatively low. Trade unions exist only in public structures, while in the private prevalence of informal working relationships and strong identification with the business on the part of the workforce.

5. *automated call centres*. This accounts for a relatively small number of call centres - usually private and often linked with computer businesses. Majority of workers are professional, such as programmers and computer scientists. Call centre agents make up a very small number - usually some 80 percent of telephone calls are dealt with automatically. This also means that existing staff carry heavy workload and have a perception of minimal social relations within the workplace. Trade unions are absent.

Common Features

In addition to the specific components of the typologies described above, many call centres present a series of common features which can be seen as typical. We can list the following:

- Location in urban areas or special sites (techno parks, industrial zones)
- high incidence of women and young workers
- reduced management structure
- little opportunity for promotion in any traditional sense
- minimal training
- high turnover
- work based on rigid team organisation

- high level of fixed-term work and flexible contractual arrangements
- widespread use of flexible working hours, wide range of part-time models and shift working
- minimal presence of trade unions

Here is an overview of the main results that emerged from our analysis. First of all, contrary to what might be believed, call centres do not usually spring up in virgin territory, but tend to perpetuate the existing concentration of service activities, reproducing existing disparities in the geographical division of labour. Although the factors determining location range from a vast pool of workforce, level of telecommunications infrastructures, availability of premises in techno parks or close to clients' markets, to factors of logistic convenience in relation to the parent company, including fiscal and financial incentives, empirical evidence shows that European call centres tend to be located in major urban centres, with some in techno parks or industrial zones. Places where there is the virtuous interaction of an ample availability of educated workforce and suitable technological infrastructures.

Call centre workers are essentially young, often students, but primarily women with an intermediate level of education. The most common level of educational attainment is the high school diploma. What links the labour force in every case is the fact of being able to respond to the need for flexibility, even if workers might have diverse social profiles.

The overrepresentation of women suggests a new form of female segregation where old stereotypes combining with taken-for-granted female aptitudes and new media images. More job applications come from women, but the employers prefer them to men, both because of their greater flexibility and because they are regarded as being more capable of learning interpersonal skills required by agents. For men call centre work tends to be temporary and related to entry into the labour market, while for women it is a way to enter the market but also to remain. It also allows many women to re-enter the labour market after a period of absence.

But is the call centre the new technological version of the Fordist production line or is it an example of knowledge-based organisation? At such a regard it has been said: 'Call centres are complex organisations, a socio-technical system where social density is equal to technological density which is equal to information density and know-how'[4]

---

[4] Donati E., *I call centre: una nuova opportunità di business e di lavoro nell'economia della conoscenza*, paper per "office automation n. 3, March 1999

Empirical analysis shows that call centres are not homogeneous and the majority of those studied can be located somewhere between the models of "minute factories" and the so-called "knowledge based organisation". At one extreme there are call centres organised as production lines following a taylorist model, where work is highly individual and relatively poor in content, breaks are rigorously calculated and supervisors closely monitor the agents' work; one the other hand, there are call centres where agents have relatively high skills, work is organised in teams and monitoring is goal-oriented, rather than process based.

There are various organisational models, from individual work to team-based. However even in team organisation there is still a high degree of isolation rather than integration, to such an extent that the work model can be defined as "individual working in teams".

In general, while functions such as inquiries, booking, debt-collection, sales and telemarketing seem to require fairly simple tasks, in those such as credit and insurance sectors, social health services, technical assistance and so-called creative centres, skills seem to be more complex.

In call centres that work as knowledge-based organisations – although not so common in this universe – traditional skills are combined with ICT skills.

In actual fact, the case studies have enabled us to highlight the determining role of technology in the work process. On the one hand, ICT has made it possible to carry out tasks and offer services which would have been unthinkable until recently, but on the other hand the ways in which skills and know-how are transmitted are increasingly incorporated into machines. This makes the agent's work easier as the information necessary for the task can be easily accessed but at the same time reduces the subjective contribution to the productive process. On the whole, this means that workers become easier to replace, while on the other hand their value grows in proportion to the tacit or implicit knowledge and skills which they can amass during their life course and professional activity. The possession of complementary skills (tacit) therefore becomes significant. On the other hand technological developments also change the structure of employment in terms of skill-based qualifications. There is the need for highly specialised and low skilled workers. This is the so-called "technological bias".

To allow call centres to become more evolved, the technological view of the call centre needs to be overcome and its value has to be assessed in strategic terms. At present, call centre work is highly structured and does not permit workers to acquire additional skills.

Even the training provided does not permit the agents to grow professionally, although there are some exceptions. The companies are not willing to invest in the single worker which also means exploiting the social capital of the company. There is also the common conviction that agents should be transitory. Companies therefore give the workers a sort of 'disposable' training, very short-lived and specific to the task at hand. Agents are trained rapidly to carry out the tasks (average time 1 to 2 weeks) so they can be immediately productive. This situation gives rise to an apparent paradox, managers lay great stress on human resources in a highly labour-intensive sector, and yet work organisation is firmly centred on technology and it is the technology that attracts the greatest investment.
This aspect is particularly critical as career opportunities are rare, especially in the call centres in outsourcing. This is due to various reasons, ranging from the presence of short hierarchical chains to the fact that there is an unbalanced ratio between management and the number of agents. But prospects are not significantly better within in-house call centres. Very often the call centre agents are not sufficiently integrated with the other company divisions so the call centre is not always an entry point for work within the company, contrary to what many young people employed there would hope for.

The final result is that the only mobility allowed in call centres is through the 'door'. Agents leave either to go to another call centre that offers better working conditions but with similarities and common features to the previous job or else the worker goes elsewhere in the labour market, but without any particular enhancement of prospects through the experience acquired.
In short, greater social status for the agents' job and more developed management and organisation conditions might be made possible when customer service provision becomes the core activity of the call centre in the Internet based market. We have seen the effects that technology has on work with respect to the transmission of know-how. Technology raises company productivity- through the autonomic distribution of calls, computer-telephony integration, the use of software to monitor calls handled, to register pick-up and waiting times but it also means the greater degree of control over workers.
In fact, electronic monitoring lets supervisors keep track of the precise operations of each worker, who is taking a call, waiting for a call, taking a break. Technology also makes it possible to listen in on the agent's conversations. This invasive control via technology and resulting pressure

on the worker contributes to higher levels of stress that characterises work in all call centres.
To these pressures from excess surveillance systems are added other problems, health problems arising from the monotony and repetitive nature of the tasks, the heavy workloads imposed, self-control required in dealing with the public etc. Even features of the working environment contribute, for example the technical quality of audio-video equipment, workstation ergonomics, noise levels, ventilation and microclimate, producing muscular-skeletal and vision disorders, as well as other symptoms.
It thus seems that high levels of stress in call centres are not just linked to heavy workloads, but to the overall demands of the work (from the speed of dealing with inquiries to the monitoring of results, etc). This situation has led to a new work culture to be put forward by an expert [5] so that young people will be taught how to defend themselves', allowing them to manage stressful situations.
Another highly critical aspect of the study is in relation to contractual conditions offered in call centres.
Contracts prevalent in the various call centres embody features of regulatory models in the different countries involved so the forms assumed by contractual flexibility follow different labour market models present in the various countries. Thus, in UK permanent contracts are frequent, while in Spain there are fixed-term contracts, and in Italy a sort of legal anomaly, somewhere between freelance and employed status, called 'para-subordination'.
Usually companies tend to structure employment relationships in concentric circles. Permanent staff constitute a first group, mostly managers and specialised operators, then the second group of workers on fixed term contracts, involving agents, but also supervisors. Lastly, a more fluctuating group on extremely short-term contracts. This means that in the same workplace there are subjects with different work statuses. This creates problems of a social nature, lowering the motivation of workers whose conditions are relatively inferior and reinforcing a condition of relative deprivation with respect to their stable colleagues. This is further aggravated by the fact that some in-house call centres apply different and worse contractual conditions with respect to those of the parent company.
'Unrestrained' flexibility is an overriding principle in the world of the call centre and one of the first concepts learnt by the agents. Along side contractual flexibility there is also widespread temporal flexibility.

[5] S. Bagnara, *1999*

Irrespective of the task, workers are expected to do part time and shift work, often so that the centre can be staffed on a 24-hour basis and to alleviate the stress of the job, recognised as such by the managers.
Obviously flexibility may also suit the needs of workers. Many of them are students or women with family responsibilities and appreciate having a job that takes up only a few hours of their week.
This aspect should not be underestimated when taking into account the general problems in the sector. Hourly flexibility should be regarded first and foremost as an instrument to meet the needs and requests expressed by the workers.
Indeed, for many young people call centre work is temporary and not an end in itself as witnessed by the high turnover in this sector. Nonetheless, it is worth considering that these workers have higher than average levels of schooling and consequently have expectations of professional improvement which are often not met. Our research shows that workers complain about the poor opportunities for professional growth.
The high turnover rates are also related to stress and the working conditions offered. Young people contribute in large measure to the proportion of workers who leave this sector and the average term of a call centre worker in all the countries involved is very low. Yet, isn't turnover a critical issue for call centre businesses just as it is for other companies that attempt to retain the workforce by activating polices to instil company identity in the workers and keep them loyal?
In fact from the employer's point of view the high levels of turnover have a dual aspect. On the one hand, the ideal condition for managers and employers of call centres is not to achieve any drastic lowering of turnover but merely to reduce it for the sake of saving on training and recruitment costs. Turnover gives the business those margins of flexibility which it needs to deal with the unpredictability of the market and its deadlines, without having to sustain additional labour costs.

On the other hand, there are also cases of call centres were the problem of retaining workers is beginning to be felt. The companies need a core group of stable workers who they can count on (regardless of the contractual conditions offered to them). This is why some call centres have recruited women re-entering the labour market and set up ad hoc programmes for them. Others are beginning to recruit even pensioners, and some have made the decision to employ workers on a stable basis because 'satisfied workers makes for satisfied customers'. A demonstration that though flexibility is a

strategic element, an excessive turnover in the workforce can also be a curb on the company's development.
To sum up this point, employers are not looking for maximum flexibility but a sort of optimal flexibility[6]. Whereas, for the workers, the appeal of this job is linked to the intersection of a number of subjective variables on their own social condition, such as personal experience, expectations and by objective variables like typology of call centre, contractual conditions, pay levels and the quality of the work.
There is an apparent paradox in terms of the high number of job applications received by call centres, in relation to the simultaneously high turnover.
A possible explanation to this phenomenon is the initial appeal of this job in terms of its social status. Many young people are willing to do this kind of work while regarding other jobs as beneath them, even though they might pay better. Poorer working conditions become acceptable because the work is only temporary and can be categorised as a "white-collar" job.

Another striking finding of the research is that in some cases there is a high level of identification with the goals of the company, along with a sense of responsibility. Doubtless this is also an effect of the company's emphasis on imbuing the workforce with its values right from the start. Yet the perception of working in a new sector should not be underestimated. Using ICT and perceiving the clients problems as "a personal challenge to be overcome", as one worker put it, are aspects which attract people to this job.

Problems and Recommendations for the Union

Trade union difficulties in this sector are aggravated by particular factors, as can be seen by the average low unionisation rates. The study has shown: the extent to which flexibility dictates work relationships, social and contractual fragmentation within the business, an informal and personalised style of relations between management and agents, a high turnover in workforce, widespread resignation or submission towards the company, individualistic attitudes. The workers feel extremely exposed to the risks of instability, making them less likely to undertake any commitment to act in

---

[6] Accornero A., Altieri G., Oteri C., *Lavoro flessibile. Cosa pensano davvero imprenditori e manager,* Ediesse, Rome, 2001.

defence of their rights, passively accepting their lot and reminding themselves that it is only a stopgap job.

In such a scenario, the union becomes the collective actor – more than parties or other political institutions – that bears the brunt of this new current economic conjuncture. Critical issues merge into a systemic interrelation between innovation in the economic production models, the regulatory sphere of rights and in the social values.
Economic streamlining, the reconfiguration of the workplace (outsourcing and lean production), changes in the socio-technical paradigm of work organisation, increasing flexibility in legal work definitions, changes in lifestyle (more individualistic), erode and upset the fundamentals of material conditions, the policies of organisations and trade unionism as we have always known it during the past.
New forms of social subjectivitiy and bonds of identification are being increasingly formed outside the workplace. Great importance is placed today on consumerism, lifestyle [7] and the cultural industry [8]. The "de-traditionalising of social classes" and the "individualising of unease" [9] tend to bring people together in "contingent coalitions" and for ad hoc issues rather than common, universal groups, like the traditional ones related to families, area, class, union, etc. Joining a trade union can even be experienced in this way. Although it is a weak bond, casual and instrumental favoured (or forced) by the transitory nature of work.
The trade unions themselves are ill-equipped in the face of these new forms of work and new kinds of workers as they are used to a very different kind of society on which the workings of the union movement have been developed over the decades. The prototype of the industrial worker inherited from the taylor-fordist era is slowly disappearing: male, adult, low educated, socialised within the working-class culture and movement.
Now they have to reckon with a different kind of workforce characterised by completely different elements than the ones listed above. Workers in the service sector (white collar), young, high educated, increasingly more women with cultural attitudes and values less tied to affiliation to a social class, movement, etc.

---

[7] P. Bordieu, *La distinction;* in it. *La distinzione,* Il Mulino, Bologna, 1979.
[8] M. Horkheimer and T. Adorno, *Dialectic of Enlightenment*, in It. *Dialettica dell'Illuminismo*, Einaudi, 1976
[9] U. Beck, (1986); in it. *La società del rischio*, Carocci, Rome, 2000; Z. Bauman, in It. *La società dell'incertezza*, Il Mulino, Bologna, 1999.

All this makes it 'objectively' and 'subjectively' more difficult for the union to communicate with the new tertiary workforce. Our interviews have highlighted these difficulties and this remoteness from trade union experience.

Given this situation, it is imperative for European trade unions to search for new responses so they can put themselves in a position to know how to intercept the demand for representation and protection advanced by the world of new jobs. The future of the trade unions lies on the balance if solutions are not found. The constraints and difficulties described so far need to be transformed into opportunities. This means re-thinking the entire social and contractual representation supply of individual and collective services, identities and symbols linked to affiliation. A new, original combination of good old techniques and some modern marketing tools are required [10]. The union must try to adjust its methods to suit the characteristics of the call centres using a mix of traditional and innovative instruments.

A priority is to develop initiatives at workplaces by obtaining detailed knowledge of the work organisation and conditions. Questions must be put to the workers and this information translated into real negotiating platforms.

The most frequent issues raised by workers interviewed, with some variation from country to country:

- higher salary levels
- more continuity and security in working agreements
- combating stress and work rhythms
- need to improve workstation ergonomics
- working hours and holidays
- defence of privacy

It would be useful to be able to define codes of online conduct and to establish explicit company policy on correct and incorrect behaviour, on what basis supervisory controls become necessary and in what ways codes of collective or individual identification become the attributes of the worker.

In any case, the efficacy of trade union representation in the workplaces presupposes at least two preconditions:

- legislation which does not obstruct, but favours trade union presence in workplaces

[10] A. Bibby, *Negotiating the new economy*, 2000

- statutory employment relationships which register relative stability of employment.

In the first of these there are already existing legislation and agreements within the EU countries which make this an incontrovertible right (outlining union rights and authorities/prerogatives at workplaces); in the second – statutory flexibility in employment relations – there is a need for legislative reforms in every country which will put an end to contractual abuses. Without minimum guarantees on the length of employment relationships, it is impossible for trade union to make any headway in workplaces. The use of flexible contracts as envisaged in EU and national legislation (fixed-term, temporary, part-time, flexible hours) has to be negotiated with workers representatives at company level. While the company has to maintain regular and up-to-the-minute information and consultation with the union on all aspects of industrial and technological policies and modifications to employment as well as work organisation.

A second terrain that must be updated is the capacity of the union to follow through transformations, especially related to labour market protection and employment relationships. This is particularly important if we consider that most of the workforce employed in call centres are only 'passing through' . It is thus important to construct and maintain 'employability'.

This type of intervention must occur through legislative tools that innovate the traditional welfare measures, calibrating them to suit the real requirements of the new professionals that populate the labour market. Social security and continuing training must be the two pillars of welfare reform, taking account of the need for social rights expressed by the new service and information workers. "Long life learning" in particular must be guaranteed to everyone to give opportunities to learn/upgrade skills. This research has crucially demonstrated that what agents learn in call centres has no great marketability elsewhere.

Today the call centre agent has a low status in the labour market; the skills required do not appear to be adequately defined. It would thus be necessary to individuate the new professional figures and provide them with skills upgrading, supported by specific vocational courses to give them career and advancement in all areas and sectors of customer management [11]. It would be useful to set up study courses on communication techniques, sophisticated technologies, teamwork, client management, problem solving. This amounts to structuring of a new profession which means not only training provision but work identity, social recognition, promotion

[11] Donati E. *Fare business con il call centre,* 1999

prospects, systems of skill certification. This would help the employability of these workers in the wider market. In short, it would mean constructing and certifying skills that would be able to be used across the board, for all ICT-based jobs.

If there is a commitment at the public/political level, perhaps in collaboration with companies, the unions will be able to take workers demands ahead. As for the trade union's own action, two results could be aimed for:

- incentives at a national and local level besides those directly in the workplace
- supplement traditional negotiating and collective role with more personalised and specialised individual services

British trade unions offer a good example of these two approaches, with the creation of call centres at the service of call centre agents, or else the Italian Chambers of Commerce located throughout the country where workers can get advice and support for pension, fiscal and legal matters.

An example of a telephone advisory service was launched by FIET in 1998 for "online rights for online workers". Call centres offer considerable possibilities for trade union recruitment and organisation. This is despite the fact that some call centre managements have tried to adopt anti-union policies (even where there are recognition and negotiation agreements with parent banks or insurers). A. Bibby has succinctly described what such an approach could yield: "The right of free access by employees and by trade unions and works councils to corporate e-mail systems, so that employee members can receive information and communicate with their representatives. The right of free access to the Internet (and to corporate intranet networks) by employees, to enable them to access trade union web sites and other information relevant to their rights at work." .

In terms of role outside workplace, we need a thorough revision of relationships between federations of sectors and territorial organisation of trade unions, in other words Cartesian axes (vertical and horizontal) within which trade union organisation has developed, in particular the Italian and French experience. If work is delocalised and dispersed throughout the territory trade unions need to operate accordingly, using territorial representation as a decisive platform for to launch of future organisation potential.

Last but not least, we should not forget that the majority of call centre workers are women. This means that the union must interpret the needs expressed by women workers. Flexible working hours, if sufficiently regulated, can give women opportunities to reconcile working life and

family life. Just as on-site childcare facilities could help women workers deal with shift work when public crèches are closed.
Recent comparative studies show that the provision of services as a motivation to trade union membership is relatively insignificant, whereas the ability to negotiate working conditions and bring about greater identification are much more decisive factors . Thus the European trade union must bring its political and cultural repertoire completely up-to-date, in every instance safeguarding its original heritage, towards a greater freedom, solidarity and democracy, within our advanced societies.

References

Accornero A., Altieri G., Oteri C., *Lavoro flessibile. Cosa pensano davvero imprenditori e manager*, Ediesse, Rome, 2001.

Altieri G., Oteri C., *Atipici, ma quanto?* In Altieri G e Carrieri M (a cura di), *Il popolo del 10%. Il boom del lavoro atipico,* Donzelli, Rome, 2000

Altieri G., *Lavori a distanza*, in "Lavoro Informazione", Rome, n. 22/2000

Altieri G., Oteri C. *La flessibilità chiama il call center risponde*, in "Quaderni Rassegna Sindacale", n. 3 /2001

Bagnara S., Donati E., *Call centres. Un'opportunità per riorganizzare i servizi*, Working Paper for Il Sole 24 ore, February 1999

Beck U., *Risikogesselschaft*, 1986; in It. *La società del rischio*, Carocci, Rome 2000

Bauman Z., *La società dell'incertezza*, in It. Il Mulino, Bologna, 1999.

Behrens M., Fichter M., Frege C., *Unions in Germany*, ILO, 2002

Bibby A., *Organising in financial call centres*, Report for Uni, 2000.

Bibby A., *Negotiating the new economy; the effect of ICT on Industrial Relations*, Working Paper, 2000.

Blaschke S., *Union Density and European Integration: Diverging Convergence*, in "EJIR", n. 2/2000.

Boeri T., Brugiavini A., Calmfors L., *The Role of Unions in the XXI Century*, Oxford University Press, 2001

Bologna S. and Fumagalli A., *Il lavoro autonomo di seconda generazione*, Feltrinelli, Milan, 1997

Bordieu P., *La Distinction, Les Editions de Minuit*, Paris, 1979

Braverman H., *Labor and Monopoly Capital*, "Monthly Reviw Press", New York, 1974.

Burawoy, *Manufacturing consent*, Chicago, Univ. of Chicago Press, 1979

Butera F., Donati E., Cesaria R, *I lavoratori della conoscenza*, F. Angeli, Milan, 1997

Callaghan and Thompson, Edwards Revisited: *Technical Control and Call Centres*, in "Economic and Industrial Democracy", Vol. 22, Sage, 2001

Castells M., *The Rise of the Network Society*, Tr. It., "La nascita della società delle reti", Bocconi Editore, Milano, 2002

Ciacia C., Di Nicola P., *Manuale sulle best practices del telelavoro*, L'officina di Next, 2001, Roma

Crouch C., *Relazioni industriali nella storia politica europea*, Ediesse, 1993;

Datamonitor, *Call centres in EMEA*, 2000;

De Benedetti Foundation, *What do Unions in Europe?* Rapporto della Fond. R. De Benedetti; Naples, 2000;

DG Employment and Social Affairs, *Industrial Relations in Europe* 2000, Brussels, 2001

DG Employment and Social Affairs, *Transformation of labour and future of labour law in Europe*, Final Report, Brussels, 1999

Donati E., *Fare business con il call centres*, paper presented at SMAUComm, 1° Ottobre 1999

Donati E., *I call center: una nuova opportunità di business e di lavoro nell'economia della conoscenza*, paper for "Office Automation" n. 3/ 1999

Dore R., in It. *Bisogna prendere il Giappone sul serio*, Il Mulino, Bologna, 1990;

Ebbinghaus B., Visser J., *The societies of Europe. Trade Unions in Western Europe since 1945*; 2000 ;

Ebbinghaus B., Visser J., *When Labour Institutions Matter: Union Growth and Decline in Western Europe*, 1950-1995, in "European Sociological Review", n. 15/1999;

Edwards, R. *Forms of control in the Labour Process: An Historical Analysis*, in Fischer and Sirriani, "Organisation and Bureaucracy"; Temple University Press, Philadelphia, 1984.

EIRO, *A review of developments in European industrial relations*, European Foundation of Dublin, Annual Review, 2000

EIRR, *Call Centres in Europe*, part one and two, in "European Industrial Relation Review", nn. 320 and 321/2000; IRS, London

EPOC, *Employ Direct Participation in Organisational Change*, European Foundation for improving the working and living conditions working conditions, Dublin, 1999.

European Foundation for improving the working and living conditions; *On industrial relations and change in the EU*, Report of the High Level Group, Jan. 2002.

European foundation for improving the working and living conditions, *Working Conditions in Europe: Third European Survey*, Dublin, 2001 (www.eurofound.eu.iu.)

Euro-Telework, *Report Towards Telework in call centres*, 2000 (www.euro-telework.org)

Flecker J., Kirschenhofer S., *The Emergence Company: case studies report*, 2001 (www.emergence.nu)

Foucault M., *Disciline and Punish: The Birth of the Prison*, Penguin, 1977

Gorz. A., *Metamorfhoses du travail*, Galilée; 1986

Granovetter M., *Economic action and Social Structure: the problem of embeddenes*, in "American Journal of Sociology", n. 3/1985

Heery E., Kelly J., Waddington J., *Union revitalisation in the UK*, ILO, 2002

Hoffman R. and Waddington J., *Trade Unions in Europe*, ETUI, Brussels, 2001

Hoggart R., *The Uses of Literacy*, Pinguin, 1969

Hyman R., Ferner A., *Industrial Relations in the New Europe*, Oxford, Blackwell, 1994

Ichino P., *Il diritto del lavoro e i confini dell'impresa*, in "Giornale di Diritto del Lavoro e delle Relazioni Industriali", n. 2-3/1999

ILO, in It. *Il lavoro nel mondo*, Geneva, 1998

Institute for Employment Studies, *Virtually There: The Evolution of Call Centres*; The Institute for Employment Studies for Mitel, 1999

IRES, *Pratiche di lavoro a distanza: alcuni studi di caso*, Working Paper, n. 12/2000

IRES, *La représenativité syndicale*, numéro spécial IRES, Paris, sept., 2000

Kern and Schumann, *Des Ende der Arbeitsteilung?*, Verlag, Frankfurt, 1984

Landes D.S., *The rise of capitalism*, Macmillan, London, 1966

Lange P. and Scruggs L., *Where have all members gone?*, in "Stato e Mercato", n. 55/1999

Leonardi S., *Flexible Arbeit und Krise der sozialen Repräsentativität der Gewerkschaft*, in WSI Mitteilungen, n. 12/2001

Leonardi S., *Il lavoro coordinato e continuativo: profili giuridici ed aspetti problematici*, in "Rivista Giuridica del Lavoro", n. 3/1999 (see www.ires.it – pubblicazioni/relazioni industriali)

Leonardi, S. *Lavoro, sindacato e classi sociali*, in "Rivista Giuridica del Lavoro", n. 3/2001 (see www.ires.it – pubblicazioni/relazioni industriali)

Leonardi, S., *Parasubordinazione e contrattazione collettiva*, su "Quaderni di Rassegna Sindacale", n. 3/2001 (see www.ires.it – pubblicazioni/relazioni industriali)

Merchants Group, *The 1998 International Call centres Benchmarking*, 1998

Ortoleva P., *La rete, la tecnica, il potere*, in "La tecnologia per il XXI Secolo", Einaudi, Turin, 1998;

Paoli P., *Deuxieme enquete europeenne sur les conditions de travail*; 1996

Richardson R. and Belt W., *Saved by the Bell? Call centres and economic development in less favoured regions* in "Economic and Industrial Democracy", vol. 22, n1/2001, special issue: call centres jobs and regions in the new economy.

Rouilleault H., *The workplace and the workforce in the knowledge based Economy*, presentation at the Employment week 2000, Brussels 8 th November

Sable and Piore, *The second industrial devide*, Basic Book, New York, 1984

Supiot A., *Au de là de l'emploi*, Flammarion, 1998

Taylor P. and Bain P., *Trade Unions and Call Centre*, Survey for Finance Sector Unions, 2000

Touraine A. "Dall'economia di mercato agli attori della produzione" in: A.A.V.V. *La tecnologia del XXI secolo*, Einaudi, Turin, 1998

Tozzi G. A., *Les troubles musculo-squelettriques en Europe: les syndicats en action*, BTS Newsletter, Dossier Special, "Les TMS en Europe"

Trentin B., *La città del lavoro*, Feltrinelli, Milano, 1997;

Van Vooren E., e.a., *Call center Management Benchmark 1999*, Vlerick Management School – Direct Marketing Research Center, BDMV-ABMD, 2000.

Visser J., *Il declino dei sindacati nei paesi industrializzati*, in "IRES Materiali", n. 3/1990

Waddington J., Hoffman R., Lind J., *Sindacato europeo in transizione?,* in "Assistenza Sociale", Rome, n. 2/1999

Western B., *Between class and market: postwar unionisation in the capitalist democracies*; Princeton Univ. Press, 1997;

Training and Human Capital in Companies

CARMINA PÉREZ

Introduction

Companies are undergoing considerable transformation and change, as are the other elements and institutions making up the structure of present societies. This produces new contexts that demand replies in accord with new scenarios (Castells, 1997: 179-227).

A company as an economic and social institution cannot ignore the dynamic of permanent change and transformation, for a variety of reasons. Firstly, because it is one of the primary sources of wealth generation, a fundamental factor for the economic and social welfare of citizens (Sudreau, 1975: 171-179). If the company, via its strategies and policies, does not act in accordance with the requirements of the new economic and market contexts, it is an inefficient company incapable of attaining one of its basic objectives. Furthermore, the company should provide the best working conditions for its employees. To this end, the company has no choice but to put into practice actions that, while bearing in mind the complexity, openness and competition in current markets, seek to reasonably meet the demands produced.

It is no easy matter for a company to attain these objectives in the new contexts, requiring constant adaptation and innovation; on the contrary, it demands a global and concerted attitude from each of the elements that make up the organisation in order to move in the right direction and that most likely to bring business success, though not without uncertainty and risk, inherent aspects of present markets.

One of the elements, among others, to most favour consistency, dynamism, and the company's strategic position in the new contexts referred to, is human capital, the company's human resources. Since the 1940s there has been a growing awareness of the importance of the human factor in a company and its necessary qualification (Monreal, 2001: 718-723). This has found expression in growing investment in education and training, in

confirmation that profitability obtained for the productive system through this was high and not less than that attained form other types of capital found in the company, whether physical or financial (Denison: 1964).
Throughout this fifty-year period, in-company training has come to be valued as a strategic factor for adaptation, innovation and competitiveness in company organisation. Logically, its importance, spread and intensity has not been regular over these 50 years. On the contrary, the mapping out of company competitiveness clearly shows which companies have known how to make a decisive step towards this new company culture (Prieto y Homs, 1995: 572) and those held back by the inertia of tradition. Both behaviours have had very different effects; while in the former case the outcome has been company success, in the latter it has brought with it temporary inefficiency or even definitive closure.
In Spain's case, where economic and company modernisation has taken place side by side with political modernisation, the role of education and training has gradually taken on greater weight in company strategy. Spain's incorporation into the European Union has supposed a significant impulse to education and training, since European culture had human capital sufficiently developed and rooted, so forcing Spanish companies into a swift adoption of this new culture, essential to speak the same language and attain competitiveness in the same markets.
The division of Spain into regions comes from different criteria: historical, administrative, political, cultural and economic (VV AA: 1981). From the economic criterion, the European Union catalogues the Spanish regions into two groups: objective 1 regions (12 of the 17) and the remaining five regions. The former are those that the European Union considers eligible to receive structural funds[1]. The other five regions are those considered by Europe to be more developed and therefore not eligible for this type of funding[2].
Although socio-economic differences are known to exist within each of the groups, this classification of the Spanish regions made by the European Union gives a dual Spain, economically and socially speaking, with different structures and dynamics. This forces differentiated analyses and by regional group, should available statistics allow.

---

[1] The list of Spanish objective nº1 regions is as follows: Andalucia, Asturias, Cantabria, Canary Islands, Castilla-León, Castilla-la Mancha, Extremadura, Galicia, Murcia, Valencia, Ceuta and Melilla.

[2] This group of regions if formed by: Aragon, Catalunya, La Rioja, Madrid and Basque Country.

In our case, it has been possible to analyse the role of training and human capital in companies in relation to objective n°1 Spanish regions [3], the majority, in that the relevant data is available. This allows us to evaluate what training policies and strategies have been applied in less-developed Spain and the perception held on this in relation to company and regional development.

The data analysed below have been obtained from the Research Study "Training and Company Culture in Spanish Objective n°1 Regions" of the research group directed by Professor Juan Monreal (University of Murcia), of which I am a member, and financed by the Ministry for Science and Technology (2001-2003).

The generation of data for the research has come from two field studies: a wide-ranging Questionnaire and Interviews with Privileged Witnesses, both field studies carried out in 2002. The data looked at in this study is only a part of the available Database, given that our interest was exclusively focused upon studying, on the one hand, human capital and company training strategies (First Part of the article), using data from the Questionnaire; and in the Second Part of the article, an examination of the value placed on training by the economic and social agents involved in decision-taking on company training policies. The data used in the latter case comes from the in-depth Interviews carried out.

From the methodological point of view, the samples from each field study are as follows:

For the questionnaire, the sample is made up of 527 companies distributed thus among the categories established: 194 in Industry and Energy, 161 in Construction and 172 in Services[4]. The sample population only includes companies in the industrial and energy sectors with more than 19 employees and, from the construction and market services sectors, those with more than 49 employees. The total number of companies making up the base population for the study has been determined by use of the Central Company Directory (DIRCE) drawn up by the National Institute of Statistics.

Re the Interviews with Privileged Witnesses, the total number of in-depth interviews was 48 throughout the objective n°1 regions. They always included those responsible for training from the following regional Institutions: Administration, Company Organisation, Chamber of

---

[3] Ceuta and Melilla have not been analysed because of their special circumstances.

[4] Agriculture, the primary sector, has not been chosen for the questionnaire sample given that training in the agricultural sector is scarce. The food industry is, however, represented in the sample via the industrial sector.

Commerce, Unions, Institutions and Foundations linked to the Business sphere and private companies that provide training courses.

Human Capital in Companies and Training Strategies

This section analyses the relevant questions re training in Spanish Objective 1 regions using data from the 527 companies' questionnaires. Training of the company's employees and the level of studies and specialised management training of the director or manager are examined, allowing us to ascertain the training level of company personnel. Also examined is the type of training provided in-company, the central issue in this research. Said analysis is carried out via the following questions: objective of training initiatives; type of training used by the company; where training takes place; length of training programmes.

1) Training of Employees in Companies

Between 1% and 5% of employees in companies in the Spanish objective 1 regions are graduates and more than 25% have received Technical Training. (Table 1).

Table 1 - Companies according to percentage of employees with higher-level studies (%)

	Graduates	*Technical Training*
0%	5.1	2.9
1-5%	33.5	18.4
6-10%	24.0	13.6
11-15%	13.6	10.0
16-25%	13.2	20.9
More than 25%	10.6	34.2
Total	***100***	***100***

Source: Questionnaire.

The percentage of employees with higher-level studies is linked to the type of company. Re the proportion of graduates (Table 2), it can be seen that around half the companies from the Industrial (56.4%) and Service sectors (51.6%) have between 1% and 10% graduate employees, whereas in the Construction sector almost half the companies (48.1%) have between 1%

and 5% in the lowest category with said studies. Construction is therefore the sector with fewest qualified employees.

Table 2 - Employees with university-level studies by company activity sector (%)

With no graduate employees	*Industry*	*Construction*	*Services*	*Total*
	7.2	1.9	5.7	5.1
1-5%	26	48.1	28	33.5
6-10%	30.4	16.9	23.7	24
11-15%	15.5	11	14	13.6
16-25%	16.6	9.7	12.7	13.2
More than 25%	4.4	12.3	15.9	10.6
Total	100	100	100	100

Source: Questionnaire.

In the Services Sector, 52.6% of companies have more than 25% of employees with higher level studies; in the Industrial Sector 53.7% of companies have more than 16% with said studies and in the Construction sector the largest number of companies (27%), have only between 1% and 5% (Table 3).

Table 3 - Employees with Technical Training by company activity sector (%)

Without employees with further education	*Industry*	*Construction*	*Services*	*Total*
	2.9	2.6	3.3	2.9
1-5%	16.0	27.0	12.5	18.4
6-10%	16.6	15.8	7.9	13.6
11-15%	10.9	10.5	8.6	10.0
16-25%	24.6	22.4	15.1	20.9
More than 25%	29.1	21,7	52.6	34.2
Total	100	100	100	100

Source: Questionnaire.

Re employee training by sector, we can conclude that the least qualified are those from Construction Sector and those most highly qualified from the Services Sector.

There is also a link between the percentage of trained employees in a company and that company's size. 10% of small companies have no graduate employees; in contrast, to a greater or lesser extent, all large companies have some; the largest percentage of them (37.5%), has between 6% and 10% graduates employees (Table 4).

Table 4 - Employees with university-level studies by company size (%)

	Small	*Medium*	*Large*	*Total*
Without graduate employees	10.0	2.4		5.1
1-5%	23.3	40.6	25.0	33.5
6-10%	26.7	21.2	37.5	24.0
11-15%	14.4	14.2		13.6
16-25%	13.9	11.5	29.2	13.2
More than 25%	11.7	10.1	8.3	10.6
Total	100	100	100	100

Source: Questionnaire.

Re the percentage of employees with Technical Training (Table 5), we can see that it is especially the small companies (37%), that have this type of employee, followed by the medium-sized (33.3%), and finally the large companies (25%).

Table 5 - Employees with Technical Training by company size (%)

	Small	*Medium*	*large*	*Total*
Without university graduate employees	2.9	2.8	4.2	2.9
1-5%	12.7	21.3	25.0	18.4
6-10%	17.9	10.6	16.7	13.6
11-15%	8.1	2.8	8.3	10.0
16-25%	21.4	20.6	20.8	20.9
Moe than 25%	37.0	33.3	25.0	34.2
Total	100	100	100	100

Source: Questionnaire.

2) Specialised Training of the Manager or Director Related to Company Management

Almost half the directors or managers have studied for a Masters degree or specialised course in business administration. This percentage is higher when the company profile is that of Exploratory/Creative as opposed to a Stable/Reactive profile (Table 6); in large companies there is a direct proportional link between size and specialised training of the director or manager; and when the latter has university level studies, 56.1% of those interviewed had also done a specialised course in business administration. (Table 8).

Table 6 - Possession or not of a Masters or other specialised course linked to Business Administration in relation to company culture (%)

	Stable/Reactive	*Foresight*	*Exploratory /Creative*	*Total*
Yes	39.9	47.8	58.9	48.6
No	60.1	52.2	41.1	51.4
Total	100	100	100	100

Source: Questionnaire.

Table 7 - Possession or not of a Masters or other specialised course linked to Business Administration in relation to company size (%)

	Small	*Medium*	*Large*	*Total*
Yes	45.5	49.5	58.1	48.6
No	54.5	50.5	41.9	51.4
Total	100	100	100	100

Source: Questionnaire.

Table 8 - Possession or not of a Masters or other specialised course linked to Business Administration in relation to manager or director's level of studies (%)

	Primary	*Secondary*	*University*	*Total*
Yes	38.1	36.8	56.1	48.6
No	61.9	63.2	43.9	51.4
Total	100	100	100	100

Source: Questionnaire.

3) Level of Studies of the Company Director or Manager

One of the most interesting variables to examine in a company is that of the level of completed studies of the person who, to a large extent, takes the decisions in that company.

There are two factors conditioning the training of the director or manager. One is company size: the size of the company interacts in the same direction as the level of completed studies of the director or manager: the larger the company, the higher the level of completed studies (Table 9).

Table 9 - Level of official (regulated) studies completed in relation to company size (%)

	Small	*Medium*	*Large*	*Total*
Primary	7.3	2.3		4.0
Secondary	34.6	37.0	19.4	35.1
University	58.1	60.7	80.6	60.9
Total	100	100	100	100

Source: Questionnaire.

The other factor is the activity carried out by the company (Table 10): the Service sector is where there are fewest managers with only Primary level studies (2.3%). The Construction sector is where there is the highest level of secondary qualified managers (43.5%); and in the Industrial sector is to be found the highest number of graduates (68.6%).

Table 10 - Level of official (regulated) studies completed in relation to company activity (%)

	Industry	*Construction*	*Services*	*Total*
Primary	5.2	4.3	2.3	4.0
Secondary	26.3	43.5	37.2	35.1
University	68.6	52.2	60.5	60.9
Total	100	100	100	100

Source: Questionnaire.

Finally, it is worth pointing out that 4% of the company directors or managers interviewed have Primary studies only. This circumstance is mostly to be found in small companies and more in the Industrial and Construction Sectors than in the Service Sector. 35.1% of managers have secondary level studies, small and medium-sized companies and the Construction Sector being where this predominates. University graduates are more to be found in large companies and in the Industrial sector, as previously mentioned.

4) Objective of Training Initiatives

Training sought by companies is oriented in two directions. They seek to "Extend and provide knowledge and skills of a general nature" and/or "Extend and provide knowledge and skills directly linked to the activity carried out by the employee in a company". We observe how a company deals with either one objective or the other, on a scale of 1 to 7, that is the degree to which they aim for a general or specific training.

As can be seen from Table 11, the majority of companies provide specific training on the whole, 73.4%; statistically speaking, the number whose objective is not to train for activities of benefit to the work to be undertaken is insignificant: only 1.3% of companies claim to provide training leading to a general qualification.

Table 11 -Objective of training initiatives (%)

1-2 (General training	1.3
3-5	25.3
6-7 (Specific Training)	73.4
Total	100

Source: Questionnaire.

The Sector to which the company belongs conditions the type of training provided, as can be seen from Table 12. It is in the Service sector that most employees receive specific training (78.8%), for the tasks assigned in their post, more than in Industry (73.3%) and Construction (67.7%).

Table 12 - Objective of training initiatives in relation to company activity (%)

	Industry	*Construction*	*Services*
1-2 (General Training)	1,0	1,2	1,8
3-5	25,7	31,1	19,4
6-7 (Specific Training)	73,3	67,7	78,8
Total	100	100	100

Source: Questionnaire.

Where most general training (level on the scale1-2 and 3-5), is to be found is in the Construction sector (32.5%) and Industrial sector (26.7%).
Company size, as well as activity type, also shows differences in the type of training carried out (Table 13). From the questionnaire data, it can be seen that the proportion of specific training is highest in large companies (86.7%).

Table 13 - Objective of training initiatives in relation to company size (%)

	Small	*Medium*	*Large*
1-2 (General Training)	1.1	1.7	
3-5	24.3	27.1	13.3
6-7 (Specific Training)	74.6	71.3	86.7
Total	100	100	100

Source: Questionnaire.

5) Training Systems Used by Companies

Training modes can be roughly divided into two opposing categories At one extreme we have traditional training systems (conferences, seminars….), and at the other advanced distance training systems (Internet, multimedia, virtual…).
Training carried out via the latter (advanced) systems, is of little statistical weight in the companies studied. Only 37.6% of companies have adopted these training modes, representing 15.18% of the training received by employees.
There is a direct proportional relationship between the traditional system of training and the level of studies of the director or manager (Table 14). The greater the level of studies, the more traditional the type of training provided. Conversely, an inversely proportional relationship can be seen

with company size: the larger the company, the less recourse to traditional training systems (Table 15).

Table 14 - Courses using traditional training modes in relation to the studies of director or manager (%)

	Primary	*Secondary*	*University*	*Total*
None	9.5	8.7	3.4	5.5
Up to 50%	9.5	9.2	11.2	10.5
More than 50%	28.6	20.7	21.5	21.5
All	52.4	61.4	63.9	62.5
Total	100	100	100	100

Source: Questionnaire.

Table 15 - Courses using traditional training modes in relation to company size (%)

	Small	*Medium-sized*	*Large*	*Total*
None	5.8	5.9		5.5
Up to 50%	10.5	10.9	6.5	10.5
More than50%	18.8	21.4	38.7	21.5
All	64.9	61.8	54.8	62.5
Total	100	100	100	100

Source: Questionnaire.

The companies from the Construction and Industrial sectors are those that use the more traditional training modes (Table 16). The Service sector, to a greater extent, claims to use none (9.3%), in contrast to 1.5% in the Industrial and 6.3% in the Construction sectors.

Table 16 - Courses using traditional training modes in relation to company size (%)

	Industry	*Construction*	*Service*	*Total*
None	1.5	6.3	9.3	5.5
Up to 50%	10.8	8.1	12.2	10.5
More than 50%	20.1	18.8	25.6	21.5
All	67.5	66.9	52.9	62.5
Total	100	100	100	100

Source: Questionnaire.

6) Place where Training Takes Place and Personnel Providing it

A close link can be seen between these two variables (place and trainer), such that when the majority of training is provided by company employees, the higher percentage given on company premises and vice versa.

So as not to complicate the analysis, although the tables on where training is given are provided (Tables 18, 20, 22, 24), the commentary only refers to the person giving the training, knowing that the variable re place behaves similarly.

Personnel providing training according to:

- Type of company culture: As can be seen in Table 17, with the Stable/Reactive typology there is a greater tendency to rely on trainers external to the company for employee training. In contrast, the greater the number of people linked to the company responsible for training corresponds to the Exploratory/Creative typology. An intermediate position is found when the company culture is that of Foresight.

Table 17 - Percentage of company personnel giving training in relation to company culture (%)

	Stable/Reactive	*Foresight*	*Exploratory/Creative*	*Total*
None	59.5	45.4	43.3	49.2
Up to 50%	27.6	32.2	22.0	27.8
More than 50%	7.4	12.2	14.7	11.4
All	5.5	10.2	20.0	11.6
Total	100	100	100	100

Source: Questionnaire.

Table 18 -Time given over to training, at and away from post in relation to company culture (%)

	Stable/ Reactive	*Foresight*	*Exploratory/ Creative*	*Total*
All away from post	38.7	33.3	40.4	37.1
Up to 50% at post	35.6	35.8	26.5	33.0
More than 50% at post	10.4	15.2	13.9	13.3
All at post	15.3	15.7	19.2	16.6
Total	100	100	100	100

Source: Questionnaire.

Company size. The high percentage of small companies stating that nobody from the company is responsible for providing training is noticeable (61.8%), as opposed to medium-sized (43.1%) and large (32.3%).

Table 19 - Percentage of company personnel giving training in relation to company size (%)

	Small	*Medium*	*Large*	*Total*
None	61.8	43.1	32.3	49.2
Up to 50%	17.8	34.5	22.6	27.8
More than 50%	8.4	10.9	38.7	11.6
All	12.0	11.5	6.5	11.4
Total	100	100	100	100

Source: Questionnaire.

Table 20 - Time given over to training both at and away from post in relation to company size (%)

	Small	*Medium*	*Large*	*Total*
All away from post	42.4	34.2	3.3	37.1
Up to 50% at post	28.8	33.9	45.2	32.7
More than 50% at post	12.0	14.8	12.9	13.7
All at post	16.8	17.1	9.7	16.5
Total	100	100	100	100

Source: Questionnaire.

- Company Activity Sector. The only data of note in this variable (Table 21) is the greater number of companies in the Services sector indicating that all the training is provided by the company's own personnel

(16.9%). In this area, the Industrial sector reports 11.3% and Construction 5.6%.

Table 21 - Percentage of company personnel giving training in relation to company activity (%)

	Industry	*Construction*	*Services*	*Total*
None	51.5	50.6	45.3	49.2
Up to 50%	26.8	30.0	26.7	27.8
More than 50%	10.3	13.8	11.0	11.6
All	11.3	5.6	16.9	11.4
Total	100	100	100	100

Source: Questionnaire.

Table 22 - Time given over to training, at and away from post in relation to company activity (%)

	Industry	*Construction*	*Services*	*Total*
All away from post	39.7	42.2	29.2	37.1
Up to 50% at post	34.0	27.3	36.3	32.7
More than 50% at post	11.3	18.0	12.3	13.7
All at post	14.9	12.4	22.2	16.5
Total	100	100	100	100

Source: Questionnaire.

- Manager or director's level of studies. When the director or manager has finished primary level studies only, the greater is the tendency for training to be provided by personnel within the company (table 23). It is worth highlighting that in 23.8% of companies where the level of studies of the manager or director is to primary level only, 100% of the training is covered in-house and this percentage declines considerably the higher the manager or director's education level.

Table 23 - Percentage of company personnel who give training, in relation to the education level of manager or director (%)

	Primary	*Secondary*	*University*	*Total*
None	28.6	58.7	45.2	49.2
Up to 50%	38.1	21.7	30.5	27.8
More than 50%	9.5	11.4	11.8	11.6
All	23.8	8.2	12,.	11.4
Total	100	100	100	100

Source: Questionnaire.

Table 24 - Time dedicated to training at or away from post, in relation to the education level of director or manager (%)

	Primary	*Secondary)*	*University*	*Total*
All away from post	19.0	39.5	36.9	37.1
Up to 50% at post	38.1	28.1	35.0	32.7
More than 50% at post	14.3	17.8	11.3	13.7
All at post	28.6	14.6	16.9	16.5
Total	100	100	100	100

Source: Questionnaire.

7) Length of Training Activities

Re length of training courses, they have been divided into three categories: fewer than 20 hours, between 20 and 60 hours and longer than 60 hours.

As can be seen from the training activities in table 25, out of the total number of courses given in Spanish no 1 objective regions, 40.9% are what can be termed short courses, a greater number, 47.2% medium length and 11.9% courses of longer than 60 hours.

Table 25 - Length of company training courses (%)

Courses of 20 hours or fewer	40.9
Courses of between 20 and 60 hours	47.2
Courses of longer than 60 hours	11.9
Total	100

Source: Questionnaire.

Below we will examine the characteristics of those companies who claim to provide "all" their training courses within a single category of the three i.e.

20 hours or fewer, between 20 and 60 hours and longer than 60 hours (Tables 26, 27, 28 and 29).
Short courses (of 20 hours or fewer), are most provided in the Construction sector; by those whose manager or director has only Primary level studies; by small companies; and those of "Exploratory/Creative" typology.
Course of between 20 and 60 hours are given most by companies in the Industrial sector; by those whose director or manager has Secondary level studies; by medium-sized companies and those of an "Exploratory/Creative" typology.
The longest course, those of more than 60 hours, are given in the Service sector; by those whose director or manager has University level studies ; by small companies and those that have a "Stable/Reactive profile".

Table 26 - Companies that give all training according to one of the three length categories, in relation to company activity (%)

	Industrial	*Construction*	*Service*
Courses of 20 hours or fewer	33.6	45.1	37.7
Courses of between 20 and 60 hours	55.4	48.3	50.0
Courses of more than 60 hours	11.0	6.5	12.3
Total	100	100	100

Source: Questionnaire.

Table 27 - Companies that give all training according to one of the three length categories, in relation to director or manager's education level (%)

	Primary	*Secondary*	*University*
Courses of 20 hours or fewer	54.6	41.7	35.2
Courses of between 20 and 60 hours	36.3	50.5	53.2
Courses of more than 60 hours	9.2	7.8	11.6
Total	100	100	100

Source: Questionnaire

TABLE 28 - Companies that give all training according to one of the three length categories, in relation to company size (%)

	Small	*Medium*	*Large*
Courses of 20 hours or fewer	37.2	40.9	20.1
Courses of between 20 and 60 hours	50.4	50.9	70.0
Courses of more than 60 hours	12.4	8.2	9.9
Total	100	100	100

Source: Questionnaire.

Table 29 - Companies that give all training according to one of the three length categories, in relation to company culture (%)

	Stable/ Reactive	*Foresight*	*Exploratory/ Creative*
Course of 20 hours or fewer	34.2	41.3	40.2
Courses of between 20 and 60 hours	53.8	47.9	52.6
Courses of more than 60 hours	12.0	10.8	7.3
Total	100	100	100

Source: Questionnaire.

Conclusions

The most significant conclusions from this study are that:

- Companies in the Spanish objective1 regions have a low level of employees with University level studies; the most frequent level of studies is that of Technical Training. The activity sector is related to education level; for example, workers in the Construction sector have lower levels of qualification, whereas the highest level of qualification is found in the Service sector. Company size is also linked to qualification level: there is a direct proportional relation between company size and University level education and inversely proportional between company size and Technical Training.
- Virtually half of directors or managers have done some kind of Master or specialist course related to company management. The percentage is higher when an Exploratory/Creative culture is found, the company is large and when the director or manager has University level studies.
- The manager or director's training is to University level in 60.9% of cases. This increases in line with company size. Re company activity, it is

in Industrial sector where the highest level of studies is to be found and the Construction sector, the lowest. 4% of directors or managers have only Primary level studies; this circumstance is mainly to be found in small companies and more in the Industrial and Construction sectors than in the Service sector.

- The majority of companies provide specific training; statistically speaking, the number where the objective of training is not of direct benefit to the work to be carried out, is insignificant. The company activity sector conditions the type of training given: in the Service sector employees receive most specific training in order to carry out the assigned tasks in their jobs. Likewise, the proportion of specific training is greater in large companies.
- Mostly companies carry out training initiatives via the traditional systems: conferences, seminars... There is direct proportional relation between the use of traditional training systems and the education level of the director or manager: the higher the education level, the greater the use of traditional training modes. The relationship in inversely proportional with the size of the company: as this increases, recourse to traditional modes of training decreases.
- There is a close link between the place where training takes place and the people giving it. The greater amount given by company personnel, the greater the likelihood of it being in-company and vice-versa. Training is mostly given "in-house and by company employees" when the employees linked to the company and entrusted with training belong to the culture type Exploratory/Creative, when the company is large, in the Service sector and when the manager or director has only finished Primary level studies.
- Courses given in Spanish number 1 regions of 20 hours or fewer are more given by companies from the Construction sector, by those whose manager or director has only Primary level education, by small companies and by those who fit the cultural type Exploratory/Creative. Courses of between 20 and 60 hours are mostly provided by companies from the Industrial sector, by companies with a manager or director with Secondary level studies, by medium-sized companies and those that have an Exploratory/Creative profile. Course of more than 60 hours are mostly provided in the Services sector, by those whose manager or director has University level studies, by small companies and by those who have a Stable/Reactive profile.

Evaluation of and Attitude Towards Training

This section analyses the opinions provided by different interviewees, directly or indirectly linked to the world of business or training, on the aspects detailed below and that will allow us to understand the present situation of training and how it is experienced and perceived by workers and company managers.

1) Problems and Lacks Observed in the Area of Training

There are no appreciable differences of opinion on this point between those interviewed; practically everyone agrees upon the aspects we have grouped into nine categories below:

▪ Companies and directors

It is shown that it is quite frequent to find managers and directors lacking training and, in particular, lacking what can be termed an enterprise culture, above all in small companies, family businesses and among autonomous workers.

Very small companies sometimes do not have resources to invest in training, but their very mentality prevents their seeing that investment in human resources could improve competitiveness.

The company must become more involved in the training process, become more aware of its importance and destine more resources to it, at the same time as facilitating access to employees. It is true that training is still seen as a cost rather than an investment.

▪ Co-ordination and organization of training

Those interviewed highlight a lack of organization when it comes to planning courses to be given; there is no planned strategy. Co-ordination and communication between organs is lacking. Close integration of Official Training, At-Post training and Occupational Training is called for.

The Administration worries about administering the budget; thus it complies with its objectives. Objectives need to be set, homogeneous reference points created, criteria established for analysis, planning, co-ordination, evaluation etc. Much time and money is being wasted on giving courses whose benefits cannot be seen. The true objectives that training should be pursuing are not being met; there is no link between the economic and human resources put in and the results obtained.

▪ Control and follow-up of training

When there is control, it is of procedure, when what is called for is quality control. Administration ought to establish requirements, a ruling to set out the development of training activity to attain quality.
Greater control of the trainers is needed and all the activities they carry out. The Administration should dedicate more human resources to this area, as a way of initiating a basic quality control, as much of the product of the training process as a later follow-up on the effects of the training.

- Territorial inequalities

Training is quite centralized, unevenly distributed between the rural and urban areas. Courses are concentrated in the large population centres, which contributes to the maintenance of territorial inequalities.
A re-distribution and application of different training modes is needed, in accord with different zone needs.

- Observation and studies of the labour market

The training currently offered does not meet the needs of the labour market. Because of the lack or an Observatory, decisions taken on this aspect re courses to give are taken by intuition, without a true understanding of active employment policies.
Those interviewed commented on the need for an Observatory to ensure training is structured systematically, in a rational manner. The economy is so volatile, that this must be borne in mind to enable training to be constantly adapted to the changes arising. An Observatory is necessary, therefore, to periodically examine the company fabric, company demand, training offers, etc. and to make strategic plans with a long term perspective on new employee profiles; whenever possible, anticipation of future needs is called for.

- Bureaucratizisation and Infrastructure

One of the problems of subsidised training is bureaucratic rigidity; excessive conditions are set in order to give certain teaching in specific sectors or occupations, sometimes making this unviable. Guidelines on this aspect should be made more flexible. There should also be more flexibility re specialisms to be given and where they may be given, since training has to adapt to the needs of the labour market.
There is no correspondence between the economic assignments and the cost of infrastructure needed to give the courses and these do not always have access to the necessary financing.

Lack of resources and financing limits the possibility of offering specialised courses. It is suggested that the Administration should intervene so that the infrastructure of Technical Training colleges could also be used to provide occupation Training and In-Post training.

- Finance

Training is often seen as a business, an uncontrolled business, a situation that favours poor training. Many interests have arisen around the funds available for training; some of those interviewed believe it always enriches the same groups.

Courses are offered thinking more of the resources available and profitability than the real needs demanded. There is an excess of courses that frequently are of no use or quality. The general perception is that the resources invested by the Administration are not being well used; managers with clear criteria are needed rather than politicians, as the external financing is often considerable and funds are not always reaching the courses.

- Employment and training offers

All those interviewed repeatedly stress that the employment offer is unsatisfactory. Employment offers related to trades greatly exceed demand, which often leads to completely unqualified people being contracted; even so, there are uncovered posts in many trades. There is a lack of builders, plasterers, crane drivers, excavator drivers, plumbers, workers related to the construction industry in general, catering and graphic arts; in the metal sector there is a lack of specialised solderers, fitters, boilermakers, lathe operators, milling machine operators, solderers, platers....

Good training is offered for many of these trades and an almost guaranteed job, because there is fierce competition between employees for these workers, even so, many of the courses do not fill all places.

- Deficiencies observed in training

Re Technical Training there is discontent at various levels: it is emphasized that the official system is out-dated, there is too much theory; this is true for training in general, but in the official system even more so. The teaching is not co-ordinated with company needs and does not sufficiently deal with trades, provided for mostly through Occupational Training. The problem stems from the fact that this training is not recognised: there are people with diplomas from Workshop Schools, the Training for Professional Insertion Plan (FIP) and Employment Plans that are not

recognised qualifications. Quality training that provides prestige for the qualification received is needed.
In Technical Training, there is a lack of information technology: computer programmes, Internet, e business and the new communication technologies in general. Apart from technology questions, the area of modern languages is also weak, needing planning and quality control.
On the other hand, it is also pointed out that Technical Training does not prepare students to work from the viewpoint of co-operation, to work as a team, to work in a co-operative fashion.
Re non regulated education, those interviewed point out as weaknesses that not all sectors of the population have access to it, often those under 25 with few qualifications, those over 45 and women are excluded. There is also a lack of courses designed for company heads. Re areas covered by training, important structural weaknesses are pointed out in the Industrial and Primary sectors, as well as jobs calling for specialisation.
Re Occupational Training it would be as well to make the following observation: some of those interviewed highlighted the importance of providing a basic training, not just a technical training linked to the trade, but a general cultural preparation in that, normally, the level of students attending this training is low, they arrive with many gaps, lacks that sometimes prevent their accessing the knowledge with clarity. For the most part, the trainees are young people who do not wish to continue at school and want to try something different; they tend to be poorly motivated or unemployed people who are compelled to attend in order to receive benefits.
Finally, those interviewed pointed out the need to increase the training of employees, those in work; maintenance and up-dating courses are needed to improve their post in the company.

2) Attitude of Employers to Training

Among those interviewed, it is widely recognised that there is a change of mentality re training among employers; in general terms a certain cultural change is perceptible. Company owners are starting to see the fundamental role of training; they now understand it is an investment and that, at least partly, the future lies in it. However, they are only interested in training that directly influences the productive system of their company; they see it only as a productivity element, as an investment, not as a kind of professional equipment in line with the personal expectations of the worker, as this may well imply a demand for promotion or a change of job or sector.

The entrepreneur does not deny the importance of training, but as a general rule does not wish to invest in it; it is still considered a cost and they are not willing to free their employees from hours at post in order to receive training. Subsidised training given outside working hours always meets with the approval of employers.
Large companies are obliged to include in-house training courses; agreements are signed with the Unions that compel them to provide training; they have their own training departments and invest in training for which they are well subsidised. Recently, workers have also managed to be entitled to receive some of this training in work time, but the employers are not willing for this to happen and the Unions point out that it remains difficult to negotiate.
In contrast, small and medium-sized companies continue to see training as a cost more than an investment; they are reluctant to undertake it and also have fewer resources and less training infrastructure.
Different experts interviewed coincide in pointing out that commitment and investment in training depends on company size, company sector, specific company activity and the training of the owner. If it is the Unions who mostly draw attention to the high percentage of owners who remain unaware of the importance of training to the company and employees, who see it as a threat, because the worker might leave the company, ask for a higher salary, change of status… and they are unwilling to ease this; generally there is limited collaboration.
Those private companies interviewed who provide training are those who claim with most enthusiasm the importance of training for the company's future development, whether large or small and the positive change in attitude of owners towards it. However, like the Unions, they recognize that companies treat training not acquired on the premises with suspicion and that training is provided when it is free. Thus, a company owner give the following opinion: "I am convinced that if FORCEM (Official training organisation in Spain) were to disappear right now, many of the companies who are providing training would cease to do so".
Company owners recognise that small companies are not yet convinced of the importance of training, taking it as a cost as well as seeing it as an expense they cannot always afford. Generally, it is only a minority of companies who see training as an investment, only those leaders in the production sectors.
From its privileged pinnacle, the Chambers of Commerce detect a positive evolution re training and the existence of considerable preoccupation among companies in this respect, but the working day remains untouchable.

They generally believe that the attitude towards training has changed, mostly in recent years. However, there is a mix of everything: owners who see training as an expense and those who see it as an investment. There are owners who view training as an obligation they have to meet, possibly because they have signed an agreement with FORCEM or other agents subsidising training and then do not worry if the training is suitable or not for the worker, it is something they do as a matter of routine, not because it forms part of a strategy where training is seen as fundamental.
The age of the owner influences the assessment of training. A new mentality is arising that gives greater value to having trained employees. Companies with development prospects and those linked to the new technologies are also the most motivated. The same happens in large companies, where the interest comes from the employer and employee alike; not so in the small companies where the problem is dual: mentality and economic resources.
Representatives from the Administration interviewed place special emphasis on the role to be played by the Administration in raising awareness re training. They must know how to transmit the importance of training for the labour market. An effort has been made in this direction and the results are beginning to be felt. Company owners are changing, coming to place more trust in the Administration and training; evidence for which, in the opinion of those interviewed, can be found in the number of applications and volume of activities administered. A lot of money is requested for training issues, which goes to show the growing awareness and sensitivity of companies in this area. However, those interviewed point out that it is not an easy question and permanent contact with company owners is necessary for them to believe in training.
Company owners also coincide in pointing out the fact that the age of the businessman, the company sector and its size all determine the way of looking at training, as previously highlighted.
The institutions and foundations linked to the world of the companies interviewed, as well as the Administration, also put emphasis on the change observed in the attitude of company owners. Some years ago an offer of free courses was made and there was a full rejection; today, on the other hand, they take an interest in them and actively participate, some even collaborating in their financing, though this depends upon the profile of the businessman, the technological content of the company and its size

3) Attitude of Workers to Training

We will now look, through the experts interviewed, at the attitude of workers towards training and their assessment of it.

The general opinion is that the majority of workers show an increasing appreciation of training, while at the same time having higher expectations, seeking quality and genuine usefulness. There has been a tendency to move away from a rather negative perception to a more positive perception and one of greater involvement.

The majority of workers are aware of the interest of training for their curriculum, their working future and their personal development. They see it as necessary, whether to maintain their job, to change job or company or to achieve promotion or get employment.

It is above all young people who have a most open mentality, are most highly qualified, who most ask for training, who are most aware of its importance and most eager to receive and participate in training initiatives. Older people, workers in small companies in rural areas and those who have a low training profile are the most reticent. However, if they are given prior information, if the importance of training is explained to them and later they are offered good quality courses, their attitude to training changes, according to the company experts consulted.

Those interviewed from the Administration and institutions and foundations, distinguish between workers who decide to undertake training voluntarily and those who are obliged to do so by their company. The former attend courses with high motivation, whereas the latter have a negative attitude, unless the training provides a high level of qualification or specialisation. They are basically afraid in the face of a situation frequently unknown to them and this prevents their accepting the training.

The most satisfactory training is that which is relevant to the post, is given in work hours and on work premises because it is seen as the most useful. Training outside working hours supposes effort on the worker's part that not all are willing to make; this is the problem for employees in small companies. Only large companies can free their employees in work hours to receive training, not that they are very willing to do it; there is a mix of attitudes on this.

Unions point out that they, the Administration and the employers should all make an effort to raise awareness, to make employees appreciate the benefits that training brings at both a professional and personal level. In any case, the experts interviewed confirm that applications, interest and awareness of the courses on offer are all increasing.

Conclusions

Re problems and lacks identified in the training area

1. Company owners lack an entrepreneur culture, especially the small owner, whether they have resources to invest in training or not, whose mentality prevents their seeing training as an investment in human resources that will really be beneficial for the company and its workers.
2. There is a lack of co-ordination and communication among the different agents involved in training, as well as a planned strategy. Training lacks objectives and homogeneous reference with respect to criteria for analysis, planning, co-ordination, evaluation etc.; this means that the profitability of the many economic and human resources mobilised in training initiatives is not perceived.
3. The Administration should seek quality in all training initiatives. In order to achieve this, more resources need to be dedicated to control and follow-up, both of the teaching and the activities undertaken, as well as the after-effects of training.
4. Training is unevenly distributed between urban and rural areas. Courses are mostly concentrated in large population centres; re-distribution of training is called for and the application of different modes according to the differing needs of each area.
5. An Observatory is needed so that training can be rationally structured. This would allow for periodic evaluation of company fabric, company demand, training offers, etc., and so make strategic plans adapted to the new professional profiles and which, wherever possible, would anticipate future needs.
6. Too many conditions are put for the provision of certain teaching connected to specific sectors or occupations, that sometimes makes them unviable; the Administration should be more flexible re its demands. On the other hand, a lack of resources or equipment limits the possibility of offering specialised courses.
7. Many interests have arisen around the economic funds given to training. Training is frequently seen as a business, which means that courses are offered bearing more in mind the resources available and their own profits, rather than the real needs of the training demand. The general impression is that the resources invested by the Administration are not being well used.
8. Recurrently, the question of the employment offer not being met comes up. Job offers related to trades amply exceed supply; there are many

posts uncovered in many trades. Training must bear these needs in mind, but the problem lies in the fact that in spite of offers of training courses that virtually guarantee integration into the labour market, places are not always taken up.

9. Re Technical Training it is pointed out: it is excessively theoretical, it is not connected to the needs of companies, it does not sufficiently cover trades and that it has serious areas of weakness, one of these being that of the new technologies. Re non-regulated education, the following weaknesses are highlighted: it does not reach all sectors of the population, Industrial and Primary sectors are insufficiently catered for, as are occupations requiring specialisation.

Attitude of employers to training

10. In general terms, a change of mentality is perceptible. Owners are beginning to see the fundamental role of training, though they are only interested in that with direct bearing upon the productive needs of their company that which is subsidised and which is given outside working hours
11. Whether there is a commitment to and investment in training depends upon the size of the company, the age and training of the owner, the company sector and the specific company activity; in general, however, owners are not prepared to make things easy and there is little collaboration.

Attitude of employees to training

12. Generally, workers are aware of the interest of training for their curriculum, their working life and their personal development. They are quite demanding and seek quality and genuine usefulness. The most satisfactory training is that which has direct relevance to their job.
13. Above all, it is young people and those most highly qualified who have a most open mentality, who most ask for training, are most aware of its importance and most willing to receive and participate in training processes. Older people, workers in small companies in rural areas and those with a low training profile are the most reticent in the face of training.

References

Castells, M. (1996): *The Information Age: Economy, Society and Culture*, Vol.I: The Rise of the Network Society, Cambridge, Massachusetts, Blackwells Publishers, Inc.

Denison, F. (1964): "*Measuring the contribution of education (and the residual) to economic growth*", en OCDE, *The residual factor and economic growth*, OCDE, Paris.

Monreal, J. (2001): "*Capital humano y cultura empresarial en el cambio de las sociedades*" en: Estructura y cambio social, Madrid, CIS.

Prieto, C. and Homs Oriol (1995): "*Formation, emploi et compétitivité en Espagne*", Revue Sociologie du Travail, n°4/95.

Sudreau, P. (1975): *La réforme de l'entreprise*, Paris, La Documentation Française.

VV AA (1981): *La España de las Autonomías*. Pasado, Presente y Futuro, Madrid, Espasa-Calpe.

Sustainable Entrepreneurship and Quality of Work.

A Capability Approach of Sustainable Rural Development

LAUGE BAUNGAARD RASMUSSEN

Introduction

Sustainable Entrepreneurship (SE) has becoming more and more in focus during the last decade, not at least due to different types of crises in European, rural areas. Many rural areas have been facing deepening economic, social, cultural and environmental crises during the last decades. In *economic* terms, the Gross Value of production (GVP) grewed constantly from 1950 to the late 1980's. But from the early 1990's it changed to stabilisation and in some areas even stagnation and decline (Ploeg et.al. 2002). There are several reasons for this development such as the falling prices of wheat, the increasing environmental restrictions and the sharp increase of transaction costs and energy costs. (Buckwell, 1997; Ploeg et.al., 2002). From a *social* viewpoint, the transformation of family and gender values has initiated a redefinition of relationships between men, women and children. Patriarchy has come under attack, and this trend has challenged the traditional patterns of family work, sexuality and relationships between elder and younger generations (Castells, 2000). The majority of the younger generations grown up in rural areas have preferred or been forced to leave the countryside and move to the smaller or main cities. This trend has also created a decline of *cultural identity* in rural areas and a feeling of not being given a fair share of the possibilities compared to those in the cities. Finally, the *environmental* situation has become aggravated by an over-reliance on pesticides, agricultural chemicals, artificial fertilizers and heavy farm machinery.

In general, the majority of the literature have focused on the problem of regenerating the economies at the countryside by introducing incentives to initiating corporate or family based economic activities. In this article we will focus on two additional aspects closely related to the regeneration process: (1) How are sustainable entrepreneurship and quality of work related to each other?, and (2) Which capabilities should be available to establish sustainable entrepreneurship and work quality in European, rural areas?

The following section presents a brief overview of the crises and challenges facing many European, rural areas. Then follows a discussion of the concept 'Sustainable Entrepreneurship' (SE) and its relevance for rural development. After that, the concept of 'work quality' is defined and discussed in relation to a SE-perspective. Finally, a capability approach, inspired by Nussbaum (2000), promoting sustainable entrepreneurship and work quality in European, rural areas is developed and discussed in relation to the opportunities and barriers of promoting sustainable innovations in rural areas.

Rural Development

- exogenous and endogenous approaches

During most of the former century, the conventional development trajectory of rural areas was providing food for the cities, in which capital and labour were increasingly concentrated. Cities were supposed to function as the core of specialised, regional economies, while rural areas were supposed to be dominated by large and technically advanced farms and agro-industries. The state sponsored modernisation of rural services focused on development of commercial units able to invest in new technologies and eliminate small and marginal holdings. The aim was to enhance the integration of rural enterprises into national and international markets and thus strengthen the economic activities in the rural areas. However, even areas of highly commercialised agriculture seemed destined to lose population. Stripped of still more economic and cultural activities, especially young people continued the movement to the cities, which were a clear sign of marginality and remoteness. Rural areas were believed to be technically, economically, socially and culturally distant from the urban centres of activity. They were described as 'lagging behind'. The strategy of agricultural industrialisation seemed to intensify the flow of labour out of the rural areas and pressed the rural population towards the cities as it has done before.

A second phase of rural policies, therefore, emphasised the attraction of new types of industries to rural areas. Manufacturing enterprises were encouraged to relocate from urban areas. In addition, improvements in transportation and communication possibilities should convince people in rural areas, that it would be possible to stay and still enjoy the benefits of modern technical and social services. However, that second phase of modernisation of rural areas was not quite successful neither from an economic nor from a social point of view. Some firms used regional policy incentives to locate either capital intensive or low wage companies, which offered little to the local economy in the way of transmission af entrepreneurship, skill formation, or reinvestment of profits: "*..Terms such as 'branch plant economy', 'dependent development' and 'industrialization without growth' were coined to highlight the incorporation of such regions within the global business logic of firms governed elsewhere; a logic working against any self-governing and self-sustaining regional economic development.* " (Amin, 1993 : 2). Based on these experiences, a counter-movement of endogenous approaches to rural development began to grow in significance. According to Picchi, endogenous development is to be understood as: "*...local development produced mainly by local impulses and grounded largely on local resources*"(Picchi, 1994 : 195). Picchi cites the following aspects as critical to endogenous development in the Emilia-Romagna Region: an extensive network of small- and medium-sized enterprises; the cultural orientation towards self-employment; the ability of labour to engage in new economic activities; provision of capital and labour from the agricultural sector to non-agricultural businesses; a set of political / institutional incentives that help to strengthen endogenous patterns of development. Other examples are the rural Wales, the Irish Gaeltacht, the Scottish Highlands and Islands, the Danish Island, Funen; and mountain community projects in Italy. However, it would be erroneous to describe the development as a substitution of endogenous for exogenous development. The crucial issue is the balance of external and internal elements (Olbertz, 2002; Ploeg and Long, 1994; Lowe, Murdock and Ward, 1994). This discussion started already with Marshall's concept of 'industrial districts (Marshall, 1890 and 1927) noting the economies of spatially agglomerated small firms located in particular 'industrial districts' (Johannisson, 2000; Lundvald, 1996; Lorenz, 1992) Specific agro-industrial districts are characterised by a growing integration between food production, processing and retailing. Many of them consist of clusters of small towns surrounded by rural regions with networks between farms, processors, distributors and retailers. It allows the non-agricultural enterprises of the food chain to remain within the regional economy rather than being captured by exogenous companies. (Lowe, Murdock and Ward,

1994). This network approach emphasizes an economy, in which: *"...transactions occur neither through discrete exchanges nor by administrative fiat, but through networks of individuals or institutions engaged in reciprocal, preferential and supportive actions....Complementarity and accommodation are the cornerstones of successful production networks."* (Cooke and Morgan, 1993 : 544) . However, some of these strong and successful European regions find themselves going through a typical *crisis of maturity* (Amin, 1999). They seem to lack a strategic convergence between the different actors at the macro, meso and micro levels (Garibaldo, 2003a). How is it possible to overcome such crises and develop new initiatives to sustaining a cross-sector oriented culture of entrepreneurship?

Sustainable Entrepreneurship as a Strategy for in Rural Development

The term 'Sustainable Entrepreneurship' is here defined as a *mindset* as well as a *process* to develop new activities by blending creativity, social and environmental responsibility, cultural heritage and economically sound management, within a new or an existing organisation or network. It is relevant for firms in all sectors, for small and large firms, for firms with different ownership structures as well as for non-profit given organisations and networks.

The term 'sustainability' is frequently used by politicians, planners and grassroots, but not so often questioned or defined in more operational terms. 'Sustain' implies that something last for a longer period. But what does it really mean to make something sustainable, and what is going to be sustained? – our environment, the survival of human beings, traditional cultures in rural areas including work and everyday life? Does sustainability means that everything should be preserved as it is or re-established, if it has gone or disappeared? If so, it would be a conservative and anti-change perspective, which would have no chance to cope with the developments imposed from external and internal factors. In addition, it would then be a contradiction in terms to combine 'sustainability' and 'entrepreneurship', precisely because the latter term is associated with organisation of innovation and change. Already Marshall (1842-1924) stressed four factors of production: land, capital, labour and organisation. Organisation is the factor, which brings the other factors together. The entrepreneurs, according to Marshall, are the driving forces behind such a coordination, because they are the innovators and willing to undertake the risks to implement innovations. Consequently, entrepreneurs see an opportunity, make reliable forecasts, evaluate the risks according to the possible benefits and perform natural leadership. Schumpeter (1883-1950) considered entrepreneurship as the 'primary engine of economic development'. According to Schumpeter, entrepreneurs are people with the ability to innovate new combinations, which may result in new methods of production, new products or product qualities, new markets, new resources for raw material or intermediate goods or a new organisational form. (Schumpeter,1934, 1951). Schumpeter, like Marshall, combined the role of the innovator with the role of being a 'gifted leader'. However, later studies (Sabel, 1992; Lorenz, 1992; Putham, 1993; Freeman, 1997; Woolcook, 1998) have concluded, that the quality of the enduring and developing relationships, which an entrepreneurial enterprise maintains with employees, business partners, customers, knowledge centres and public authorities, is decisive to entrepreneurial success. For instance, in a study from US, Sabel (1992) stressed the importance of creating trust by bringing in consultants in order to make groups of firms capable of re-defining their collective interests paving the way for a new quality of trust building. Lorenz (1992), in a study of the Lyon Region in France, showed that a 'partnership' strategy, based on agreements on quality of work between the client firms and the subcontractors tends to promote the qualities of trust and cooperation. Thus the non-economic factors for the performance of entrepreneurship have become more and more visible in the literature of economic sociology. An example is Putham (1993), who adopted the concept of 'social capital' as an extension of the classical economists' use of 'physical capital' (i.e. assets that generate income) and the neo-classical economists' introduction of 'human capital' (provided by the means of education and training for instance). According to Putman, social capital means "*...features of social organisation, such as networks, norms, and trust, that facilitate action and cooperation for mutual benefit*" (Putham, 1993: 35-36). It represents a set of social norms and networks, which influence the exchange-relations and creative activities among social actors in the society (Woolcock, 1998). An example of a combined mobilisation of physical, human and social capital is the strategy of '*Multi-functional Agriculture*'. This paradigm has rapidly emerged as a strategy for regeneration of European, rural areas. It was mentioned already in 1992 at the Rio Earth Summit and was further developed as a strategy by OECD in 1998. In the EU Agenda 2000 Framework, which outlines the development of joint agricultural policies over the years 2000-2007, the multi-functional principles are stated as follows:

- *The multi-functionality of agriculture, i.e. its varied role over and above the production of foodstuff. This implies the recognition and encouragement of the range of services provided by farmers.*
- *A multi-sector and integrated approach to the rural economy in order to diversify activities create new sources of income and employment, and protect the rural heritage.*
- *Flexible aids for rural development, based on subsidiarity and promoting decentralisation, consultation at regional, local and partnership levels.* (From http://europa.eu.int/comm/dg06/rur/*index_en.htm*>, *European Commission website)*

Generally, the proponents of multi-functionality are pointing to benefits like vitality of rural communities through maintenance of family farming, cultural heritage, rural employment, and skill enhancement. In addition, other benefits are mentioned like animal welfare, food quality, food safety, biological diversity, soil and water health, bio-energy, landscape, recreation and tourism.
These aspects of rural development have been structured as follows:

- *Deepening* of the agro-food supply chain
- *Broadening* of rural activities
- *Re-grounding* of resource mobilisation

(Ploeg et.al., 2002)

The *deepening* process of the agro-food supply chain includes for instance activities such as organic farming, the production of high quality products, on-farming processing and direct marketing. The idea is to deliver products that entail more value added per unit and allow the producers to increase their profits provided they fit better with the demands of the consumers (Marsden et.al., 2000; Ploeg et.al, 2002). The *broadening* of rural activities refers for instance to agro-tourism, management of nature and landscape, new on-farm care-activities and production of energy. Such activities make it possible to enlarge the income flows of the farm enterprises as long as they imply the delivery of goods and services, which consumers and societal institutions are willing to pay for.
An example is the integration of care activities on farms: "*Experiences from care farms indicate that mentally ill or disabled people are better able to develop their physical and intellectual potentials in an agricultural/farm context. Working with animals, gardening, and working on the land is no longer seen by care providers as monotonous, but as appealing,*

encouraging independence among clients and enhancing the quality of (therapeutic) labour" (Oostindie, 2002)
The socio-economic impact of care-farming is still limited in Europe. However, many care-farmers combine care activities with other rural development activities, such as organic production, small-scale processing, direct marketing through farm shops and nature/landscape management. The *re-grounding* process of resource mobilisation includes for instance off-farm incomes like job outside the farm or new forms of cost reduction like 'low external input agriculture', in which purchase of external inputs are reduced and internal inputs simultaneously increased (Ploeg et.al, 2002).
An example from Denmark illustrates the local perspectives of such an approach . A local knowledge centre, Baaring Folk High School at Northwest Funen, has decided to establish a Centre for Coast Culture (CfCC) to promote a sustainable development of the region of Funen. The objectives of CfCC is to:

- *"..improve the understanding of the human and cultural traditions of the history of Northwest Funen*
- *create a basis for experiences of the regional nature along the coast and areas near the coast.*
- *Increase the understanding of the cultural and natural values related to the coast and near-coast areas.*
- *To establish partnerships across the particular interests related to the coast and near-coast surroundings as well as improvement of sustainable development within agriculture, fishing, industries and tourism."* (Ottesen, 2003 :3, translated by LBR)

CfCC intends to create new networks within the local community through creation of partnerships between actors or agents from business, education, grassroots and public institutions. These kinds of partnerships should enhance the social, economic, environmental and cultural sustainable development of the region. For instance, they can initiate projects. which create new jobs, include local people with special handicaps, improve the environmental conditions of the region and enhance the cultural identity of the local population (Scheer, 2002). CfCC will involve local enterprises, voluntary organisations, institutions and public authorities in partnerships and networks, which address local challenges of combining economic, social, cultural and environmental concerns. It is a point to connect CfCC to a Danish Folk High School, which is acknowledged for it's 'catalyst' functions in the region of Northwest Funen. In such an environment, CfCC will be seen as a new initiative building on the entrepreneurial and networking experiences of the people employed at Baaring Folk High School, but also as a possibility of developing these activities even further on. The opportunities of mobilising adequate skilled people, material resources and combining them into viable networks depend on one or several regionally based 'dynamos' like a Folk High School or a similar, regionally based knowledge centre. CfCC is an illustrative example of combining exogenous and endogenous strategies in a regional context. Like other endogenous approaches, CfCC intends to focus on the (re)vitalisation of the regional cycles of economic, social, cultural and environmental activities, creating synergy and strategic convergence between business activities, culture, environment and improved social life / work conditions by considering the natural and human resources of the region as it's basic 'materials' for development. However, CfCC is exogenously oriented too. For instance, Baaring Folk High School has already well established networks with regions for instance in Romania, China, India, South Africa and Chile. These *inter-regional networks* promote cultural and educational interrelationships based on mutual exchange of teachers and students and fund-raised resources of specialist knowledge and money to build 'dynamo' centres in the foreign regions like it has been developed at Northwest Funen. In addition, CfCC will also be based on networking with several Universities of Denmark as well as other Centres for Coast Culture in Scandinavia and other parts of Europe. Finally, the intension of CfCC is also to function as a 'cultural lighthouse' attracting new, sustainable companies and institutions to Funen.

Entrepreneurship and Quality of Work in Rural Areas

The relationships between company strategies and quality of work have been analysed in the literature of industrial sociology and management theory. In particular from the early 1990s, the connection between innovative company strategies, new forms of organisations and quality of work has earned itself growing recognition in the European Union (Arzeni and Pellegrin, 1997; Bettis and Hitts,1997). The documents of the European Commission, such as the EU Green paper on 'Partnership for a New Organisation of Work'(1997) underline the role of work organisation for the improvement of competitiveness and the increase of employment. In Lisbon in 2000, The European Council defined its objectives in terms of employment, economic reform and social cohesion. In 2001, The European Council agreed on a strategy for sustainable development and added an environmental dimension to the Lisbon strategy. The Council recognised the need for radical transformation of the economy, in order to create some 15 million new jobs by 2010 (COM (2000)
9. final) At the Barcelona Spring Council in 2002, the Council took note of the Commission's intention to present a Green paper on Entrepreneurship in Europe (COM, 2003) 27 final) The importance of entrepreneurship for jobs and growth, through knowledge, innovation and business dynamism has been reaffirmed in the Commission's 2003 Spring Report (COM (2003) 5).

Because the crises, observed in European, rural areas, contain economic, social, cultural and environmental aspects, the new responses to overcome these crises must take these four aspects into consideration too.

- The *economic* dimension of sustainability includes a profitable production and sales of products and services in short and long terms.
- The *social* dimension of sustainability focuses on satisfactory employment and working life conditions.
- The *cultural* dimension of sustainability defines beliefs of identity according to acceptable values
- The *environmental* dimension of sustainability comprehends the possibilities of regeneration of natural resources and protection of the needs of the future generations.

An example may clarify, how economic, social, cultural and environmental aspects of work quality are reflected by a sustainable oriented entrepreneur. Henrik, a dairy engineer with a craftsman background, was manager at a large dairy until 1999. His work was purely administrative, but in 1999 he became weary of 'all that paper work' and of working in a large organisation 'with little freedom'. He felt it unsatisfactory for a craftsman working with computer controlled cheese production, in which one does not 'come close to the milk'. In 2000 he established a little, organic cheese creamery together with a farmer. He wanted to produce a better quality of cheese products by using the artisan way of producing cheese. Which qualities of work were significant to Henrik, when he made his decision to shift from a manager position in a large dairy to be an entrepreneur in a small dairy? *Firstly,* he was concerned that he was able to produce a better quality of cheese by using the artisan method compared to the automated mass-production. He wanted to produce a product, which would be evaluated as a high quality product. He found some recipes of traditional cheese production, which has been given up in the 1970s, because they were not suitable for mass-production. He began to feel himself as part of an artisan culture and felt it very satisfactory being able to use his skills as a craftsman again to produce a high quality cheese product. *Secondly,* he wanted to shift from conventional to organic cheese production, because he believed that it was more in accordance with his concern for environmental sustainability. According to Henrik, environmental concerns are not something in addition to quality of working life, but a 'must', if he should be able identify himself with his work. *Thirdly,* he prefers to be a part of a small dairy and an entrepreneurial teamwork with a spirit of experimentation and innovation. He really likes the challenge to build up a new factory from the very beginning working creatively with product as well as process development. He believes, that his knowledge and skills as a craftsman and engineer are matched much better with the job requirements as an entrepreneur than as an administrative manager in a large, automated cheese dairy. *Fourthly,* he anticipated, that he could sell the high quality cheeses to a higher price than the industrialised cheese products. The values of sustainable entrepreneurship play a core role in Henrik's imagination of work and employment quality. It is clearly a matter of professional as well as personal satisfaction. So is the communication with the consumers. School classes and other groups are invited to come and see and hear about the creamery. In this way it has become a meeting place for communication and discussions of certain life style values and how the people at the Creamery have tried to realise these values. It functions as a social catalyst for development and shaping of identity and meaning. At the same time it is a kind of social experiment. In addition, it is also a way of making the consumer aware of the qualities of the product, and to convince them buying these products. Industrialism developed a mindset seeing work as a purely economic activity. Sustainable entrepreneurs like Henrik see work as a social, cultural and environmental activity as well. The ability to determine one's own job content as well as a certain amount of flexibility appear to create personal satisfaction and partly to outweigh possible monetary disadvantages compared to a manager position in a larger company. This tendency is confirmed by Welter and Peistrup (1999) in their six case studies carried out in Germany: "*The subjective quality of work depends on a number of different elements such as the kind of activity in terms of degree of specialisation, the motivation of the self-employed and/or the working family, the satisfaction with the household situation as well as professional satisfaction of owners and the 'external' employees. Self-employment and employment in micro-enterprises conceal a huge array of different economic and social situations which render any generalisation problematic.*" (Welter and Peistrup, 1999 : 27). Even if a strict generalisation from case studies is ‚problematic', at least they indicate that lower work quality cannot per se be associated with smaller companies. Personal networks and the psychic and physical assistance provided by partners and/or family members seem to play a major role in determining the subjective feeling of work quality. Small farm creameries contribute to revitalise the spirit of entrepreneurship from the period of the origin of the Danish dairy cooperatives in the 1880's and 1890's. These small farm creameries, focusing on cheese recipes not suitable for mass-production, do not compete directly with the large, multinational cooperatives, because they create their own niche markets consisting of consumers, who accept to pay a higher price for a better product quality. Their real competitors are the small cheese producing creameries for instance in Italy, France and The Netherlands. A number of organic farm dairies and farm creameries have been established in Denmark during the last decades, despite the fact that more than 90 percent of the total dairy activities in Denmark are concentrated in a large, Danish-Swedish, multinational concern, Arla Foods.

Sustainable entrepreneurship is not restricted to small companies, even though some of these companies seem to be most visible in this regard at the moment. Some large companies have developed formal strategies on Corporate Environmental and Social Responsibility. These strategies include integrating environmental and social concerns into their business operations and in their interaction with stakeholders. It seems to be a growing recognition, that such strategies directly or indirectly can support business success, and even result in reduction of production costs (COM, 2003, 27 final). The large companies within the agro-industrial sector may even possess better opportunities to implement sustainable entrepreneurship, because they have more comprehensive resources to formulate long term visions, strategies and planning of implementation. However, some of the large companies in the agro-industrial sector seem to be dominated by managers with a mindset, which allows little space for curiosity and risk-taking activities. Another barrier is lack of skilled employees, who are able or willing to take more responsibility, despite being offered to take on more challenging job assignments. Here is a dilemma. On the *one* side, one could argue that the entrepreneurial role model creates more challenging jobs and thus better quality of working life. Following this argument, it should in principle be the role model for all employees (Amit, Brighan and Markman, 2000). On the *other* side, from a social policy viewpoint, quality of working life should not be measured by the standard of the highly intelligent and creative employees only. The European Social Model includes a 'welfare society for all people'. In accordance to this Model, it is intolerable to allow individuals or groups of people to fall below a 'respectability level' without adequate assistance being provided. A part of the strategy of sustainable entrepreneurship is to create jobs and working life conditions, which make it possible to employ the potentially economic and social excluded groups. The objective of sustainable entrepreneurship is not only development of a 'smarter' organisation or to increase productivity. It is also the task to develop and maintain a culture, in which employees think and act creatively within a holistic perspective of sustainability. By generating diverse heuristic methods for problem solving in multi-functional teams entrepreneurial processes like improvisation, experimentation, co-adaptation, regeneration, patching and time-pacing (Eisenhardt, Brown and Neck, 2000; Brown and Eisenhardt, 1998; Morris, 1998) can be introduced as innovative competencies and job requirements of employees in the agricultural and the agro-industrial sector:

"...Our new role model is no longer the corporate manager but the entrepreneur. No one needs to tell the small company owner of the need to stay close to the customer, to remain flexible, to reduce non-value-adding overhead, to respond quickly to new situations....that success a tone thing means nothing without success at everything else. " (Hammer, 1996 : 31)

Such an entrepreneurial approach is not only a strictly economic one, but also a social, cultural and environmental approach. These four aspects are considered as separable only for analytical reasons. In practice, they are inseparable, because sustainable entrepreneurship are based on a holistic paradigm, including all four aspects into one frame . Therefore, capabilities of developing sustainable entrepreneurship are much more than just being an innovative businessman in the strict economic sense of making profit. What else is needed is the subject of the next section.

Capabilities of Sustainable Entrepreneurship in Rural Areas

The capability approach, (Nussbaum,2000), builds on philosophers like Aristotle, Marx, Mill and Sen. Nussbaum has developed a number of mutually interrelated capabilities. In particular two of these capabilities are relevant for sustainable entrepreneurship: affiliation and practical reason. *Affiliation* is defined as dynamic relationship between self-confidence and empathy. Self-confidence is seen as a pre-condition for being able to take initiatives and being acknowledged by other actors. Empathy is the capacity for experiencing the feelings and thoughts of another as one's own. Affiliation is more than being able to communicate and making social contacts. The core of affiliation is creation of *trust* among social actors of a network based on mutual respect and justice. There are at least three reasons why social actors in a network might act in transactions as they are supposed to. One reason is social and/or economic self-interest to do so. Another reason is that they believe it is a moral right to do so. Still another reason is, that it is considered as a part of the regularised expectations that characterise their personal relations with their network partners (Granovetter, 1985, 1992). If only one or two of the reasons are manifest to the network partners in question, they may face a dilemma, either morally, socially or economically. If all three reasons point in the similar direction the cohesion of the network will -ceteris paribus- be relatively more reliable and trustworthy. The entrepreneurs with affiliating capabilities are able to create network relationships, which combine all three dimensions of trust. They typically spend an incredible amount of time to communicate with customers, sub-contractors, employees, planners, politicians or NGOs. However, affiliating capabilities do not necessarily imply creative abilities. As an affiliative person, one can be so well adjusted to a specific role pattern, that he/she would not even think of making changes. Therefore, becoming an entrepreneur another capability is needed too, namely practical reason, which here is defined as the capability to form a conception of possible and desirable futures as well as to develop strategies realising one or more of these futures. Entrepreneurship depends on both capabilities. For instance, a person may be able to establish a huge array of social networks, but not to create any new ideas. Or he may be 'gifted' as a creative person, but without affiliation to create trust and convince other persons to see the innovative aspects of his/her idea. Entrepreneurship depends on affiliation as well as on practical reason to create trust and creativity. An example is PP, the director of a middle-sized dairy in Denmark. PP is aware of the importance to communicate his ideas and projects to the farmers. He does not invite them very often to participate in formally arranged meetings, only once a year, but he spends a startling amount of time of informal communication. Though it is rather time-consuming, he finds it is a 'must' for the quality of the raw milk and the stability of the supplies delivered from the farms. Consumers are part of the business network too. PP does not offer many resources on traditional marketing. According to PP, a good reputation depends on spectacular stories in the media, rather than on conventional advertisement. Thus he is very engaged in creating 'good stories' of new products in a way that appeals to newspapers and TV. For instance, when a new product called 'jersey mini milk' was introduced, PP was in the TV-News. In addition, he has also been invited as guest in several radio and TV programmes. In that way PP has become very visible to the Danish consumers. Another link in the business network is the relationship between his dairy and FDB, the biggest supermarket chain in Denmark. For instance, the dairy key account manager in FDB suggested PP to produce low fat drinking milk, because he could foresee a promising market for such a product. PP reflected the idea for some time. After a while he elaborated the idea to a new quality product combining the concept of low fat milk with a special quality of jersey milk. This example is typical for the way product innovation is handled at his dairy : informal discussions with other partners of the network initiate new product ideas. Another part of the business network is the suppliers of dairy technology. Through his many years of experiences as salesman of dairy technology, PP has established a comprehensive network to companies producing and selling dairy technology. These contacts are very useful for him when he plans to invest in new dairy technology. It is easy for him to update his knowledge about new dairy technologies by using his informal networks of dairy technology producers. He does not just buy dairy technology 'of the shelves'. Instead he identifies his specific needs of technology adaptable to the size and production structure of his dairy. Then he discusses with the suppliers of dairy technology how the specific needs of his dairy can be satisfied. Just as important as the business network seems the *development network* to be. Already when PP studied at The Danish Agricultural University he made personal friendship with another student, who later became professor at that university. As a medium-sized enterprise, his dairy cannot afford a separate research and development department. Instead PP makes use of his personal relationships to one of the professors at the Danish Agricultural University, suggesting him to carry out experiments at the university, for instance to find out if a special new product or process development is possible or not. The research is paid by the state, but the results are usable for private companies. PP is also a member of the Dairy Branch Research Fond and makes use of this position to update his knowledge within the dairy sector. In addition, PP has been involved in several, public financed projects too. The partners or consultants have been different Universities, technological information centres and private consultants. The *regulation network* is also useful for PP to acquire new knowledge. As an experienced dairy engineer and dairy manager, sometimes he is asked to represent the Danish State as advisor, when new kinds of regulation within the dairy sector are supposed to be elaborated. Normally PP accepts to participate in such advisory functions of several reasons. One is that he then knows beforehand what is likely to become a new regulation within the dairy business. Another is that he is held a jour with 'whom knows what'. Later on he may utilize this knowledge if the relevant situation should occur to him. *If* he is confronted with a problem, that he himself is not able to handle, he knows to whom he should direct his questions. However, PP is not alone. He has established his own internal network. These other managers at the dairy are important sparring partners, when PP suggests new ideas. Sometimes they counterbalance his creativity and sometimes they supplement and elaborate his ideas to 'sound' business. The point is, that without that internal network, the enterprise would be much less productive and innovative. Though PP is a typical example of a creative entrepreneur, the entrepreneurship of the dairy is based on teamwork and network rather than on the creativity of one bold person only. (Rasmussen and Nielsen, 2004, forthcoming).Thus, using his affiliating capabilities, PP is able to combine economic interests, the ethics of organic production and a set of trust-sustaining mutual expectations between the agencies of the different networks, of which he is an active part. As the description indicates, he is a very creative person, able to receive critics and reflect on that, before he makes his decision to implement the idea or not. In other words,he is using both affiliation and practical reason in his entrepreneurial activities

Affiliation and practical reason are core capabilities. They enable the entrepreneurs to act immediately, when needed in certain situations. For instance, i*mprovisation* is a way of managing seemingly chaotic, unpredictable and/or critical situations (Eisenhardt, Brown and Neck, 2000; Brown and Eisenhardt, 1998). In general, it refers to flexible operations within constraints of minimum rules and procedures. Metaphorically, entrepreneurial improvisation can be compared with improvisional theatre, in which the actors adapt to the suggestions from the audience and change their roles as the performance progresses (Crossan et. at., 1996). When entrepreneurs improvise, they try to adapt to suggestions from customers, subcontractors, or other actors in their network. Improvisation in Jazz provides further insight of the interaction between affiliation and practical reason. When jazz musicians improvise together, they listen to and experience the feelings of one another and make on-the-spot adjustments to the music they hear from each other, As they sense the direction of that interwoven sounds, they synthesise their impressions and make a new sense of it, adjusting their performance to these new sounds. How can they do this? Because they make use of a common melodic and metric schema, which is familiar to all the musicians and gives a certain kind of predictability to all the pieces. Besides, each of the participants is able to deliver a repertoire of special musical figures at appropriate moments (Schön, 1973) . Improvisation may not necessarily be an innovative act, but an improvising act may in some instances create innovation depending on the synthesising abilities of the actors. When entrepreneurs improvise, they seem also to follow a kind of schema and deliver a 'repertoire' of ideas or plans, some of which are transcending the prevailing ways of doing things. In difference to the jazz musicians, the entrepreneurs are supposed to be innovative, while the jazz musicians most often combine and recombine a set of figures within the schema, which bounds and gives coherence to their performance (Schön, 1973). *Patching* is another entrepreneurial process (Eisenhardt et.al., 2000). A 'patch' is a piece used to mend or cover a hole, a weak point or a 'white space'. For instance, managers in football clubs continuously keep an eye on the talent pool of possible players to make the best match between the available players and their opportunities to win the games against the other football teams in the league. In a similar way, entrepreneurial managers in firms, public institutions or NGOs continuously match for the 'white spaces' between existing possibilities for resource mobilisation and the prospective opportunities to expand or re-arrange their activities to their prospective fields (customers, clients, focus groups). Effective patching depends on the affiliative capability of social interaction to get the correct information about their operational fields. In addition, it presupposes the capability of practical reason to engage in critical reflection about strategies and action plans to cover the 'weak spots' or 'white spaces'. An example of patching is the creation of the Centre for Coast Culture (CfCC). Baaring Folk High School experienced a

‘white space’ in the region of North West Funen. They spotted a number of local initiatives but also a lack of coordination and systematic integration of these initiatives. In addition, CfCC is also seen as an opportunity to increase the material, human and social capital at Baaring Folk High School and thus strengthening it’s position in the region of Funen.
Another example of patching is the Japanese car producing company, Honda (Brown and Eisenhardt, 1998). In 1993 and 1994, Honda’s care sales fell due to the strong yen and the missing of the sports utility vehicle craze. Then Honda began to do patching. First, the Honda engineers broke the market into more finely grained market niches or smaller patch sizes. Then, the Honda managers selected some unique patches, and new car models were developed to fit across some of these selected patches. For instance, their Odyssey vehicle was patched across the traditional station wagon and the minivan markets. By late 1996, 60 percent of Honda’s new car sales in Japan came from the models developed through their patching, and Honda moved from number five to three in their domestic market (Brown and Eisenhardt, 1998). The point is, that typical capabilities of entrepreneurship such as improvisation, patching, networking, experimentation and regeneration are based on the synergy of affiliation and practical reason. Taken separately, none of them will result in sustainable entrepreneurship, but the combined effort of them may have astonishing impact on innovative activities. Quality of sustainable entrepreneurship depends on how well potential entrepreneurs may be qualified handling these two core capabilities.

Educational Approaches Towards Sustainable Entrepreneurship

The question is, how young, potential entrepreneurs may be prepared in the education system to take into consideration the sustainable view of entrepreneurship? Of course, educational policy and curriculum content that emphasize technical skills, accounting, finance, marketing and human resource management may provide potential entrepreneurs with basic skills needed to start and run a business. Likewise, creative problem solving, communication and leadership are entrepreneurial skills that may be built up through the educational system and further developed through training in a practical context. However, we do not believe, that these suggestions are adequate for education and training for sustainable entrepreneurship. Though some universities have introduced courses of entrepreneurship, a cross-cultural, multidisciplinary approach has still to be developed. It must focus on the core capabilities of entrepreneurship by the mean of continuous networking between universities and practical entrepreneurship cultures. The overall objectives should be improvement of the reciprocal understanding, mutual awareness and knowledge exchange between academic institutions, communities and enterprises. Interaction and linkages of these kinds could be promoted by the development of new, multidisciplinary curricula, that combine the knowledge of universities and entrepreneurship cultures embodied in professionals, knowledge centres and enterprises at the regional and local levels. Development of such a professional education system requires integration of two types of activities:

- An establishment of linkages and collaboration between teachers and researchers from different social science and technical disciplines at higher education institutions.
- Networking between multidisciplinary teams of researchers and entrepreneurship cultures in regional contexts.

So far, the efforts of educational institutions enrolling entrepreneurship professionals have remained isolated from each other. In order to promote a more systematic and integrated approach for sustainable entrepreneurship, it is necessary to establish an institutional frame- and network enabling pooling of isolated attempts into incorporate experiences and understanding of different entrepreneurship cultures into the educational curriculum as a cumulative process.

One example of how it is possible to combine the learning of affiliation and practical reason as well as the other entrepreneurial capabilities is the Participatory Scenario Workshop (PSW). In general terms the aims of PSW are:

- To identify and clarify the problems of the present situation relevant for the involved participants of the workshop.
- To generate new visions and ideas for action and initiatives
- To identify and discuss the barriers and the possibilities of change
- To suggest strategies and action plans to realise one or more of the elaborated scenarios at local, regional, national and / or international levels. (Rasmussen, 2003)

Thus the PSW method can improve:

- *The relational praxis* of the organisation or network by improving the participants' capabilities to collaborate, communicate and solve conflicts.

- *The reflexive-creative abilities* of the organisation or network as an effect of participating in problem stating, vision making, backcasting and action planning processes of the scenario workshop.
- *Plurality of knowledge.* The scenario workshops are not restricted to oral or written words, but they may as well use techniques or tools from the worlds of photography, video, theatre or dance. The development of knowing in the scenario workshops may be more valid, if it is based on the participants' experiences, expressed through images, models, role play or physically created models.
- *Engagement into significant work.* The processes established during the scenario workshops often create a deep feeling of release and empowerment and thus enhance the participants will to change their mindsets and behaviour either individually or collectively as a group.
- *Long termed perspectives.* The scenario workshops address problems and questions within a long term perspective. They provide the opportunity to get a broad perspective of desirable futures. Such an increased awareness may improve the capabilities of the organisations of elaborating long termed strategies and action plans as well as handling possible constraints against the realisation of the action plans (Rasmussen, 2003).

Confronted with the total complex of rural and regional development, the students may learn that entrepreneurial processes like patching, improvisation, experimentation and regeneration should be used as tools within a much larger approach of balance between economic, social, cultural and environmental aspects of rural and regional development. In other words. sustainable entrepreneurship challenges the classic and neo-classic economic concepts of entrepreneurship as being primarily an individual activity carried out for pure economic reasons. It must include social, cultural and environmental aspects too, and focus on activities at more aggregated levels too, such as networks of enterprises, knowledge centres, politicians, planners, and voluntary organisations in the region. Such kinds of regional approaches could be connected to each other by Information and Communication Technologies (ICTs) mediated systems within networks of cross cultural, open knowledge centres and cultures of entrepreneurship.

Conclusions and Perspectives

How is it possible to manage globalisation from the point of view of the European Social Model? How is it possible to develop a policy approach capable of reinforcing economic development as well as employment, social cohesion, cultural identity and environmental concerns? One answer seems to lie in the role of sustainable entrepreneurship as a strategy to enhance quality of life and work. Quality is considered one of the key elements in the European Social Model. It links the two basic objectives of competitiveness and cohesion and it represents a driving force for a combined approach of economic development, social inclusion, cultural identity and environmental protection. Sustainable entrepreneurship implies that the goals of moving towards full employment has to be pursued by trying to create not just more jobs but also jobs at a higher quality level. It implies that the creation of new jobs should occur within a combined development strategy of economic, social, cultural and environmental sustainability. For instance, quality in work does not only depend on a productive labour force or efficient structure of an organisation. Nor is it sufficient to reach a high standard of health and safety in work. In addition, quality in work should also include the aspects of promoting cultural identity and environmental protection as illustrated in the examples from the organic dairy sector. Therefore, the crucial questions concern how the enterprises develop their strategies as well as how public or private agencies coordinate and sustain a combined regional approach of sustainable entrepreneurship? The basis hypothesis that there exists a dynamic link between company strategies and quality in working life is confirmed by empirical studies in may sectors including the studies in the Danish dairy sector (Netterstroem, and Rasmussen, 2003; Rasmussen and Nielsen, 2004, forthcoming). However, the abstract notion of 'low road' and 'high road' strategies towards innovation should be considered more as artifice developed for heuristic and analytical purposes than examples from a real life context. (Garibaldo, 2003b). In fact, there appears to be a number of companies, which seems to be 'low road' at some aspects and 'high road' at others. For instance, in the Danish organic dairy sector, some companies appear to be very innovative regarding product development without large amounts of resources of research or a very advanced organisation of production. Other companies may not score very high marks on the quality of health and safety, but they nevertheless occur to be in front regarding continuous improvements of their external environmental activities.

The concepts of sustainable entrepreneurship widens the quality in work including not only economic and social dimensions but also cultural and environmental dimensions. If this strategy is developed as a combined deepening, broadening and re-grounding approach (Ploeg et. al. 2002) such

an increase of quality can promote the development of new sustainable products and services, a higher level of productivity, a better quality of health and safety activities and environmental impacts. In addition, they might support the improvement of living standards increasing local identity among interacting stakeholders in rural areas and communities.
The establishment of enterprises and communities, which integrate these concerns, is one of the most promising development trends in the rural areas (Nussbaum, 2002; Ploeg et. al., 2002). A comprehensive approach to promoting sustainable entrepreneurship and quality of work must work at several levels:

- If *individuals* are going to be motivated to become entrepreneurs, it requires, that they should be equipped with the right skills and competencies turning creative ideas into environmentally and socially responsible business ventures. In order to do this, educational institutions at all levels in the society should teach and train the students becoming aware of the principles and practices of sustainable entrepreneurship.
- For entrepreneurial ventures developing into sound and responsible businesses, supportive *services and networks* should be encouraged expanding at intra- as well as inter-regional levels. Risk-taking and partnerships between public and private sectors can help to overcome some of the entry barriers.
- The growth of entrepreneurial activities depends on positive appreciations of entrepreneurs in the *society* as well. Entrepreneurial initiatives should be valued and the stigma of failure reduced. The development of such positive appreciations depends on how entrepreneurial ventures are communicated and evaluated by mass-media, educational institutions as well as by politicians and other opinion leaders.

A pure cost based company or community strategy, will not be able to meet the prospective market demands. However, the sustainable oriented entrepreneurs do also face serious problems, in particular if they are small of size and with relatively few financial resources. Therefore, it is important to create special funds for the small companies to apply for resources to do research, development and marketing. An additional possibility is to strengthen the virtual and material networking among the knowledge centres and the small enterprises as well as between these companies themselves. The most successful development may be one, in which traditional skills in the region change through a process of hybridisation of knowledge, external techniques and cultures without loosing the wealth of traditional knowledge and skills (Garibaldo, 2003a). The birth or regeneration of such cross-sector networks can be supported by modern ICT's, but the effects depend on how we might do it. If ICT's are going to be used simply to enhance inherently deficient existing practices, it will at best be a modest improvement with little or no innovative perspectives. But if ICT's are implemented as part of a new, cross-sector, entrepreneurial culture-creating approach, it may have the potential to transform the lacking strategic convergence within or between sectors and regions, and be one of the prime factors of integrating local entrepreneurship with globally available partnership in order not only to attain the competitive edge of tomorrow but also to design and develop a sustainable future for the rural areas in Europe and elsewhere.

References

Amin, A.(1999): *The Emilian Model,* IpL-working paper Http://www.ipielle.emr.it/ita/index.html

Amin, A.(1993): *The regional development potential of inward investment in the less favoured regions of the European Community.* Paper presented at the *Conference on Cohesion and Conflict in the Single Market.* Newcastle upon Tyne. UK

Amit, R.H.; K. Brigham and G.D. Markman (2000): *Entrepreneurial Management or Strategy.*

In: Meyer, G.D. and K.A. Heppard: *Entrepreneurship as strategy-Competing on the entrepreneurial edge.* Sage publications, London, UK, p.83-100

Arzeni, S. and Pellegrin, J.P. (1997): *Entrepreneurship and Local development*, *The OECD Observer, no. 204, Feb.-March, 1997*

Bettis, R.A. and Hitts, M.A. (1995): *The new competitive landscape. Strategic Management Journal* , 16, 7-19

Brown, S. L & Eisenhardt, K.M. (1998): *Competing on the edge: Strategy as structured chaos.*

Boston: Harvard Business School press, US

Buchwell, A.(1997): *Towards a common agricultural and rural policy for Europe. European Economy 5* (Brussels: Directorate for Economic and Financial Affairs)

Castells, M. (2000): *The Information Age: Economy, Society and Culture. Vol. I: The Rise of the Network Society" (sec. Edition)* Blackwell Publishers, Oxford, UK

Cooke, P. and K. Morgan (1993): *The network paradigm: new departures in corporate and regional development.* In: *Environment and planning D: Society and Space,* 11 pp. 543-564

Crossan, M.M., White, R.E., Lane, H.W. and Klus, L. (1996): *The improvising organisation: Where planning meets opportunity. Organizational Dynamics* 24 (4), 20-35

Eisenhardt K.M., Brown S.L., Neck K.M. (2000): *Competing on the Entrepreneurial Edge.* In: G.D. Meyer and K.A. Heppard (Eds.): *Entrepreneurship as strategy.* Sage Publications, Inc. US

European Commission Green paper (1997): *Partnership for a New Organisation of Work*

http://europe.eu.int/comm/employment_social/soc-dial/green_en.htm

European Commission (2002): *Increasing labour force participation and promoting active ageing*

COM (2002) 9 final, 24.01.2002

European Commission (2003): *Communication from the Commission: Choosing to grow: Knowledge, Innovation and Jobs in a Cohesive Society.* COM (2003) 5, 14.01.2003

European Commission Green Paper (2003): *Entrepreneurship in Europe.* COM (2003) 27 final
http://europe.eu.int/eur-lex/eu/com/gpr/2003/com 2003_0027en01.pdf

Freeman, C. (1997): *The 'national system of innovation' in historical perspective.* In: D. Archibugi and J Michie (eds.): *Technology, Globalization and Economic Performance*; Cambridge University Press, UK, 24-49

Garibaldo, F. (2003a): *Clustering and networking in Italy: A Critical Reflection on Emilia-Romagno and Bologna.* In: Brandt, D. (ed): *Navigating Innovations – Indo-European cross-cultural Experiences. Vol. I* India Research press, New Delhi, India

Garibaldo, F. (2003,b): *Globalisation, Company Strategies and Quality of Working Life in Europe.*

Unpublished paper, International Conference: *Prospects for the Social Conditions and the Role of Work in the Italian and European Society.* Bologna, 18-21 june, 2003.

Garrison, D.R. and Anderson, T. (2003): *E-learning in the 21th Century* Routledge Flamer, US

Granovetter, M. (1992): *Problems of Explanation in Economic Sociology.* In: Nohria,N. and R.G.Eccles (eds): *Networks and Organizations: structure, form and action.* Harward Business School press, Boston, US

Granovetter, M. (1985): *Economic Action and Social Structure: The Problem of Embeddedness,* American Journal of Sociology 91(3): 481-519

Hammer, M. (1996): *The new loyalty. Leader to leader* 2, pp. 20-35

Johannisson, B. (2000): *Networking and Entrepreneurial Growth.* In: Sexton D.L. and Landström, H.: *The Blackwell Handbook of Entrepreneurship.* P. 368-386. Blackwell Business, UK.

Lowe, P., J. Murdock, and N. Ward, (1994): *Network in Rural Development*: Beyond Exogenous and Endogenous Models. In: J.D. van der Ploeg and G. van Dijke (eds.): *Beyond Modernisation.*Van Corcum & Comp. A.A. Assen, NL

Lorenz, E. (1992): *Trust, Community and Cooperation: Toward a theory of industrial districts.* In: M. Storper and A.J. Scott (eds): *Pathways to Industrialization and Regional Development. (p. 195-204)* Routledge, UK

Lundvall, B. (1996): *The Social Dimension of the learning Economy.* DRUID Working Papers No. 96-1, Aalborg University, DK

Marsden, T.K., Banks, J and Bristow, G. (2000): Food Supply chain approaches: exploring their role in rural development. *Sociologie Ruralis,* vol. 40 (4), 424-438

Marshall, A. (1890): *Principles of Economics.* Macmillan, London, UK

Marshall, A. (1927): *Industry and Trade.* 3rd edition, Macmillan, London, UK

Miles,G., K.A.Heppard, , R.E. Miles, and G. Snew (2000): Entrepreneurial Strategies – the Critical Role of Top management. In: Meyer, G.D. and K.A. Heppard: *Entrepreneurship as strategy – Competing on the Entrepreneurial Edge.* Sage publications, London, UK, 101-114

Morris, M.H. (1998): *Entrepreneurial intensity –Sustainable Advantages for individuals, organisations and Societies.* Quorum Books, UK

Netterstroem, S. and L.B.Rasmussen (2003): *Development of Small Enterprises through Networking: A Case Study from the Danish Dairy Sector.* In: Brandt, D. (ed):

Navigating Innovations – Indo-European Cross-Cultural Experiences. pp. 133-148. India Research Press, New Delhi, India

Nussbaum, M.C. (2000): *Women and Human Development –The Capabilities Approach* Cambridge University Press, US

Olbertz, E. (2002): The Region of Aachen as a 'Learning Region: A Case Study.*AI & Society*, 16 (?): 224-242

Oostindie, H. (2002): The integration of care activities on farms. In: Ploeg, J.D. van der, Long, A. and Banks, J.: *Living Countrysides: Rural Development Processes in Europe: The State of the Art,* Koopmans, NL

Ottesen, B. (2003): *Centre for Coast Culture.* Unpublished paper, Baaring, Funen, DK

Picchi, A. (1994): *The Relations between central and local powers as Context for Endogenous Development.* In: van der Ploeg, J.D. and A. Long (eds): *Born from Within: Practice and perspectives of Endogenous Rural Development.* Pp. 195-203. van Gorcum, Assen, NL

Ploueg, J.v.d. and Long A., (1994): *Endogenous Development: Practices and Perspectives.* In: Ploeg, J.D. van der, and Long A.(eds): *Born from Within: Practice and perspectives of Endogenous Rural Development.* Pp. 195-203. van Gorcum, Assen, NL

Ploeg, J.D. van der, Long, A. and Banks, J.(2002) : *Living Countrysides: Rural Development Processes in Europe: The State of the Art.* Koopmans, NL

Powell, W. (1990): *Neither market nor hierarchy: network forms of organization.* In: *Research and organizational Behavior.* 12, pp. 94-96

Putham, R. (1993): *Making Democracy Work.* Princeton University press, US

Rasmussen, L.B.(2003): *Action research Toolkit II: The Scenario Workshop.* In: Brandt, D. (ed):

Navigating Innovations – Indo-European Cross-Cultural Experiences. Pp. 241-258 India Research Press, New Delhi, India

Rasmussen, L.B. and Nielsen, T. (2004, forthcoming): *Entrepreneurial Capabilities: Is Entrepreneurship Action Research in Disguise?* (*AI & Society, special Issue, 2004)*

Sabel, C. (1992): *Studied Trust: Building New Forms of Co-operation in a Volatile Economy.* In: Pyke, F. and Sengenberger, W. (eds.): *Industrial istricts and local Economic regeneration.* International Institute for Labour Studies, Geneva, 215-250

Scheer, H. (2002): *A Solar World Economy* (Danish translation) Hovedland, DK

Schumpeter, J.A. (1934): *The theory of economic development.* Cambridge, M.A., Harvard University press, US

Schumpeter, J.A. (1951): *Essays on Entrepreneurs, Innovations, Business Cycles, and the Evolution of Capitalism.* (ed. By Richard V. Clemens. Transaction Publishers, US and UK

Schön, D.A. (1973): *The Reflective Practitioner – How Professionals Think in Action.* Basic Books, US

Welter, F. and Peistrup, M. (1999): *Self-Employment: The quality of work in micro enterprises in Germany.* ILO.
www.ilo.org/public/english/employment/finance/reports/germany6.htm

Woolcook, M.(1998): Social Capital and Economic Development: Toward a theoretical Synthesis and Policy Framework. *Theory and Society* . 151-208

World Commission on Environment and Development (1987): *Our Common Future,* Oxford University Press, UK

Training in Organisation and Sector Development

JUAN MONREAL

Introduction

The new economic and social contexts through which we are living demand permanent change (Monreal, 2001: 717), as well as a flexible outlook to enable continuous adaptation to the constant transformations taking place. This openness to change is required not only from people, but also from institutions, organisations and groups in these times marked by profound and constant change.

Certainly, a propensity towards change today exists more than at other times due to the general pervading culture; however, we should not overlook the natural tendency to resist change inherent in both human beings and organisations. Hence, instruments to foment a positive attitude towards change are required, given that this does not occur through inertia or spontaneity. Training in whatever form (education, continuous education, vocational training), is precisely the most appropriate mechanism to feed and maintain permanently-activated a favourable outlook towards change and innovation as prompts towards personal and organisational development and, why not, development of the production system in any of the sectors in which it expresses itself. This potential in training explains why it is considered a strategic factor and basic agent for any process of change that has to be undergone, above all in the productive sector which is where greatest upheaval and competition is being experienced. This special context in which training plays a part is well described by H. Ceri (1995:466): "Companies are systematically preparing themselves to tackle an increasingly turbulent and unpredictable environment and are developing key resources to carry through strategic actions that include technology, co-operation, information and human resources. The full utilisation of these resources requires prevision and planning: improvisation and an ad hoc approach do not work. Leading companies undertake this process, develop these resources and take action

in the face of events and development opportunities of such importance to them.
Uncertainty and turbulence are the essence of the contemporary scene and the capacity to undergo change the key to success. This means that it is fundamental to create, through education and training policies, the capacity in the workforce for innovation and flexibility. European companies can only triumph with the support of education and training infrastructures that encourage these capacities".

Training in Emergent Societies

The experience derived over recent years, as well as data emerging from recent behaviour patterns in society, only go to show the increasing scale of change taking place, whether at global, regional or local level.
Three basic factors intervene in this change process:

1) Information technology is becoming an indispensable factor in the economic re-structuring processes observed in recent years.
2) The new style of capitalism taking over, characterized by globalisation of economic activity, organisational flexibility and greater company power in reference to their workers. These new behaviours in the economic system have led to a reduction in the Welfare State, whose existence was the outcome of economic and social policies applied by social-democratic parties after the end of the Second World War.
3) The emergence of a new culture resulting from the factors previously mentioned creates a new orientation in economic and social relationships, principally marked by an increase in inequality, unemployment, social polarization and the resulting situations of insecurity and social exclusion. Bourdieu, speaking of the Neo-Liberal project (1999:141) expresses it in these terms: "the bottom line of all this economic order to be found under the banner of individual liberty is, effectively, the structural violence of unemployment, instability and fear inspired by the threat of dismissal: the "harmonious" working of the individualist micro-economic model and the principle of individual "motivation" to work lie, at the end of the day, in a mass phenomenon, the existence of a reserve army of unemployed, an army in name only in that unemployment creates isolation, atomisation, individualisation, breakdown and insolidarity".

The issue of social exclusion cannot be understood in isolation from the work sphere. In effect, companies and their instrumental decisions create problems of social exclusion. It is in this sense that Robert Castel (1995:28) puts forward the notion of social vulnerability as a social process expressed through the work crisis, employment and politics, with situations of impoverishment and social exclusion: "it would be better to bring into relation what is happening in situations of extreme margination, social isolation, absolute poverty with the configuration of situations of vulnerability, insecurity that frequently precede and foment them".

2.1. What is the Role of Training in These Societies?

One of the differences to highlight in contemporary social change is the growth of uncertainty and flexibility as traits of the "new economy" (of information, of dematerialisation etc.), as opposed to the search for a highly-computerised administration in the social and economic world of the rationalist-bureaucratic movement as laid out by the advance of inter-war capitalism. Max Weber dedicated much time to the study of this process. This 'cage' bound individuals within space-time co-ordinates where risk and insecurity were reduced to the minimum. This arrangement is precisely the founding characteristic in the growth of welfare capitalism. Full employment, salary growth, job stability, bureaucratic organisation, State control, expanding markets, large companies etc. make up the elements of a Social Welfare Society.

Following the 70s economic crisis, the welfare edifice was considerably shaken. The new regime of flexible accumulation (Harvey, 1998), based around information technology gave rise to a very different space-time horizon. Uncertainty and risk, the immediate and ephemeral, flexibility and permanent movement are the defining traits of the new order. Leaders in the new information economy celebrate the characteristics of what they have baptised "the great disruption" (Fukuyama, 2000), in which flexibility, constant innovation and permanent risk are attributes highlighted as belonging to the management culture that has to meet the challenge of globalisation and the Internet era.

Business management discourse shows an unhidden enthusiasm for this flexible capitalism that sweeps away the established certainties of the Welfare State Society, breaks with planned timescales and structured time and views risk not as an area of uncertainty to be avoided, but rather as something to seize upon as the motor of creativity and novelty.

Sociology, fortunately, has not lost one of its most emblematic identity signs, that principle of healthy suspicion. This is clearly to be seen in a good number of studies that, beyond the glorious future of the flexible, information society, show that the game rules for the new economy do not have to be experienced in the same way over the whole social spectrum, especially those who find themselves in the lowest, most vulnerable layers. Thus, it is evident that "less routine" types of work may have very negative effects on the daily life of people who feel that flexible timetables, work teams and polyvalence add new forms of degradation to their working and living conditions. In short, if some believe these new ways imposed by flexible capitalism worthy of celebration, for employees this might translate into greater intensity of work or "character corrosion" as tellingly analysed by Richard Sennet (2000:10) in his recent essay that, through a series of questions, perfectly poses the dilemmas faced by many people on a daily basis in this time of uncertainty and risk: "How do we decide what is of lasting value in ourselves in an impatient society centred around the here and now? How can we pursue long-term goals in an economy given up to the short- term? How can we maintain loyalty and reciprocal commitment in institutions in continual disintegration and re-organisation?"

Training is considered strategic in the information economy and society. For example, in the White Paper on Education and Training (1995:23) it states: "Information technologies help to eradicate some routine, repetitive jobs which can be codified and programmed by automatic machines. Work will increasingly be made up of intelligent tasks requiring the spirit of initiative and adaptation".

However, sociological studies have shown that these individual traits based upon initiative and adaptation are not homogeneously distributed throughout the social fabric, but instead tend to accentuate social polarisation as Manuel Castells points out (1997a : 280): "The increase in training, whether general or specific, demanded by the re-skilling of posts in the work structure, further divides the workforce by virtue of education, already a highly segregated system, since to some extent institutionally it depends upon a structure of separated residence. Then there is degraded work, especially those dreary jobs undermined by a new generation of women, ethnic minorities, immigrants and young people concentrated into a range of poorly-qualified and badly-paid activities such as temporary work or various service industries".

Furthermore, the emphasis placed on the individual's responsibility for determining their own training paths and professional up-dating may act as an incentive for many people on certain rungs on the employment ladder, enabling them to personally take control of their social and working careers, but a considerable number cannot or experience more difficulty in so doing: "When individuals find themselves in situations of existential insecurity, lack of perspectives and confidence re improvement in their work situation, the minimum necessary conditions for taking responsibility for renewal of their abilities are not met. Only when an individual finds themselves, within their work context or life in general, in a position in both the internal and external job market that gives confidence, that stimulates future projects and at the same time provides the possibility, interest and capacity for self-directed learning is this responsibility-taking made possible." (Kovács: 1998:18).

Even among those people with the ability to assume responsibility for personal training projects, the sensation of insecurity and vulnerability does not disappear, as has been shown (Sennet: 2000). This is one of the characteristics of social relationships in flexible capitalism: training, qualifications or human capital do not guarantee safe pathways for social mobility, unlike in the phase of welfare capitalism where security demanded promotion prospects and mechanisms for the negotiation of working conditions. Vulnerability is no longer the exclusive trait of unqualified workers, but also those in possession of a higher level of qualification and human capital can experience the vertigo of time moving too quickly, where the risk of getting left behind is very high: "Never were workers more vulnerable in that they have become isolated individuals, subcontracted within a flexible network with horizons unknown to that same network (Castells, 1997a: 309).

It is no coincidence, and even less so if we adhere to the diagnosis of re-emergent societies sketched out, that one of the most widespread concepts of contemporary sociological theory is that of risk. Sociology, with a much more rigorous view of emergent societies than that provided by the apologists for the regime of flexible accumulation, in fact characterises the profiles of social change which Ulrich Beck has come to conceptualise as a "work society of risk" (Beck, 2000). Beck has theorised that the present social change is the transformation of an Industrial Society, based upon the social production of wealth into a Risk Society based upon the social production of risks (Beck, 1998a).

However, what is risk? Risk is the undesired consequence of modernisation. For Beck (1998b:143), the extent of the sphere of risk and uncertainty is the most outstanding feature of late capitalism. Thus, a new social structure emerges defining itself around the production, definition and distribution of risks. By means of a perception of the probability of a damaging event, the Risk Society is built up as permanent insecurity where ... "the past loses its influence on the present and the future takes centre stage".

If in the Industrial Society the axis of production defined the distribution of resources between capital and work, what characterises the Risk Society is a new kind of social stratification generated by the production and distribution of risk.

Training and the Society of the Future

In considering training for the society of the future, we must start by asking it means to talk of a society of the future. The task of thinking about the society of the future, as we understand it, should lead to:

- Identifying those tendencies that it would seem reasonable to take as characterizing society in the next few years. Looking to the future forces observation of the present and past. Tomorrow comes from today and today from yesterday.
- Analysing the past and present, as well as trying to perceive the outline of future tendencies, must be carried out from a systematic vision of reality. Everything is inter-connected.
- Understanding that reality is structured and made up of economic, political and social factors and whatever happens in one area is linked to the rest. The specific logic has to be explained by the general logic.
- Accepting the fact that the future is not a reproduction of the present, though both are connected and conditioned.

From these beliefs and bearing in mind the behaviour traits of current societies, it would seem that the most significant tendencies marking future society will be:

1) An increase in complexity and uncertainty. If current societies are already complex, it is only reasonable to assume that future society will increase in complexity, obliging us to believe that the probable behaviour scenarios of the twenty first century will further accentuate the complexity and uncertainty.
2) Knowledge, information and technology will remain the fundamental pillars of future society and will even more emphasize their impact upon the entirety of organisation and lifestyles of the population, related to work, consumption and personal relationships.

3) Some of the present tendencies that most characterize the organisation of production, such as flexibilisation and decentralisation will proabably be intensified.
4) Human labour will continue to increase the process of fragmentation and atomisation evident at present.
5) Globalisation of the economy will intensify its present trend, possibly bringing with it improvements in production and the generation of wealth, but could predictably also suppose an increase in territorial imbalance and social inequality.

The society of the future with the specific forms it will take in production and consumption must continue to value the central role to be played by training. Specifically, in probable future scenarios, work will even more be positioned as a strategic production factor thanks to the expected increase in knowledge, information and technology, basic elements of human capital. This is illustrated in the observation of M. Castells (1998b: 375): "An important difference concerns what can be labelled as the generic worker as opposed to the self-programmed worker. The crucial quality distinguishing these two types of worker is education and the capacity to gain access to the higher levels of education: that is, the incorporation of knowledge and information... they who have education in a suitable organisational context can re-progamme themselves for the ever-changing tasks of the production process. On the other hand, the generic worker is assigned to a set task, with no capacity for reprogramming, which does not presuppose the incorporation of information and knowledge beyond the ability to receive and carry out directions".

In any case, for an educated worker to function within the terms demanded by present and future scenarios requires submission to a situation of training and continuous change that will prepare him for new economic contexts where the behaviour of the company, employment and the very same economic sectors find themselves enmeshed in permanent transformation processes. At the same time, this will require far more assimilation and growth in the general capacity for change in the activity carried out, the post held and the sector in which employed.

Do not let us fool ourselves into believing that the tomorrow of our society could be the outcome of well-meaning hopes, dreams and prophecies. On the contrary, it will be the product of development achieved in current society's human capital. Those societies that continue to invest heavily in this field will have great potential in human and economic resources and consequently their competitiveness will likewise be great. However, this investment and effort cannot be sporadic and casual; on the contrary, they should be a permanent goal and a life-long development project. Thus, the concept of education must go beyond the regulated education taking place at a set period in life. It must be extended into a life-long process, with the different forms and labels it can take, such as vocational training, continuous education or simply education for life. As Díez Hochleitner (2002:36) affirms it is not a question of "merely ensuring more education with the consequent greater expense to "carry on as before", but rather a much greater effort towards a renewed education and life-long learning with a rigorous demand for tangible outcomes and at the service of social, cultural, scientific and technological results, as well as economic. Life-long education, as well as the most novel learning processes, must address the issue of the type of society it hopes to serve and the type of society it wants to shape".

From this perspective human capital should be understood, in the words of J. Delors (1996:14), "as a constant process of enrichment of knowledge, technical capacity, but also, and above all, as a privileged building of the person and relationships between individuals, groups and nations". Leading on from this is the need to "base education on four pillars: learn to know, learn to do, learn to live together, learn to be" (UNESCO report, 1996:109). To conclude, it could be said that the evolution of future society is closely linked to policies, to strategies such as investment in human capital made by present societies. We do not expect miracles, but the logical results of the actions undertaken now in a sector as productive as that we label human capital. As H. Ceri (1995:481) affirms, working along those lines "is an opportunity to look towards the twenty first century, but with realism and a dose of optimism because human capital means people. The problems of people in the world have changed considerably. Collaboration within the European Community will help all citizens and workers to lead a more active life because training will provide them with initial qualifications and these will be renewed throughout their lifetime".

The role of Training in Organizational Development

There is nothing new about the link between organizational development and training, but rather it forms an essential element in the process of an organization's make up and formation in that organizations undergo constant change, as does society as a whole.

Today, as has happened at other unique moments in history, we experience and perceive the reach of changes taking place in organizational modes of production and consumption that shape population lifestyles, as much in the individual as in the collective sphere.
Sociology and economics have especially concerned themselves with the identification of explanatory factors for organizational change, highlighting human capital, as much through formal education as via training, as making up a mediating factor in the change process within organisations, even though its relevance has not always been sufficiently valued.
The interest aroused in training of human resources in organisations has always been justified, and now even more so, by the contextual conditions that organisations create and operate within: factors such as market globalisation, the imposition of technological innovation, the creation of new products and services that requires high levels of efficacy and efficiency from the human resources. These demands will be met if the training factor is constantly to the fore. We take as a given that training, like the majority of an organisation's strategic decisions, is clearly influenced by the reigning culture.
As a general rule it can be claimed that both at the theoretical and practical level a dependency relationship is established between the terms organisation and training in acknowledging and accepting that the internal dynamic of each influences the other.
Training has been considered in a wide sense, that is, formal education in all its levels and training not only profession-ruled, but also occupational and continuous.
How can the relationship between these two terms be explained? Both elements are what permit a project or company's fulfilment, they determine and set the quality level. On the one hand, a company needs organisation, as well as other elements, to establish itself as such and be competitive (survive in time and space); on the other hand, training as the driving force of the company culture allows for the sharing of goals and acquisition of values essential to the organisation.
Furthermore, if we speak of organisational development in relation to training, this means emphasizing even more the importance and relevance of this factor as a part of company culture when it comes to finding the most appropriate organisational applications, whether at the individual, group or functional level.
There is no single model but rather a range of organisational development models. Consequently, different training models need to be set in motion in accord with the diverse goals aimed for by the organisation.

We live in an age marked by great change; logically, organisations do not escape the upheavals shaking the social fabric as a whole. If organisations have always expressed and applied the different company projects that have arisen over time, emergent and existent organisations will aim with more intensity and flexibility for the company's goals in the globalised context in which we live.

Nowadays, organisations favour companies that show (Castells, 1997a: 180-200):

- light production (more production with fewer permanent workers), as opposed to traditional production.
- flexible production (client choice), as opposed to mass production.
- growing importance of small and medium-sized companies.
- importance of territorial networks in companies of greater industrial weight than that involved in the traditional so-called mass economies.
- use of new working and management methods (rapid production response to market demands, use of advanced electronic media).
- emergence of net-worked business co-operation.
- move in large companies from a vertical to a horizontal corporation: company de-centralisation (relative autonomy of departments, divisions, countries operating with almost total autonomy).
- use of strategic alliances between companies (at a given moment and for a specific product or space).

However, for organisations to incorporate these new methods, so allowing companies to fulfil previously established objectives, the global (involving all agents) and permanent mediation of training is necessary, training as the instrument of change in the organization as a whole.

Training as a way of transmitting knowledge has always been a necessary instrument in relation to organisations, but nowadays it has become a strategic factor of the highest order because of the nature of the societies in which we live, where information, innovation and knowledge form the very foundations of their being and organisation.

This is why the evaluation made by social agents of the role of training has changed so much. In the past, training, like human capital, did not receive due attention, in contrast to other types of mediating capital in the production processes (physical and financial capital). It is from the 1940s onwards, especially since society has placed high value on knowledge and information, that training has found its place as a fundamental factor in the transformation of society. Thus, the significant change in perception undergone by social agents in relation to the role played by training in organisational change should come as no surprise.

A Case Study: Training in the Organisational and Productive Sectors′ Development of Spanish nº 1 Regions

As a clear example of the re-evaluation of the role of training in organisational change, we will present the results obtained from a research study "Training and Managerial Culture in the Spanish Objective 1 Regions" (the less-developed Spanish regions) ., financed by the Spanish Ministry of Science and Technology and carried out by 12 Spanish universities with Professor Juan Monreal as the main researcher.
The conclusions are drawn from data obtained from a wide-ranging questionnaire through statistical sampling in the relevant regions of companies that had previously confirmed their participation in training-linked activities.
The sample population only includes companies in the industrial and energy sectors with more than 19 employees and from the construction and market services sectors those with more than 49 employees. The total number of companies making up the base population for the study has been determined by use of Central Company Directory (DIRCE) drawn up by the National Institute of Statistics.
The sample is made up of 527 companies thus distributed between the categories established: 194 in industry and energy, 161 in construction and 172 in services . The field study was carried out during the month of February 2002.

Conclusions

Below are presented both the most relevant conclusions in relation to entrepreneurial organisation in Spanish objective 1 regions as well as in the Spanish productive sectors.

Training and Entrepreneurial Organisation

- Training sought by companies is two pronged. They seek to " Increase/provide knowledge and skills of a general kind" and/or "increase/provide knowledge and skills directly linked to the work carried out by the employee in the company".

From the data obtained, most companies principally provide specific training 73. 4%; statistically speaking, the number whose aim is training for activities with no direct repercussions on the work to be carried out is insignificant. Only 1. 3% of companies claim to give training with the principal aim of providing workers with a general qualification.

- The results from the questionnaire state as priority motives for training provision: the need to adapt the company to new technologies (55. 8%), followed by request both from management personnel (45%) and non-management personnel (41. 4%) and analysis of future company plans (34. 9%).
- Company directors interviewed principally identified themselves with the management style that seeks to "plan for the future" (47%), "continually adapt and change" (31. 6%), "be prepared for changes that arise" (20%). On the other hand, the attitude of resistance to change is minimal (1.3%).

The order reflected in this data reflects the role assigned to training in the development process of the company organisation.

- The predominant company culture is that of "foresight" (39.5%) followed by those that show a "stable/reactive" cultural typology (31.4%). Thus, the majority of companies analysed are forward-looking and have a tendency towards change provided this is progressive and controlled or towards stability.
- The smaller the company size, the greater the tendency towards stability.
- The higher the level of education of the director, the greater is the tendency to develop a "foresight" culture in the company, while at lower levels of education e.g. basic education only, the greater the tendency towards a "stability" culture.
- With respect to company management orientation and its relationship to the cultural typology developed, those companies with an orientation towards planning and marketing develop an "exploratory/creative culture, while a "foresight" culture is clearly dominant among companies with an orientation towards the product, market development and diversification and, to a lesser extent, towards production, costing and finance where companies tend to come closer to a "stable/reactive" culture. This is the predominant orientation among the companies analysed.
- Permanent adaptation to change, firstly, and reaction to this when presented are the fundamental characteristics of the companies analysed in relation to their environment.
- Regarding the most significant aspects of management, great importance is attached to the ability to work as part of a team, and co-operation and problem-solving in conjunction with other company colleagues.

However, less interest is demonstrated in the capacity to delegate in strategic decision taking and the capacity to assume risk.

Training in the Spanish Productive Sectors

Industry

- The industries forming part of the sample can be characterised as small and medium-sized companies, a factor related to their possibilities for commercial outreach to international markets. In this respect, the majority of companies do their buying and selling within and for the internal market. Similarly, the majority carry out their production processes entirely within our country.
- In general terms, the number of companies that can count a significant number of university graduates among their staff is not very high, the majority of employees having technical college level training. The educational level of managers interviewed tends to be to university level and to a lesser extent secondary schooling/technical training. Approximately half of managers have received training specifically designed to develop management ability.
- The level of training coverage in half the companies lies between 0 and 25% of trained employees among the total workforce, with an increase in this percentage for the last two years of the analysis. In the majority of cases, the training content is eminently specific and relevant to the activities carried out by employees within the company. This training is mainly provided via short courses (between 20 and 60 hours' duration) and mostly given by personnel external to the company and post. The predominant reason for provision of training is the adaptation of the company to new technologies, then management request and analysis of the companies' future plans.
- Around 38% of industries invest none of their own funds in training, which indicates the importance of subsidies to carry through training initiatives. At the same time, over the last two years, a tendency to increase the resources devoted to such initiatives can be discerned.
- In their evaluation systems, companies normally include all those aspects suggested in the questionnaire, though they are particularly interested in assessing the degree of application of the knowledge and skills acquired via the training process to the post. The level of employee satisfaction and the assimilation of knowledge and skills transmitted via training are also frequently assessed.

- With regard to attitudes of owners and managers to the role to be played by training in regional economic development, those responsible for this area within companies interviewed did not show any high level of agreement with the claim that unemployment in the region was due to a mismatch between training and work tasks to be carried out. More consensus was shown with the idea that expenditure on training created significant increase in regional economic development. Finally, the third statement put forward for evaluation that "the effort workers put into training is suitably reflected in the salaries received" achieves even lower levels of support than previous claims. This result may indicate that, on the whole, the training workers receive in companies does not represent an investment linked to salary increases.
- The last aspect analysed, that of company culture, measured via a series of variables, shows the following results: production, costs and finance make up the dominant factors towards which management is oriented in more than half of companies. They are followed in importance by management focused upon the product, market development and diversification. If we consider the attitude towards change, the overriding tendency is towards gradual change and the assumption of a moderate level of risk, results in consonance with the prevailing catchphrase of industrial organisations " the future must be planned for, we look for new ways of satisfying new demands", a suitable phrase for a culture of foresight.
- In line with the cultural typology put forward in the questionnaire, nearly 40% of companies had a stable/reactive culture, 37% that of foresight and 23% exploratory/creative. The prevailing culture in a company influences the manager's evaluation of the basic directions that management should take. In this respect, the most highly valued dimensions are those of ability to work in a team and willingness to collaborate with other members of the organisation. Aspects less highly valued were risk-taking and the delegation of strategic decisions.

Construction

- The majority of companies consulted in the construction sector are: young companies with fewer than 20 years in the market, of medium-size, who carry out their buying, production and sales in the national market and care about the quality of their products.
- The level of preparation of employees confirms that in the majority of companies only a minimal percentage have higher education or technical training.

- Among the managers interviewed, a large number are graduates and enjoy specific training in company management.
- Training initiatives undertaken aim to extend and provide knowledge in a wide sense and, to an even greater degree, extend and provide job-specific knowledge.
- Training is generally provided by personnel external to the company for which it is given and usually takes place away from the normal working post, although it is sometimes also given there.
- Of courses given, it is significant that in a quarter of companies all courses are of fewer than 20 hours' duration and in the remainder training courses are of between 20 and 60 hours, that is, short and medium-length courses and almost in their entirety using traditional formats.
- A greater number of men have permanent contracts and development 2000-2001 reveals that while men's stability increases, women remain on temporary contracts.
- When the number of workers receiving training in the years 2000 and 20001 is compared, a considerable increase in numbers can be observed.
- What stands out when companies' training costs are analysed is that a great number invest no money in this area and of the others, although more money is dedicated to training each year, the total amount remains low.
- When we look at data relative to the percentage of subsidy for training received, it is clear that a large percentage is subsidised in its entirety, but there is virtually no change in the total subsidy allocated.
- Where an increase in funding can be observed, it is in the quantity of their own resources companies dedicate to personnel training, with more than half showing this trend.
- Concerning the relationship between training and development, it is worth pointing out that, unlike the previous view, in this sector many companies believe: a mismatch between training provided and the post to be held is the cause of unemployment, expenditure on training leads to important increases in regional economic development and the training effort is reflected, to a greater or lesser degree, in the workers' salary retributions.
- The most important motives behind choice of training are: adaptation to new technologies, management proposals and workers' request.
- Aspects most valued by the companies in their training evaluation are: consistent attendance and uptake from courses, application of knowledge and skills to the post and the knowledge and skills themselves.

- Companies have improved most in the areas of: quality of products/services, employee motivation/satisfaction, commitment and identification of workers with the companies and innovation.
- Company management has been mostly directed towards production, costs and finance.
- The majority of companies tend to change in a gradual and planned manner, continually adapting to change.
- Management is most affected by: ability to work as a team, willingness to co-operate with other organisation colleagues and come up with joint solutions, assumption of risk, introduction of innovation and the delegation of operative decisions.

Services

- The service companies interviewed are of relatively recent creation with almost 50% set up within the last two decades.
- The companies are oriented towards the internal market and have virtually no purchasing or sales contact with abroad (more than 70%).
- With respect to training, in more than 50% of companies, more than 25% of employees have technical training and 16% are graduates. More than 50% of management have received courses or specialist Masters degrees (52%) or have a first degree (60.5%).

A great majority (78.8%) seek objectives related to the worker's post from training.
As yet, training is not given by their own employees (45.3%) or only to a limited extent (up to 50%: 26.7%).
Regarding the place where training is given, the majority of courses are taught outside the workplace (all outside: 29.2% and up to 50% inside: 36.5%). Only 22.2% of training is given at post.
Training courses mainly last between 20 and 60 hours, although it is worth highlighting that 66.5% are developing longer courses (more than 60 hours).
The majority of course are traditional in delivery mode.

- With reference to training and gender, in spite of what may be thought about the figures for female employment in the service sector, almost 50% of companies have a male workforce on permanent contracts and in more than 80% of companies less than 25% of employees are female, whether on fixed or temporary contracts.
- With respect to finance, the perspective is dismal. Although service sector industries are interested in their employees' participation in

training initiatives, they are unwilling to pay for it; around 32% are prepared to spend more than 120 euros (per worker). 35% are not even prepared to invest a single cent in training

At the same time, 50% of companies complain that the Administration finances less than 25%. However, 29.1% are lucky enough to receive help of between 70% and 100% of the investment in training costs. With this prospect, if the majority of companies are not committed to investment and the Administration does not contribute with responsible policies, no development can take place.

There is, however, a new trend in that half of companies claim to have perceived a change in the last two years and an increase in the resources given over to training.

- Concerning the relationship between training and development, we can highlight that these companies believe:
  - that the mismatch between training and jobs is the cause of unemployment (1.2% say somewhat and 22.4% a little)
  - that the increase in expenditure on training is relative (the somewhat and little replies make up 66.5% of the companies claiming this. That is, service industries do not sufficiently value training as a factor for development, confirming their opinion on the commitment of finance
  - the majority of companies (57.4%), state their perception of little interest among workers in training (the somewhat and little together make 70%).
- With regard to the assessment of training, the reasons most mentioned for training needs are focused upon adaptation to new technologies (51.7%) and to a lesser degree the needs of the employees (45.3%) and managers (45.9%). In identifying needs, the human resources department (19.8%) and production department (18%), carry less weight. Finally, it is worth pointing out the scant importance in determining needs on the part of the Unions with only 5.2% of companies identifying their input.

Concerning the outcome of training, it would seem that especial significance can be attached to the factors of employee satisfaction (85.9%), attainment of knowledge (86.%) and improved results (81.7%).

- With reference to the company's development and projection, it is possible to claim that, in the majority of areas identified, companies claim to tend towards maintenance (from 51.5% for "innovation in products and services" to 71.5% on "average employee salary"). Furthermore,

30% claim to have perceived improvement in all the indicators put forward.

- When company culture is considered, the prevailing model is centred upon "production, costs and finance" (37.3%) and to a lesser extent upon "production, development and diversification" (29%) and marketing (26%). Research and new technologies are little valued (7.7%).
- The majority of companies discern a path towards progressive change (58.1%) and, to a lesser extent, stability (39%). Radical change is not contemplated (2.9%).
- In line with the above, the level of risk that companies can assume is situated at mid interval (from 1 to 7), that is more than 50% of companies place themselves between 4 and 5, though with a slight tendency towards 7 (maximum risk).
- In consonance with the above, the most suitable motto for service sector companies is "the future must be planned for" (47.1%) and the motto "continuous adaptation is necessary" (32.9%).
- Finally, more than 50% of companies are committed to objectives such as the need to work as a team (59.2%), and solving day-to-day problems (55.6%). These points are slightly above those of introducing innovation (49.7%), delegation of operative decisions (41.7%), acceptance of risk (39.9%) and delegation of strategic decisions (31.7%).

References

BECK, U. (1998a): *La sociedad del riesgo*, Barcelona, Paidós.

BECK, U. (1998b): *¿Qué es la globalización?*, Barcelona, Paidós.

BECK, U. (2000): *Un nuevo mundo feliz. La precariedad del trabajo en la era de la globalización*, Barcelona,.Paidós.

BOURDIEU, P. (1999): *Contrafuegos: Reflexiones para servir a la resistencia contra la invasión neoliberal*, Barcelona, Anagrama.

CASTEL, R. (1995): "De la exclusión como estado a la vulnerabilidad como proceso", Archipiélago, nº 21, verano.

CASTELLS, M. (1997a): *La era de la información. Economía, sociedad y cultura.* Vol. 1, Madrid, Alianza ed.

CASTELLS, M. (1998b): *La era de la información. Economía, sociedad y cultura.* Vol. 3, Madrid, Alianza ed.

CERY, H. (1995). "El papel de la educación y de la formación en el ciclo de vida", en *El capital humano europeo en el umbral del siglo XXI*, Madrid, Ministerio de Trabajo y Seguridad Social.

COMISIÓN EUROPEA (1995): *El Libro Blanco sobra la Educación y la Formación*, Bruselas.

DELORS, J. (1996): "La educación o la utopía necesaria" en UNESCO: *La educación encierra un tesoro*, Madrid, Santilla-Ediciones UNESCO.

DIEZ, R. (2002): *Educar para la convivencia democrática*, Madrid, Periódico EL PAÍS, 4 de Noviembre.

FUKUYAMA, F. (2000): *La gran ruptura*, Barcelona, Ediciones B.

HARVEY, D. (1998): *La condición de la posmodernidad*, Buenos Aires, Amorrortu.

INFORME UNESCO (1996): *La educación encierra un tesoro*, Madrid, Santilla-Ediciones UNESCO.

KOVÁCS, I. (1998): "Trabajo, cualificaciones y aprendizaje a lo largo de la vida. Ilusiones y problemas de la sociedad de la información", en *Sociología del Trabajo*, nueva época, nº34, otoño.

MONREAL, J. (2001): "Capital humano y cultura empresarial en el cambio de las sociedades" en: *Estructura y cambio social*, Madrid, CIS.

SENNET, R. (2000): *La corrosión del carácter*, Barcelona, Anagrama.

The Industrial Development Dynamics and Work in Selected Sectors in Europe. An Introduction

GIUSEPPE STRINA

Prologue

"The increasing dynamics and turbulence of today's markets...", "The ongoing globalisation, the increasing requirements and the impacts for enterprises..." These are standard phrases at the beginning of nearly every other article dealing with the actual situation of doing business and work in the industrial context. Of course there are some strong indicators that this increasing phenomenon is not totally wrong. But nevertheless sometimes the question is obtrusive: Is it a true description of the real situation or is it a scenario becoming a self-fulfilling prophecy when repeated enough?
Let us presume the first possibility is true with some influence of the second one. The question then arises: why is it so or at least why do we have the impression that it is so and what can we do to prevent it?

The ICT Development as one of the Main Drivers for Increasing Dynamics

Simply to look on relevant figures might only give some useful information. But combining this information with the experience and the knowledge of how comparable things went in former times makes this view on figures quite instructive. In this sense the following statements might help to get an impression of the fast-paced changes going along with the ICT development (see Fig. 1):

Fig. 1: The dynamics of modern ICT

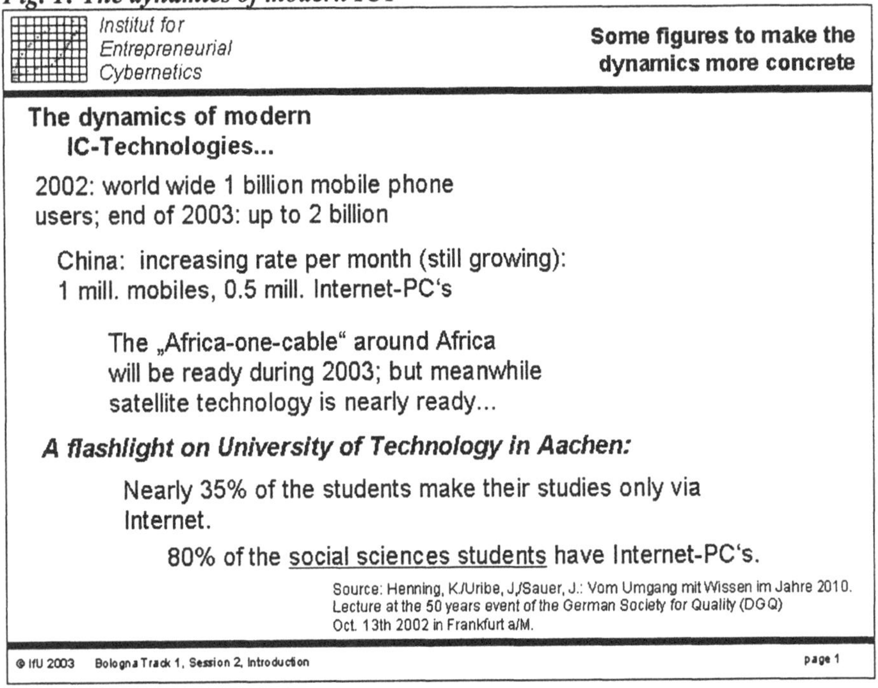

- Between 2002 and 2003 the word wide number of mobile phone users will be doubled from one billion to two billions. This means nearly a third of mankind has switched within a decade to this new technology. Considering the new technical opportunities that are going to be developed with the mobile phone as the central communication tool, the total change impact on private and business communication behaviour is at the moment not predictable.
- Looking at China, the increasing rates for mobiles and Internet-PC's are so impressive that the final outcome going along with the fact that this big country will be one day more or less totally "on-line" is not imaginable.
- With the "Africa-one-cable" and meanwhile with satellite technology, too, a complete continent, so far nearly forgotten, will be "connected with the modern world". In this case, too, the end results for the development of these still poorest countries are not predictable at all.
- But not only in the so far called "Third World" the communication attitudes will be changing dramatically. In our daily surroundings, too,

there will be drastic changes. A small flashlight on the actual situation on Aachen Technical University, one of the major technical universities in Europe, shows the tendency: today already a significant (and of course increasing) number of students, in some faculties more than a third, are making their studies only via Internet. And even the students of social sciences, well known for their affinity to written texts, are already more or less on-line. Changes that "happened" within a couple of years...

As mentioned before, these facts give us a small impression of what is coming soon. And of course, this has an important impact on how to organise work and industrial relations.

Managing the Unmanageable?

Under these circumstances it seems that managing social and working conditions in a proper way becomes more and more impossible. The balancing act between the industrial development dynamics and the increasing degree of interconnections, and the unspecific impression that all is any way interrelated with everything, is the so called "dynaxity", which is becoming more and more unbearable (see Fig. 2). There could be only two strategies to solve this problem: To reduce velocity and/or complexity wherever it is possible and reasonable and at the same time to increase the ability to handle the dynaxity, to increase the "dynaxibility" (Rieckmann/ Weissengruber 1990; Henning/Marks 1989). On an organisational level one answer for this need is to create a corporate culture in an organisation or in an enterprise, based on the idea that skills and competencies of its employees and staff people are the most valuable treasure they have. This is the reason why the "old" concepts of participation are discussed again.

Fig. 2: Corperate Dynaxibility as success factor

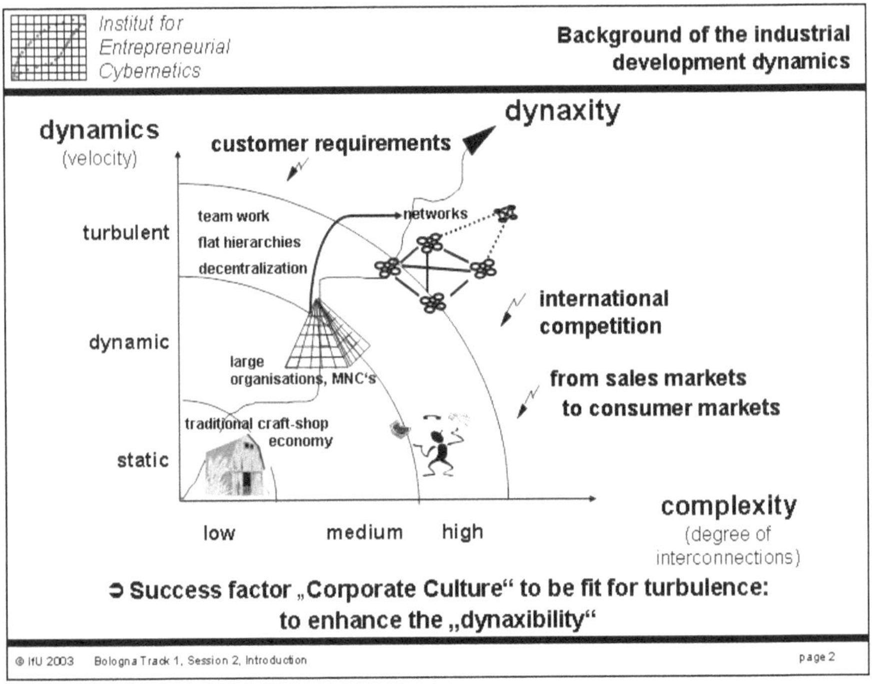

New Old Leadership Approach: Participation and Empowerment

Due to discussions about Participation and Empowerment (P&E) in the USA, P&E is increasingly being debated across Europe as an important aspect in changes to the working environment. Regarding this topic, a partially standardised survey was carried out by experts on P&E all over Europe; the results of which have been summarised as follows (Scheve/Strina 2003). According to P&E experts, it was aimed at certain active members of the "International Society for Participation and Empowerment" (InSPE) as well as other people, who are bringing forward the application of P&E internationally. All together nine experts from about as many countries were questioned.

Naturally from this random sample of people who were questioned, we cannot draw an overall and representative evaluation. The dialogue with representatives from different countries and also with experts of the different (business) cultures shows however a complex insight into the prominent features of P&E.

Participation for all those questioned is a matter of demonstrating the possibility, influencing the planning of work ("planning up to competence level"), accepting responsibility and participating. The extent of influencing and taking responsibility should not depend on the hierarchy, but on the competence of the employee.

Regarding Empowerment, we understand from the majority of European experts who were questioned, that it is possible for employees to reach a high competence level in the concrete fulfilment of duties (ability to participation). Participation is therefore a step that periodically takes place before Empowerment.

In most countries Participation is most likely seen as a trade-union-bottom-up concept, and Empowerment is most likely seen as a top-down constructed idea representing the side of the employer. We come to the conclusion that concepts such as Lean Management or the approach of humanising work are in fact related to P&E. P&E attempts, however, to agree upon the advantages of the different and already mentioned approaches and therefore to face up to the negative aspects, such as negative physical effects in connection with Lean Production.

Amongst those who were questioned, two main uses of P&E are evident: improving the well being and the increase of the competition capability of the enterprise. The improving of the well being of the individual is thereby attributed to a better quality of working life. An increase in the competition capacity in enterprises will attribute to a stronger motivation, an improved learning and an increased trail of though amongst the workers.

The survey of P&E in a European comparison shows that there are both similarities and differences in the international understanding of P&E concepts and its implementation. In particular we can see the similarities in the treatment of the combination of P&E and the benefit of the implementation of this concept. In basic terms there exists a more or less similar understanding of P&E within Europe.

Above all, differences can be seen in the areas of the practical implementation of P&E notions in the various countries. In this case, the necessity of a European agreement at the highest possible level is very clearly deduced as a question of research and operation. A crucial strategy to get to this agreement will be combining the knowledge spread over countries and, above all, the knowledge on how to transfer experience.

Scanning the Management Philosophies: the Case of Automotive Industry

In the past we often have seen the automotive industry to be the leading edge of new organisational and management philosophies. So it makes sense to scan, by looking at the below seen diagram, the trends over the last decades and to draw some important conclusions from it for the tendencies over the coming years (see Fig. 3).

Fig. 3: The Management Philosophies in Automotive Industries (Strina 2002)

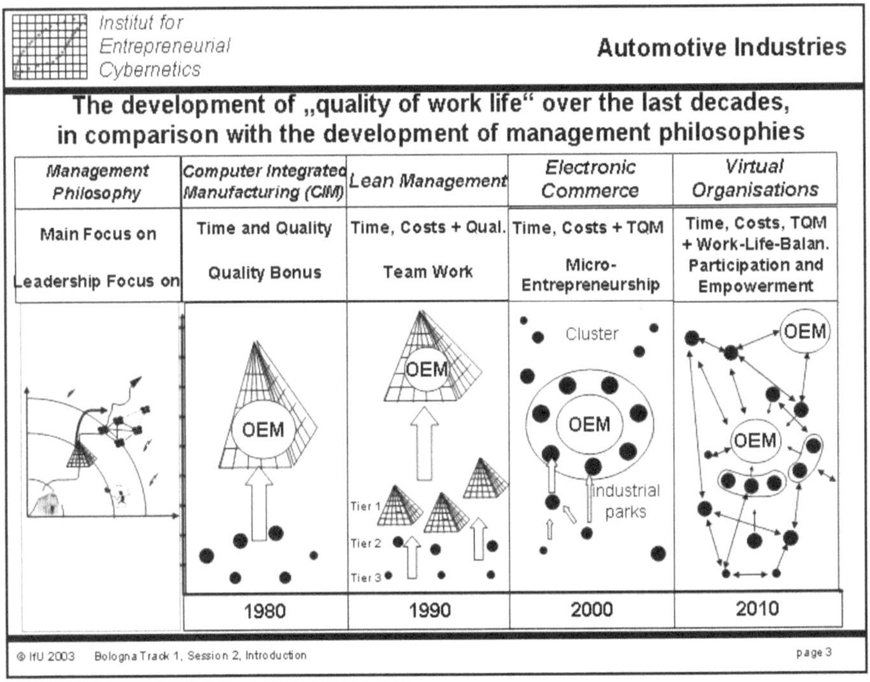

In comparison with the 1980ies where the Computer Integrated Manufacturing was the focus, the Lean Management Philosophy of the 1990ies centralised the idea of teamwork and at the same time emphasised cost targets. The first, second and third tiers appeared, but the Original Equipment Manufactures (OEM) put a strong pressure on them mainly in terms of cost cutting. In the actual situation the tier concept is more and more transformed into "industrial park" concepts, where the suppliers are considered semi-partners, without loosing control over the cost target. The logistics are dominated by Electronic Commerce solutions – of course those of the OEM's (procurement portals etc.); meanwhile the organisational focus is on emphasising the core competence aspects (out-sourcing, out-placement etc.). The response of the suppliers is on the one hand to organise themselves more and more in networks and clusters, and on the other hand inside to foster the idea of employees as "entrepreneurs within enterprises". In the future we see an increasing relevance of all forms of virtual organisations, going along with the fact that the work-life balance becomes more important (Brandt et al. 1999; Strina/Honecker 2003). Thus, within enterprises, leadership models of Participation and Empowerment could be regarded more than in the past; in the inter-organisational field the network and cluster idea will become predominant.

Conclusions and Questions Marks

If the above outlined tendencies are at least in some way becoming true there are of course a lot of questions arising from this point of view:

- If it is true, that P&E is one answer for the increasing dynaxity, how to give assistance to employees to manage their balance of self-realisation and self-exploitation?
- What about the relation of P&E and salaries?
- Do we need a new corporate conflict culture in enterprises for a real P&E?
- Could we see here a new action field for unions? What are their roles in this game?
- What are the impacts for change processes in organisations?

At least for some of these questions we find possible answers in the following contributions. Martin Upchurch is presenting reflections on the future role of unions in this context. The contribution of Peter Totterdill discusses the question of the impact that these upcoming change processes will have for enterprises and organisations.

References

Brandt, D.; Hartmann, E.; Sander, C.; Strina, G. (1999): *Designing and Simulating Sociotechnical Systems – Concepts and Strategies*. In: Human Factors and Ergonomics in Manufacturing, Vol 9 (3) pp. 245-252, 1999

Henning, K.; Marks, S. (1989): *Application oc Cybernetic Priciples in Organizational Development. 2nd International Symposium on Systems Research, Informatics and Cybernetics*. Baden-Baden, 1989.

Rieckmann, H.; Weissengruber, P. H. (1990): *Managing the Unmanageable? oder ... lassen sich komplexe Systeme überhaupt noch steuern? -Offenes Systemmanagement mit dem OSTO-Systemansatz*. In: Kraus, H.; Kailer, N.; Sandner, K. [Hrsg.]: *Management Development im Wandel*. Wien: 27-96.

Scheve, P./ Strina, G. (2003): *Das Konzept und die Implementierung von Partizipation und Empowerment im europäischen Vergleich*. In: Isenhardt, I./Hees, F./Henning, K. (Hrsg.): *Partizipation & Empowerment*. Aachen, 2003, S. 74-79

Strina, G. (2002): *Participation and Empowerment at Work. Keynote Lecture on the 4th Conference of the European Academy of Occupational Health Psychology*, December 5, 2002, Vienna, Austria.
see URL: www.inspe.net, InSPE-news.

Strina, G.; Honecker, N. (2003): *Changing Socio-Technical Systems – The Case of the John Deere Plant*. In: Brandt, D. (Ed.): *Human-Centred System Design. First: People, Second: Organization, Third: Technology*. Aachen (Mainz), 2003, pp. 162-172

Globalisation and Corporate Turbulence: Trade Union Response in UK Manufacturing[1]

MARTIN UPCHURCH, MIKE RICHARDSON, ANDY DANFORD

Internationalisation of the world economy has been associated with widespread restructuring of industry. This restructuring has involved corporate take-over, merger, joint ventures and strategic alliance formation as individual capitals have sought to readjust their position within an expanding international product market. In its extreme version, the associated 'globalisation thesis' has become all-embracing, with footloose capital making national regulatory regimes irrelevant if not defunct. For labour the consequences of such a scenario are extreme. Trade union power is, according to this thesis, emasculated, as workers become powerless in the face of capital's threat to withdraw and relocate. Critics of the 'globalization' thesis, such as Hirst and Thompson (1996), have already pointed out the overstated nature of the trends evident in the world economy. Sutcliffe and Glyn (1999) remind us that inward foreign investment (including intra-) in the first half of the 1990s to the EU was only 5.6 per cent of domestic investment. Similarly, only a 'clear minority' of workers in the UK are employed in industries that are directly or indirectly (as suppliers) subject to international competition through imports or exports. Far from being cowed by the forces of 'globalisation', British workers might have their power enhanced by the inter-relatedness of production and JIT, whereby one workplace stoppage can have quick repercussions in other production locations (Auerbach,1989).

---

[1] A more detailed account can be found in *New Unions, New Workplaces: A study of union resilience in the restructured workplace* by A. Danford, M. Richardson and M. Upchurch (London, Routledge 2003)

Nevertheless, as Hirst and Thompson (2000:336) suggest, the UK is 'the most internationalised of the major industrial countries' and, within the globalised economy, is 'far ahead of the game' in terms of its dependence on overseas trade and investment. In international comparative terms the degree of inward investment to the UK is very high, when compared to total GNP, and the level of overseas investment is also very high. UK manufacturing industry is thus more prone to the decisions of foreign owners and British capital, conversely, has more propensity to shift investment abroad. Barrell and Pain (1997), from their research of FDI into the EU, also claim distinctions in the type of inward investment between EU countries. They conclude that 'whilst the UK has clearly been able to attract relatively labour-intensive investments, it has fared relatively poorly in attracting more capital-intensive investments, and it has not been particularly attractive for sectors where R & D has been more significant'.

Secondly, within the global theatre, changes of corporate ownership and control have been commonplace and a new corporate instability has emerged. In addition the 'short-termism' associated with a relatively open and de-regulated financial markets which predominate in the UK has added to instability (Cosh et al, 1990; Marsh, 1991). This has led in turn to an increasing divorce between patterns of corporate ownership as a legal entity and the everyday decision-making structures in individual enterprises. The increased dominance of holding companies, strategic alliances and joint ventures has further confused patterns of corporate governance, producing a high degree of diversification and divisionalisation of corporate structure (Edwards et al, 1992). Such instability leads Hirst and Thompson (2000:352) to argue, in extremis, that the UK manufacturing sector at least 'is in danger of becoming a greater Canada, a branch-plant economy dependent on the decision of foreign owners'[2].

Third, the process of neo-liberal labour market and financial deregulation began earlier in the UK than in competitor nations and has been more intense in response to the high degree of internationalisation. As a result the impact on patterns and processes of managing the employment relationship has been severe. Standing (1997:11), and Capelli et al.(1997: 43-4) have argued that globalisation and deregulation have increased job insecurity. Concomitant with increased competitive pressures have also been employer initiatives to introduce new forms of work organisation to intensify work as

[2] This is arguably an exaggerated assessment. The UK remains second to the US in the rate of overseas direct investment and as such is a major player as a world source of FDI.

a precursor to raising labour productivity and cutting unit labour costs (Casey et al 1997; Gall, 1998; Howell, 1999; Upchurch and Danford 2001; Danford et al 2002a).

For British trade unions these processes, lasting through the 1980s and 1990s, when combined with Government legislative attacks on rights to organise, have created a cold and inhospitable industrial relations climate in which trade union membership and density has declined and industrial stoppages have plummeted to an all-time low[3]. The 1997 election of a New Labour Government has not fundamentally reversed or altered the orientation on market internationalisation. Prime Minister Blair, in his introduction to the 1998 Fairness at Work White Paper, outlined that the new UK employment legislation 'seeks to draw a line under the issue of industrial relations law....even after the changes we propose, Britain will have the most lightly regulated labour market of any leading economy in the world ' (DTI, 1998)[4].

The decline in union membership and the associated 'crisis of representation' have for a decade or more been the source of debate about the future of trade unions which has thus been of particular relevance to British unions with membership in the manufacturing sector. The trend towards more insecure and precarious employment associated with both corporate instability and new forms of work has posed UK trade unions with a series of problems (Heery and Abbott, 2000). At one level pessimistic conclusions have resulted linked to ideas of creeping individualism of the worker (e.g.Valkenburg, 1996), a fragmented working class (Phelps Brown 1990), and the impending decline of unions as solidaristic 'movements' (Crouch 1992). On the other hand a substantial body of empirical evidence seems to contradict these conclusions (Lind in Denmark, 1996, and Waddington and Whitson in the UK, 1997), suggesting, for example, that there is no evidence to confirm a shift from collectivism to individualism. In particular it has been argued that trade unions in the workplace must engage in the 'new politics of production' if

---

[3] Some caveats need to be expressed here. The latest returns on a membership of trade unions affiliated to the TUC in 1999 indicates a rise in membership for the first time since 1985, although density has fallen by 0.1 % over the year .Whilst the number of days lost through work stoppages has declined a TUC Survey (2000) reports a doubling in the number of strike ballots in the year up to May 2000 compared with the previous year.

[4] Quoted in G. Monbiot (2000) *Captive State: the Corporate Take-over of Britain* p7.

they are to continue to stake their claim (Stewart and Martinez Lucio 1998).

Whilst analysis and research has focussed on the response of trade union leaderships in the UK little has been reported on workplace union response to industrial restructuring (Ackers et al 1996; Mueller et al 2002). Fairbrother (2000) exceptionally argues that British manufacturing unions have been generally reactive, basing their strategies on survival. We attempt to begin to redress this lack of knowledge (see also Danford et al 2002b). In particular we argue there is a need to address the particular problems for workplace unionism caused by the exceptional instability of corporate governance and control described above. Is it possible for British unions to establish partnership discourse, for example, when they are faced with unstable ownership patterns and more change than continuity? Furthermore, is it not the case that the decentralisation of industrial relations and the emergent 'mosaic' of management styles and ownership patterns make it difficult to generalise experience of UK union renewal on a sectoral or industry wide basis? Could it be the case that the old certainties of centralised union approaches to recruitment and organising, based as they are on spheres of craft or occupational influence, are now becoming increasingly meaningless in a more unstable corporate environment with ever changing employer initiatives on production methods and processes? The research presented in this paper attempts to explore some of these questions with respect to three British trade unions at the workplace level with substantial membership in the manufacturing sector. Patterns of changing ownership and control of fifteen manufacturing enterprises are sketched together with their employment profiles. Continuity and change within management -union relationships and working practices are recorded before moving on to explore in more detail the resultant workplace union responses, providing further empirical evidence to inform the ongoing debate on prospects for trade union renewal.

The Research Base

Union representatives in fifteen manufacturing establishments in the west of England were interviewed between 1998 and 2000. The fifteen companies in the survey vary in products and ownership. Four of the companies were part of UK based MNCs, four were US based MNCs, two were Canadian based MNCs, two German based MNCs, one an Irish based MNC, one a joint venture (Swiss/UK), and one was a UK private limited company.

Table 1. Company profiles

Company	Union(s), (surveyed in bold)	Ownership and business	Working Practices
RubberCo	**AEEU** (60 members, 94% density), TGWU	UK based auto and technical products	Flexible working hours, teamworking, *kaizen*. Considerable union influence evident on work organisation. Recent attempts by union to negotiate introduction of multi-skilling (mechanical/electrical) rebuffed by management.
PagerCo	**AEEU** (80% density)	UK based MNC (Blick International), computerised timing products (e.g.pagers)	'Empowerment' and increased functional flexibility.
CerealCo	**AEEU** (98% density)	Anglo-Swiss Joint Venture, breakfast cereals	
CheeseCo	**AEEU** (100% density), formerly TGWU	Irish MNC, cheese manufacturing	Fully automated production process after introduction of computerised 'menus' for cheese manufacture. Tight monitoring and control of worker output.
BrakeCo	**AEEU** (50 members), TGWU	German based MNC. (formerly UK owned). Manufacture of hydraulic brakes.	Teamworking. JIT for last twelve years.
InjectorCo	**AEEU**	US based MNC,	

Company	Union(s), (surveyed in bold)	Ownership and business	Working Practices
	(50% density) single union agreement	manufacturing injector bodies.	
OptoCo	**AEEU** (300members) non-recognised for bargaining but recognised for disciplinary cases.	Canadian based MNC, optoelectrics.	Teamworking abandoned after worker opposition connected to peer assessment.
CopyCo	**AEEU** (669 members, 66% density), GMB (413), MSF (140) **MSF** (140 members, 66 % density)	US based MNC, document processing systems.	Assembly and testing outsourced. Semi-autonomous teamworking (contradicts temporary working). Polarisation of skills.
AlloyCo	GMB, **AEEU** (110 members), MSF	US based MNC. Nickel alloy manufacturer.	Teamworking and multi-skilling introduced ten years ago. Continued reluctance to accept multi-skilling by workforce.
HydraulicCo	**AEEU** (180 members, 82% density)	US based MNC, aircraft hydraulic systems.	Teamworking proposed by union but opposed by management
ComponentCo	**GMB/APEX** (80%:50% density)	Canadian based MNC making auto components. Formerly UK owned.	'Japanese' practices introduced - *kaizen* group problem solving. Cell managers and team leaders. Close surveillance and control through team leaders.
PaperCo	**GMB**	Ex family firm owned since 1995 by UK based MNC ,	Stalled attempt to introduce teamworking. Foremen still remain. Job and

Company	Union(s), (surveyed in bold)	Ownership and business	Working Practices
		making high quality security paper e.g. travellers' cheques.	skill demarcation persists.
PlasticCo	**GMB** (90 members)	Private limited company making plastic mouldings.	Traditional managerial structure. Lack of teamworking. Computerised systems introduced with no effect on work organisation. Payment by results.
ValveCo	**MSF** (250 members, 50% density)	UK MNC making thermosatic valves and water control systems.	Flatter management structure, breakdown of demarcation barriers, multi-skilling, teamworking, empowerment, increased responsibility, outsourcing
CarCo	**MSF** (430 staff members, 33 pattern makers and 18 craft)	German MNC owned (at time of survey). Formerly Japanese owned. Now part of UK based consortium.	Flatter management structure, Japanese philosophy, team work, empowerment

MSF = Manufacturing, Science and Finance; AEEU = Amalgamated Engineering and Electricians Union

Most of the companies had experienced recent changes of ownership, and only the British private limited company, had a stable ownership history. The nature of products made is identified in Table 1, and express a heterogeneous mix including SIC categories in food manufacture, paper products, metal manufacture, rubber, plastics, autos, auto components and other machinery. Unions were recognised and had full bargaining rights in all of the establishments except one (OptoCo), where the union had representative rights only. The unions on which the research is based are the Manufacturing, Science and Finance union (MSF), the general workers' union GMB, and the engineering and electrical union AEEU [5]. The MSF was chosen because of its multi-occupational base representing mainly technicians, specialists and supervisory staffs within the manufacturing sector. Both the GMB and AEEU represent contrasting examples of trade union spheres of influence within the British context. The GMB representing mainly manual and production workers in public utilities and manufacturing, and the AEEU representing skilled and semi-skilled production workers primarily in the engineering industry (but with some public sector membership). AEEU representatives were interviewed in ten of the establishments, GMB in three and MSF in three. In comparative terms, they exhibit somewhat different trade union profiles and history and as a consequence provide a rich source of variables for research analysis. The MSF was one of the first UK unions to officially adopt the organising model, despite apparent tensions in the relationship between national and regional officials in its interpretation and implementation (Carter, 1997). Branches retain a relatively high degree of autonomy when compared to other unions, reflecting the dominant tradition of the old ASTMS within the new union (Carter, 1991). The AEEU has long had a system of shop steward representation at the workplace. A tightening of control from above in the areas of industrial policy and political activity has weakened the devolved district power structure that existed in the union's old engineering wing. The GMB adopted a steward system relatively late, as a move to a more open style and as an alternative to the over concentration of power with regional officials that has long characterised the union (Maksymiw, 1990; Fairbrother, 2000: 38-40).

Corporate Turbulence and Restructuring of Work

All bar one of the manufacturing establishments researched for this study has been subject to a change in ownership in recent years, either through joint partnerships, acquisitions, mergers or disposals. This corporate

---

[5] Since conducting this research a new union, Amicus, has been created from a merger of the AEEU and the MSF. However, for the time being, there remains relative autonomy of the two sections.

turbulence shows little sign of seriously slowing. Echoing this point, it has been confirmed since the completion of our fieldwork that CarCo, one of the sample establishments examined, was bought by a UK based consortium after being sold by its German owner. The parent company of another, ValveCo, has called an extraordinary meeting of its shareholders to obtain their support for the disposal of the whole of its plumbing arm, which includes ValveCo.

WERS (Workplace Employment Relations Survey) 1998 has identified a number of distinctive features associated with establishments that have undergone ownership change in the 1990s, two of which are particularly relevant here. First, a change in ownership was cited as a notable cause for significant downsizing, although a reduction in product demand was the main reason given. Second, WERS found that in a minority of cases a move to the centralisation of managerial decision-making followed corporate restructuring. This latter development was frequently accompanied by shifts in managerial attitude and behaviour in respect to industrial relations, especially in the private sector (Millward et al, 2000; 24, 27, 78—79) [6]. Our findings show a similar pattern, although another variable, a fall in profits, emerged to stake a strong claim as one of the drivers behind workforce reductions, restructuring the organisation of work and the transformation of management-employee relations. The regularity of corporate restructuring was often found to be destabilising, weakening employee morale.

Nearly half of our survey had been subject to ownership change in the 1990s, subsequently suffering a significant reduction in the number of workers employed. Between 1998-1999 AlloyCo cut 200 jobs, which amounted to 18% of the workforce. This reduction trailed the disposal of the business by a Canadian multinational to an American multinational in 1998, a decision that was no doubt also influenced by severe financial losses, registered at over £1,000,000, in the subsequent 12 months. Proportionately BrakeCo endured similar job losses but within a more concentrated period, 1989—1999, under the direction first of an American and then a German multinational. Redundancies and natural wastage reduced the numbers employed from 1,410 in 1989 to 370 in 1999. InjectorCo has been subject to two take-overs in recent years, the first in 1996 by an Anglo-American engineering group and the second by an American multinational in 1999. At the time of the interview in 1999

[6] This shift in managerial attitudes, according to WERS, was even more likely when workplace mergers or splits accompanied a change in ownership.

InjectorCo employed 450 people. However, nine months previously staff levels were as high as 700 but due to the loss of a major contract all temporary workers were dismissed along with 96 permanent staff. It is too early to say what impact the recent change in ownership will have but in its wake jobs have been shed in two other UK plants in the group. Ownership change, job cuts and losses of £1.9m were recorded at HydraulicCo. CopyCo experienced a reduction in the number of core workers following the American buy-out of its European partner and the transfer of some production work to a Greenfield site in Ireland. ComponentCo was acquired by a Canadian multinational in 1996 but only recently has it shed jobs. It slashed its workforce by 28% in response to the fall in demand from Rover's threatened Longbridge plant. Finally, two years after being taken over by a UK multinational in 1995 PaperCo restructured and rationalised its business reducing via redundancy its shop floor staff by 10%.

It is not the intention here to review the overall union response to job cuts but simply to highlight two key issues where some degree of collective anti-corporatism was apparent. The first example occurs at CopyCo where one of the unions surveyed (MSF) had adopted a form of community unionism by organising marches and demonstrations within and with the help of the local community against the threatened transfer of jobs from the west of England plant to Ireland. This outside campaign supplemented lobbying of the local M.P.s. The strategy met with partial success in that job transfer was limited.

At BrakeCo fears of plant closure following take-over by a German MNC, had prompted a narrower 'constitutional' campaign with the AEEU and TGWU jointly pursuing the issue, with the help of the local Labour M.P. and MEP, through the UK and European Parliaments. The plant has faced constant redundancies in the last ten years. The site is split into four manufacturing divisions, which have been subject to some recent 're-unification'. The main UK plant has since been closed with some limited manufacturing/assembly taking place in a new and smaller local site.

The German parent is clearly responding to tight product market competition in the supply of air brakes to lorry manufacturers. All low tech (old-fashioned brake manufacture) is being transferred to an Indian plant and all high tech (new specification) manufacture to a French and a Hungarian plant. Manufacturing is therefore to be concentrated in global production units despite the fact that the UK factory was once the world leader, produces high quality products, is profitable, and has over-full order books. Whilst the two plant unions were able to co-operate at UK level the experience within the EWC has been less fruitful. The TGWU Convenor, who sits on the EWC, was cold shouldered at EWC meetings by reps. from the French and German plants, reflecting a more sectionalised response in the face of intra-national plant competition for jobs. As the AEEU steward explained:

> *The last time C. went[to the EWC], they told him we're not interested in BrakeCo in Bristol, that's going. They've been told in their various factories that its closing. When he bought up the subject, he felt as though he was the odd man out, there was the old feeling that - you're going, we don't need to talk to you.*

Such intra-national plant competition provides the MNC with an opportunity to exploit divisions in the workforce by introducing 'coercive comparisons' between plants based on a cost basis (Müller and Purcell, 1992) and thus divide and rule with respect to employee relations strategy (Marginson, 1994).

Turning to look at the impact of the examples (HydraulicCo, CopyCo, AlloyCo and PaperCo) where the centralisation of managerial decision-making clearly accompanied changes in ownership, our evidence suggests that in three of the four cases divisions opened up between 'old' and 'new' within organisational hierarchies. This development has had serious implications for union organisation and strategy. The GMB senior steward at PaperCo, for example, noted that:

> *There's been a lot of redundancies. There's been a lot of restructuring on a major level within the workforce right across the Group, right across the world where they are multi-nationa....What they tend to do, listening to the Directors and Chief Executive, is leave everything to local management. They are basically telling them you have to cut this and cut that, and it's up to him how he finances it and does it. They seem to be mill by mill or site by site negotiations.*

Despite the apparent delegation of corporate governance to local managers, under the direction of a new managing director they had to work within strict financial parameters and a set of strategic goals, which was often the cause of antagonistic relations between management and the GMB representatives.

At AlloyCo the AEEU senior steward was damning in his depiction of local managers' subjection to central control from the plant's head office in America:

R&D is carried out in America, product development is carried out here, but the basic structure...I don't even think anyone knows what the hell is going on.

In two of these cases the extent to which the centralisation of managerial decision-making curtailed the authority of local managers impacted on the nature of industrial relations. In the case of AlloyCo this development led to frustrated attempts by AEEU to forge a partnership arrangement. And at PaperCo it helped to create a more hostile environment, which contributed to the outbreak of a prolonged industrial dispute involving a positive strike ballot. In this dispute GMB members imposed its workplace collective identity by seeking to negotiate local bonus arrangements on top of the national agreement.

Restructuring of Work: Re-active and Pro-active Union Responses

The intensification of global competition and corporate restructuring in the manufacturing industry has impelled many companies into reorganising their production processes. The manufacturing establishments visited were no exception, although divergent practices between and within establishments existed. The differing experiences are explored below beginning with the situation at the three manufacturing establishments where kaizen practice has been introduced.

Testimony from the senior stewards from ComponentCo, RubberCo and InjectorCo reveal some contrasting reactions in regard to the implementation of kaizen as a specific practice.[7] The workforce at ComponentCo have reconciled themselves to changes in the way in which work is organised, having been subjected to more flexible working, labour discipline and labour control than most other manufacturing firms visited. It was under the previous ownership that the process of replacing the traditional operational management practices and culture with the Japanese model first began. ComponentCo accelerated the process of change, drawing on a range of Japanese management techniques but with a particular focus on kaizen group problem solving. This change of strategy was based on the expectancy, suggested by influential commentators such as Womack et al (1990), that benefits such as increased productivity and improvements in quality would follow. The GMB senior steward was in

---

[7] At InjectorCo kaizen was implemented under the *leitmotif* Total Quality.

little doubt that the company used kaizen to reduce non-productive time and intensify the pace of production. He believed the company was able to achieve this because many of his members were beguiled by the 'work smarter, not harder' notion:

Every time you do a kaizen the gap widens between the number of people actually doing the job and they amount of work they are supposed to do....Yes, and if anybody complains, they say it's not our suggestion, people on the line suggested this.

Despite the scepticism of the senior steward, and some long service union members, towards kaizen there was an absence of organised factory-wide union strategy to deal with its impact.
The reaction from the AEEU convenor to kaizen practice at RubberCo was more pro-active, largely based on the fact that the union had secured a degree of involvement from the beginning. Since 1994 the company has employed a procedural type agreement with AEEU to ensure that a broad consensus was reached before any changes in relation to continuous improvement were introduced. This is how the senior steward detailed its operation:

On our engineering team now, we have a document where we make modifications on the way we work ...I make sure the changes are OK with the membership and we all go back and sign on the dotted line. We started with issue 1 going back a number of years, and now we're up to issue 9.

The fact that the union is able to sanction changes in work organisation reveals that it has maintained some influence at this plant and is able to mollify to some extent the way in which kaizen can be used as a tool of labour exploitation. Moreover, that kaizen has, according to the senior steward, not been applied in a deterministic fashion, as only 'the bits' thought to be beneficial have been utilised, adds weight to this point.
At InjectorCo in 1997 a Total Quality (TQ) strategy was introduced as a process of continuous improvement. Interestingly an AEEU shop steward interviewed was a TQ facilitator, which no doubt contributed to the emergence of conflicting views of TQ. He remarked that 'at least now there's a formal structure by which people can suggest improvement ideas, they will be actioned one way or another.' The deputy convenor, however, had a different perception:

Now they want you to make too many suggestions. Whether they want you to make 2 suggestions a day or week, I'm not sure. They can actually downgrade you on assessment if you haven't given enough ideas. I've had 2-3 people come to me on recent assessments, so this is something we've got to look into.

All employees had received basic TQ training, including a two-day course. Managers and TQ facilitators had received between four and ten day's tuition. A principal aim of this TQ strategy was to target the elimination of idle time or to be more precise to purge the effort, movement and use of time that did not add value. Given the association of TQ and kaizen with the intensification of work (Delbridge et al, 1992) it is interesting to note that that the shop steward, who was also a TQ facilitator, posed the opposite view claiming that kaizen 'made work easier for people because they are having to do less unnecessary tasks.'
Although kaizen embraces a number of methods and aims, after two years of operation the signs are that the workforce at InjectorCo is losing interest. Fewer suggestions are coming through despite the fact that workers' appraisals incorporate involvement with TQ and team managers are assessed on the number of ideas that their teams generate. In fact this coercive attitude may well have contributed to alienating the workforce from proactively engaging with TQ as implied by the deputy convenor's comment that the inclusion of TQ on appraisals is 'why we're seeing all the pitfalls from it.'

Team-working was present in all bar three establishments, PlasticCo, HydraulicCo and OptoCo. At PaperCo team-working was in place but according to the senior GMB steward was not fully operational. Apart from these exclusions the extent to which the implementation of team-working could be described as fully autonomous (see Cully et al, 1999, 43) varied. Team-working in most but not all of the establishments functioned to breakdown traditional ways of working in order to increase flexibility through the promotion of multi-skilling, multi-tasking and to a lesser degree job rotation and empowerment. Old lines of demarcation have been eroded exposing as inadequate the traditional workplace unionism organised along skilled, semi-skilled, white-collar, or blue-collar lines. At CopyCo MSF has taken cognisance of this by reorganising union representation so that each team has a shop steward as teams have been empowered to handle a whole range of industrial relations issues. This reorganisation of union representation did not occur elsewhere. For instance, at InjectorCo, despite the existence of team-working since the opening of the plant, union representation was still organised along craft and blue and white-collar lines.

The principal outcome of team-working has been the erosion of traditional demarcation lines and associated restrictive practices. This was evident at PagerCo, CopyCo, ComponentCo, ValveCo, CarCo, BrakeCo, InjectorCo, and CheeseCo. A few developed examples illustrate this point. At PagerCo teams are cross-functional with labour flexibility between as well as within teams. The reduction of the workforce by 33% in 1998, a response to a fall in profits, triggered an extension of multi-tasking and multi-skilling. According to the senior steward:

> *Because of the low numbers of staff, it's a case of it's essential now for people to do other work...They [managers] are encouraging more self-development because it used to be one person would do one type of job all the time.*

Experimentation of a new form of teamworking was underway at CopyCo. Based on a system employed at its sister plant in Holland all team leaders and managers are in the process of being replaced by a much smaller number of coaches. The idea is to 'empower' teams to manage themselves with a coach come mentor to consult, guide and advise them. The AEEU convenor explained that teams were empowered to 'sort out everything, the day to day running of their section, they will run themselves.'

However, there is an apparent contradiction in CopyCo's's approach. Given the increased use of agency workers (see below), who do not enjoy job security guarantees, commitment to semi-autonomous teamworking may well be weaker. And the success of management initiatives involving 'empowerment' depends heavily on procuring employee commitment (Wilkinson et al, 1992; Guest 1992). Moreover, given the rationale for using agency labour — the reduction of labour costs — and the temporary nature of the employment contract it is less likely that capital investment in the training and development of these workers would be at the same level as that given to permanent staff. These factors are potentially divisive in the shift to team empowerment

At ComponentCo, team leaders are appointed from the factory floor by higher management, rather than democratically elected by the workforce. Supervisory line managers have been abolished. The GMB senior shop steward implied that the selection of factory operatives as team leaders was based on the servility of the employee to switch loyalties and become the eyes, mouthpiece and defender of management governance. This is how the he put it:

> *[They] take ordinary people from the shop floor-you are now a team leader. You are now on the first rung of the ladder for promotion. But, you must report any wrong doings that are done by your colleagues. We've actually had instances where union members are instrumental in another union member being disciplined.*

Such discipline by peers is at least as coercive as the more traditional way of organising the production process.

Other brief examples capture a wider spectrum of problems associated with new working practices. The major contentious change at ValveCo, where team-working has been operating for five years, was the switch from an individual to a team bonus scheme. Team-working and continuous improvement was incorporated into an agreement at CarCo in 1992, an arrangement that continued after a change of ownership in 1994 as guarantees of job security given in 1992 were renewed. Subsequent disposal of the plant by its German owners raised new doubts on the agreements' future. At BrakeCo, just-in-time (JIT) and team-working had been operational for at least 12 years but the new management could not meet previous allied practices such as employee involvement, team briefing and so forth because its commitment to the future of the plant was again in doubt. This gave rise to rumours that the plant would close. To a limited degree evidence also emerged of an association between downsizing and a subsequent widening of functional flexibility. For instance, since redundancies at InjectorCo functional flexibility has increased although workers who demonstrated a special aptitude for a particular function were less likely to move from one function to another because team leaders 'know they're going to get output'. Similar findings emerged at PaperCo but at AlloyCo, despite significant job losses over many years, the use of multi-skilling has contracted rather than expanded as a result of worker reticence. This is how the AEEU senior steward put it:

> *We've got multi-skilling...it was a brilliant idea when it was taken on, but it's never really come to fruition in so far as everybody wanted to do everybody else's job at the start because it was something different, now nobody wants to do somebody else's job, only their own.*

The changes in work organisation described above suggest widespread use by employers of new management techniques designed simultaneously to encourage quality consciousness and to cut production costs. Such initiatives can be linked with a drive to improve organisational competitiveness in an internationalised product market. Our survey reveals a mixed union response, which is generally defensive and sometimes contradictory. There are examples, however, of more pro-active union initiatives designed to wrest back some organisational control and to engage in the 'new politics of production' (Stewart and Martinez Lucio, 1998). Examples of this are the development of procedural rules over the implementation of kaizen, the re-organisation of union structure to accommodate team-working, and developing reticence to engage in quality initiatives and group suggestion. This ability of unions at the workplace level to move from re-active to pro-active will depend to a certain extent on changes in management-union relations, and it is this aspect which we now record.

Management-Union Relations

The characteristics of management-union relations in the fifteen companies varied reflecting past organisational strategy and culture as well as the entrenchment or otherwise of the trade unions in the process of job regulation and control. In most of the AEEU recognised workplaces, for example, union density is high and traditions of job demarcation and joint regulation have been established. However, in both InjectorCo and OptoCo recognition (or partial recognition) is recent and management maintain a hostile attitude to the unions. Differences can nevertheless be discerned on two spectrum - firstly, that of hardening/softening relationships and secondly, the degree of partnership implementation - and it is these differences and possible explanations for the differences which are explored below.

Hardening and Softening Relationships

Questions were asked during the interviews as to whether or not relationships between union and management at the workplace have improved (softened) or deteriorated (hardened) in recent years. Responses were evenly divided, with some of the 'softening' respondees reporting moves towards a 'partnership' agenda. At RubberCo a hardening relationship was linked by the AEEU stewards to a cultural change in the company from a 'family firm' paternalist orientation to one where management had adopted more strategic human resource approaches including the adoption of kaizen. As the steward explained:

> *I think over the last few years, they've become less caring... It used to be, once upon a time, if you worked at RubberCo, it was a very family oriented thing, you felt you were part of a big family. I don't think that is now in place.*

The steward attributed the adoption of this new strategic focus to a shift in financial values within the company whereby shareholders had paramount importance above the needs of the workforce.
A similar hardening approach can be discerned from the GMB stewards at both PaperCo and ComponentCo. At PaperCo there remains a strong tradition of job demarcation and attempts to introduce team-working have previously stalled. The change in management attitude was claimed by the stewards to be a direct product of the take-over of the company by a British based MNC:

> *When D LR took over, it was what I classed as welcome to the 1990s syndrome. All of a sudden you were going to get things that would never have happened before.*

Interestingly, this approach involved DLR bucking the trend to decentralise collective bargaining to divisional or plant level. It seems that rather than draw the association between increased productivity and pay closer the company actually favoured the elimination of local pay bargaining. Whether this was a conscious strategy in order to reduce the power of shop stewards and the rank and file at its individual sites is hard to say.

At ComponentCo new control and ownership was accompanied with a less consultative management style. In contrast to PaperCo, however, it chose to decentralise pay bargaining, which had a deleterious effect on cross-plant contact between the union. 'Best practice' had not prevailed and collective union approaches to pay and conditions appear to have evaporated. One rare contact visit by the ComponentCo steward to a sister plant highlighted the differences. He explained:

> *I couldn't believe it - fire exits with motorbikes stored in them. Horrendous it was... When he came round here he couldn't believe it.*

He said he just didn't believe the facilities we've got here. I said we weren't handed them. We bloody fought for them.

The decentralisation of collective bargaining exposed a potential for re-igniting collective workplace identity, but this had yet to materialise. Only examples of sectional disputes were given, associated mostly with team-based targets or changes to working arrangements. The 'new collectivism' associated with team-working and fractured collective bargaining thus had an impact on employees in this instance, and whilst there was evidence of a more sectionalised worker response it was also evident that the union still formed the focus of worker orientation in addressing discontent.

At InjectorCo the shift towards a more hardened adversarial relationship was associated with a hard fought recognition campaign where AEEU is now the sole recognised union. The first ballot for recognition was lost but in the run up to a second ballot two years later the management had taken the opportunity with a move to a 'greenfield' site to tighten surveillance and control and to impose tighter work regimes. The existing staff association clearly could not cope with these attacks and in the second ballot the AEEU won on the basis of the ability to provide more effective representation

In these plants where a hardening relationship has been experienced management-union relations are strongly adversarial. Whilst all of them have experienced recent changes of ownership the trigger for a more aggressive management approach to unions appeared to be different, suggesting that wider contextual factors than ownership change configure employers' employee relations' strategies. Prominent among these wider factors are changes in the organisation of work, shifts in organisation culture away from paternalism, and employer response to emergent union organisation.

Companies exhibiting a softening approach were PagerCo, CheeseCo, BrakeCo, PlasticCo, CarCo and ValveCo. In the case of ValveCo the MSF stewards reported an attempt by management after changes in ownership to introduce an open and consensus based TQM programme to replace traditional hierarchical authority. The introduction of teams was used to replace foremen and a training programme introduced ("First in Service") to inject quality consciousness. However, there was a distinct fragility in this new consensus which was exposed as soon as management decided to implement immediate closure of the toolroom. As the steward explained:

> *The whole of FIS was all about frankness and openness and all that. But when you had a situation where they shut the tool room over night and they'd been negotiating it for the last 2 years, FIS went out the window.*

The other companies all shared the new discourse of partnership to a lesser or greater extent and it is to this second dimension of similarity and difference that we now turn.

Partnership?

One specific open question asked in interviews was the degree to which 'partnership' may or may not have been introduced into the companies. No single definition of partnership was offered by the interviewers other than that which suggested notions of management and union 'working together' as an alternative to 'them and us'. The question was asked with the objective of probing changes in employee relations as well as assessing the diffusion of partnership discourse to the workplace level. Of the fifteen companies a total of seven recorded interviews where stewards referred to a partnership agenda. However, in two of the companies, OptoCo and AlloyCo, partnership agendas and issues had been suggested by the unions and rebuffed or ignored by the management. The only actual written and jointly agreed partnership agreement was in one company - CarCo. In three of the other companies (CerealCo, CheeseCo and BrakeCo) partnership was claimed by the stewards to exist either in non-written form or as part of a new discourse between management and union. The final example, CopyCo, deserves special attention as two distinctly different responses to the partnership question emerged from the two separate sets of stewards interviewed (AEEU and MSF).

Attention here focuses on this range of 'partnership' responses and their contextual triggers. At OptoCo the AEEU stewards had proposed a partnership approach against a background of attempts by management to increasingly marginalise the union and to exploit the use of temporary and contract labour. The union had not achieved full recognition at the plant but was given time to represent members in disciplinary and grievance hearings. Approximately ten per cent of the 3000 strong workforce were members of the AEEU. The union were clearly frustrated by the lack of progress in establishing working relations with management and had used a partnership approach as a strategy to bring management to the negotiating table. However, the rebuff by management clearly demoralised the union in a situation where 'partnership' may have been seen as a short cut to legitimacy by the union at the expense of building up membership by more traditional means. As the steward reported:

Now we're getting more and more champing at the bit, we want to go forward now, we want our recognition. We've worked long and hard for what we've got and they won't give an inch. They just will not react to us.

At AlloyCo the AEEU stewards were similarly proactive in attempting to introduce a partnership arrangement driven by the recent history of compulsory redundancies and substantial financial losses. As such it might have been responsive to suggestions for crisis management and partnership approaches as part of a 'survival pact' between management and union (see Knell, 1999 for other such examples). The steward explained the strategy:

We allowed our company to be reduced from 2,500 people and a world leader to 900 people with an infantry line trying to hold it back. What we're saying to you is we want to get involved with you in a partnership. We want to see arbitration instead of industrial action. We want to see flexible working patterns. We want to see lifelong learning and education. We want to see single spine structures. We want to see the ability to utilise the resource we've got within the plant to the best of its ability and to utilise best practice. The things that will make this company successful.

The lack of interest by the UK based manager has led the union to suspect that he is acting on 'orders from above' and that one of the employers' strategies may be to marginalise the unions in advance of closure.
At CarCo the original written and agreed partnership agreement was signed after ownership of the company passed from a British to a Japanese based MNC. The national partnership agreement was narrowly accepted by the joint unions in a ballot and was accompanied by a 'japanisation' programme and the removal of a lower level management and supervisory tiers. Distinct changes in management style had preceded and followed the agreement. As the MSF senior steward explained:

The old management style was totally confrontational. As soon as you'd got a shop stewards card the local manager was intent on dominating you and deliberately set you up for things...I think the Japanese profile was the team leader would replace the shop steward and once they'd done that, they would have gone after the activist I think, no doubt about that. But I don't think the CarCo management really wanted to play that game and now of course we are in with the Germans, you've got European law backing you and all the rest of it, so we're a necessity to them now.

The commitment to a partnership approach by the senior management was undoubtedly sincere and would involve disciplining lower tier managers who continued to operate in the old ways. The employers' strategy was to seek to raise productivity at the plant by adopting a 'win-win' mutual gains partnership approach whereby new methods of working were traded for job guarantees and a more comprehensive benefits package. A downturn in the companies' fortunes and a corporate take-over triggered the opportunity. However, since the interview new German owners have sold off part of CarCo, and the plant has been subject to a management buy-out.

At CerealCo, where the AEEU has 98 per cent membership, a partnership 'arrangement' exists whereby some support is given by management to new entrants in terms of encouraging them to join the union. In this case the stewards saw partnership as little more than an attempt by management to develop a better understanding with the union and to seek more co-operation. Differing interpretations of partnership were apparent at both PagerCo and BrakeCo, with no real substantive agreement attached to the claimed new or emerging 'partnership' approach. At PagerCo the AEEU steward argued that he thought partnership 'was developing' whilst at BrakeCo the senior AEEU steward's vision of partnership included co-operation, transparency of decision-making and the harmonisation of working conditions. In practice this had meant that a newly arrived Managing Director:

...did away with private parking spaces' [and] 'did away with a lot of barriers and their door was always open... What he wanted from us, the workers, was the way we could participate as trade unions in a joint venture of making this company profitable so we could keep our jobs.

However, the new German owners of BrakeCo later forced this particular British manager out of the company and the new management has since abandoned any partnership-type approach to industrial relations. Fears were expressed by the steward that corporate plans included the probable closure of the UK factory as work was shifted abroad to other plants owned by the parent German based MNC.

The examples above illustrate that a wider corporate context predetermines the possibilities for partnership arrangements or agreements. In particular, if a remote corporate HQ is seeking to run down operations then the prospects for a 'survival pact' approach from the union are remote. Similarly if corporate ownership changes, or corporate strategy changes, then any partnership agreement becomes fragile and tenuous.

'Community Unionism' at CopyCo?

CopyCo is interesting in relation to the exploration of the 'partnership' experience. The sister plant in the USA, with about 4,000 employees, has a partnership agreement with the Union of Needletrades, Industrial, and Textile Employees (UNITE). Its attraction to the union has been the commitment of the organisation to providing job security. However, the company is now under intense pressure to outsource more of its production to lower-cost manufacturers around the world. In short this means to sustain the partnership agreement the union would have to deliver increased productivity, quality and flexibility over and above the levels demanded in the past (Kochan, 1999).

CopyCo provides an example whereby the lead given by the MSF and AEEU convenors, in keeping with the tradition, style and strategy of their respective unions, differed. The impact of these differences was not so great as to harm the operation of the combined activity of the MSF, AEEU, GMB and APEX on both the joint shop steward committee and the joint negotiating committee. However, if these variances are translated into a diagrammatic line of continuum between moderation and militancy (Kelly 1996) we would observe that the MSF holds a relatively more militant perspective than the AEEU.

Contradictory accounts of management/union relationships emerged from the interviews held with the convenors at the plant. One concern of the ('militant') MSF convenor was that the transfer of the Human Resource function to business councils, in regard to negotiating changes in working conditions, enabled the company to circumvent convenors and senior stewards and reach agreements with inexperienced junior stewards within the divisional forum. The particular worry was that agreements made in isolation might prove to be detrimental to the interests of the membership as a whole. A second concern was that since the American arm of CopyCo bought out its European partner in 1997 higher levels of organisational decision-making have been increasingly subject to central control. According to the MSF convenor contact with American decision-makers is difficult:

You can get to them [decision-makers] if you kick up a stink. The one thing that this company doesn't like is any bad publicity. So it depends on how far you are prepared to go on how much access you can get. But, the Americans do not like dealing with British trade unions. They totally detest it and if they can avoid it, they will do.

Given the misgivings expressed by the MSF convenor it is unsurprising to find that MSF stewards perceive CopyCo as a non-partnership establishment. Yet AEEU stewards signified the contrary which was supported by the inferences and observations of the AEEU convenors reflected in the following remarks of the deputy convenor:

We haven't got a formal Partnership agreement, but we have been referred to at various meetings as "partners". I believe we are partners in these ventures even though we haven't got a Partnership agreement.

In essence the four business councils are consultative bodies made up of senior managers (including the human resource manager), accountants and senior and junior shop stewards. Non-union staff are denied representation. The aim of the business councils is to find ways of improving aspects of the organisation such as operations, strategy and so forth but their remit forbids encroaching on issues subject to negotiation between management and the unions. According to the AEEU deputy convenor, however, these councils are important sources of knowledge useful for negotiating purposes and developing union policy.

A further sign that AEEU convenors viewed themselves as tied into an informal partnership agreement was their willingness to withhold the release of information flagged up by the company as confidential. This seems to be a clear rejection of membership mobilisation in favour of greater dependence on the employer. The AEEU convenor revealed:

It's given us the opportunity to divert some major decisions, to find some innovative ways between joining management that we can avoid some major confrontations.....People come up to you and ask you what their future is and you know you can't say anything.

However, early in 1999 the company announced that it was to switch 500 jobs from the UK factory to a new plant in Dundalk (Ireland). Significantly, only the interview with the MSF convenor revealed the community campaign that took place in an effort to save these jobs: 'We've had marches through the village, mass meetings out there where we've invited all the local media, all the locals.' The European Works Council was involved and the issue was raised in the European Parliament. The MSF membership at CopyCo was balloted, voted in favour of taking industrial action and embarked on a course of non-co-operation. The AEEU convenors made no reference to this campaign of action. At a later date an acting convenor confirmed that AEEU was involved with MSF and GMB in this campaign but did not ballot its membership or embrace any form of industrial action. The end result was that the company pledged $30 million investment and agreed to make no enforced redundancies among permanent staff at the plant. Ostensibly, by offering job security to the 'core' workers the company was edging closer towards a partnership agreement based on mutual gains with the unions similar to the arrangement it had with the Union of Needletrades, Industrial, and Textile Employees (UNITE) at the company's manufacturing plant in America (Kochan 1999). However, CopyCo management only responded after workers, and the local community, were mobilised into action, suggesting that 'partnership' from a management perspective offered a block to worker radicalisation in the plant.

Discussion and Summary

This paper has attempted to trace the connections between corporate restructuring, changes in work organisation and the union response to such changes. The UK manufacturing sector has formed the research base of the study and reference has been made to the exceptionally intense rate of change experienced within the UK as a consequence of its embededness in the world economy. The manufacturing establishments surveyed did, indeed, exhibit an exceptionally high degree of corporate change with fourteen engaging in recent partnership, acquisition, merger or disposal activity. Half of the establishments subject to corporate ownership change also experienced significant downsizing, confirming other evidence that corporate restructuring invariably involved job loss. Associated with corporate restructuring were significant introduction of new methods and ways of organising work, such that continuous improvement (kaizen) and team-working were frequently mentioned in the workplace representatives' interviews as important recently introduced changes. One particularly striking aspect of this has been the implicit and explicit erosion of job demarcation lines and a shift away from 'traditional' working practices. Such changes have, as would be expected, posed enormous challenges for trade union organisation at workplace level. However, there is sporadic evidence in the survey that the unions have managed to retain some control and authority and to be pro-active in determining new organisational and bargaining strategies. For example, in some cases (e.g CopyCo) one union (MSF) re-organised itself at the workplace to encourage the election of union representatives within each team. At PaperCo the introduction of team-working has been successfully resisted by the GMB and job demarcation retained. This contrasts with other examples (e.g ComponentCo) where management has replaced line managers with appointed team leaders from the factory floor, based, according to the GMB, on the 'servility' of the individual operative. With continuous improvement programmes our evidence shows that in some cases (e.g. AEEU at RubberCo) the union has negotiated the schemes and has become actively involved in their implementation whilst attempting to 'soften' their impact on workload. In other cases (e.g. ComponentCo), no union strategy has evolved to either oppose or co-operate and consequently schemes have been introduced which have been clearly detrimental in terms of work intensification. Our evidence on union response to changing work organisation has therefore been mixed, with examples of emergent pro-active, re-active or passive union strategies.

An obvious consequence of intense corporate change has been instability in corporate culture and management employee relations' strategy. Evidence of 'remote control' appeared in a number of establishments, particularly those with US ownership. In some workplaces there was also some evidence of emerging 'partnership' discourse, although a written partnership agreement was only found in one establishment (CarCo). What is interesting is that the driving force for partnership agendas came from different sources. In two cases ((OptoCo and AlloyCo) the issue had been raised by the union and rebuffed by management. In three other companies it was a joint initiative whereas in the divergent case of CopyCo management had accommodated the issue with one union (AEEU) whilst at the same time the other union (MSF) had distanced itself. In these latter cases there emerges a tendency for the union side to become involved in partnership discourse either as an extension of a moderate (c/f militant) approach or, alternatively, as a perceived need to establish a 'survival pact' framework to negotiations when the individual plant is faced with potential closure or a financial 'crisis' (either real or perceived).

Finally, the issue of job insecurity was also widespread and in two cases (CopyCo and BrakeCo) had led to union led public campaigns to save the plant. However, the nature of these campaigns was different. In the former case a 'community unionism' approach had emerged with the unions going outside the plant and union structure for help, whereas in the latter case a more 'constitutional' approach was used by concentrated lobby support from the local M.P. and M.E.P and through the parent companies' EWC. In both these cases the more threatening aspects to organised labour of 'globalization' were apparent, with, in these instances at least, the 'community union' approach proving more successful as a strategy to preserve jobs .

In total the study suggests a high degree of corporate change and a variegated union response to the effects of that change. However, there is undoubted resilience of union organisation from which the possibilities of union resistance remain.

Acknowledgements:
The research project has been funded by a grant from the Leverhulme Trust (RF&G/7/9900487).

References

Ackers, P., Smith, C. and Smith, P. (1996) *'Against All Odds? British Trade Unions in the Workplace'* in Ackers, Smith and Smith (eds.) *The New Workplace and Trade Unionism*, London, Routledge: 1-40.

Auerbach, P. (1989) *'Multi-nationals and the British Economy'* in F.Green (ed.) *The Restructuring of the UK Economy*, Hemel Hempstead: Harvester Wheatsheaf

Barrell, R., and Pain, N. (1997) *'Foreign Direct Investment, Technological Change, and Economic Growth within Europe'* , The Economic Journal,107 (November) : 1770-1786

Capelli, P., Bassi, L., Katz, H., Knoke, D., Osterman, P. and Useem, M. (1997) *Change at Work,* New York: Oxford University Press

Carter, B. (1991) *'Politics and process in the making of Manufacturing, Science and Finance'*, Capital and Class, 45, 35-72

Carter, B. (1997) *'Adversity and Opportunity: towards union renewal in MSF'* Capital and Class, 61:8-19

Casey, B., Metcalf, H., Millward, N. (1997) *Employers' Use of Flexible Labour*, London: Policy Studies Institute

Cosh,A., Hughes, A., Singh, A., Carty, J. and Pender, J. (1990) *Take-overs and Short-termism in the UK*, London: Institute of Public Policy Research

Cully, M., Woodland, S., O'Reilly, A. and Dix, G. (1999), *Britain at Work*, Routledge, London.

Danford, A., M. Richardson and M. Upchurch (2002a) *'Trade union strategy and renewal; the restructuring of work and work relations in the UK aerospace industry*, Work, Employment and Society, 16, 2: 305-327

Danford, A., Richardson, M. and Upchurch, M. (2002b) *'Crisi del sindicato o suo rinnovamento? Le riposte dei sindicati all'individualizzazione delle relazioni sul posto di lavoro*' in *Sociologia del Lavoro; Lo Stao del Dibattito in Italia ed in Gran Bretagna* 86-87 ed. G. Bonazzi, M. La Rosa and V. Pulignano, Bologna

Darlington, R. (1994) *The Dynamics of Workplace Unionism*, London: Mansell

Delbridge, R. (1998) *Life on the Line in Contemporary Manufacturing*, Oxford: Oxford University Press

Delbridge, R., Turnbull, P. and Wilkinson, B. (1992), *'Pushing back the frontiers: Management control and work intensification under JIT/TQM factory regimes'*, New Technology, Work and Employment, 17:2, 97—106.

Delbridge R. and Lowe J. (1998), *Manufacturing in Transition*, London: Routledge

Department of Trade and Industry (1998) *Fairness at Work*, Cm 3968, HMSO, May

Edwards, P., Hall, M., Hyman, R., Marginson, P., Sisson, K., Waddington, J. and Winchester, D. (1992) *'Great Britain: Still Muddling Through?'* in A.Ferner and R.Hyman (eds.) *Industrial Relations in the New Europe*, Oxford: Blackwell

Fairbrother, P. (1994) *'Privatisation and local trade unionism'*, Work, Employment and Society, 8,3: 339-56

Fairbrother, P.(2000) *Trade Unions at the Crossroads*,London: Mansell

Fosh, P. (1993) '*Membership participation in workplace unionism: the possibilities of union renewal*' in British Journal of Industrial Relations, 31 (4), 577-92

Gall, G. (1998) *'The changing relations of production: union derecognition in the UK magazine industry'* Industrial Relations Journal, 29, 2, :151-61

Guest, D. (1992), *'Employee commitment and control'* in F.J. Hartley and G.M. Stephenson (eds.) *Employee Relations*, Blackwell, Oxford.

Heery, E. and Abbott, B. (2000) *'Trade Unions and the Insecure Workforce'* in E. Heery and J. Salmon (eds.) *The Insecure Workforce*, London: Routledge

Hirst. P, and G. Thompson (1996) *Globalization in Question* London: Polity

Hirst. P, and G. Thompson (2000) '*Globalization in One Country? The Peculiarities of the British'* Economy and Society, 29, 3: 335-356

Howell, C. (1999) *'British Trade Unionism in Crisis'* in A.Martin and G.Ross (eds.) *The Brave New World of European Labor*, New York and Oxford: Berghahn

Kelly, J. (1996) *'Union Militancy and Social Partnership'* in P.Ackers, C.Smith and P.Smith (eds.) *The New Workplace and Trade Unionism*, London: Routledge pp 77-109

Kelly, J. (1998) *Rethinking Industrial Relations: Mobilization, Collectivism and Long Waves*, London: Routledge

Kochan, T.(1999), *'Rebuilding the social contract at work: lessons from leading cases'* Institute for Work and Employment Research, Sloan School of Management.

Knell, J. (1999) *'Partnership at Work'*, Employment Relations Research Series, No.7, Department of Trade and Industry

Lind, J. (1996) *'Trade Unions: Social Movement or Welfare Apparatus ?'* in P. Leisink et al (eds.) *The Challenges to Trade Unions in Europe*, op cit.

Maksymiw, W. (1990) in *The British Trade Union Directory*, London: Longman

Marginson, P. (1994) *'Multinational Britain: Employment and Work in an Internationalised Economy'* , Human Resource Management Journal, 4,4: 63-80

Marsh, P. (1991) *Short-termism on Trial*, London: Institutional Fund Managers' Association

Millward, N., Bryson, A. and Forth, J. (2000), *All Change at Work?*, London: Routledge

Monbiot, G. (2000) *Captive State: the Corporate Takeover of Britain*, London: Macmillan

Müller, F. and Purcell, J. (1992) *'The Europeanisation of Manufacturing and the Decentralisation of Bargaining: Multinational Management Strategies in the European Automobile Industry'* , International Journal of Human Resource Management, 3.1: 15-44

Müller, F., Proctor, S., and Buchanan, D. (2000) *'Teamworking in its context(s): Antecedents, Nature and Dimensions'* , Human Relations, 53,11: 1387-1424

Phelps-Brown, H. (1990) *'The Counter-revolution of our time'* Industrial Relations, 29,1:1-14

Standing, G. (1997) '*Globalisation, labour flexibility and insecurity: the era of market regulation*' European Journal of Industrial Relations, 3, 1: 7-37

Stewart, P. and Martinez Lucio, M. (1998) '*Renewal and Tradition in the New Politics of Production*' in P.Thompson and C. Warhurst (eds.) *Workplace of the Future*, London, Macmillan

Sutcliffe, B. and Glyn, A. (1999) '*Still Underwhelmed- Indicators of Globalization and their Misinterpretation*' Review of Radical Political Economy, March

TUC (2000) *Trade Union Trends*, September

Upchurch, M., and Danford, A. (2001) *'Trade union response to industrial restructuring: sectoral case studies from the South West of England'* in D. Foden, J. Hoffman and R. Scott (eds.) *Globalisation and the Social Contract*, Brussels, ETUI.

Valkenburg, B. (1996) *'Individualisation and Solidarity: the Challenge of Modernisation'*, in P.Leisink et al (eds.) *The Challenges to Trade Unions in Europe*, Cheltenham, Edward Elgar

Waddington, J. and Whitston, C. (1997) *'Why do people join unions in a period of membership decline?'* British Journal of Industrial Relations, 35,4: 515-46

Wilkinson, A., Marchington, M.Ackers, P. and Goodman, J. (1992), *'Total quality management and employee involvement'*, Human Resource Management Journal, 2:4, 1—20.

Womack, J.P., Jones, D.T. and Roos, D. (1990), *The Machine that Changed the World: The triumph of lean production*, New York: Rawson Macmillan.

Health Care Work in Europe - Introduction to the Workshop

WOLFGANG POTRATZ

The service sector in general and health care and health industry in particular in the last decades have been the motors of structural change of European economies. This certainly goes for Scandinavia, but continental Europe is catching up[1].They have left their imprint even on 'old industrial areas' such as Northrhine-Westphalia, where meanwhile almost 2 mio. people work in the health industry; 180.000 of these jobs have been created only during the last decade. This may justify to speak of the health industry as a "job machine" and the "hidden champion" of structural change.

Bottle Neck Working Conditions.

Yet there is some water in the wine. The job machine splutters, not due to demand but due to supply shortages. Staff is lacking in more or less all health service professions, doctors as well as nurses and medical and non-medical assistants. So far there are no comprehensive and comparative studies about reasons and causes[2], but a few are evident: there is a lack of junior staff, limited income perspectives and above all unattractive working conditions.

One aspect should be noted beforehand: the demographical factor. Populations are shrinking all over Europe, with the consequence of lower numbers of potential recruits for a job in the health and related services. However, politics apparently prefers not to acknowledge this simple fact and to include it into respective considerations for reform or reconstruction of health services.

---

[1] Cf. Smith 2002, table 2, p.288

[2] For a comprehensive international data set see OECD Health Data 2003; for a comparative study on employment see Schneider et al. 2002, who analyse employment differences in relation to organisational and financial structures of health systems

A few data from Germany, which is the third biggest spender on health (behind the USA and Switzerland) among the OECD countries, may highlight this situation[3]. The largest groups of employees in the health sector are nurses and doctors. Between 1991 and 1999 demand for nursing training and education programmes has diminished by 6.5%, while the number of offered trainee places has gone down only by 1.7%. An almost dramatic situation is to be stated for auxiliary nurses, where interest in training has gone down by 55.6%!

Concerning doctors, the situation is a little bit different. Interest in the respective university courses is relatively constant over time, but large numbers of the graduated young doctors afterwards do not show up in the medical professions, be it in clinics or practices. Between 1991 and 2000 the share of under 35-year-old doctors has dwindled down from 27.4% to 18.8%, which indicates a process of geriatrisation of this core staff group.

In contrast to these two medical staff groups in the remaining health service professions or professions close to medical and care services (dieticians, physiotherapists, laboratory assisants, health protecting professions etc.) the situation is somewhat better. Qualification and training capacities during the 90ies have gone up by 12.6%, but still this growth cannot compensate for the general loss.

A second reason certainly are income perspectives, even in a high-wage country like Germany. On the whole employees in the health services in West-Germany have lower incomes than their counterparts in the industrial part of the economy, and also average growth rates are smaller. In the period of 1986 to 1995 hospital doctors had an average yearly growth in income of 3.3%, and nurses/doctor's assistants of 4.3%; a comparable employee to the latter enjoyed a growth rate of also 4.3%, but starting from a roughly 35% higher basis (1995). If you correct for an exceptional rise in 1990 and 1991 the yearly growth in income for a hospital doctor is reduced to 2.6%, and 3.7% for a nurse and 3.8% for the fictitious employee in industry. In east Germany the situation is different: it is devastating.

A third and probably the trigger reason is working conditions. Working conditions in the core health services are almost traditionally bad. Long and irregular working times, shift work, and high physical and mental strains are the rule and lead to broadly spread burn-out-symptoms, above-average fluctuation and job leavers[4]. The ranking of reasons suggested here, with

[3] Data and information are taken from Dülberg/Hilbert/Fretschner 2002, p.42 ff.; see also Statistisches Bundesamt 2002

[4] for an in-depth-analysis of working conditions in the nursing sector (in Germany) see DAK-BGW 2000; also ver.di 2003 and Büssing/Glaser 2003

working conditions on top, can be underpinned by a survey conducted on behalf of IAT[5], which displayed that in spite of the working conditions employees in the health services evaluated participation, cooperation, room for initiative and work place autonomy higher than the average of all service sector employees. In other words: employees work with high intrinsic motivation, but they are defeated by external conditions.

"Customer orientation" is a strategy, where these factors cumulate and make for a subjective feeling of exploitation. Measures to improve information, consultation and support for patients/"customers" have been and are at the core of endeavours to enhance efficiency and productivity of clinics. The findings of a benchmarking study[6], which comprised 30 clinics as well as 7370 patient and 6827 employee questionnaires (valid questionnaires) showed a remarkable contrast between patient/customer satisfaction and employee satisfaction: where patient/customer satisfaction was high, employee satisfaction was low. Main causes for employee dissatisfaction were found in a lack of coordination and support by superiors and management as well as in uncertainties about the policy and strategy of the institution. This leads to a number of interfaces and communication problems with the large set of instances involved in a given case; employees are able to cope with these problems, however, at the price of additional working time needed for search and finishing activities, which adds to the already existing intensity and strains of work.

This little encouraging situation may, by and large, be assumed for continental Europe and the UK, while concerning working conditions Scandinavia is somewhat ahead. Still, also Scandinavia suffers from an even more severe lack of staff in this sector, which hampers economic development as well as novel forms of health service governance and organisational and workplace innovation.

However, innovation and the opening of new perspectives for the health sector is also hindered by short-sighted political reactions to general budgetary strains. The common answer in most European countries is plain cost-cutting, without sufficiently acknowledging that the health sector for long has become a driver of value added and employment nor of the precarious relation between value added and employment[7] and the role of

---

[5] cf. Born 2000, special analysis for IAT

[6] Bandemer/Born/Middendorf/Scharfenorth 2003

[7] An exception is the report of the German Council of Experts for Concerted Action in Public Health of 1996 and the report of the German Council of Experts for Economic Development of 2001, which analyse the health sector as a branch of the service industry

work organisation for enhancing efficiency both on operational and the system level. Some of these issues and aspects are explored in the papers presented in this workshop.

From Compliance to Innovation: Clinical Re-organisation as a Reflexive Process

The above notes are mainly based on German observations, but with their opening statement that "surprisingly work organisation achieves little recognition in the NHS policy agenda" *Rosemary Exton* and *Peter Totterdill* confirm this as a core issue. In their case study *"Partnership, Governance and Innovation at Nottingham City Hospital"* they point out the consequences of implicit but nevertheless widespread neo-Tayloristic thinking especially in clinical middle management, which fosters a mechanistic view of organisational behaviour, the perpetuation of traditional forms of work organisation and hierarchy, and, if it comes to change, top-down target setting. Given the present turbulent environment for social policies in general and a growing pressure for enhancing efficiency in particular, and confronted with recruitment problems and employees' dissatisfaction with working conditions, clinics, which are governed the traditional way, soon find themselves in the "quality assurance without quality improvement trap". As a way out *Exton and Totterdill* outline a new initiative "Improving Working Lives" (IWL) introduced by the NHS and evaluate the first outcomes using the case of Nottingham City Hospital.
Somehow the authors' findings remind of the situation as we know it from change processes in industry: the new initiative is welcomed as a new policy, but the point is rather how to implement and embed it across the organisation and to ensure participation across all hierarchical layers in order to not only recognise but make best use of the "valuable resource represented by the skills and knowledge of the employees". Yet here, the conclusion in the Nottingham case goes, both management *and* unions still have a way to go to leave their well-trodden paths and to recognise and accept their specific role and competencies in such a complex change process. The question is, what happens until they have found their way?

---

with considerable multiplyer and value adding effects. However, these insights have not yet translated into strategies of restructuring and reform of the German health system.

This is the starting point in the contribution by *Palle Banke* and *Annemarie Holsbo*, who, nomen est omen?, head their paper *"Can apnea be avoided when developing work organisation in hospitals?"* Again, the four change processes they observe and analyse take place against a background of increasing pressure for more efficiency, to be interpreted as lower costs, and decreasing supply of labour, to be interpreted as "voting by feet" on the working conditions. Patient processes and interdisciplinary coordination were identified as the key variables to be improved in order to achieve better quality and efficiency which would benefit both patients, the hospital enterprise/management and employees.

Similar to the Nottingham case, interdisciplinarity and cooperation primarily presents a challenge to hierarchy. Mutual recognition of roles and functions, and in consequence information and knowledge sharing as a prerequisite for cooperation to the benefit of work processes and coordination to the benefit of patients in the first instance appears to be a matter of perception. "Each staff group has and has had its eyes on the process and their special challenges. ... So, although in most of the projects the doctors have been invited to participate, they have typically not come to feel committed to the matter or to have the opportunity to think of themselves as a part of the basis for changes." So the actual change process is more about the reconciliation of perceptions of roles, work assignments, qualifications and competencies between staff groups. The danger of "apnea" comes in, when these processes take too long and what is so special about the project gets lost in everyday routine[8].

Perspectives for Further Research

What then are the conclusions for further research in "Health&Care Work in Europe"?

The starting point clearly is the hypothesis, which is also sketched out in the presented papers of this workshop, that personnel development is one of the crucial bottlenecks of further economic and social development of health and care as service to the public as well as a branch of the service industry. To do something in this direction is necessary and the more urgent since

[8] "apnea" means "respiratory standstill"

- there is an ideological warfare about the dismantling of the welfare state which necessarily will lead to the erosion of the financial structures of health and care
- the internationalisation of national health and care services is progressing (international suppliers, labour migration) despite the needs and demands of an ageing population
- there is simply a lack of knowledge about intelligent solutions to comparable problems.

What is needed is a Europe wide "Programme for Modern Work in Health and Care in Europe", based on systematic comparative analysis and design of model solutions. Methodologically from the research side an action research based approach would be appropriate, and from the side of actual change strategy and implementation an inclusive participative approach would have to be applied. Exemplary themes following the discussions in the workshop and the conference might be

- cross-enterprise quality management and benchmarking methods, procedures and projects to improve efficiency and quality of health & care in respective institutions (public and private)
- further development and dissemination of work related and support technologies (e.g. documentation systems)
- linking-up of care (outpatient, inpatient) with neighbouring services, to avoid ghettoisation, and also to support work load balancing by rotation and exchange possibilities for personnel

More specifically work related issues are:

- qualification and training schemes for management personnel in organisation and management (leadership, mediation, personnel policies), applied technology and marketing
- modern design of working time schemes and flexibilisation; usage/application of job rotation schemes
- development of assessment schemes to identify required future personality profiles of personnel in health & care
- solutions for child care of employees' children during working hours to improve the employability (and recruitment) of employees
- development of subcontracted labour schemes to better balance cases of sick leave, to balance work overload and to give room for rotation and for further training and qualification
- mobilisation, recruitment and qualification of personnel from other branches (loosing employment); recruitment and integration of foreign staff

References

Bandemer, Stephan von/Born, Andreas/Middendorf, Anja/Scharfenorth, Karin 2003: *Schlussbericht für das BMBF geförderte Projekt Benchmarking in der Gesundheitswirtschaft*, Institut Arbeit und Technik, Gelsenkirchen.

Born, Andreas 2000: *Gemeinsam oder einsam? Arbeitsorganisation im Dienstleistungssektor*, in: Nordhause-Janz, Jürgen/Pekruhl, Ulrich (Hg.): Arbeiten in neuen Strukturen? Partizipation, Kooperation, Autonomie und Gruppenarbeit in Deutschland, (Hampp) München u. Mering, p. 103-138.

Büssing, André/Glaser, Jürgen (Hrsg.) 2003: *Dienstleistungsqualität und Qualität des Arbeitslebens im Krankenhaus*. (Hogrefe) Göttingen et al.

DAK-BGW 2000: Krankenpflegereport 2000. *Arbeitsbedingungen und Gesundheit von Pflegekräften in der Bundesrepublik*. Hamburg.

Dülberg, Alexandra/Hilbert, Josef/Fretschner, Rainer 2002: *Rahmenbedingungen und Herausforderungenn der Gesundheitswirtschaft* (Ms.) Gelsenkirchen.

Sachverständigenrat für die Konzertierte Aktion im Gesundheitswesen 1996: Gesundheiswesen in Deutschland: Kostenfaktor und Zukunftsbranche. Sondergutachten, 2 Bde., (Nomos) Baden-Baden. (internet version: www.svr-gesundheit.de)

Sachverständigenrat zur Begutachtung der Gesamtwirtschaftlichen Entwicklung 2001: Jahresgutachten 2000/01 "Chancen auf einen höheren Wachstumspfad" (W. Kohlhammer-Verlag) Stuttgart/Mainz (internet version: www.sachverstaendigenrat-wirtschaft.de)

Schneider, Markus/ Hofmann, Uwe/Jumel, Séverine/Köse, Aynur 2002: *Beschäftigungsunterschiede in ausgewählten Gesundheitssystemen der EU*. (Basys) Augsburg.

Smith, Mark 2002: *Dienstleistungen und Zugang zur Beschäftigung in Europa*. In: Gerhard Bosch, Peter Hennicke, Josef Hilbert, Kora Kristof, Gerhard Scherhorn (Hg.): *Die Zukunft von Dienstleistungen. Ihre Auswirkungen auf Arbeit, Umwelt und Lebensqualität*. (Campus) Frankfurt/New York, p. 282-304.

Statistisches Bundesamt 2002: *Gesundheit. Personal 2000*. Wiesbaden. (internet www.destatis.de) ver.di 2003: *Die Situation der Beschäftigten im Gesundheitssektor - zwischen wachsender Nachfrage, steigendem Kostendruck und tariflicher Flexibilisierung. Transparenzstudie, gefördert durch die Hans-Böckler-Stiftung*. Düsseldorf.

Partnership, Governance and Innovation at Nottingham City Hospital

ROSEMARY EXTON, PETER TOTTERDILL

Background

This paper has three main objectives:

- to explore the relationship between workplace partnership, innovation and governance;
- to identify obstacles to workplace partnership and staff involvement;
- to identify effective strategies for participative workplace innovation.

The paper grows from the collaboration of the two authors in a government-sponsored initiative to improve quality of working life for staff at Nottingham City Hospital. It is based on a reflective account of workplace innovation, combining the perspective of an active trade unionist and clinical midwife in the hospital with that of an action-researcher concerned with dialogue-based organisational development.

Outcomes from this collaboration will also contribute to the *European Hospital Network* funded under the Swedish SALTSA programme.

Introduction

Policies for National Health Service (NHS) reform seem detached from wider European trends in work organisation. Recent surveys indicate that the introduction of new forms of work organisation such as empowered teamworking improves performance and innovation. For example the Employee Participation and Organisational Change survey of 6000 workplaces in Europe which confirms that direct employee participation and teamworking can have strong positive impacts on both productivity and quality of products or services (European Foundation, 1997). EU policy calls on employers to modernise work organisation as a means of enhancing innovation in products and services (Commission of the European Communities, 1997).

Surprisingly work organisation achieves little recognition in the NHS policy agenda even though the need for workplace change is recognised. *Shifting the Balance of Power: securing delivery* (DoH, 2001a, p24) argues that:

"A real shift in the balance of power will not occur unless staff are empowered to make the necessary change . . . Staff need to be involved in decisions which effect (sic) service delivery. Empowerment comes when staff own the policies and are able to bring about real change."

However there is little evidence that the scope of such a transformation is adequately recognised or resourced within the NHS policy agenda. *Shifting the Balance of Power* has little to say on the hard realities of organisational innovation, of how to build effective workplace dialogue and participation, of job redesign and empowerment, of implementing and sustaining genuine teamworking, of creating a work environment which values reflection and creativity, of achieving convergence between quality of working life and performance. While these issues are recognised in principle, concrete interventions may prove to be poorly matched with the scale of the need.

The Limits of Performance Management

Clinical governance has become the foremost driver of innovation and change within the NHS, reflecting such government priorities as risk management, clinical effectiveness, patient involvement and enhanced professional competence. Its practice is largely defined by the controls with which government requires hospitals to regulate their activities. Hospital Boards have to account to external, government-appointed auditors for performance against some 400 indicators including mortality rates, bed occupancy and the quality of patient food. Such targets play a powerful role in directing the focus of managers' attention. Arguably they induce reactive management cultures, stifling innovation and preventing the ability to build sustainable change. The fulfilment of short-term targets has become almost the sole preoccupation of politicians and health service managers with worrying consequences for the reflexive and innovative capacity of the NHS. Over-emphasis on targets may lead to quality assurance but is unlikely to secure real quality improvement.

Whilst the regulation of hospital activity reflects aspirations and standards widely accepted amongst NHS employees, this paper argues that it is not sufficient to ensure the reflexivity and organisational innovation required for safe, patient focussed care. Clinical governance must set itself a more strategic vision, laying the foundations for long-term learning and adaptation in an increasingly unpredictable and turbulent environment. There is a need for a significant shift in management focus, one in which the delivery of targets is achieved as the by-product of wider and sustained improvements in service quality. Such a shift from short-term target chasing to building the organisational competencies associated with adaptive, innovative organisations would represent a radical transformation of the NHS.

An approach to clinical governance in which health service organisations do indeed achieve external targets as a 'by-product' of their inherent organisational competence and values might be characterised as the 'high road'. The defining characteristics of the high road lie in the creation of organisational spaces and the liberation of the tacit knowledge, experience and talent of the entire workforce in ways which achieve a dynamic balance between service and process innovations. Crucially the high road seeks to reunite job satisfaction and patient satisfaction. In contrast the 'low road' – arguably the dominant mode of clinical governance for most NHS hospitals in the present environment - is driven by cost, performance measurement, punishment and reward. For NHS staff it frequently results in deterioration in the quality of working life (Meadows et al, 2000) which purely remedial HR initiatives cannot redress. Apart from increasing problems with recruitment and retention, this failure to involve staff at all levels of service provision represents a lost opportunity for innovation and improvement

Obstacles to Workplace Innovation

Building partnership between management, trade unions and the workforce is an essential precondition for sustainable change in the NHS. Within such a culture of partnership, teamworking is a key building block for effective involvement, workplace innovation and service improvement. This is often understood at the strategic level, but has yet to filter through to middle managers.

Traditional forms of work organisation and middle management culture in hospitals prevent effective teamworking. 'Teamworking' is a term often used when a line manager leads a group of workers - even when he or she is deeply reluctant to relinquish traditional authority and thereby inhibits autonomy, innovative practice and the ability of staff to promote change.

The nature and benefits of real teamworking in hospitals need to be better understood, an issue addressed later in this paper.

Within the government's NHS modernisation programme (DoH, 1997) there has been increased emphasis on leadership development for middle management with the aim of improving patient care through teambuilding, networking and enhanced political awareness. Likewise the nursing, midwifery and health visiting national strategy (DoH, 1999b) set out action plans to improve recruitment and retention, reform education, improve working lives, modernise career paths and pay, enhance quality of care and work in new and more effective ways. The implementation of the government's NHS Plan (DoH, 2000a) promises well-publicised changes in investment and reforms. These include ambitious plans for changing the Health Service around the needs of the patient, as well as providing a better place in which to work.

Despite this mounting crescendo of change, many ground floor staff are oblivious to the existence of such initiatives, not being consulted or involved in the plans for their department or hospital. It is middle management who are leading and shaping changes at local level - and with only minimal involvement, if any, of frontline staff.

Evidence based on interviews during 2002 (Exton, 2003) demonstrates that many initiatives for change have yet to make an impact on staff. Many continue to experience problems affecting their working lives including stress, frustrations with work/life balance, shift patterns, unfairness, ineffective communication and inadequate support:

"Travelling long distances to work is very expensive. If I could do fewer, longer shifts I would reduce my petrol costs. My ward manager will not allow 12 hour shifts on her duty rota."

"On site affordable childcare, that would accommodate my irregular, part time shifts, would reduce my stress levels."

"My manager doesn't seem to understand our staffing problems and workload. Some support, feedback and acknowledgement would be appreciated."

"There is inequity in the provision and accessibility for training courses in my (hospital)."

"Some departments are so understaffed there is no one to provide cover for training sessions, yet other departments seem to manage."

"I don't know what is happening in my unit and the (hospital). I work mostly nights, and find it difficult to attend unit or team meetings. I have

little chance to access the bulletin board on our computer system as there are too few terminals in our busy work area."

Many of these comments are echoed by recent research on why midwives leave their profession (Ball, Curtis & Kirkham, 2002), which concluded that:

"... while the need for greater flexibility in working patterns within (NHS organisations) was frequently articulated, the need for profound cultural and organisational change has also to be recognised."

Quality of working life depends on the extent to which people feel empowered to influence their work environment and to use their professional knowledge and experience to the full. Indeed Ball et al demonstrate that lack of ability to influence work is a major reason for midwives leaving the profession:

"Many midwives felt that they had insufficient control over their working lives. Frequent dislocations at work made it difficult to build and maintain confidence and expertise, and difficult to develop and sustain relationships with colleagues and clients. Fuelling these concerns was a frequently articulated need for more effective support within the work environment... Moreover, not only were midwifery managers not seen by many clinical midwives as a source of support, they were often perceived to be an integral part of the problems that midwives face in the modern health service."

Removing Obstacles to Staff Involvement: the Case of Flexible Working

Experience shows that trade union stewards can become a vital link in two way communication between management and staff. Union representatives are also a largely untapped source of expertise with detailed knowledge of their professional and service areas and a clear understanding of the likely impact of change. They are in a unique position, combining their experience as members of the workforce and their active involvement with senior management in deliberating the implementation of hospital policies.

These stewards make a major contribution to supporting and counselling staff, since many managers are not readily accessible to the workforce and are often not involved in the day-to-day provision of clinical services. Issues affecting clinical risk and quality of patient care are often raised initially with the union steward or representative, whereas in an effective teamwork environment they would be discussed and dealt with in a team forum. However this requires managers to work as part of the team, encouraging dialogue, supporting staff and representing their views across the hospital.

In practice the steward's role often extends to that of facilitator for staff issues, especially in ensuring the equitable implementation of hospital policies. For example, one NHS hospital has clear policies for staff involvement, flexible employment and work-life balance, yet different models of leadership in two adjacent departments demonstrate different consequences for their implementation. In one department, the staff have established a system of shared governance and have designed their own approach to self-rostering. Just next door, staff suffer a management-dominated system, with line managers reluctant to allow empowerment or attempts to enhance work-life balance by introducing new working practices. Trade union representatives held discussions with management highlighting discrepancies in working practices throughout the hospital. Despite acknowledgements at Board level that the introduction of the EU Working Time Directive would necessitate changes to shift patterns, the manager of this particular department was reluctant to address the recommendations for self-rostering of the duty rotas.

Many staff contacted the union steward requesting a system of self-rostering for their shifts. There is evidence that this can work effectively in nursing and midwifery, aiding recruitment and retention and improving working lives. Despite the steward's request for the implementation of self-rostering, supported by evidence of improved work/life balance and the application of a Flexible Working Practices policy in other areas of the hospital, two of the four team managers refused to accept the potential benefits to staff and continued to manage the rostering themselves. Meetings with staff subsequently identified a number of negative reactions:

"We are made to feel that we have let the team down when we put requests in. We can't say they are for childcare because the manager then suggests that childcare dominates the rota and other people have needs."
"My line manager's answer to my requests for flexible shifts to accommodate my child care problems, was to say I had to reduce my hours worked. Thinking I had no option I now don't earn enough to cover my childcare. I have since heard of other staff in my (hospital) who can self roster their own flexible shifts."
"My line manager refuses to let me do 12 hour shifts which would help with my childcare - she says the ward can't be run around childcare, but other wards in the (hospital) have these shift patterns"

In the same unit some staff requested shorter shifts to suit childcare arrangements, while some wanted to improve their work-life balance by working fewer but longer 12-hour shifts. Line management were reluctant to consider these different shift patterns that would accommodate this even though this would have provided a means of ensuring compliance with the European Working Time Directive.
Together the staff and their trade union steward arranged a series of meetings. A group of enthusiastic staff prepared a pilot rota, based on the results of a questionnaire completed by the majority of unit staff. A team leader was approached and reluctantly agreed to trial it. The first pilot rota incorporated the self-rostered duties and the 12-hour shifts, providing adequate staff cover at all times. Feedback from the staff unit meeting was positive, and the member of staff who managed the rota was told by her colleagues that the team leader had thought it a success and that she was requested to manage the next rota.
However the team leader altered the next rota, without consultation with any of the staff and failed to provide adequate cover for all shifts. The other team leaders then complained that the pilot rota was not workable, and many staff were asked to work extra shifts. The steward and staff involved met to discuss the problems with middle management, since two first-line managers were reluctant to consider further trials of the 12 hour shift pattern despite many requests from staff.

The steward later received a copy of a letter sent from the manager to the team leaders and staff members involved in the pilot, requesting them to attend a meeting to discuss these problems. The steward's copy clearly stated it was for information only - she was excluded from the meeting and received no management feedback from it. The two staff members who had led the trial rotas attended the meeting, but were so disillusioned by lack of management support for flexible working patterns and self-rostering that they declined to be involved further.

The twelve hour shift trial was continued over six months but there was resistance from management to extend it to include all the staff in the unit who wanted to work these shifts. Despite the efforts of the steward, some first line managers refused to change traditional shift patterns and relinquish control of the duty rota. The inequity for staff in this department led to low morale and discontent, with some staff leaving for more flexible arrangements elsewhere.

The steward discussed her concerns with senior managers, who were unaware that flexible working policies were not being implemented equitably within this part of the hospital. Meanwhile, an external NHS assessment team evaluating the hospital's employment practices had arranged an open meeting with staff in this directorate. The steward informed the manager that they would be interested in the trial for flexible working patterns in the unit. A week later a letter was sent from the manager to the steward informing her that flexible working patterns, including twelve hour shifts, would be available to all staff within the unit.

This case study of middle management resistance to agreed policy measures demonstrates the difficulties faced by trade union representatives and senior management alike in making change happen, even where a clear and agreed policy framework is in existence.

Clinical Governance and Workplace Innovation

As we have argued, one of the key challenges is to avoid the 'quality assurance without quality improvement' trap. This requires the establishment of a strong link is established between clinical governance, staff involvement and workplace innovation.

We have argued that measurement of *performance* against clinical governance indicators provides does not in itself permit assumptions to be made about the nature of effective *practice* at clinical team or management levels. It implies a highly mechanistic view of organisational behaviour, a

'black box' perspective in which outputs directly mirror commands. The pervasive cultural influence of FW Taylor's 'scientific management' (Taylor, 1911) is apparent: the hospital is a machine whose activities respond directly to the performance criteria against which it is measured.
Taylorism's origins lie in the emergence of mass production in the early 20th Century and are closely associated with Ford. Taylor himself proposed a management system that sought to eliminate inefficient variations in work procedures by prescribing the 'one best way' of carrying out individual tasks. However the division of tasks did not only relate to distinctions between different manual skills. Taylor advocated that:

"All possible brain work should be removed from the shop floor and centred in the planning ...department ... " (Taylor, 1911).

Workers would concentrate on manual tasks freeing up managers' capacity for intellectual activities, thus opening a deep chasm between the conception and planning of work on the one hand and its manual execution on the other. It fundamentally challenges the ability of employees to exercise control in their working lives (Hague, 2000); equally it denies access to employees' knowledge and experience.
While the NHS is far removed from an early twentieth century automobile factory, parallels are clear in terms of task separation, the division between conception and execution, and the unidirectional nature of target setting. In the wider world Tayloristic practices are increasingly recognised as a constraint on the adaptability and innovative capacity of organisations, especially in an increasingly uncertain (social, political, economic) environment. Less tangibly neo-Tayloristic thinking imposes intellectual constraints on governmental and managerial ability to reconfigure health service organisations.
Hospitals are complex organisations: day-to-day processes involve responding to non-standard problems in conditions of uncertainty. Moreover day-to-day problem solving and innovation has to recognise the often competing claims of multiple stakeholders. Effective clinical governance must therefore place a considerable premium on the ability of organisations to harness the tacit knowledge and creative potential of employees. This involves much more than the ability to recruit and retain staff with necessary competencies. The emphasis on developing individual competence needs to be matched by *organisational* competence – building an approach to work organisation which engages all levels of employee in planning, quality assurance, problem solving and innovation (Cooke &

Seely Brown, 2000). Establishing this work environment involves a complex and contextualised process of dialogue, learning and organisational innovation based on interdependent processes which embrace workplace partnership, job design, teamworking, and quality of working life (Totterdill, P., Dhondt, S., Milsome, S., 2002).
Work organisation must be seen as a reflexive process, not an end state. Data from the Hi-Res[1] project, a European research review and analysis of some 120 case studies of organisational innovation, were examined for relevance to the NHS. The Hi-Res findings suggest that that workplace innovation cannot be defined in terms of the identification and implementation of a series of blueprints to change discrete aspects of an organisation. Although the traditional way to accomplish change is through the application of generalised concepts to specific problems according to a predetermined set of rules, it is now increasingly argued (see for example Fricke, 1997; Gustavsen, 1992) that this is a roadblock to real change. Rather it is important to understand the complex learning paths which characterise change in real situations. Pettigrew (1987) for example argues for greater focus on the internal and external contexts which drive, inform and constrain change. Such commentators criticise the common perception of change within management texts as rational and incremental, thereby supporting the use of normative change models. They argue that change is a dynamic and uncertain process which emerges through the interplay of many factors. Successful change involves research, negotiation, experimentation, reflection and redesign over many cycles (Totterdill, P., Dhondt, S., Milsome, S., 2002).
Hi-Res recognises the importance of learning from case study experience but seeks to avoid prescription or the dubious claims of universality embodied in 'key learning points' (Hague, 2002). Rather there is a need to understand the untidiness of real-life change processes embodied in the dilemmas, contradictions and choices faced by practitioners. Work organisation is essentially contested, reflecting complex interactions between internal and external drivers, influences and learning. In this analysis, organisational innovation struggles towards a virtuous circle in which reflexive practices capture employee knowledge and experiences to create a dynamic interaction between product or service innovation and

---

[1] Hi-Res: *Defining the **High** Road of Work Organisation as a **Res**ource for Policy Makers and Social Partners*. Project undertaken for the European Commission by a consortium of partners from 6 Member States led by The Work Institute at Nottingham Business School. See Totterdill, P., Dhondt, S., Milsome, S., 2002 (available at www.hi-res.org.uk).

organisational change. Hi-Res therefore identifies and explores the 'arenas' in which work processes are negotiated and tested.
The following section draws on the Hi-Res analysis to identify the specific organisational dimensions of clinical governance. Figure 3 (below) identifies three principal high road arenas: knowledge as a resource for improvement and innovation; partnership and involvement; job design and multidisciplinary teamworking.

Arenas of Organisational Learning and Change

A) Knowledge as a Resource for Improvement & Innovation

As earlier sections of this paper have argued, effective clinical governance places knowledge, innovation and learning close to the heart of the work process at all levels of the organisation. While clinical procedures are codified to minimise risk and maximise effectiveness, judgement and discretion are central to the day-to-day process of dealing with patients. Service improvement and risk management depend on the ability to capture learning and experience from practice, create spaces for reflection and innovation, and distribute knowledge as an organisation-wide resource. This goes far beyond the narrow 'learning from mistakes' approach within the NHS *Organisation With a Memory* (OWAM) initiative (DoH, 2000b).

Garvin (1993, p.80) refers to the "learning organisation" as:

"an organisation skilled at creating, acquiring and transferring knowledge, and at modifying its behaviour to reflect new knowledge and insights."
At the most basic level, organisational learning can emanate from repeated tasks and activities which result in progressive adaptation and greater efficiency. At a higher level however the learning organisation progressively modifies its structures, technologies, practices and cultures to maximise and utilise the learning capabilities of its people (Shapiro, 1998; Stalk et al, 1992). Critically:

FIGURE 3 - Arenas of organisational learning and change

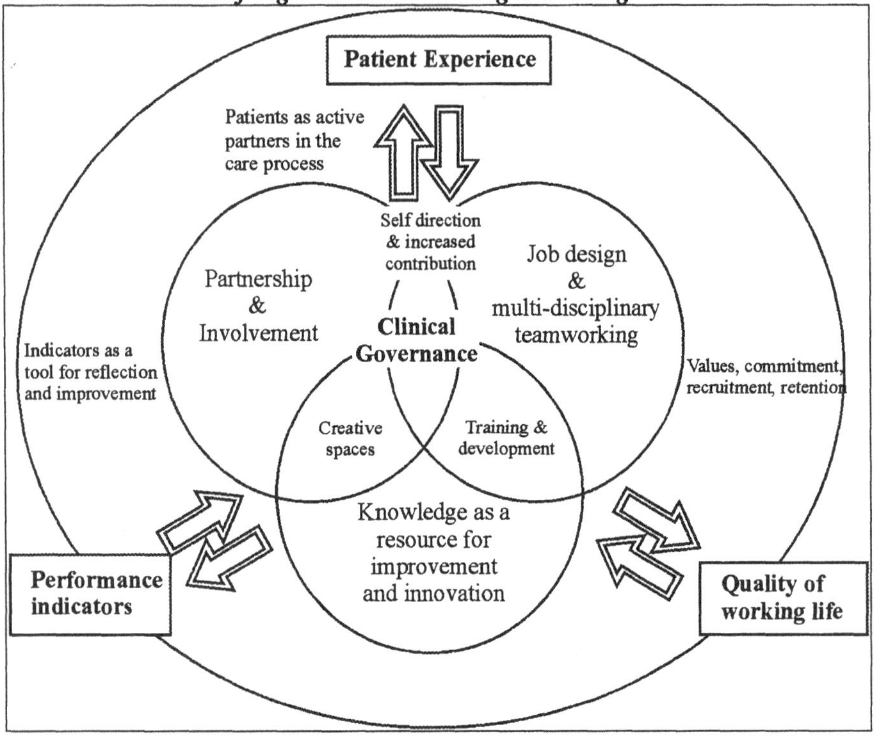

"Although organisational learning occurs through individuals, it would be a mistake to conclude that organisational learning is nothing but the cumulative result of their member's learning. Organisations do not have brains, but they have cognitive systems and memories." (Hedberg, 1981, p3).

This re-emphasises the importance of the distinction between individual and organisational learning. Argyris (1977) distinguishes between single-loop learning (in which the need for improvement is identified by individuals but where the objectives and policies of the organisation remain essentially unchanged) and double loop learning in which the organisation has the capacity to reflect on itself and to develop appropriately adaptive behaviour. Double-loop learning can be identified with the reflexivity characteristic of the high road of clinical governance, creating a collective knowledge resource to support the dynamic balance between organisational innovation and service innovation. However the bridge between single loop and double loop learning can be seriously impeded in the hospital context by professional demarcations and organisational divisions. Recent illustrations can be found in the Kennedy Report (2001) into children's heart surgery at the Bristol Royal Infirmary, and the Toft Report (2001) into a death at the Queen's Medical Centre, Nottingham.

Organisational structures, technologies, practices and cultures either help or hinder organisational learning and improvement. The Hi-Res study identifies several cases where new approaches to work organisation have been introduced to overcome identified obstacles to learning and improvement, ranging from the introduction of semi-autonomous teamworking to the physical integration of R&D and production functions.

While these concepts are acknowledged within the NHS Modernisation agenda, the capture, analysis and distribution of knowledge in the hospital context is not simply about the creation of centralised 'good practice' databases. Rather it focuses on two dimensions of work organisation: the establishment of workplace practices conducive to partnership and dialogue between management and employees, and the establishment of effective multi-disciplinary teamworking.

B) Partnership, Involvement and Participation

In many hospitals, forms of workplace partnership have been established to deal proactively with industrial relations issues, ensuring early consultation on pay and conditions, employment changes and organisational restructuring. However emergent thinking moves partnership away from a specific focus on industrial relations, recasting it as a potentially important driver of, and resource for, organisational innovation (Dawson, Hague, Knell & Totterdill, 2002). In Ireland, for example, social partners and government identify workplace partnership as central to the modernisation of work organisation. In particular it is seen as a vehicle for initiating change, ensuring its widespread 'ownership' by employees thereby enhancing effectiveness and reducing risk of innovation decay (Savage, 1999; Sharpe & Totterdill, 1999). In the Health Service this is recognised by the *Report of the NHS Taskforce on Staff Involvement* (DoH, 2000a) which argues that opportunities for active participation in the workplace help staff to "feel valued and make a better contribution to service delivery". However the resulting *Action Plan* reveals only limited measures to support implementation at hospital level (DoH, 2000c).

Employees increasingly expect rewarding work and a high quality of working life, a key component of which is the ability to influence their own work environment (Knell, 2001; Hague, Huzzard, den Hertog & Totterdill, 2002). Meaningful work has always offered the NHS an important advantage in attracting and retaining employees, even where quality of working life is problematic (Meadows et al, 2000; Ball, Curtis and Kirkham, 2001). 'Health service values' have always been one of the Health Service's most important intangible assets, though one which can no longer be taken for granted without more explicit staff recognition, involvement and self direction.

Partnership in its fuller sense has to permeate all levels of the organisation. Representative measures (such as partnership agreements, management/trade union panels or employee directorships) may play an important role in anchoring partnership firmly within the practice and culture of an organisation. However they do not ensure opportunities for the direct employee involvement that, in clinical governance terms, can enable the full knowledge and experience of staff to be utilised in identifying risks and opportunities for improvement. In part such direct employee involvement is a product of effective job design and teamworking (see below) but in complex organisations such as hospitals 'dialogue structures' which cut across and by-pass line management channels could become an important mechanism for challenging established practice and promoting innovation. Dialogue structures can include organisation-wide events such as Change Conferences designed to inform corporate strategy, ad hoc project groups or inter-team forums. In each case they need to be governed by agreed procedures designed to ensure full participation by all levels of employee, thereby enabling the force of the better argument to prevail (Gustavsen, 1992). Above all there needs to be an acceptance by management that lean, cost-driven organisations are not innovative organisations: people need slack to be creative together.

As the flexible working case study (above) shows, employee involvement and participation challenges management prerogative, exposing decisions and styles to much greater scrutiny. At a minimum this requires the acquisition of new competencies by many mangers, and in many cases the resign of the management function within organisational structures (for a radical example in healthcare of the elderly see Sherrin, 2002a).

'Bottom up' approaches to organisational and service innovation require careful preparation and resourcing, using evidence-based tools to promote dialogue, trust and the transformation of traditional management practices. As we have seen this, as yet, is scarcely recognised in the government's approach to staff involvement.

C) Job Design and Teamworking

Traditional approaches to job design and work organisation are no longer sustainable in a hospital context which demands greater responsiveness to patient needs. As recent Commission for Health Improvement audits illustrate (www.chi.nhs.uk) professional demarcations, poor inter-professional communication and lack of autonomy in non-medical staff roles are obstacles to the delivery of safe, effective and patient-focussed care.

Teamworking has been one of the defining characteristics of new forms of work organisation, with deep roots in European thinking about management and organisation dating back to the 1940s (Sherrin and Procter, 2002b). The current interest in teamworking dates back to its rediscovery in the North American manufacturing sector in the mid-1980s, since when the concept has spread widely into other areas of work. However the term is increasingly used to describe such a diverse range of workplace situations that arguably it has become meaningless. Mueller and Purcell (1992) attempt to clarify the modern conception of teamworking by drawing on the definition used in GM/Opel:

- the team works on a common task;
- its work is spatially concentrated and it has a recognisable territory;
- the allocation of tasks is largely organised by the team;
- the team encourage and organises the acquisition of multiple skills;
- it has decision-making power over time and appropriate means;
- there is team spokesman/leader;
- the team has some influence on who will join it.

What distinguishes a team in the sense used here from a collection of workers who merely work in the same department is the degree of autonomy it enjoys in relation to formal line management structures. However – and this is particularly pertinent to the health service context – it is also necessary to consider the quality of dialogue and innovation which takes place inside the team. If teams are to be more than decentralised units for the production of a given service, all team members must have the potential for a high level of reflexivity unconstrained by internal demarcations and privileges (Gustavsen, 1992).

Within the NHS progress has been made in certain areas of job design, notably the expansion of nursing roles into areas of practice traditionally reserved exclusively for doctors. However the nature of clinical work organisation remains largely neglected and considerable variations in practice exist even within individual hospitals.

At a clinical level, the distinction between team-based and non team-based approaches to patient care was clarified in a study of five paediatric renal units in different European countries (Centre for Work & Technology, 1995). Although each of the units described themselves colloquially as 'teams', two broad organisational approaches could be distinguished:

- In the more traditional model patients and their families are seen by the medical consultant, who decides whether they should then be referred to other professionals such as dieticians, clinical psychologists or social workers. These referrals could involve patients and their families in multiple visits to the hospital, often with significant gaps. Eventually the consultant will receive reports on the patient from the other professionals and will use them to make a diagnosis and prescribe treatment on the basis of his or her own judgement. In many cases the consultant and the other professionals will be located in different parts of the hospital or even on different sites and will meet only rarely. Separate patient notes will be kept by each professional so there is no integrated case history.
- In the much rarer team-based model (only found at one hospital in the paediatric renal study) each professional group is located within a common area, at least on relevant clinic days. Depending on the case history all the relevant professionals will be present at the consultation, or will be available for referral shortly afterwards. The different professionals will confer on the spot and ensure that the patient leaves with the benefit of an integrated diagnosis and treatment plan. Clinic sessions are followed by case meetings at which both the medical and psycho-social aspects of each patient's condition will be considered. Diagnosis and prescription are therefore a continuously negotiated process based on high levels of mutual trust and understanding between the different professions. For patients and carers this provides a relatively seamless route through the different aspects of care. The different professional groups (including doctors) involved in the team-based model each reported enhanced levels of job satisfaction compared with their previous experience of more traditional approaches. In part this reflected improved clinical results generated by the more effective pooling of expertise; in part it grew from a sense of mutual support and sharing between team members. Nurses and other professionals commented on their ability to use competencies to the full in a team setting, enjoying higher levels of discretion and respect. Interaction between professionals in a team environment also generates high levels of innovation in terms of service improvement and team development. The team was also a

potential (though largely untapped) resource as a 'dialogue structure' to promote wider employee engagement with corporate strategy.

Significantly although the team-based model demonstrated tangible patient benefits, there was no hospital-wide strategy to adopt the approach as the norm for clinical work organisation. Indeed the wider organisational environment in which the paediatric renal unit existed acted as a significant constraint on teamworking, particularly because of:

- limited control over budgets;
- tension between vertical line management based on professional groups and team accountability;
- limited ability to recruit its own membership (team members were often recruited by line managers without wider involvement);
- the lack of corresponding team practices in related parts of the hospital (for example ward staff) leading to broken lines of communication;
- poor information technology support, preventing the creation of integrated, multi-professional case notes.

At corporate level the hospital's understanding of team principles was limited and there was little evidence of central support to develop the team further or to avoid innovation decay. Stronger support was required for non-medical staff in developing teamwork competencies including facilitation skills; arguably this should eventually lead to a separation in roles between *medical* leadership and *team* leadership in order to reinforce open dialogue and extended participation.

Teamworking should not be restricted to the point of service delivery (a wider conclusion drawn from the Hi-Res research) but needs to become a defining characteristic of all aspects of work, both routine and developmental, at all levels of the organisation. In this sense teamworking emerges not as a formulaic model but as an approach to work organisation that broadens job design and challenges both hierarchical and horizontal demarcations in order to optimise levels of agility and innovation. It also provides the day-to-day context for enhancing quality of working life.

Improving the Working Lives of NHS Staff

At a time when the health service struggles to rise to the challenge of staff recruitment and retention, the NHS Plan (DoH, 2000a) announced the government's commitment to improve the working lives of staff. All NHS organisations are being assessed against new performance measures as part of an 'Improving Working Lives' (IWL) initiative (see figure 1):

FIGURE 1 - Key Strands of the Improving Working Lives initiative

- Flexible Working Patterns
- Staff Benefits and Child Care
- Communication and Staff Involvement
- Healthy Working Practices
- Equality and Diversity
- Training and Development
- Human Resources Strategy and Management
- Staff Attitude Survey

Source: DoH (2002)

While IWL is to be welcomed, senior NHS managers recognise that the difficult task is not to design the appropriate policy framework but to make sure it is implemented equitably across the service. Hospitals are already required to have policies for flexible working, equal opportunities, healthy workplace practices and personal development. Although the IWL initiative addresses these same issues, amongst others, hospitals will now have to demonstrate that policies are being implemented effectively and that they have begun to make a real difference to the working lives of staff. IWL performance measurement for the interim 'Practice Standard' assessment only allocates a maximum of 25% weighting to the written portfolio of evidence based on hospital policies. Much more emphasis is placed on evidence collated from interviews with a cross section of staff from the hospital, which accounts for the remaining 75% of the assessment. The intention is that all hospitals should have been assessed for 'Practice Standard' by 2003. To achieve this they must be able to demonstrate evidence of *plans* to address the eight key IWL standards outlined in figure 1. However they would also have to achieve the advanced 'Practice Plus' standard by 2005, requiring evidence that these plans are being implemented effectively and that they are actively improving the working lives of staff.

IWL is important as a new initiative, but improving the quality of working lives of staff needs to be embedded into all areas of hospital management and practice. It should not become yet another initiative geared to the achievement of narrowly defined performance targets. There is evidence that many middle managers interpret and apply their hospital's policies in arbitrary ways (see for example Exton, 2003). This new standard will highlight areas of poor communication, the uneven application of human resource policies and insufficient staff involvement. More positively it will demonstrate areas of good practice and service innovation.

As a key part of the NHS Plan, the IWL initiative will only be successful if it effectively engages and involves frontline staff, providing the opportunity for them to develop their professional, service and working conditions. The eight key areas to be assessed within the IWL standard (listed in figure 1 above) address some of the most important reasons given by employees leaving the Health Service. Involving staff at all levels of the IWL initiative would empower them to make a difference within their hospital, shaping future health services and lead to improved retention and recruitment. These improvements will ultimately influence their work environment, increase their quality of working life, enable work-life balance and lead to improved standards of patient care.

Shifting the Balance of Power

For the IWL Standards to be implemented effectively, the dominant management culture in the NHS needs to be challenged. *Shifting the Balance of Power: securing delivery* (DoH, 2001a, p24) argues that:

"A real shift in the balance of power will not occur unless staff are empowered to make the necessary change . . . Staff need to be involved in decisions which effect (sic) service delivery. Empowerment comes when staff own the policies and are able to bring about real change."

This represents a massive change from the way most staff work at present and these changes won't happen without a struggle. By achieving IWL accreditation, hospitals will not automatically create real changes in working life - there have been plenty of examples in the NHS where performance measurement has led to quality assurance without quality enhancement. Even when hospital Boards are fully committed to improving the quality of working life, there is no guarantee that this will be realised at workforce level.

Many trade union representatives experience the present system of implementing hospital policies as inadequate, ineffective and inequitable. Directorate managers or even lower line managers have considerable discretion in interpreting how (or sometimes whether) policies will be implemented, based on their personal assessment of 'the needs of the service'. Employees are therefore often unable to benefit from hospital policies on issues such as family friendly flexible working patterns. As the previous case study demonstrates, many trade union representatives and their colleagues strive to bring about changes at ground floor level. Unfortunately this can cause a considerable increase in stress for those individuals. Management often gives little more than token verbal support for involvement in issues traditionally seen as part of their own remit. For these ground floor staff, involvement in improvement programmes and other initiatives is often undertaken in their own time because there is rarely cover to release them from their clinical or service commitments. Will the IWL initiative crash onto the same barrier reef of middle management?

The costs of non-involvement are great. Even if IWL performance targets are seen to be met, staff will leave the Health Service in even greater numbers if policies continue to be inequitably implemented and staff are able to participate. Change will only be achieved if the NHS embeds the principles of partnership, involvement and participation in the very culture of each hospital.

Staff involvement must ensure that real life issues are heard and addressed. Staff experiences of both good practice and the need to address bad practice can be identified to support improvement. Consultation with and feedback from the work force will identify the real issues of working in that hospital. Managers need to be accountable to their teams and accept the challenge of engaging with staff to steer the NHS through much-needed cultural change.

The IWL initiative was first discussed with the trade union representatives at their joint meetings with management as early as March 2000. Formal endorsement of the hospital's commitment to IWL had already been agreed at senior level but there was little appreciation of the volume of work required to achieve the 'Practice Standard' by 2003.

The first impact the IWL initiative had on trade union representatives and staff alike was the allocation by Government of a £25,000 grant to each NHS organisation enabling small, practical improvements designed to benefit staff and improve their working lives. Staff members were asked by their line managers to make suggestions, and as usual the more proactive teams benefited first!

In January 2002 trade union representatives were invited to join with hospital executives, non- executives, clinical staff and managers at a time-out morning to develop a framework for the implementation of the IWL initiative. This was a notable milestone in the development of effective trade union involvement, working in partnership with hospital management rather than being forced into a reactive role. An initial framework for the achievement of IWL Practice Standard proposed involving middle management as the main channel of communication within the hospital. However the union side suggested that this was not appropriate because employees would simply dismiss IWL as yet another management-led initiative. A more effective framework based on much wider staff involvement was proposed by trade unions at the time out and subsequently adopted (see figure 2, below):

FIGURE 2 - IWL Staff Involvement at Nottingham City Hospital

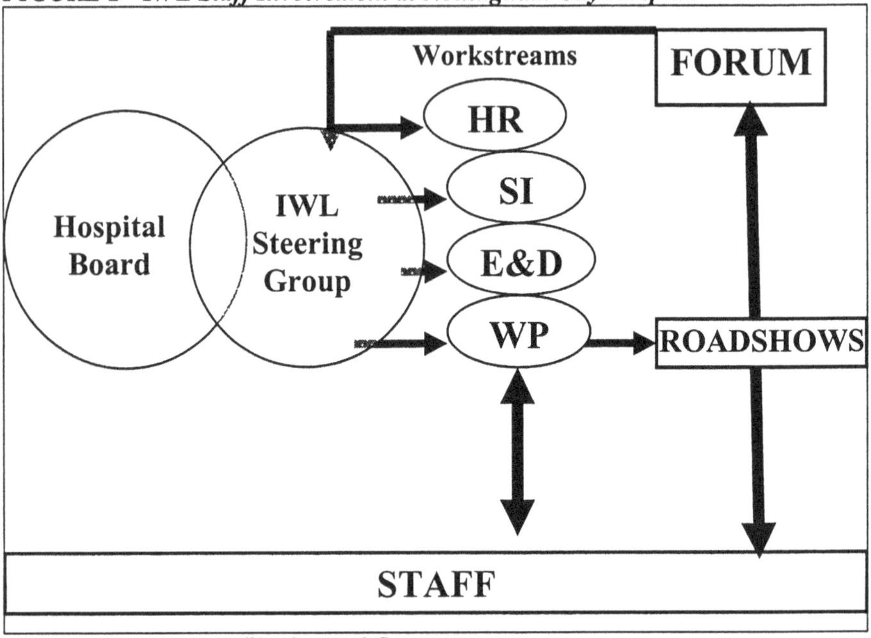

HR: Human Resources SI: Staff Involvement & Communication
E&D: Equality & Diversity WP: Working Practices

Trade union participation at this meeting added new insight to the discussions, drawing on wide knowledge of management practice across the hospital. Union representatives identified good examples of management style and team working, but also drew attention to the arbitrary interpretation and implementation of hospital policies by some middle managers.

It was becoming clear to trade union representatives that they had everything to gain by involvement in an initiative that addressed many of their concerns and could be a driver for real change. Moreover the emphasis of the assessment system on staff interviews ensured that the hospital would not be allowed to see IWL merely as a paper exercise in which it could just tick present its portfolio of evidence. Real staff involvement was crucial to its success.

IWL Steering Group

Following the time-out session a Steering Group was established, chaired jointly by an executive and non-executive director. The chairman and secretary of the joint trade union committee were invited to join the Steering Group, together with managers from each clinical directorate plus human resources and other service departments. Higher management representation from each clinical division on the Steering Group was secured in an attempt to secure a communication pathway to the traditional line management structure. However dissemination through traditional line management often proved ineffective, resulting in poor local support and understanding of IWL.

Partnership with leading union representatives at the strategic level was a clear acknowledgement that the hospital considered staff involvement essential to the success of the IWL initiative. However these representatives struggled to balance the huge demands on their time attending meetings and organising events with their clinical and service support commitments. Union representatives initially struggled to achieve recognition of their problem with balancing work commitments given the limited resources available in their clinical and service areas to cover their absence.

The Steering Group was created initially to set the direction for achieving the IWL Practice Standard and has continuing responsibility for encouraging wider change within the organisation. It ensures that initiatives are co-ordinated and communicated across the hospital. The Group is responsible for agreeing work programmes of four thematic Workstreams (see below) and for managing their performance. Responsibility for ensuring effective responses to staff suggestions also lies with the Steering Group

IWL Workstreams

Four Workstreams were established to address key organisational issues:

- Human Resource Strategy and Management
- Staff Involvement and Communication
- Working Practices
- Equality and Diversity.

Membership of the Workstreams initially consisted of members of the Steering Group, HR managers, union representatives and a cross section of hospital management. This was altered at the request of the unions, who expressed serious concerns that membership was weighted towards the management perspective. More involvement from all grades across the hospital was sought, and over 70 staff members were eventually included in these Workstreams. Workstream action plans included an assessment against the IWL Practice Standard, the evaluation of hospital policies

including the effectiveness of their implementation, and the active engagement of staff at all stages of the process. Discussion within the Steering Group quickly led to agreement that capturing the views of staff across the hospital and responding to them effectively was a key priority.
Staff involvement at this level created a new challenge for the leadership of these Workstreams, recognising that the formality of meetings, structured agendas and the presence of managerial and non-managerial staff could inhibit participation. It would require openness, trust and familiarity to encourage some staff to attend and speak out, without fear of being penalised by line managers. Feedback from one frontline worker attending her first meeting was that she felt intimidated by the formal agenda and the format of the meeting, and she subsequently left the group. This highlights the continual struggle that Workstreams face in balancing the need for structured discussions to complete formal business on the one hand with open dialogue designed to capture staff experience of working life on the other.

IWL Roadshows

To address the challenge of involving all hospital staff in identifying opportunities for improvement, the secretary of the joint trade union committee proposed the concept of 'Roadshow' events designed to take the IWL initiative out to the workforce at times and venues accessible to all. A series of seven Roadshows was held during November 2002 in two key locations on the hospital campus. Some 576 staff attended the first cycle of Roadshows, and this participation of 10% of the workforce was considered a good result for such an innovative project.
The Roadshow is designed as a relaxed informal drop-in forum for staff consultation and participation, with visual displays and a refreshment area where staff can sit and chat. On arrival they are welcomed with coffee and biscuits, and invited to complete a questionnaire comprising short multi-choice questions designed to evaluate their quality of working life. The results of this and future questionnaires will assist in monitoring trends following the IWL assessments.
The questionnaire sets the scene for a series of displays which provide visual explanations of the IWL initiative in ways that are exciting, informative and designed to stimulate comment. Staff are encouraged to share examples of good practice from their areas of work and to write questions and comments about their working lives. Each Workstream's display introduces its members and offers a brief resumé of its work. A representative from each group is available to answer questions and explain

the IWL initiative in greater detail, highlighting the importance of staff involvement.
Within the traditional culture of the NHS some staff may fear recrimination when commenting on their quality of working life. Union representatives acted as facilitators at the Roadshows, encouraging and enabling staff to share their thoughts and experiences in the knowledge that they wouldn't be identified. Graffiti wall charts and marker pens proved a successful media for staff to express ideas and suggestions, and anonymous boxes were available for written comments. Roadshow participants were encouraged to share examples of good practice, identify shortcomings and discuss ideas for improvement to their working lives. Many comments were received, covering a wide range of issues.
A number of experienced facilitators were asked if they would lead informal discussion with staff at the events. An area for these informal groups was arranged near to the refreshments and staff were encouraged to engage in discussions. Posters on the walls prompted the sessions with statements such as *'What makes you feel good about your job?' 'What does the hospital do really well... and not so well?' 'How is your knowledge and experience valued at work?'* and *'What stops your job from being rewarding?'* The question *'How can we do things better?'* was introduced throughout the discussion to generate ideas and suggestions. Ideas introduced were tested on other staff members in the group, for example *Would this work elsewhere in the hospital?* or *How could we make this work across the whole organisation?* This information was collected on flip charts and collated for review by the Workstreams.
Other features included in the Roadshow were displays introducing the members of the hospital Board, the IWL Steering Group and the unions. Many staff commented that this was beneficial because they would not otherwise have recognised some of these key people. Roadshow events also proved successful in promoting staff involvement in key issues relating to changes within the hospital. The proposed new hospital uniform was displayed for staff to see and comment on. Other issues such as changes to car parking and site reconstruction are planned for future Roadshows.

IWL Forum

The first Forum meeting was held on 6 December 2002, and sought to examine in greater detail the key issues that had been identified at the Roadshows. The event was well supported, with 41 staff attending from a wide range of professions and areas of the hospital. Participation in the Forum is open to all employees, and managers from each department were asked to ensure that at least one member of their area took part. Facilitated by members of the Steering Group, staff suggestions arising from the Roadshows are clustered and peer-reviewed. Conclusions are then refined and tested, eventually emerging as specific proposals to be addressed by the Workstreams.

Key points from the Roadshow flipcharts and graffiti boards were summarised under the following headings:

- **Work organisation** - the way the hospital works including management style, decision-making forums and staff involvement, training and development.
- **Work environment** - including car parking, buildings, security and health and safety.
- **Communication, involvement and partnership** – information, communication and participation mechanisms within the hospital, and how these can be improved.

The overall evaluation of the Forum was positive, with the participants concluding that it represented a good start to addressing issues raised by staff.

Reflections and Lessons from the IWL Initiative

The IWL initiative encompasses all the areas that influence our working lives. Staff should be represented and involved at every level of discussion about IWL within the hospital because without staff involvement the standards will not be met. The IWL Roadshows provide a forum for staff participation across the organisation, separate from the traditional line management structure. Discussion within workforce teams about the IWL initiative can identify issues relating to good practice, the need for improvement, team performance, communication and the promotion of ideas for change.

The valuable resource represented by the skills and knowledge of the employees of the National Health Service needs to be recognised. There must be a positive culture for change and innovation, motivating employees to initiate and embrace change and challenge traditional processes within the NHS. Breaking down the barrier of middle management and building a workplace partnership of management, trade unions and professional representatives with the workforce is necessary to create this culture of change in the NHS. To achieve a high standard of patient care hospitals need to identify issues that will improve the quality of working lives for their staff and not aim simply to achieve their performance targets.

Building workplaces that improve the quality of working life of employees so that they are involved, feel valued, and are less stressed will be the cornerstone for the future National Health Service.

Conclusion: Clinical Governance as a Reflexive Process

In summary, the arenas of organisational learning and innovation described above offer the scope to shift clinical governance from emphasis on compliance to improvement and innovation. If the current focus on performance management implies a mechanistic view of hospital organisations, the high road in contrast emphasises their organic nature and their potential for learning, risk-taking and innovation. Indeed it offers a profound challenge to the Tayloristic separation of planning and delivery that lies at the heart of current policy.

This paper argues that distortions in the implementation of Clinical Governance result in quality assurance without quality improvement. While there is recognition of the importance of staff in achieving effective Clinical Governance, there is little practical understanding at hospital level of how to achieve this by reuniting patient satisfaction and quality of working life.

Likewise there is little evidence that hospitals recognise the need to strengthen the basic, interdependent building blocks of post-Taylorist work organisation: knowledge creation and distribution, partnership and involvement, and multidisciplinary teamworking. The prioritisation and resources given to enhancing these building blocks simply do not match the obstacles encountered in attempting to change traditional forms of work organisation and management practice.

Acute hospitals need to formulate a more strategic role for Boards, to value staff involvement and participation as a core strategic value, to build team-based practice throughout their organisations, to redefine the roles and competencies of managers, and to build the skills required to make new forms of work organisation successful.

Likewise the health service trade unions need to understand both the potential and the implications of their emerging role as knowledgeable participants in workplace innovation. The flexible working and *Improving Working Lives* examples in this paper show how union representatives can play an important role in identifying opportunities for change, in informing change processes, in animating and sustaining dialogue with employees, in challenging obstacles to change and in guarding against innovation decay.

However there needs to be open acknowledgement of the value of this role by management and union officials alike. In particular the front line steward needs to be adequately prepared and resourced to take on these challenges.
Few hospitals can achieve these changes on their own. The question is whether government can develop modes of policy intervention capable of animating and resourcing such widespread organisational innovation.

Acknowledgements

The authors are grateful for ideas and contributions received from several colleagues, especially Jeremy Hague, Annette Sharpe and Jessica Sherrin (The Work Institute), Gilly Shapiro (CENTRIM, University of Brighton) and Elaine Moss (Nottingham City Hospital).

References

Argyris, C. (1977) "Double Loop Learning in Organizations" *Harvard Business Review* September – October, pp 115 - 125.

Ball, Curtis and Kirkham (2001) *Why Do Midwives Leave?* RCM Report for the DTI Partnership Fund. London: Royal College of Midwives.

Centre for Work & Technology (1995) *Women and Teamworking in the Health Services of Europe* Project Report, The Nottingham Trent University.

Commission of the European Communities (1997) *Partnership for a New Organisation of Work* Green Paper, Brussels.

Dawson, S., Hague, J., Knell, J., & Totterdill, P. (2002) *Partnerships for workplace innovation? A UK WON Dialogue Report* UK Work Organisation Network, Woking.

DoH (1997) *The New NHS: Modern, Dependable* London: HMSO.

DoH (1999a) *Agenda for Change: Modernising the NHS Pay System.* London: Department of Health.

DoH (1999b) *Making a Difference: Strengthening the nursing and midwifery and health visiting contribution to health and healthcare.* London: Department of Health.

DoH (2000a) *The NHS Plan*. London: Department of Health.

DoH (2000b) *An organisation with a memory* DoH, London.

DoH (2000c) *NHS Taskforce on Staff Involvement* DoH, London.

DoH (2001) *Shifting the Balance of Power: Securing Delivery.* London: Department of Health.

DoH (2002) *Improving Working Lives National Audit Instrument.* London: Department of Health.

European Foundation for the Improvement of Living and Working Conditions (1997) *New Forms of Work Organisation - can Europe realise its potential?* Office for Official Publications of the European Community, Luxembourg.

Exton, R. (2002) *Midwives take the lead, not leave.* Midwives Journal (Dec 2002).

Exton, R (2003) Case study of service redesign in an acute hospital Trust. Forthcoming.

Fricke, W. (1997) "Evaluation of the German Work and Technology Programme from an action research point of view" in *Workplace innovation: a way of promoting competitiveness, welfare and employment* Alasoini, T., Kyllönen, K., & Kasvio, A. Eds., National Workplace Development Programme, Helsinki.

Garvin, D. (1993) "Building a Learning Organisation" *Harvard Business Review* July – August.

Gustavsen, B. (1992 *Dialogue and Development* Van Gorcum/ Maastricht: The Swedish Centre for Working Life, Stockholm.

Gustavsen, B. (1996) "Action Research, Democratic Dialogue and the Issue of 'Critical Mass' in Change" *Qualitative Inquiry*, 2 (1).

Hague, J. (2000) *Work Organisation: new wine in old bottles?* Innoflex Working Paper, The Nottingham Trent University.

Hague, J. (2002) *Arenas of Change* Hi-Res Working Paper, The Nottingham Trent University.

Hague, J., Huzzard, T., den Hertog, F. & Totterdill, P. (2002) *Better Rich and Healthy than Poor and Sick* Innoflex Project Report, The Nottingham Trent University.

Hedberg, B. (1981) "How can Organizations Learn and Unlearn?" in P. Nystrom and W. Starbuck (eds) *Handbook of Organizational Design* Vol. 1, OUP, Oxford.

Iles, V. & Sutherland, K., (2001) *Organisational Change: a review for managers, professionals and researchers* NCC SDO, London.

Involvement & Participation Association (2002) *IPA Response to the DTI Consultation Paper on High Performance Working.* London: IPA.

Kennedy, Professor Sir Ian, (2001) *Report of the Public Inquiry into Children's Heart Surgery at the Bristol Royal Infirmary 1984 - 1995* DoH, London.

Knell, J. (2001) *The Quiet Birth of the Free Worker*: Industrial Society, London.

Meadows, S., Levenson, R., Baeza, J. (2000) *The Last Straw: Explaining the NHS nursing shortage* King's Fund, London.

Mueller, F. and Purcell, J. (1992) "The Drive for Higher Productivity" *Personnel Management* pp 28 – 33.

NHS Confederation (2002) *Update* August.

Pettigrew, A. M. (1987) Context and Action in the Transformation of the Firm *Journal of Management Studies,* 24 (6), 649-670.

Savage, P., *New Work Organisation in Ireland* Irish Productivity Centre, Dublin.

Seely Brown, J. and Duguid, P. (2000) *The Social Life of Information* Harvard Business School Press, Boston.

Shapiro, G. (1999) *Inter-project knowledge capture and transfer: an overview of definitions, tools and practices* CENTRIM Working Paper, University of Brighton.

Sharpe, A. and Totterdill, P. (1999) *An Evaluation of the New Work Organisation in Ireland Programme* Irish Productivity Centre, Dublin.

Sherrin, J. (2002) *Arboga* Case Study at www.ukwon.net.

Sherrin, J. & Procter, S. (2002) *The Team-Based Organisation* Hi-Res Working Paper, The Nottingham Trent University.

Stalk, G., Evans, P. and Schulman, L. (1992) "Competing on Capabilities: The New Rules of Corporate Strategy" *Harvard Business Review* (70).

Taylor, F. W. (1911) *The Principles of Scientific Management* Harper, New York (1947 edition).

Toft, Professor Brian, (2001) *External inquiry into the adverse incidents that occurred at Queen's Medical Centre, Nottingham, 4th January 2001* DoH, London.

Totterdill, P., Dhondt, S., Milsome, S., (2002) *Partners at Work? A Report to Europe's Policy Makers and Social Partners.* The Work Institute, Nottingham.

Can Apnea be Avoided when Developing Work Organisation in Hospitals?

Examples from a partnership project

PALLE BANKE, ANNEMARIE HOLSBO

Preface

The co-operation in development of hospitals - (Samarbejdet om Udvikling på Sygehusene) - SUS - was established by employers and employees in the hospital sector: the Association of County Councils, The Danish Confederation of Municipal Employees, the Healthcare Confederation and the Junior Hospital Doctors' Association. Therefore, the project had a double perspective: To de-velop the hospital enterprises to the benefit of patients as well as employees. The basic idea was that by developing the way the work was organised and the responsibility and competencies were allo-cated, the result would be hospitals where a better quality and efficiency was obtained through in-ter-disciplinary collaboration. Thus, the parties entered the project with the idea that together they could promote the interests of the individual organisations, and the financing did come from the la-bour agreements.

There were two rounds of SUS projects. The first one was in 1997-1999 and the second one which this report is about, went on from spring/summer 2000, and the project related part was concluded by year-end 2001-2002. From central quarter the project could offer assistance from a private consultancy company to the employees and departments that wanted to participate in order to imple-ment the project and have the possibility to exchange experiences in networks with other develop-ment departments. Finally, it was a part of the local SUS project to participate in the evaluation. The evaluation and reporting was implemented by Danish Technological Institute.

A steering group of managers from the organisations was set up. The initial procedure was that de-partments wishing to become a SUS project forwarded an expression of interest. The steering group especially emphasised the inter-disciplinary backup and involvement in the project and that the pro-ject had potentials for a subsequent demonstrational value. Moreover, it was a wish to have a
diversification on different types of departments - and thereby types of problems - as well as a cer-tain geographical diversification. Since there was both finances and prestige attached, the trade un-ions and the Association of County Councils of course wanted the projects receiving SUS support quite certainly to be implemented successfully.
Based on the above five development projects from five central hospitals were chosen:

- The medical ward M 130, Central Hospital Nykøbing Falster;
- Esthesiological ward NR, Silkeborg Central Hospital;
- Casualty ward, reception, Central Hospital in Grenå;
- Surgical ward 252, Central Hospital Esbjerg Varde;
- Neurological ward N, County Hospital in Gentofte.

The projects at the departments of course developed quite differently. Different types of problems had made the departments want to participate in the SUS process. The ambitions of the projects were different as were also their experiences in development project work. Some projects had been inspired by the possibilities in SUS while others were based on current activities. None of this was wrong, but the consequence was that the projects operated very time staggered and very much so in relation to the concluding evaluation. Therefore, the report is mainly based on knowledge gained from four projects.

Method of Evaluation

The SUS II project (in the following referred to as the SUS project) has been process evaluated which means that experiences from the individual projects regarding results and target compliance were gathered during the process. This report is based on the current contact with the projects - with managers and employees at the wards and project co-ordinators and their external consultants, if any. Therefore, it is not an evaluation intending to access whether something was good enough or too poor based on some external premises. On the contrary, the dialogue with the projects was based on their own targets and wishes as regards courses of development, of course within the over-all idea of SUS - i.e. that the project must at the same time result in benefits to the patients, the hos-pital and the employees and that this can be brought about by strengthening the inter-disciplinary collaboration.

Concrctcly, thc cvaluation took place in such a way that after the initial meeting with representa-tives from management and employees at the various workplaces a draft was prepared for a collabo-rative agreement regarding the targets and means within the frames of the project that the depart-ment would try to reach. The collaborative agreements were discussed and adjusted in the project steering groups and did, in so far as they were drawn up operate as a good management tool. All projects were visited at least three times, and moreover the evaluators participated in single project seminars as well as in SUS' collective activities. At all workplaces interviews were implemented with management and employees from all the staff groups being involved in the project. Likewise, efforts were made to talk to representatives from steering groups as well as staff groups and em-ployees who had not been involved in the development of the project. This was in order to measure the degree of anchoring and any obstacles etc. to the success of the project. After each visit the pro-ject received a feedback with points of attention which they could choose to utilise in their further development.

This evaluation has not collected information from patients or the hospital top managements - statements about these two groups were, as mentioned, based on interviews with managers and em-ployees. This means, of course, that the report is mostly focussing on the employee and union per-spectives and less on the patient view. At the same time, exactly these three interests have been im-portant guidance points in the evaluation: Which benefits are there in SUS for patients, hospital and employees?

Patients	Hospital	Employees
	Surgical ward – Esbjerg Central Hospital *Whole patient processes and development of team organisation*	
• Meet fewer employees and more competent staff. This gives more peace and continuity • Earlier discharge • Are assigned contact persons. This makes the ward less complex and gives a better contact to the staff	• Better control of the care • Shorter hospitalisation time - reduced cost per patient. The hospitalisation period has been reduced from 12-14 days to 7-8 days. • Fewer/no patient complaints • More rational operation • Improved knowledge sharing between the staff groups • More inter-disciplinary task processing • Function and procedure descriptions	• Have a less complex job area with more influence. This gives more satisfaction and good patient processes • Co-operates better within the staff groups • Improved possibility for systematic competence development and professional concentration • New colleagues receive a formalised introduction and there is a follow-up • The social and health service assistants get more challenging tasks. The nurses get more time for their specialities • The secretaries are closer attached to the care
	Casualty/reception/out-patients' clinic – Grenå Central Hospital *Inter-disciplinary competence development*	
• Meet a more co-ordinated staff • Have appointments at the out-patients' clinic that are kept • Meet the operating surgeon at the out-patients' clinic	• Improved co-operation between doctors and nurses • Better utilisation of the doctor resources at the out-patients' clinic • Greater efficiency • Procedure descriptions • Systematic knowledge sharing within the group of nurses	• Are able to better overview the tasks by means of the procedure descriptions • Get more systematic knowledge sharing. This results in more mutual respect and more job satisfaction • Younger doctors and consultant doctors collaborate better. This gives more satisfactory working conditions • The service assistants get better job development possibilities • The secretaries get better/more information

Patients	Hospital	Employees
Esthesiological ward – Silkeborg Central Hospital *Inter-disciplinary teams*		
• Meet calmer, patient focussed processes • Get fewer and punctual notices of delayed operations • Get quicker and better bedding	• Fewer and punctual notices of delayed operations • Greater efficiency • More inter-disciplinary respect and better co-operation in teamwork • Better utilisation of knowledge and knowledge sharing within the staff groups • Better co-ordination. In the operating room via the ward foreman and at the department via the co-ordinator • Better resource utilisation with the service assistants' new competencies	• See that focus on the patient gives a better working climate • Meet inter-disciplinary respect and co-operation in teamwork. This gives greater job satisfaction • Have better knowledge sharing between the staff groups. This gives greater job satisfaction • The service assistants' competencies are developed
The medical ward – Central Hospital in Nykøbing Falster **Inter-disciplinary project on mobilisation of patients**		
• Are mobilised quicker, more and better – by the same person	• Quicker, more and better mobilisation of patients • Better resource utilisation for the nursing staff, physiotherapists and the orderlies • Less absence due to sickness among the orderlies	• The department orderlies have new tasks and are integrated in the department. That gives bigger job satisfaction for the orderlies, the nursing and therapist groups • Better working conditions give less absence due to sickness among the orderlies
Neurological ward – Copenhagen County Hospital in Gentofte *Co-ordination and continuity in the patient process*		
• Get information material. Also material for the relatives • Have a regular contact person	• Better information to patients and relatives • Better communication about the patients, among other things due to the Barthel-scoring	• Better co-operation among the nursing staff and in relation to the physiotherapists and the ergotherapists

Obstacles and Levers Across of the Projects

The work at a hospital ward has some characteristics that are special for this sector and that means something for the kind of possibilities and obstacles there might be to implement projects meant to develop work organisation. These conditions are seen at all hospital wards - also those having par-ticipated in the SUS project.
The hospital sector has increasingly been placed in the limelight during the latest ten years. The in-creasing demand from the government for more effectiveness and a starting lack of personnel in general - but also within the hospital sector – result in great management and organisational challenges and also in many ways difficult working conditions. - A mildly speaking challenging 'cock-tail' within a sector with a rather complex framework for market conditions, 'production' and work organisation.
At the same time, the hospital sector is exposed like any other industry. All of us are interested par-ties and (potential) clients - patients and relatives - and have an opinion which we feel entitled to express at any time. The sector is one of the really heavy, public responsibility and resource sectors, and thereby the hospitals are being targeted. And politicians as well as journalists love hospital sto-ries, usually with a negative angel focussing on for instance waiting lists and (mis)treatments. It is seldom that the media and politicians are occupied with the complexity of running a hospital, not to speak of all the, after all, daily, successful patient processes – which form the typical picture.
To the staff there are some ruthless demands for finalised treatments in the shortest possible time. At the same time, patient treatment, nursing and patient contact as a whole make some special de-mands on the employees. It lies in the character of the work that it is difficult to 'get through' and to 'have enough time' - which is especially true for the nursing staff. This is enhanced by the patients' increasing demands and expectations of a good process. As they said at one of the hospitals: "It has only been a good day for the patients if the consultant doctor has been on the round and had time to talk".

About the Inter-Disciplinary Challenges

The doctors, nurses, social and health service assistants and the other staff groups handle each of their particular part of the patient process, and therefore they do not necessarily need to have an overall perspective. There is no doubt that everyone has the patient in focus, but with such sharp job demarcations the patient will still easily disappear in the staff flow and practical nursing and treat-ment.

Patient processes and co-ordination therefore become key words in the development of the hospital as a workplace and enterprise. However, the job demarcations can make the development process awkward. Each staff group has its own challenges in the development against more inter-discipline and delegation of responsibility.

Work-sharing and the many staff groups at the hospital ward are the greatest challenges for actual organisation development. This has been taken up in all the SUS projects - and it was the core chal-lenge in the development work.

Often 'inter-discipline' at the hospitals is dealt with as a question of hierarchy. As a one way dele-gation and task sliding from above (from the consultant doctors) and downwards (to the service as-sistants/orderlies).

Although in practice there can be much truth in the overall perspec-tive, it can crumble away if it is the only perspective. The better one is at adhering to the col-lective task related to the individual patient, the more flexible and varied the inter-disciplinary development will be. It is more about the overall co-operation (in the patient process) than about the competence development or relief of some (more than others).

Each staff group has and has had its eyes on the process and their special challenges. Generally, the SUS projects have been characterised by the fact that to a high degree the drive has come from the nursing staff - especially the nurses. So, although in most of the projects the doctors have been invited to participate, they have typically not come to feel committed to the matter or to have the opportunity to think of themselves as a part of the basis for

About inter-discipline

At the same time it is both more and less visible professional standard. One does not insist so much on ones own professional standard, and con-currently one can see the others' specialist education and their profes-sional standards.
(Doctor)

Inter-disciplinary co-operation fosters some special resources - everyone has got something - based on their own professional standard and with re-spect and understanding for the oth-ers'. But one has to move ones own mono professional standards.
(Manager)

One must control ones mono profes-sional standard competencies in order to share within a team.
(Nurse)

changes. The other staff groups - for instance physiotherapists and ergotherapists and service assistants/orderlies - have participated at several occasions - with the orderlies of Nykøbing Falster being the most offensive. In this section the individual staff groups are given the floor and are describing the SUS project from their point of view. The SUS projects have shown that it is important to recognise the various preconditions in order to work more transfunctionally. The inter-disciplinary process runs most smoothly if all staff groups are involved - with each of their interests and challenges as regards a more patient-orientated and inter-disciplinary organisation of the work. In other words, one must rest on ones own professional standard in order to be able to really work transfunctionally.

The doctors

By tradition the doctors are 'their own masters' in the professional track of qualifications while at the same time it is they who have (by tradition) the final responsibility for the treatment. This means that the doctors - at their many different levels - to a high degree are concentrating on education, technical-professional development and, of course, the actual treatment work – which is closely connected to the two first mentioned issues. The big responsibility and professional standard make many doctors 'technicians' rather than organisers or managers. This also applies to the managing doctors who, therefore, often leave much of the management tasks with the managing nurse.

Therefore, the doctors can been hesitant in relation to staff questions - and thereby also to develop-ment tasks. Since, otherwise, the doctors are regarded as the 'strong' staff group, also as regards management, their colleagues from other staff groups might overlook that the doctors can feel just as uncertain as other non-nursing staff groups. The doctors will easily become targets while at the same time they often withdraw from the inter-disciplinary discussions which take place in for in-stance development forums. And the management lets them do it.

The doctors are very different; they are at various educational levels and have different specialities. The doctors - of course especially those having completed their education - generally see them-selves as the central actors in the 'production' of patient processes. They are 'delivering the core output' while the rest of the staff is not less relevant but has tasks generated from the treatment as such. At the same time, the doctors are far from acting as one group but rather like single-person specialist enterprises - arranged around the very different professional specialities.

Seen from the doctors' perspective

The doctors are afraid of the new way of working. And to be tied down - that their freedom will be taken away. When working in the team one is tied by the department. [...] We have resigned; we have said that we want this, but you can not force people... (Manager)

When the doctor has been on the round he says: "I am finished". [...] You have to push them, but we have two open doctor vacancies, and that will be the excuse - that nothing can happen until after January the 1st. [...] The doctors are free birds, but it is no good with the old fashioned consultant doctor with a tie. But the problem is that they can get a job anywhere. [...]

(Manager)

The greatest problem in the project is that it has not been made clear from the beginning how the staff groups are operating. Inter-discipline is ok, but now there is too much focus on the nurse group. [...] I don't know what the project has done for me - the rounds have become more troublesome.... The team thought is good, but we have not been involved.

(Doctor)

Generally, the doctors have been very absent in the SUS projects. There has been a big difference in the extent to which the doctors as a staff group have been involved in the project from the start and how much they have participated during the process. At the same time, the changes will have conse-quences - also for the way in which the doctors can perform their job. However, if the doctors cannot see the benefits of SUS' objective and means, they are in a position to make it difficult for the rest of the wards and the staff to obtain the full benefits.

With various expressions and forms the doctor group has at some stage in the five projects had a tendency to become the scapegoats of the departments - on the part of the other staff groups - the reason that the development could not proceed. Part of the explanation that the doctors have not been involved is that although the project as a starting point is meant to be transfunctional and the doctors therefore are formally included, the starting point for the doctors has not been sufficiently represented. That might have made them uncertain as to the space volume for their participation - and to the project as such.

Generally there is a big difference in the status and self-knowledge of consultant doctors and senior registrars. Therefore, they have also participated or not participated in SUS in different ways, and therefore they are also dealt with separately in the next sections.

Consultant doctors

The consultant doctors have generally not recognised the great benefits in the participation in the SUS projects. (In Nykøbing Falster they were not involved). The exception is the esthesiological department which is the only department where the managing consultant doctor has insisted that 'his' doctors - the esthesiologists - have participated. At the same time, the doctor collaborators here, the surgeons, have not participated actively. So, generally the consultant doctors have not been very visible in the SUS picture although being central actors in the patient process.

The senior registrars

The doctors in educational/rotation positions are rather a part of the hospital as an educational sys-tem than of the hospital as a workplace. They are at the departments for at short period - 6 months - and their tasks are highly directed by the educational requirements. They are amply occupied with the technical-professional as well as the work related challenges. Also, their relation to their 'men-tors' and teachers, the consultant doctors, often requires much energy, because the rotating doctors can feel more uncertain than the consultant doctors have time for or energy to hold.
This means that several of the SUS steering groups have prioritised to save the resources of involving one rotating doctor after the other in the projects. At the esthesiological department and the casualty ward/reception/out-patients' clinic the rotating doctors have participated, and it has turned out that there is a potential in the rotating doctors' transmission of experiences to other hospitals and wards.

In the younger doctors' perspective

There is too far between the small doctors to the big doctors.

(Younger doctor)

We think the department is very nurse-managed, among other things because they are experienced. Yes, they have scraped a lot together, and then it can be very difficult as a group of doctors to fight our way back on ground.

(Yngre læge)

Thus, in the SUS projects younger doctors have participated to a various extent. In the projects at the esthesiological department and the casualty ward/reception the younger doctors were, as men-tioned, very integrated in the projects - but due to the timewise length of the project it was, of course, different persons. At the medical ward the doctors have been kept advised of the project, but they have not participated. At the surgical ward it was chosen to concentrate on involving the con-sultant doctors. And at the neurological ward the younger doctors were from the beginning consid-

rological ward the younger doctors were from the beginning consid-ered a part of the project, but they did not themselves feel to be involved.

The nurses

- have the organisational and staff related tasks which makes them important managers also at lower levels in the organisation. The nurses have over the years defined still more tasks under their pro-fessional standards - comprising nursing, administration and management. Although it has been discussed for several years, the nurses are not always interested in letting other staff groups come in over 'their' duties. Professionalisation of the nursing discipline - with for instance increasingly more theory in the education - 'helps' the nurses to argue professionally for their 'right' to the tasks.

About prioritising development

We talk a lot but that is about the patients. Not about the bigger things and the department. I must admit that we down-prioritise that. We spend time on the students and training the new ones. And at the rounds.
(Nurse)

However, it must be mentioned that the allocation of competence and tasks between nurses and social and health service assistants typically changes from day to evening duty. Many tasks handled by the nurses during the day are taken over by the social and health service assistants in the even-ing.

The nurses as a staff group fill a lot in the hospital landscape and have also been the driver in most of the SUS projects. This driver often consists of a requirement for technical-professional continued qualification, and the interest in mono professional training has been large in several of the SUS projects.

The nurses see themselves as those in the wards being responsible for the patients. And this also seems to be a part of the basis 'upbringing' in the education at the nursing schools. The SUS pro-jects have depicted a picture of the nurses considering themselves as educated to take on responsi-bility, to possess the knowledge about nursing requirements, plan and take on tasks that require vigilance. Operational tasks - handling of nursing tasks - fill a lot. And although there is a lot of meetings during the working day, development tasks like the SUS projects are not always legiti-mate. 'Development' is easily downgraded among the many urgent duties.

It seems as if it is sometimes difficult for the nurses to clarify which are their special, professional competencies. This can contribute to make it difficult to work transfunctionally - and to delegate to other staff groups.
In relation to the social and health service assistants the nurses sometimes seem to lack confidence in the competencies of the other staff group.

> **Seen from the nurses' perspective**
>
> *We are also interested in the doctors becoming more involved. Many times we feel a bit on our own, but if the doctor came down and showed us something about a leg instead of just dealing with it over the phone.... There is a need for the registrars but also for the nurses. We feel that we have a big responsibility for medical matters, because we perform a great deal of treatment guidance.*
>
> (Nurse)
>
> *We nurses are especially trained to take on tasks that require vigilance. The social and health service assistants can take care of the patients when they are stabilised and the care has been organised by the nurse.*
>
> (Nurse)
>
> *I have begun to appreciate that many things which I thought only I could do, can actually be done by others also.*
>
> (Nurse)

The social and health service assistants

- are in may ways a very different group - also within SUS. The assistant nurses who have been trained can find it difficult to be allowed, or to allow themselves, to have new nursing tasks - to take over tasks from or to co-operate in tasks with the nurses.
The newly educated social and health service assistants generally have a clear feeling of their professional standards and are very ready to utilise them in the nursing tasks which are otherwise the nurses field. However, it can be difficult for them to get enough space to make use of and develop their new qualifications. Not necessarily because the nurses do not want to, but typically because that kind of organisational and competence development is not prioritised within the very operation-oriented organisation.

Seen from the nurses' perspective

We are also interested in the doctors becoming more involved. Many times we feel a bit on our own, but if the doctor came down and showed us something about a leg instead of just dealing with it over the phone.... There is a need for the registrars but also for the nurses. We feel that we have a big responsibility for medical matters, because we perform a great deal of treatment guidance.

(Nurse)

We nurses are especially trained to take on tasks that require vigilance. The social and health service assistants can take care of the patients when they are stabilised and the care has been organised by the nurse.

(Nurse)

I have begun to appreciate that many things which I thought only I could do, can actually be done by others also.

(Nurse)

At the surgical ward new job descriptions are prepared for the newly trained social and health service assistants.

The service assistants

- are also a very mixed group. A group of older, female cleaning assistants and younger service assistants - both men and women. SUS has observed several active service assistants, especially at the casualty ward/reception, who have been very offensive - though perhaps less towards the end of the project. Often SUS will come on top of a service assistant project which has put together the former cleaning assistant and orderly functions.

The service assistants generally have a clear picture of their position in the bottom of the hierarchy. Literally speaking both service assistants, orderlies and cleaning assistants are typically placed in the basement. And they do not expect anybody to start on their own asking to take over their duties.

Some of the younger service assistants seem to have a good mind to take on more various types of tasks - and to develop their professional standards.

The orderlies

The old group has its own clear professional identity which is enhanced by the increased risk to be forced into a service assistant overall and be send out to clean. Orderlies at the medical ward ex-pressed exactly this.

The orderlies have been used to 'live their own life' in the orderlies' centre (in the basement) and can therefore become invisible and 'forgotten' in development projects. The surgical ward is an ex-ample of this.

The SUS project at the medical ward has given the participating orderlies - affecting their colleagues - bigger dignity in the job. This at the same time means that they have generally become more visible and that those who might want to do so will find it harder to 'hide' in the future.

Seen in the orderlies' perspective

It is nice to become visible - to have a job that is actually making a difference.

(Orderly)

The secretaries

- are involved in several SUS projects. They typically have a very specific working area with the administrative tasks while at the same time they make up the putty - an organising link - between other staff groups.

At the surgical ward it has been discussed that the secretaries could step in to relieve the nurses but that was easier said than done.

In the secretaries' perspective

The nursing staff must get to know the secretaries, and we must train ourselves to express what is important to us, so that our job can become good for us.

(Secretary)

It is good to belong to a team. Then you know whom to turn to, and the services are handled twice as quickly.

(Secretary)

Once we get the time, we can take over the duties.

(Secretary)

The physiotherapists and ergotherapists

Like many service assistants the two therapist groups have duties at the department, but organisationally they are attached to their own professional managements. The physiotherapists and ergotherapists have a clear, professional profile which they defend but which does not cause conflicts at the departments, because the therapists are not a part of the individual department's finances.

In SUS they have participated in two projects: At the medical ward they played an outstanding role based on the theme 'mobilisation', and in Gentofte a large part of the group actively participated in the project and common meetings.

Adding New Problems to Old Ones: Public Sector Management in Social Services in the Age of Neo-Liberalism and the "Third Way"

RAINER GRECA

This article starts with a description of the origins of the welfare states in Europe and examines the measures taken to combat the economic and social problems which became apparent in the age of industrialization and mass production. In the second part the emerging new problems resulting from a shift in economic, social and political factors in post-modern societies in the 20th century will be discussed. Finally the results of two empirical comparative research projects about the re-organization of social services in Bavaria, Germany and South Tyrol, Italy will be used to reflect new problems resulting from this reform.

The Origins of Welfare States in Europe

The early forms of social help and social protection starting from ancient and mediaeval times to early modern states can be described as antecedents of the modern welfare state; they form sediments on which the institutional constructions of modernity are erected. If we separate the question of legitimization of help from the facts of helping processes, we get in a long-time historical perspective an interesting picture: until the 15th and 16th century the recipients of help are seen in an abstract way as objects of an universal moral: the clients are involved in interpretations of the Holy Bible like artificial figures. The prosecution of help as part of the Christian morality is more important than the result of the good deed. A progressive tendency toward rationality in the time before and after the Protestant reformation helps establishing specific regulations for people in need, which is measured on definite criteria. At the same time the group of recipients is restricted. The national states in the 17th and 18th century again enhance the group of those seen as clients of the institutions of a paternalistic state because of the application of codified regulations. Repression, education and alleviation of need follow the idea of a "good order" which is ensured on the basis of a comprehensive legislation; therefore in Europe a predecessor of the modern welfare state can be seen in the so called "*poor law period*". At that time poor relief becomes a matter of national concern and care for the welfare of the citizens is counted as belonging to the obligations of the state.

The French Revolution formed the theoretical fundaments -- basing on the fundamental principles of human rights -- for the modern national states. In the revolutionary period social care was not seen to be an impressive mission of governments; the decrees from March 19th and June 28th 1793 determined subsidies only for those in need. But from another point of view the French Revolution was very important for the development of the welfare state: the establishment of a rigid, hierarchical ordered administration which observes rational criteria. In France already under the reign of Louis XIV and Richelieu a reform of the administration had taken place. In the Napoleon era the central administration -- weakened by the revolution -- was reconstructed. The classical ministries were multi-graded, the administration for the inner affairs was organised up to the level of the communities. This model was copied in many European countries.

The personal completion of the public services is focused at first on the administration of inner state affairs, in the 19th century additional the service administration was developed, but social services were scarcely included. This "lag" in the creation of social services follows the liberal ideology, which was expressed in Germany for example by the influential Wilhelm von Humboldt as follows: "The state should abstain from all care for the positive well-being of the citizens and should not go one step further than it is necessary to protect them against themselves and against foreign enemies." (Humboldt: 1792, III,7) The liberal state conceptualization led in most countries in the citizens' lives as disadvantageous. Instead of public institutions the growing cities support a system of caring for the poor, which is based on the principles of voluntaries and neighbourly help; e.g. the "Elberfelder System" in Germany. In France the concept of "solidarité" describes a compromise between a liberal approach for freedom and the necessity of state interventionism. (Kaufmann: 2003, 212)

But it became obvious that the liberal concept fails obviously in combating the effects of industrialisation and the growing poverty in the industrial zones of Europe. For the first half of the 19th century the term "pauperism" is convenient to describe the economic and social situation of a huge part of the population. Traditional forms of poverty in the agricultural regions summed up with the social problems of poverty in the metropolitan areas. Finally facing the evidence that the market is not able to regulate itself -- a most important experience in this sense was the crash of the Vienna Stock Exchange in 1873 -- the liberalism was no longer the leading economic theory. (Grimm: 1983,52) Moreover the example of the 'Parisian Community' of 1871 had rose anxiety amongst the rulers and thereby promoted the readiness for integrating social security systems. (Kirsch: 1980,15) The ruling elite in all European countries were forced to establish new politics to secure mass loyalty. Under the influence of the philosophy of Hegel in Prussia leading reformers began to define the role of the state in a new way, for Lorenz von Stein for example, the state had the task to "further the non-possessing classes." (Hansmeyer: 1957,13)

Resistance against these negative developments of a liberal market conceptualization rose also from political and moral positions, especially the socialist movement organised the fighting back of the losers of the capitalistic society. Differences in the strength of working class parties and trade unions are most important for explaining variations in welfare state developments. "To some extent, differences in the strength of labour movements are a function of religions, linguistic and/or ethnic cleavages..." (Flora/Alber: 1981,43) The Christian churches, too, started opposing the ideology of the liberal market economy. The capitalism was not called in question, but the state was asked -- as in the Papal social encyclicals -- to compensate the evil developments. The subsidiary principle became prominent in the Christian tenets: the welfare state activities should be brought into action only if the small social units could not care for themselves. In many countries the catholic social tenets influenced the legislation, the funding of voluntary programs was supported significantly, the same is valid for the concept of social partnership, the concept of property creation for workmen and the model of intensive wages (Greca: 1994,355). Also in the Protestant and Calvinistic churches a "radical shift" (Kirsch: 1980, 14) took place toward a perspective of a social compensating state, because the leading ideas of liberalism had shown themselves as insufficient. (Lampert/Bossert: 1992,11)

The concept of the welfare state was practised in a double sense: internally it served to combat labour movement, externally it was practised for national dispute with other national and governmental systems (Flora/Heidenheimer, 1981, 17ff). By this way the modern welfare state was disunited and disuniting because of this political calculation.

It seems not to be appropriate arguing that "the modern European welfare states really began in the last decades of the nineteenth century" and that Bismarck and the German 'Kaiserreich' was "the pioneering country", (Flora/Alber: 1981, 37,60) even if an indirect impact from the establishment of the German system of social policies to other national concepts seems to be provable at this time, e.g. in Sweden (Henningsen, 1986,90), or France (Kaufmann: 2003,228). The most European countries have developed systems of social protection of their own, which can again be shown with the Swedish (Henningsen: 1986,94), British or French example (Kaufmann: 2003,126,229).

Numerous organisations for care were founded in the European countries. Ecclesiastical, political and social groups establish themselves and develop different institutional perspectives and goals of aid. Among these groups are the socialist workers movement, the Christian social movement, the liberal social movement and the co-operatives. Some of these organisations had an international character from the beginning, e.g. the 'Caritas', others remind in their activities of former European territorial formations, e.g. the 'Raiffeisen' organisation all over the territory of the former 'Habsburg Empire'.

Several traditions from the times before the welfare state was established have survived and still demonstrate and date back to different cultural and religious convictions. The priority given to forms of residual help in traditional catholic countries in contrast to the extension of institutional care in protestant countries (e.g. a Mediterranean model vs. a Scandinavian model) can be explained by these cultural diversity (Flora/Alber: 1981,43).

In general one could say that the development of social protection systems follows the impacts of the political, social and economic processes of the 19th century and is not simply the product of one European government:

France, Great Britain, and Germany had simultaneously the same development of national revenues and state expenditures in the 19th century. (Hansmeyer: 1957, 69) This indicates that they all were touched by objective external processes they had to react against. An increase of the population of more than 40 percent from 188 to 267 million people happened in Middle Europe. Only a small part of the population pressure could be alleviated by emigrations. (Grimm: 1983,46) The rapid growth of the population led to a remarkable increase in the number of working forces, which affected droppings in the wage-rates to a minimum living standard. (Kirsch: 1980,12)

In all European countries the economic liberalism had failed to solve the social problems. Poverty, especially in the new industrial areas, pauperisation of many groups of the population was not intended and unexpected consequences of a liberal 'Manchester Capitalism'. Child labour, lack of ownership, poverty, physical misery, housing

shortage, lacking security in times of crisis (unemployment, illness, old age) are the key words which enlivened the debates at a time when the industrial labour force was coming into existence.
The economic development of the 19th century dissolved the old solidarity: people, affected by illness or age and therefore not capable to work, were abruptly endangered in their existence. On the other side no institutions against risks like accidents, illness, incapacity, age, mental or physical handicaps existed.
The human labour force was not sufficiently protected against physical and psychical exploitation. Although people were equal in legal sense, they remained unequal in social affairs. (Lampert/Bossert: 1992,9)

The following measures were taken in many European countries:

- Restriction to working time and protective labour legislation reduced exploitation and risks
- Elementary interests of working people were protected by rights of co-determination
- The excessive supply of working force, caused by population growth, was limited by legal injunctions and prohibition (prohibition of child labour, women and mother protection, holiday regulation, illness and pension insurance)
- Financial transfer systems were established to fund benefits and social services
- Savings were founded which aimed to support members by means of money which has been saved by the members for these purposes
- An important column of the welfare system was established with the social insurance system
- In the education system new chances were offered in spite of different social and personal presuppositions

The effects of all this measures consist in an "equal distribution of room for material freedom, in a more equal distribution of chance for participation in economy, culture, sports and politics, and in a more equal distribution of the economic and social progress in society." (Lampert/Bossert: 1992,14)

An important financial redistribution in favour of needy parts of the populations does not take place before the beginning of the 20th century. E.g. the expenditures of the German Empire for social care were not more than 6.2 thousand millions RM. At the beginning of the 'Weimar Republic' they had increased up to 1,619 thousand millions RM. "In that, not in the Bismarckian social policy lies the beginning of transfer payments." (Hansmeyer: 1957,44)

The welfare state thereby modified the economic market forces in three directions:

- It guaranteed individuals and families a minimum income "irrespective of the market value of their property"
- It narrowed the extent of insecurity "by enabling ... to meet certain social contingencies, ..,which lead otherwise to individual and family crisis"
- It offered all citizens "a certain agreed range of social services". (Briggs: 1961,228)

These programs were introduced programmatically in many European countries, but not in the same way and not at the same time.

A comparison of European welfare systems shows clearly that the different political systems and parliamentary regimes had a significant influence on the construction of the diversity of welfare state politics and conceptions, as is shown in the table below:

Enfranchisement, Parliamentary, and Social Rights

Parliamentary regime	*LIBERAL DEMOCRATS* Public assistance as disqualifying alternative to political (and civil) rights	*MASS DEMOCRACIES* Social rights as democratic corollary of political rights and as a consequence of party competition for votes
Non-parliamentary regime	*CONSTITUTIONAL - DUALISTIC* Poor relief as paternalistic responsibility for needy 'subjects'	*MONARCHIES* Social welfare as authoritarian defence against (full) political citizenship and as a consequence of a competition for loyalty
Suffrage	Limited (manhood) suffrage or estate representation	Extended (manhood or adult) suffrage

(From: Flora/Alber: 1981,46)

It is obvious that liberal democrats thinking leads to other conceptions as do social-democratic visions in parliamentary regimes; while liberal democrats regard political and civil rights first and social rights as disqualifying, in mass democracies with parliamentary regimes social rights are established to the same degree as political rights. In constitutional monarchies without parliamentary regime either under conditions of limited suffrage poor relief will be given only to a limited group of persons or under condition of extended suffrage as a defence against full political participation and as a mean to sustain loyalty benefits will be given to extended groups of people.

These different constitutional and ideological concepts in Europe have lead to a mosaic of different regulations, which were established at different times. This tessellated pavement in Europe does not only show differences between nations, but also the succession of different parliamentary and political majorities within one country.

As the most important dimensions of institutionalisation of the European social security systems we respect (1) the juridical-normative codification of provisions, (2) the introduction of regularities in financing and support (e.g. the introduction of a complementary insurance for employees and employers), and (3) the cognitive interpretation and legitimisation of benefits.

The table below compares the different types of institutionalisation of social insurance for 'Industrial Accident', 'Sickness Insurance', Pension Insurance' and 'Unemployment Insurance' in various European countries between 1887 and 1967:

Social insurances for 'Industrial Accident', 'Sickness Insurance', 'Pension Insurance' and 'Unemployment Insurance' in various European countries (1887 – 1967)

Country	Industrial Accident		Sickness Insurance		Pension Insurance		Unemployment Insurance	
	A	B	C	D	C	D	C	D
Austria		1887		1888		1906 (employees) 1927 (workers)		1920
Belgium	1903		1894 1944		1900 1924		1907 1944	
Denmark	1898	1914	1892	1933 (semi.-compuls.)		1891 (national pensions) 1922 (national pensions rev.) 1933 (invalid ./old age insur.)	1907	
Finland		1895 1917		1963		1937	1917	
France	1898	946		1930	1910	1930		1914 (unemployment. assistance) 1959 (collective labour agreements) 1967
Germany		1884		1883		1889		1927
Italy		1898	1886	1928 (collective labour agreements) 1943	1898	1919		1919
Netherlands		1901 1921		1913 1929		1913	1916	1949
Norway		1894		1909		1936	1906	1938
Sweden	1901	1906	1891 1910			1913	1934	
Switzerland		1911		1911		1946	1924	
United Kingdom	1906	1946		1911 1946		1908 (national pensions) 1925		1911 1920

Notes: A = employers' liability; B = compulsory insurance; C = subsidized voluntary; D = compulsory (From: Flora /Alber: 1981:59)

At the end of the last and the beginning of the 20th century in many European countries four main social insurance systems were developed in relation to different risks: industrial accidents, sickness and invalidity, old age, and unemployment.
In the case of accident insurance five countries introduced workmen's compensation schemes: Belgium, Denmark, France, Sweden, and the UK, seven others started with compulsory insurance schemes: Austria, Finland, Germany, Italy, The Netherlands, Norway, and Switzerland. Six countries introduced voluntary sickness insurance schemes. Three countries introduced subsidised voluntary old-age insurance: Belgium from 1900 until 1924, France from 1856 until 1910, and Italy from 1898 until 1919. Unemployment insurance was generally introduced late. Three countries established an only subsidised voluntary scheme: Denmark, Finland, Sweden, five other countries have retained such schemes for a long period: Belgium until 1944, the Netherlands until 1949, Norway until 1938, France until 1967, and Switzerland until 1976. Four countries introduced compulsory insurance systems: Austria, Germany, Italy, and the UK.
Between the two world wars an extension of regulations happened. Social insurance was adopted in additional countries and was extended to cover more risks as well as new groups. At the beginning of World War II, the majority of the European countries had made accident and sickness insurance compulsory, all had introduced some kind of unemployment insurance, and, with the exception of Switzerland, provided for old age.
But it was not before the end of World War II the idea of the welfare state became universal. Lord Beveridge stands for this new concept of society. England had walked through a period of deep economic recession, accompanied by extreme rates of unemployment between World War I and II. During World War II the British nation again found a unity. Accompanying a new consensus about social security arose. After world war II the concept of the welfare state expressed the believe of people in a new social order "a new kind of society"

(Marshall: 1992,137). The support of poverty was discharged by concepts of prevention.

Indispensable in this concept the idea of citizenship is related to the idea of the welfare state: "Citizenship is a status bestowed on those who are full members of a community. All who possess the status are equal with respect to the rights and duties with which the status is endowed." (Marshall: 1964,84)

In the growing of the welfare state three fundamentals can be described, which guarantee the status of the citizen:

- The civil element consists from rights which are necessary to secure the individual freedom: freedom of the person and of thought, liberty of religion, speech, and possession, and of fair court proceedings.
- The political element consists from rights for the participation and the use of political power.
- The social element stands for: the right for a minimum of economic welfare and security, for a full participation in societal goods, and to share a life under civilised conditions according to the normal standards. It is especially the education system and the social services which guarantee these rights (Marshall: 1992,38).

In the 1960s and 1970s the welfare state became the most dominant characteristic besides industrial capitalism and representative mass democracy in all western industrial societies. Measures were institutionalised for:

- Regulations of the consumption markets, e.g. for prices and rents, subventions for goods, industry and housing
- Health care
- Aid against misery and poverty and guarantee of a subsistence level necessary for a life in human dignity
- Reduction of wealth discrepancies and dependencies for the creation of actual (and not only legal) equality
- Social security against the risks of accidents, illness, untimely incapacity of earning one's living, unemployment, old age, and the loss of bread winner

- Increase of prosperity and a just distribution of prosperity (Zacher: 1989,29)

Instruments of the welfare state are:
- Direct payment of cash benefits (e.g. income maintenance for typical phases of non-employment in the life-cycle),
- Direct provision of services (e.g. education, medical care, social care and advisory services),
- Indirect benefits (e.g. tax credits). (Flora/Heidenheimer:1981,25-26)

Comparative studies from the 1980s identify that various types of welfare regimes were established in Europe at this time. The following table presents the results of an examination, which describes four types of European welfare states: Scandinavian, Bismarck, Anglo-Saxon, and Latin-rim with specific characteristics and rights:

Types of European welfare regimes

<table>
<tr><th></th><th>Scandinavian</th><th>Bismarck</th><th>Anglo-Saxon</th><th>Latin rim</th></tr>
<tr><td>Type of welfare regime</td><td>Modern</td><td>Institutional</td><td>Residual</td><td>Rudimentary</td></tr>
<tr><td>Characteristics</td><td>Full employment; welfare state as employer of first resort and compensator of last resort</td><td>Full growth; welfare state as compensator of first resort and employer of last resort</td><td>Full growth; welfare state as compensator of last resort and tight enforcer of work in the market place</td><td>Catching up; welfare state as a semi-institutionalised promise</td></tr>
<tr><td rowspan="2">Right to:</td><td>Work</td><td>Social security</td><td>Income transfers</td><td rowspan="2">Work and welfare proclaimed Implemented only partially</td></tr>
<tr><td colspan="2">Backed up by an institutionalised social concept of citizenship</td><td>No such back-up</td></tr>
</table>

(From: Leibfried: 1993,142)

Typical for the Scandinavian type is: modernism, full employment and a fundamental right to work; for the Bismarck type: institutionalism, full growth politics and social security rights; for the

Anglo-Saxon type: residualism, full growth, and right to income transfers; for the Latin type: rudimentarism, catching up and proclamation of work and welfare. The Scandinavian and the Bismarck model share an institutionalised concept of social citizenship, the Anglo-Saxon and the Bismarck type see both the welfare state as compensator in the labour market (but with different stages of resorts).

Analysing the institutionalisation of the welfare state principle we can distinguished four different types:

- A universal und egalitarian social security system with large-scale financial transfers and extended social services; the financing is made by general taxation (e.g. Sweden)
- A universal und egalitarian social security system with low-scale financial transfers and few social services; target of the welfare politics is to avoid poverty, the reasons for poverty are not touched (e.g. UK)
- A comprehensive social security system by means of different protections which aim at the securing of social status of different professional groups; financing is made by contributions and taxation (e.g. Germany)
- Limited and regional variable social security; insurance is supplement to private providence (e.g. Switzerland)

The following table presents a comparison of the standard of welfare institutions in different western countries in the second half of the 19th century:

League table of standards of seven social security schemes

	Employment Injury	Temporary Disability	Invalidity	Old Age	Unemployment	Family Endowment	Health Service	Scores T	Scores B
Austria						T		1	-
Germany	T	T		T	T			4	-
Ireland				B			B	-	2
UK.							T	1	-
Denmark			T	T			T	3	-
Netherlands	T	T	T		T	T		5	-
Canada		B	B					-	2
USA	B	B	B		B	B	B	-	6
New Zealand								-	-
Australia	B			B	B	B		-	4

Notes: T=top; B=bottom   (From: Kaim-Caudle: 1973,301)

It is evident that the standard of social security was highest in all European countries in the table compared with those from the US, Canada, Australia or New Zealand. In the case of 'Employment Injury', 'Temporary Disability', 'Invalidity', 'Old Age', 'Unemployment', 'Family Endowment', 'Health Service', the Netherlands reached five times, Germany four times, and Denmark three times top scores. While on the other side the US had six times, and Australia four times the bottom score. Only Ireland had the same (low) status as Canada.

The Crisis of Welfare States

These findings can not support the thesis of a general acceptance of the welfare state concept in the post-war period. Neo-Marxists, liberals, social democrats had different arguments in describing the purpose and outcomes of social policy at that time (Room: 1979). Critics of the development of the welfare state already arose in the 1960s. It was argued, that the societies were choked on welfare, especially because it hindered the progress of economy and society (Marshall: 1992, 187). A massive inflation of pretension occurred, because the price for services seemed to be to low from the point of view of the individuals. “The state becomes more than ever that kind of illusion in which everybody intends to live on the spending of others.” (Kirsch: 1980,16) From a more formal point of view the welfare state was criticised for its inefficiency, ineffectiveness, bureaucratic structures and the shortcomings that result from the variety of services offered without sufficient co-operation. Also among the potential recipients of welfare benefits – the citizens – a discussion was started in the 1970s on the welfare regime’s provision principle. Self-help movements resulted and the discussion came to include the demand for smaller administrative territories of welfare services. As opposed to the state planning euphoria of the 1960s and 1970s, there was now a demand for a participation of the citizens.

On a scientific level the conflict between independent formal economy, state institutions and individual as well as collective action was discussed as a growing dilemma of the welfare state: “... the (market) economy, which stimulates competition, gives freedom in terms of destroying links and opening up choices, yet creates all kinds of inequalities; the state, which is able to counteract the latter, to enhance equality and to accentuate common interest beyond particularism and individualism, might yet limit freedom of choice and space for self-organization; the social sphere can create all kinds of lively solidarity but also dependence on communities and local egoism. The utopia of welfare is in fact nevertheless characterized by the aim of abolishing markets or independent economies like the socialist utopia wanted to; vice versa it seems evermore unrealistic to minimalize state intervention by maximizing the impact of market rules as it has been envisaged in liberal utopias. And the social-democratic compromise between state and market seems to be seriously threatened with respect to the role of the social sphere: by citizens who want to become acknowledged as participants, not only in political terms but also in terms of being co-producers of goods, services and benefits.” (Evers/Wintersberger: 1990,401)

Also on the level of political guiding principles the central political believe of the leading parties of the 1960s and 1970s – social democrats and Christian unionists – in an optimal guidability of these systems by the state in economic and social terms becomes an outlived utopia. The consensus of the 1960s and 1970s broke up and lead to a new "Unübersichtlichkeit" in public discussions and political conceptualizations (Habermas: 1985). The ideas of the function and tasks of the social welfare state changed internationally. Criticism of the "social network", of the goals of social intervention and of the possibility of harmonizing political goals with employment, the economy, and social services led to a vehement discussion of the limits of the conceptualization at work.

A neo-liberal position became popular, and from this point of view the welfare state itself was accused as being one main reason for economic and social decline, the debate was lead by "hard-nosed neo-classical economists espousing high unemployment, lower wages, and reduced fringe benefits and welfare state programmes." The neo-liberal attack against the welfare state became most popular throughout Europe. "Welfare state policies have shifted from relatively easy acceptance of expansion to criticism, reform or change, retrenchment and privatization." (Miller: 1990,373)

The points of liberal criticism against the social welfare state principle were:

- the negative impact on the population's motivation for performance
- the reduction of the strife for independent security through the accumulation of assets; the reduction of social efficiency because of bureaucratization

Social politics of the neo-liberal state follows new strategies can be described in three points:

- Selectivity refers to the stricter definition of respective groups of the welfare benefits
- Rationalisation is defined as „the attempt to cover the tasks in the field of social services with less manpower, changing teacher-pupil ratios, working organisation in hospitals, etc."
- Externalisation characterises efforts to substitute central welfare institutions by private households, private-for profit or local institutions of help (Evers/Wintersberger: 1990,392)

The liberal's camp reform ideas are based on a stronger market orientation, which creates bearable risks of self-procurement, introduces deductibles for social benefits to be paid by the recipient, reduces welfare benefits which decrease the recipients' motivation to performances.
Ideas for a reform of the welfare state were also developed from the political left. They emphasize the satisfaction and integration goals of social policy which – without fundamentally removing the contrast among social classes – are meant to adapt the labour force in the system through the compensatory and stopgap function of social policy, which compensates the risks of the production and reproduction system in collective insurance systems, reduces the risks of individual producers and defuses the problems of the labour market enough to not endanger the political system as a whole; the use of the systems of social security as controls to attain the motivational adaptation to the constraints of the modern industrial and labour world; the advance and constitutive function, which takes over tasks which promise no gain but which constitute the infrastructural preconditions for production. (Greca: 1996,17)
Because of these reasons even in the traditional welfare countries - like Sweden - a change in welfare politics happened. This is illustrated in the following table about retrenchments in the national welfare politics:

Retrenchments in welfare statistics in five industrialized countries

	USA	Britain	France	Germany	Sweden
Tax cuts	*	*	(*)	(*)	
Regressive shifts in the tax load	*	*	(*)	*	(*)
Reduced benefits for recipients of state transfers	*	(*)	(*)	(*)	(*)
Reduced eligibility for state transfers	*	*	(*)		
Reduced social services		*			
Residualization of benefits and services at the poor	(*)	*		(*)	
Reduced formation of social capital		*	*	(*)	
Reduced coverage of occupational benefits	*				
Reduction in favour of private provision		*			
Rising unemployment		*	*	*	
Rising inequality	*	*	(*)	(*)	

**=policy shift; (*)= policy move of minor importance; a blank space indicates that the policy did not apply or that the opposite policy was carried out (From: Esping-Anderson: 1990, 248)*

The table shows that starting in the 1980s a remarkable shift in welfare policies had taken place in most of the analysed countries. Regressive shifts in tax loads happened in a more or less strict way in all countries: US, UK, France, Germany and Sweden. Only the latter had no tax cuts. Rising unemployment became a problem in Britain, France and Germany, rising inequality took place in all countries, except Sweden. To a more or less degree reduced benefits for recipients of state transfers occurred in every country, reduced eligibility in the US, UK, and France. Reduced staff was only found in Britain, while residualization took place in US, the UK and Germany. Reduced formation of social capital could be seen in Britain, France, and Germany, reduced coverage of occupational benefits only in the US, reduction in favour of private pensions only in Britain. The most remarkable shift in welfare policies happened in Britain (in 8 fields), US (6), France and Germany (5), while Sweden did not have such a rapid change.

But also under this quite dramatic circumstance the welfare state did not vanish, it still exists and - compared with the development in the former communist countries it helped to keep the political stability of the Western world. (Klein: 1993,12)

Comparing the resulting strategies for political action to reform the welfare state, five models of change can be distinguished:

- "Defend-and-change": Because of the fundamental attacks on the welfare state defenders of this concept "want to maintain or restore the welfare state exactly as it was." The motives for defending are widespread, e.g. the staff of welfare state institutions fear cuts in the number of jobs, the recipients worry about the quantity and quality of services.
- "Participation and Economic Transformation": Self-help movements and other political groups have continued the criticism of the 1960s and called for greater participation of the clients in welfare state activities. "Neighbourhood control", "empowerment", "localism", "network-construction" are the themes, which are supported partly also by some conservative critics. This position is joined by analysts who follow the assumption that full employment will not be a realistic target on a national level; instead they underline the possibility of local activities.
- "The Social Integration Approach": This view focuses on the necessity of social integration, because the main problem of the present situation is said to be the "excessive individualism, atomism and anomie". At the political level a target is empowerment of family activities, at the organisational level the aim is to make a shift from the bureaucratic social programmes to non governmental, non-profit agencies, which are locally based. The social integrationists call for an institutionalised non-governmental voluntary sector.
- "Privatisation": The supporters of the concept of privatisation seek efficiency, less governmental expenditures, and increase choice through market competition. Therefore they favour a shift to market relationships. Competition of providers and choice by "enabled" purchasers would reduce costs and promote efficiency; "it would also assure better treatment of the users of the service because they would be customers, not clients, who could move their business elsewhere." (Miller: 1990,383)
- "The third way": A concept, which wants to formulate a new social "enabling" social democracy, taking into account the economic,

political and social changes in all industrialized nations, accepting some of the critical remarks about the negative outcomes of massive inflation of expenditures and services for the welfare state recipients, but also avoiding the new social problems caused by neo-liberalism. (Giddens: 1998)

A historical "Ungleichzeitigkeit" could be observed because old and new conceptualizations were implemented at the same time. With the example of Germany it can be demonstrated that the historical background of the concrete shape of the welfare state, especially its institutional implementation, was already being criticised in the Federal Republic in the mid-1960s. Particularly the Social Democratic Party, which for a long time held the opposition to the Christian Democratic Union of Adenauer, criticised the lack of effectiveness and efficiency, the bureaucratic structures and the one-sided orientation of social policy toward Christian family values. After the change in political majorities and the execution of reform policies, various German towns that had Social Democratic governments started reforming the legal and institutional framework of social services in the early 1970s. However, these planned reforms failed in 1974, when those projects could no longer be financed because of an economic crisis.

The socio-political arguments of that time advocating a change in the organization of social services on the community level can be summarized as follows:

1. Democratization: There was a demand for a stronger democratization of procedures. Among the issues were a more intense participation of citizens in the decision-making processes, a weakening of the hierarchies of decision-making processes, and a social policy geared toward the wishes of the citizens rather than the ideas of distanced decision-makers.
2. Decentralisation: The slogan of decentralisation was to account for the fact that in the immediate contact with those requiring assistance a large capital of knowledge had been accumulated by social workers and that it ought to be made use of. Decentralised planning was also meant to help confront the negative experiences

of long and insufficient planning processes that had been gathered until then.

3. Anti-Institutionalism: According to many of its critics, the bureaucratic organization of social work, its official structure, the work according to case principles, and diversified areas of responsibility had led to the lack of a holistic view of the problem. Instead, the assisting institutions concentrated on certain aspects of individual or family problems, on manageable difficulties, on situations that corresponded to the regulations. This situation was to be remedied through a co-operation among employees of various service providers, which was to be co-ordinated from a holistic perspective on persons and cases.
4. Pluralism: The pillar principle of social provision in the Federal Republic of Germany had led to various carriers of social institutions (welfare organizations) specializing in certain groups of clients, while their ideological orientation remained unchanged, although their task was to provide for all citizens. The critique of this model stressed that from the perspective of the clients, who required assistance; this meant that there was no free choice, that they were forced to consult the (ideologically biased) institutions in the vicinity of their place of residence.
5. Conceptualization based on needs: The programmatic model of social work was accused of not meeting the genuine needs of the population. From a socio-political perspective, it was additionally argued that antiquated concepts dominated, e.g. that of the priority of family institutions as the primary source of assistance. On the other hand, the development potential of children and adolescents, but also of women and other disadvantaged social groups, was not taken into account adequately. What was favoured instead, was to make the clients' needs the basis for social work.
6. Community conceptualization: Another demand in social politics, finally, referred to the creation of new communities. Those should unfold on a communicative basis, and social work was to contribute to the creation of network structures geared toward communication, which were to serve as bases of the new communities.

During the period of Social Democratic government these concepts began to be implemented on a national and regional level.
In the 1980s, then, the Federal Republic witnessed a considerable rise in the output of social services: the increase in new positions being filled exceeded evens that for technological or economic professions. In this phase, when the public coffers were rather full, many demands articulated by various social groups could be met. Apart from providing for the basic needs of socially disadvantaged parts of the population, there was now an increase in services rendered voluntarily by the communities and aiming at a general improvement in the quality of life for individuals, groups, and the community.

The Re-Organization of the Public Administration

Beside these theoretical and political debates about the legitimization of the welfare state a definite shift in the basic economic circumstances and social developments changed the conditions for public welfare and enforced pragmatic action:

1. The history since the 1980s "returns to normality": economic instability and social crisis are customary again. (Habsbawm: 1996,503) The collapse of the former communists' regimes diminished the necessity of legitimating the capitalist model by means of a welfare state program. Priority in politics and for financial transfers is given to support the economic system. Economic performance, technical development and global investments are interwoven factors, which – in combination with the demographical factor – effect global migration. (Le Monde diplomatique: 2003,54)
2. While the supranational economy developed global dimensions, the national governments lost more and more the possibility to control its own affairs. Health care, education, financial support and other forms of social protection can no longer be calculated within traditional national frontiers.

3. In a first and second wave of an export of working places not only low skill jobs but also qualified information and communication working places have been exported from European to low wage countries. In this respect one can argue that in the global economy China has become the shop-floor and India the brain laboratory of the world economy (Möllhoff: 2003,23), while all Western countries have to bear a high rate of unemployment of unskilled and qualified labour force.
4. The end of the full employment period came in the 1980s. High unemployment rates emerged in all European countries, increased welfare state outlays, and reduced governmental funds for welfare were a consequence. (Mishara: 1993,24) Lower wages, taxes and fringe benefits in order to increase the national competitiveness were introduced. Under these conditions, expanding the welfare state was no longer seen to be a realistic political possibility.
5. Additional a demographic crisis came into view: low birth-rates brought a shift to the demographic structure of societies. More and more elder people burdened the welfare infrastructure. Over-expenditures in parts of the social programs were obvious, especially in the health care services. (James: 1993,19)
6. Deregulation, flexibility of work, and priority to economic standards became most popular terms also for the majority of ruling parties. A shift from class politics to plural politics could be observed. (Mishara: 1993,27) Irregular and changing employment patterns became more frequent. Flexibility and adaptability, growing of low wages jobs had important negative effects on unions, and their possibility to protect members from the negative economic development.
7. The process of segregation and differentiation produces poverty and social exclusion for specific groups of the population. Unemployment, low wages and job shifts became especially a problem for specific groups: long-term unemployed, women, youth, ethnic groups and immigrants. But also new and old inter- and intra-regional differences are emerging: even in the richest and developed countries of the world the daily picture of beggars

or homeless people on the streets became normality. An analysis of the development of poverty in Europe indicates social differentiation and exclusion on different levels but with similar qualitative effects. (Fabian: 2003,222)

8. A shift in the normative foundations of every day life and in life-styles happened. Individualism and egoism became prominent, while community-orientation, collectivism, group orientation were not present at all any more in the real life. (Habsbawm: 1996,532)
9. In the 1970s and 1980s there is a dramatic increase of the cases covered, of institutions, and of specialised personnel in social services. What had been expressly created as an expanding sector in times of economic prosperity now turned out to be a considerable burden in times of economic crisis. Savings programs were announced and carried out; they put pressure on the social sector in terms of finances and legitimacy. (Greca: 1995,89)
10. Risks are privatised, help is offered in a system of a "mixed economy of welfare". The welfare state is becoming economised in two senses: efforts are made to reduce welfare state expenditures (e.g. by contracting the services or demanding payments for services especially for medical care); more and more economic criteria are used to make decisions about the organisation and number of services. Social programmes are increasingly used to combat unemployment or to reduce the official unemployment rates (e.g. early retirement for older workers, temporary work programmes to promote youth employment). "This tendency to use social policy as a micro-employment policy has some positive effects but it is part of the increasing push to make all things subservient to economic pressure." (Miller: 1990,374)

In short we can say that today we face a similar situation as in the middle of the 19th century: a radical shift in economic, societal, juridical and political conditions imposes a new social landscape that asks for new visions in social politics. (Kaufmann: 2003, 260)

During the old liberal period one will find a universal interpretation of civil rights, which brings with it also a deregulation of concrete help. Instead of this in the last phase after of "the short century", again the arguments for help get an universal approach, the progressive globalization makes it difficult, to locate the group of recipients within the boundaries of the national states. Residual forms of help get priority again. The future of the welfare state is connected to a convincing answer to the question, who should be the carrier in times in which moral basis for welfare is located in a global society.

But instead of answering to this questions and combating the fundamental reasons for the negative outcomes of the global change and its effects (e.g. globalized financial markets, migration of work from and to the western countries, reduction of the potential of national politics, etc.) the problems are placed in the social security systems and efforts are made to individualize and to segregate them from the economic system. (Luhmann: 1979)

Consequently the organization of social services became a prominent target of welfare politics and the repercussions of the welfare state brought new envisioned goals to the regional and local level of services favouring the concept of New Public Management (NPM).

NPM refers to a combination of old and new tools in managing public services (Greca: 1998), e.g.:

- Integration and co-ordination of services. The concept of re-organizing the co- operation between different social welfare providers and purchasers was introduced because a reduction of costs was expected by removing bureaucratic obstacles and procedures and reducing an over-supply of services and gratifications.
- Support of self-help groups. Instead of expensive professional care voluntary help was expected to strengthen the empowerment of local communities and to save expenditures for care as well.
- Decentralization. Reducing the welfare administration hierarchy and favouring locally based decision structures seemed to be the adequate instrument to develop a "real" need orientated and less expensive supply of social services.

- Budgeting. Taken from the private industry and applied also to the public administration the micro-economic funded concept of budgeting should help to control efforts related to cost in social services.
- Privatization. It was argued that private providers would be able to offer social services less expensive and more effective.
- Mixed economy of welfare. The competition between various providers seemed to be an appropriate way to lower the costs and improve the quality of services at the same time.

Not in all European countries these efforts were made at the same time and with the same concepts. A mosaic of narrow locally based reform experiments were established, as it has already happened in the United States where "the landscape is littered with experiments that became approach roads to nowhere." (Miller: 1990,385)
Several comparative research projects (Greca 1998; 1999, 2000, 2001) in the regions of Munich (Germany) and Bozen/Bolzano (Italy) make it possible to reflect the outcomes of this NPM re-organization:
From 1993 to 1998, a reorganisation process of the traditional social welfare system was undertaken in four boroughs of Munich in Bavaria in order to overcome the traditional hierarchical pillar system of services. On the basis of a formal decision made by the city council to develop new forms of co-operation the main social service carriers entered into a contractual agreement on the modes of collaboration among their institutions on a decentralised, regional level. The main target of this programme was described as: "The creation of an excellent quantitative and qualitative network of services for all social problems within a region by empowering local responsibilities and competences" (Landeshauptstadt München:1993,27). This co-operation is to include not only the professional basis of the city administration as well as the private welfare organisations but it is supposed to extend also to regional political institutions, private businesses, grass root movements and traditional self-help organisations.

In 1997, a reform debate in public sector management in the autonomous province of "Bozen Südtirol - Bolzano Alto Adige" resulted in a new conceptual framework for the re-organisation of social service provision. Part of it, the decentralisation and co-operation program, is a copy of the Munich model.
Both projects were evaluated with quantitative and qualitative methods for more than six years.
The result of the comparing research can be summarized as follows:
The concept of NPM and the linked tools were copied and not orientated at local needs and traditions. The term "isomorphism" was introduced by the neo-institutional paradigm to describe the fact that for institutions a structural change can result because of different reasons, and in diverse ways. Scott (1995) describes seven mechanisms through which environments can have a direct impact on the structural development of organisations: imposition, authorization, inducement, acquisition, imprinting, incorporation and bypassing. In 1992, public administration in Munich was re-organised according to new conceptualisations. Social welfare administration was the first area to be restructured with an eye to regionalising and decentralising social services (Greca: 1993, 1994, 1995, 1997). In 1995, a further step in reorganising public administration was taken, when a proposal was implemented that was based on a conceptualisation which had been developed by a leading organisation for administration reform in Germany (KGSt: 1993) and that favoured the budgeting approach. Although this concept was criticised (Boumil/Kißler: 1996) and considerable problems like an increase in bureaucratic structures, centralisation and higher costs arose (Stadtbild:1997) the new concept called NSM (Neues Steuerungsmodell – New Steering Model) was institutionalised (Der Oberbürgermeister der Landeshauptstadt München: 1994). The project "Sprengel unterwegs – Distretto in cammino" started in 1999. After various discussions about the re-organisation process and visits to Munich in the spring of 1999, the local authority decided to transfer Munich's "REGSAM" to this region and to implement it over a two years period. Later in 1999, in order to facilitate this implementation, an official who had already

been in charge of the re-organisation process in Munich was invited to manage the project in "Südtirol - Alto Adige". Therefore, in 1999 and in early 2000, the same structural concepts that had previously been implemented in Munich were introduced in this part of South Tyrol. The program was partly financed by the European community. The funding was possible because the re-organization project application outlined some of the mainstream key-words favoured and supported by EC programs.

In the South Tyrol program we could observe that EC programs had a significant impact on the re-shaping of public administration. Not the local situation, but funded programs were the reason to start projects. In this and other cases the program's conceptualization was orientated at "key words" of the EC programs like "privatization", "public-private-partnership", "budgeting", which had to be mentioned adequately in the application to find the positive response from the evaluators. It can be said that the EC bureaucracy administers main stream concepts that were developed several years ago; outcomes of the programs are not evaluated adequately to verificate the original concepts and theories. Most successful projects therefore are those where "key-word" specialists within the local agencies or private institutions meet "key-word" evaluators on the national or the European administration level.

The new concepts are not cost saving: expenditures are increasing for single institutions but also for all over costs for social care. Contradictory to the original targets in no case we could observe a reduction of expenditures for social care within the observed period.

This can be demonstrated with the overall expenditure for the social budget in Munich, as is illustrated in the chart below:

Budget for Social Care, Munich (1990-2002)

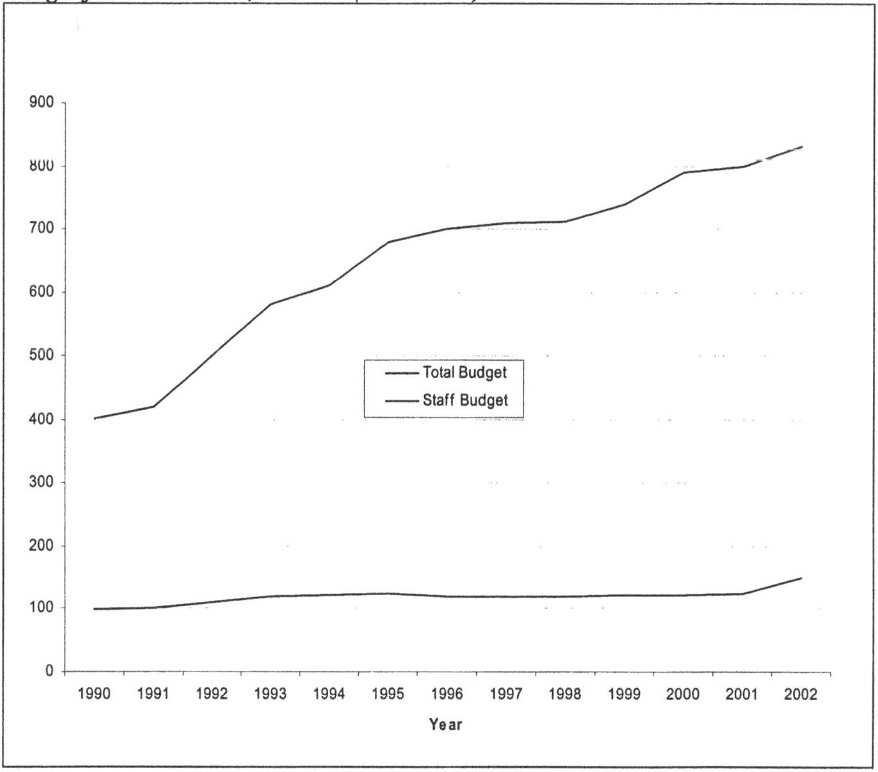

Although the budgeting concept was introduced at begin of the 1990th a continual rise of total expenditures for social services took place from 409 million € in 1990 to 830 million € in 2002 (+ 101%). Also the expenditures for employees of social services rose from 90 million € in 1990 to 153 million € in 2002 (+ 70%). The reason for this explosion of costs lies for the most part in the extremely rising numbers of persons who need financial support, which can be illustrated with the next chart:

Social welfare recipients, Munich (1993-2001)

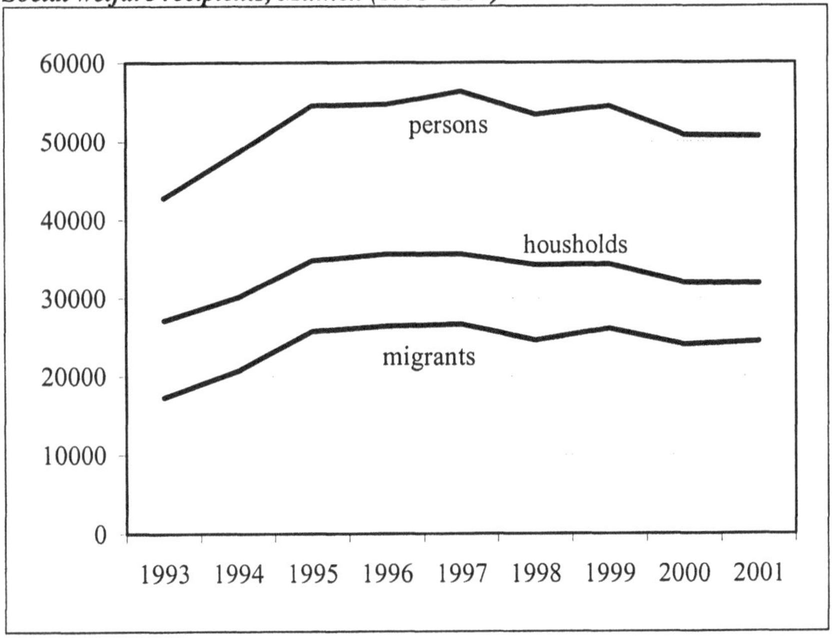

From 1993 to 2002 the number of persons depending on welfare in Munich rose from 42,751 to 52,983 (+24%), the number of households from 27,100 to 33,246 (+ 22.7%). The share of immigrants related to all persons being dependent from social aid increased from 40 percent in 1993 to 48 percent in 2001 (24,401 persons).

This illustrates with the example of Munich that not the organizational structure of services but the outcomes of the globalized economy creates the problems that cannot be tackled adequately by local, regional or national governments. Unemployment and migration have a major impact on the growth of the social budget and therefore reorganization concepts were not able to turn back this development. A comparison between German municipalities demonstrates that the case of Munich is not exceptional: only Dresden has less people depending on welfare; cities like Hamburg; Hannover, Berlin and Bremen have a poverty density which is twice as high as it is in the Bavarian capital. A study, which compares 3 European regions: East Hungary, Northern Italy and Southern Bavaria in Germany demonstrates that similar social exclusion and differentiation processes happened in the last ten years in all these areas. (Fabian: 2003)

Defenders of the NPM argue that without the implementation of this reform concept the cost explosion might have been much higher. But similar to research results in other countries we found that the organizational re-shaping was expensive itself and in contradiction to the envisioned goals not less but more bureaucratic procedures take place to today, which are time-consuming. Additional for the steering and management for the organizations economists, advocates and other specialists had to be employed, which enhanced the expenditures for the staff. Time codes for the organization of work are changed; less time for help and care and more time for control and bureaucratic procedures is resulting. Implementing economic control instruments like "budgeting", "evaluation", "controlling" lead to centralization instead of the promised decentralisation of decision processes.

In many sectors of social help – especially in the case of care – the outcome of privatization is an increase of expenditures and a worsening of the quality of services.

The reason for this development is cost pressure, which forces public and private institutions to oblige nurses to deliver services under time pressure. Quality management systems are introduced to "get more from less". Therefore we observed that for a majority of employees the motivation to work after the introduction of the NPM dropped significantly and the job-turn-over increased significant.

The economic standards effect not only less time for help and care but also for the "new" reorganisations programs. The former "mixed calculation" of the public health care institutions and private welfare organizations had to be given up. Instead "lower budgets" for normal care and "higher budgets" for extra care sum up to more expensive expenditures. The neo-institutional approach describes this as the effect of the "silence inside the eye of the hurricane". This picture paints the curious situation that although cost explosions are partly effected also by the new micro economic steering concepts itself the new managers are convicted that their extra costs will amortizes on the long run. But on the long run everybody will be dead (Keynes).

References

Alber,J., 1989, Der Sozialstaat in der Bundesrepublik 1950-1983, Frankfurt a.M./New York.

Baldwin,P., 1990, The Politics of Social Solidarity: Class Bases of the European Welfare State, Cambridge.

Beveridge,W., 1942, Social Insurance and Allied Services, London.

Böhm,W. (ed.), 1992, Europa 1993: Supermarkt oder Sozialraum?, Berlin.

Bös,D./Seidl,C. (eds.) 1996, Welfare Economics of the Second Best, Berlin.

Borscheid,P., 1987, Geschichte des Alters I, 16.-18.Jahrundert, Münster.

Boumil,J./Kißler,L., 1996: Moderne Zeiten im Rathaus. Risiken und Chancen der Einführung eines Neuen Steuerungsmodells (NSM) für die lokale Demokratie, Marburg.

Briggs,A., 1961, The Welfare State in Historical Perspective, in: European Journal of Sociology, 2, 221-258.

Cochrane,A./Clarke,J. (eds.), 1993, Comparing Welfare States, Britain in International Context, London and Beverly Hills.

Commission of the European Communities, MISSOC 1993, Social Protection in the Member State of the Community. Situation on July 1st 1993 and Evolution. Brussels.

Der Oberbürgermeister der Landeshauptstadt München: 1994, Das Neue Steuerungsmodell für die Stadtverwaltung der Landeshauptstadt München, München.

Dixon,J./Scheurell,R. (eds.), 1989, Social Welfare in Developed Market Countries, London.

Dorwart, R.A., 1971, The Prussian Welfare State before 1740, Cambridge, Mass.

Duby,G., 1977, Krieger und Bauern. Die Entwicklung von Wirtschaft und Gesellschaft im frühen Mittelalter, Frankfurt a.M.

European Commission, 1991, Final Report on the Second European Poverty Programme 1985 - 1889, COM (91) 29, Brussel.

Engels,W., 1985, Über Freiheit, Gleichheit und Brüderlichkeit. Kritik des Wohlfahrtsstaates, Theorie der Sozialordnung und Utopie der sozialen Marktwirtschaft, Bad Homburg.

Esping-Andersen, G., 1990, The Three Worlds of Welfare Capitalism, Cambridge-Oxford.

Evers,A./Wintersberger,H. (eds.) 1990, Shifts in the Welfare Mix. Their impact on Work, Social Services and Welfare Policies, Frankfurt a.M., Boulder Co., US.

Evers,A../Wintersberger,H., 1990; Main Findings and Common Orientations in the National Reports, in: *Evers,A., Wintersberger,H.* (eds.) Shifts in the Welfare Mix. Their Impact on Work, Social Services and Welfare Policies, Frankfurt a.M. ,Boulder, Col.,.

Fabian, G., 2003, Die relative gleiche Differenzierung. Inaugural Dissertation zur Erlangung des Doktorgrades der Geschichts- und Gesellschaftswissenschaftlichen Fakultät Eichstätt, Eichstätt.

Flora,P./Alber,J., 1981, Modernization, Democratization, and the Development of Welfare States in Western Europe, in: Flora,P.,/Heidenheimer,A.J., 1981; The Development of Welfare States in Europe and America, New Brunswick (U.S.)/London (UK).

Flora,P./Heidenheimer,A.J., ,The Historical Core and Changing Boundaries of the Welfare State in: Flora,P./Heidenheimer,A.J., (eds.) The Development of Welfare States in Europe and America, New Brunswick (U.S.) and London (U.K.).

Flora,P. ,1982, : Krisenbewältigung oder Krisenerzeugung? Der Wohlfahrtsstaat in sozialhistorischer Perspektive, in: Mommsen, W.J., (Hrsg.), Die Entstehung des Wohlfahrtsstaates in Großbritannien und Deutschland 1850-1950, Stuttgart, S.352-398.

Flora,P., 1993, Europa als Sozialstaat? In: *Schäfers, B.* (ed.), Lebensverhältnisse und soziale Konflikte im neuen Europa, Frankfurt a.M./New York.

Giddens,A., 1998, The Third Way. The Renewal of Social Democracy. Cambridge.

Ginsberg,N., 1992, Division of Welfare. A Critical Introduction to Comparative Social Policy, London and Beverly Hills.

Girvetz,H., 1968, Welfare State, in: International Encyclopedia of the Social Sciences, Vol. 16.

Goodin,E.E., 1988, Reasons for Welfare. The Political Theory of the Welfare State, Princeton, N.J.

Greca,R., 1989, Handlungsmuster in der Sozialarbeit I. Zur Verberuflichung sozialer Hilfe, München.

Greca,R., 1994, Wirtschaft, in: *Dunde,R.* (ed.) Wörterbuch der Religionsoziologie, Gütersloh.

Greca,R., 1995, Innovation und Verknappung, in: *Greca,R./Erath,P.,(*ed.) Regionalisierung sozialer Dienste in Deutschland, Eichstätt.

Greca,R., 1996, The Reorganization of Social Services in Germany, Birmingham.

Greca,R., 1998, Evaluating the change in social work organization. Rhetoric, Institutionalization and Political Decision making, in: The International Journal of Public Sector Management, Vol.11, 4-5.

Greca, R., 1999, Solving Problems by Creating Opportunities: Integrating Social. Ecological, and Economic Targets in Social Work, Bozen/Bolzano.

Greca,R., 2001. Modellprojekt „Sprengel unterwegs", Abschlussbericht, Eichstätt und Trento.

Grimm,D., 1983, Die sozialgeschichtliche und verfassungsrechtliche Entwicklung zum Sozialstaat, in: *Koslowski,P./Kreuzer,P., Löw,R., (eds.)* Chancen und Grenzen des Sozialstaates, Staatstheorie - Politische Ökonomie - Politik. Tübingen.

Habermas,J., 1974, Können komplexe Gesellschaften eine vernünftige Identität ausbilden?, in: *Habermas,J./Henrich,D.,* Zwei Reden. Aus Anlaß des Hegel-Preises, Frankfurt a.M.

Habermas,J., 1981, Theorie des kommunikativen Handelns, Band 1, Handlungsrationalität und gesellschaftliche Rationalisierung, Frankfurt a.M.

Habermas,J., 1995, Die neue Unübersichtlichkeit, Frankfurt a.M.

Habsbawm,E., 1995, Das Zeitalter der Extreme. Weltgeschichte des 20.Jahrhunderts, München-Wien 1995. Engl.: Age of Extremes. The Short Twentieth Century 1949-1991, London.

*Hansmeyer, K.-H.,*1957, Der Weg zum Wohlfahrtsstaat. Wandlungen der Staatstätigkeit im Spiegel der Finanzpolitik unseres Jahrhunderts, Frankfurt a.M.

Hasenfeld,Y., (ed.) 1992, Human Services As Complex Organizations, London.

Henningsen,B., 1986, Der Wohlfahrtsstaat Schweden, Baden-Baden.

Humboldt, W.v., 1792 (1982), Ideen zu einem Versuch, die Grenzen der Wirksamkeit des Staates zu bestimmen, Stuttgart.

Jones,J., (ed.) 1993, New Perspectives on the Welfare State in Europe, London/New York.

Jordan,W.K., 1961, The English Background of Modern Philanthropy, in: American Historical Review, vol. 66, no.2.

Kaim-Caudle,P.R., 1973, Comparative Social Policy and Social Security. A Ten Country Study, Bath.

Kaufmann,F.X., 1996, Steuerungsprobleme im Wohlfahrtsstaat, in: *Kaufmann,F.X.,*1996, Modernisierungsschübe, Familie und Sozialstaat, München..

Kaufmann,F.X.,, 2003, Varianten des Wohlfahrtsstaates. Der deutsche Sozialstaat im internationalen Vergleich, Frankfurt a.M.

KGSt- Bericht 5/1993: Das neue Steuerungsmodell. Begründung, Konturen, Umsetzung, Köln.

Kirsch,G., 1980, Der Wohlfahrtsstaat, in: Die Orientierung, Nr. 75, Bern.

Kleinhenz,G. (ed.), 1993, Soziale Integration in Europa, Berlin.

Kohl,J., 1993, Der Wohlfahrtsstaat in vergleichender Perspektive, in: Zeitschrift für Sozialreform 39, 1, pp. 67-82.

Koslowski,P./Kreuzer,P./Löw,R., (Hrsg.), 1993, Chancen und Grenzen des Sozialstaats. Staatstheorie - Politische Ökonomie - Politik, Tübingen.

Landeshauptstadt München, Sozialreferat – Abt. Sozialplanung: 1993, Regionalisierung sozialer Arbeit in München – Modellversuch. Konzeption und Stadtratsbeschluss, Beiträge zur Sozialplanung 007, München.

Lampert,H./Bossert,A., 1992, Sozialstaat Deutschland, Entwicklung - Gestalt- Probleme, München.

Lee,P./Raban,C., 1988, Welfare Theory and Social Policy, London and Beverly Hills.

Leibfried,S., 1993, Towards a European welfare state? On integrating poverty regimes into the European Community, in: Jones,J., (ed.), New Perspectives on the Welfare State in Europe, London/New York.

Le Monde diplomatique, 2003, Atlas der Globalisierung, Berlin.

Luhmann,N., 1979, Formen des Helfens im Wandel gesellschaftlicher Bedingungen, in: *Otto, H.-U./Schneider,S.* (Hrsg.), Gesellschaftliche Perspektiven der Sozialarbeit, 1. Halbband, Neuwied und Darmstadt.

Marshall, Th.H., 1950, Staatsbürgerrechte und soziale Klassen, engl.: Citizenship and Social Class - and other Essays, Cambridge.

Marshall, Th.H., 1964, Class, Citizenship, and Social Development, New York.

Marshall, Th.H., 1981, The Right to Welfare and other Essays, New York.

Marshall, Th.H., 1992, Bürgerrechte und soziale Klassen. Zur Soziologie des Wohlfahrtsstaates. Frankfurt/New York. Herausgegeben, übersetzt und mit einem Vorwort versehen von *Elmar Rieger.*

Merten,D./Pitschas,R. (eds.), 1993, Der europäische Sozialstaat und seine Institutionen, Berlin.

Miller,S.M., 1990, The Evolving Welfare State Mix, in: *Evers,A., Windersberger,H. (eds.)* Shifts in the Welfare Mix. Their Impact on Work, Social Services and Welfare Policies, Frankfurt a.M. ,Boulder, Col.

Möllhoff, Chr., 2003, "Wir sind die Gewinner". Die zweite Globalisierungswelle rollt. Banken und Software-Firmen verlagern jetzt auch immer mehr hoch qualifizierte Arbeitsplätze nach Indien, in: Die Zeit Nr. 44, 23. Oktober 2003.

Offe,C., 1993, Zur Typologie von sozialpolitischen „Regimes", in: Zeitschrift für Sozialreform 39, 2, pp. 83-86.

Rimlinger,G.V., 1971, Welfare Policy and Industrialization in Europe, America, and Russia, New York.

Romano,R., 1980, Versuch einer ökonomischen Typologie, in: *Romano,R. u.a.* (Hrsg.), Die Gleichzeitigkeit des Ungleichzeitigen. Fünf Studien zur Geschichte Italiens, Frankfurt a.M.

Room,G., 1979, The Sociology of Welfare. Social Policy, Stratification and Political Order, Oxford.

Schulz-Nieswandt, F., 1993, Einführung in die wohlfahrtsstaatliche Landeskunde der Bundesrepublik Deutschland, Weiden und Regensburg.

Scott, W.R./Christensen, S. (eds), 1995: The Institutional Constructution of Organizations. International and Longitudinal Studies, Thousand *Oaks,/London/New Delhi.*

Scott,W.R., 1995: Institutions and Organizations, Thousand Oaks/London/New Delhi.

Sievernich,M., 1991. Die Option für die Armen aus pastoraltheologischer Sicht, in: *Bucher,A./Fornet-Betancourt,R./Renker,J./Sing,H. (Hrsg.),* Forum „Vorrangige Option für die Armen der Katholischen Kirche in Lateinamerika, in: Concordia, Internationale Zeitschrift für Philosophie, Reihe Monographien, Eichstätt.

Sorokin,P, 1969, Altruistic Love. A Study of American „Good Neighbors“ and Christian Saints, New York.

Staub-Bernasconi, S.,1995, Das fachliche Selbstverständnis sozialer Arbeit - Wege aus der Bescheidenheit. Soziale Arbeit als „Human Rights Profession“, in: *Wendt,W.R.* (Hrsg.), Soziale Arbeit im Wandel ihres Selbstverständnisses, Freiburg, S.57-104.

Vincent, J.M., 1935, Costume and Conduct in the Laws of Basel, Bern, and Zurich 1370-1800, Baltimore.

Stadtbild: 1997. Zeitung für Mitarbeiterinnen und Mitarbeiter der Stadtverwaltung, Ausgabe 7, Oktober 1997. Verwaltungsreform. Wie geht es weiter? München.

Weber-Kellermann, I., 1987, Landleben im 19.Jahrhundert, München.

Zacher,H.F., 1989, Vierzig Jahre Sozialstaat - Schwerpunkte der rechlichen Ordnung, in: *Blüm,N./Zacher,H.F.* (eds.), 40 Jahre Sozialstaat Deutschland, Baden-Baden.

Zacher,H.F., 1992, Stand und Perspektiven der Forschung und Lehre auf dem Gebiet der Sozialarbeit, insbesondere im Rahmen kirchlicher Fachhochschulen, Schriften des Deutschen Vereins für öffentliche und private Fürsorge, Allgemeine Schrift 29, Frankfurt a.M.

Work-Life Balance in the Public Sector – The Irish Experience[1]

ALMA MCCARTHY

Introduction

The reconciliation of work and family life has become increasingly important in recent years across the European Union (The European Foundation for the Improvement of Living and Working Conditions, Foundation Paper No.1, 2002). Work-life balance has come to the fore in contemporary debates because the increasing, and sometimes excessive, demands of work in developed societies are perceived to present a distinctive problem that needs to be addressed (Guest, 2001). The implications of sometimes, conflicting work and family responsibilities for people management and work structures are wide ranging (Fisher, 2000). These issues not only operate at policy level, but work-life balance, family-friendly work practices, employee-friendliness, flexible working arrangements are contemporary work related terms impacting social partnership, policy-making both nationally and at EU level, and people management and strategy decisions.

Changes impacting on the work environment over the previous ten to fifteen years such as globalisation of competition, changes in the patterns and demands of work and the fast pace of technological innovations (Coughlan, 2000; DFEE, 2000; Fisher, 2000) have put extra time demands on employees. Coupled with these organisational and work design changes, are increased female participation rates (Houston, 1999; Bates *et al* 2002), growth in the diversity of family structures (Duxbury and Higgins, 2002), long commuting journeys (Coughlan, 2000), and changing worker expectations (Zemke *et al.,* 2000; Greenblatt, 2002). The latter set of developments have increasingly made the issue of balancing work with personal life essential to all employees.

---

[1] Paper presented at the 4th conference of the Regional and Local Development of Work and Labour Network, Bologna, Italy, June 2003.

The increasing number of dual career couples in the workforce is also presenting more difficulty for managing the work-family interface than that experienced for families where only one parent partakes in full-time paid employment (Bernas & Major, 2003; Brockwood *et al.*, 2003; Drew *et al.*, 1998; Duxbury & Higgins, 2001; Frone *et al*, 1997). This paper explores the concept of work-life balance and how it impacts quality of working life. Firstly, it aims to clearly establish what is meant by work-life balance and sets out some definitional problems that exist regarding the terminology used. The discussion then turns to an examination of work-life balance across the EU. Thirdly, the paper examines a number of work-life balance initiatives that have been adopted in Ireland, looking specifically at the Irish public sector. Drawing on experience in other countries, the paper concludes by discussing the key issues that impinge on the achievement of acceptable work-life balance and highlights some recommendations for change.

Exploring the Work-Life Balance Construct

Work-life balance is built on a belief that while work is important to each individual, and to society as a whole, achievement and enjoyment in everyday life beyond the workplace are essential to human and societal well-being (Joshi *et al* 2002). Guest (2001: 11) defines work-life balance from a subjective standpoint as "a perceived balance between work and the rest of life". Legislative and social attempts to define balance more objectively have occurred because of the consequences of certain patterns of behaviour such as very long working hours (Guest, 2001). Clark (2000: 549) defines work-life balance as "satisfaction and good functioning at work and at home with a minimum of role conflict". Furthermore, Greenblatt (2002: 179) defines work-life balance as "the absence of unacceptable levels of conflict between work and non-work demands". In practice it can be seen that definitions on work-life balance focus on time, role enactment and conflicting demands.

Despite widespread recent attention, the concepts of work-life balance and family-friendly work arrangements remain theoretically and empirically ill-defined (Felstead *et al.*, 2002). Guest (2001) also notes that debates on work-life balance often occur without any clear and consistent definition of what is meant by work-life balance. Drew *et al.* (in press) make a clear distinction between the terms, arguing that family friendly working arrangements involve measures to "support or assist employees in managing the dual responsibilities of work and family life". They propose that work-life balance involves seeking "a balance between an individual's work and their life outside work, and that this balance should be healthy, that personal fulfilment is important inside work, and that satisfaction outside work may enhance employees' contributions at work". Work-life balance is thus a more inclusive concept as it does not discriminate on the basis of family.

Traditionally, the emphasis at national and EU level was on reconciling work and family responsibilities. However, all employees, irrespective of their family situation or personal responsibilities, need and want to have a better balance between their lives, both within and outside the workplace (Fisher, 2000). Observers of contemporary society in the UK, such as Handy (1993) and Pahl (1995), have argued that societal cohesion is dependent upon the re-discovery of a more appropriate balance amongst the competing demands that individuals face. By implication, Guest (2001) argues that many commentators believe that work has become too dominant.

For the purpose of this paper, the term work-life balance will be adopted since the focus of the paper is not on differentiating the causal effect of family *per se* on work-life balance but, rather, it is concerned with general perceptions of work-life balance irrespective of family situation. Of course, many work-life balance initiatives are, nevertheless, developed and implemented specifically for employees with children. The term work-life balance is broader and embraces the needs of all employees in reconciling work and non-work responsibilities (Greenblatt, 2002). The following section of the paper reviews the developments which have led to an increased focus on work-life balance considerations across the EU and briefly compares some work-life balance metrics between selected member States.

Work-Life Balance Across the EU

The 1998 Amsterdam Treaty detailed the promotion of employment as one of the key Community objectives in its European Employment Strategy. The aim of the European Employment Strategy is "the achievement of a high level of employability for all groups, including those most distanced from the labour market; to develop skills of those already in work, especially in exposed or vulnerable sectors; to broaden the capacity for entrepreneurship and to ensure the equal participation of women and men in the labour market" (p. 4). It is commonly believed that a greater focus on work-life balance will significantly positively impact the latter of these objectives.

In 2001, the European Council guidelines for member States regarding employment policies emphasized the following key point concerning reconciling work and family life. "Policies on career breaks, parental leave and part-time work, as well as flexible working arrangements which serve the interest of both employers and employees, are of particular importance to women and men" (The European Foundation for the Improvement of Living and Working Conditions Foundation Paper No.1, 2002: 6). The paper goes on to suggest that the implementation of the various directives and social-partner agreements should be accelerated and monitored regularly. The challenge for member States is to ensure these aims are translated into effective action at national and local level. By definition, these new forms of arrangements should enhance employee perceptions of work-life balance.

Within this political backdrop, there are a number of indicators which can be considered in an investigation of the state of play of work-life balance across the European member States. One comparable metric is average weekly working hours. In the recent European Foundation's Working Conditions[2] survey (2001), authored by Paoli and Merllié, the average weekly hours of work for all workers ranged from 32.9 in the Netherlands to 42.4 in Greece (EL). The difference of almost ten hours a week is quite significant. The average for the 15 EU countries was 38.2 (see figure 1). The report goes on to explain that part-time work arrangements may explain some of the 10% variation, since the uptake of part-time working is highest in the Netherlands. The proposition for this statistic is that the greater the number of hours worked, the greater the challenge to balance work and life. However, this remains to be tested empirically.

[2] Paoli, P. & Merllié (2001) Third European Survey on Working Conditions 2000, European Foundation for the Improvement of Living and Working Conditions, Dublin.

Fig. 1 Average Weekly hours of all Workers in the EU by Country

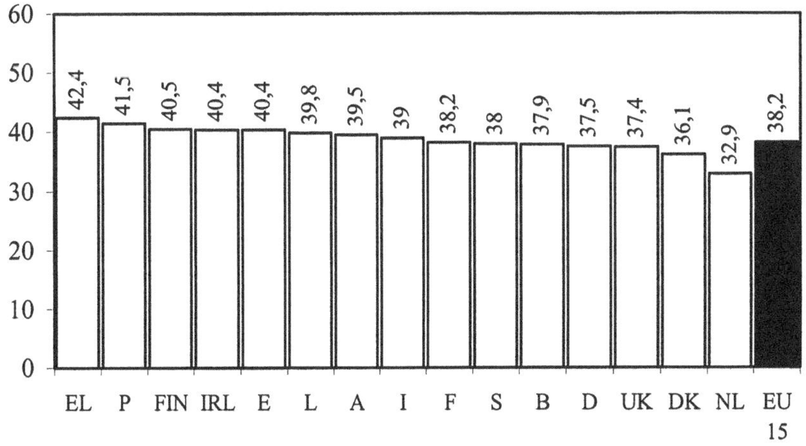

Source: *Third European Working Conditions Survey, 2000*

Part-time working and job-sharing are two of the most common work-life schemes in existence (Fine-Davis et al., 2002; Fynes *et al.*, 1996; Humphreys *et al.*, 2000). It is commonly believed that the provision of part-time working arrangements by employers will positively impact employee work-life balance. However, the empirical support for this assumption is extremely limited. Much of the research on work-life balance to-date is mostly concerned with assessing the various work-life balance initiates which exist and the documentation of up-take rates among men and women. Fagan and Burchell (2002) is a notable exception and this study is referred to below.

Figure 2 presents the percentage of part-time work across the EU countries. It is evident that this form of flexible working arrangement is most popular in the Netherlands, where 33% of employees work part-time, and least popular in Greece, the figure being only 5%. It has been suggested that some reasons for this variation across the member States include differing tax systems, varying childcare arrangements, and institutional policies (Fagan & Burchell, 2001).

Fig. 2 Part-Time Work in the EU by Country (%)

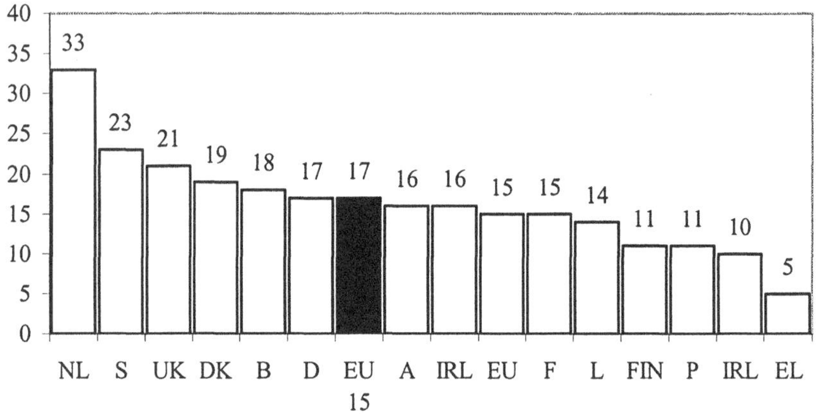

Source: *Third European Working Conditions Survey 2000*

Fagan *et al.* (2002) provide some employee self-report data in terms of the compatibility of working hours with family and other non-work commitments across the EU states. Table 1 presents these findings by parenthood. The table demonstrates that mothers employed part-time report significantly higher levels of compatibility between work and family than mothers who are employed full-time. Fagan *et al.* (2002) do not report the corresponding figure for men working part-time.

Table 1 Compatibility of Working Hours with Other Commitments by Parenthood (%)

	Father	Men without dep children	Mother employed full-time	Mother employed part-time	Women without dep children
Very well	27	31	27	50	40
Fairly well	48	49	48	41	45
Not very well/not at all	25	20	25	8	15

Source: *Fagan & Burchell (2002)*

However, what is also interesting is that 15% of women who have no dependent children report a poor compatibility between work and life commitments. The corresponding figure for men without dependent children is 20%. Furthermore, there are no significant differences in responses between employees with or without children. This relates to one of the limitations that exists in the work-life literature which is the assumption that it is work and family which cause conflicting interfaces in one's life. However, this is too narrow a definition of the issues at play in terms of balancing work and non-work commitments. These findings would corroborate the use of the term work-life balance rather than family friendly work arrangements as argued above.

Teleworking is another flexible work arrangement in the EU which is espoused to help employees balance work and life activities. Proponents of teleworking would argue that work is an activity and not a physical place. The Third European Survey on Working Conditions 2000 reports that occasional teleworking is more popular among northern European countries. The UK has the highest incidence of teleworking (10% of employees partaking in this arrangement) while Italy reports the lowest level, only 2% (see figure 3).

Fig. 3 Teleworking from home in the EU by Country (%)

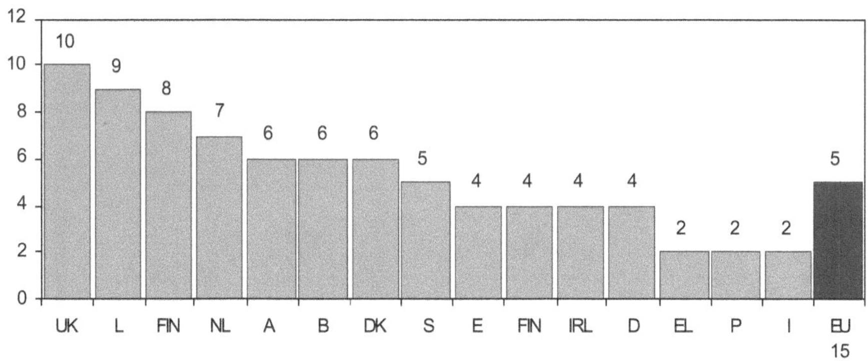

Source: Third European Working Conditions Survey 2000

The report also discusses the impact of work on respondents' health. 60% of respondents consider that their work negatively affects their health. This figure has increased by three percentage points on the 1995 survey. Exploring this area further, Paoli and Merllié (2001) report that overall fatigue rates in the EU have increased in the five years between the two surveys from 23% in 1995 to 29% in 2000. Where work-related stress is concerned, 29% of females and 28% of males reported that they suffer from stress. Greece, Sweden, Italy and Luxembourg are at the top of the list in terms of worker stress (Paoli & Merllié, 2001).
Research has indicated that higher levels of work-related stress lead to less favourable perceptions of work-life balance (Kopelman *et al.*, 1983). However, it could be argued that the cause and effect may work in the opposite direction, namely that a poor work-life balance causes stress (Stoeva *et al.*, 2002). This is an area which needs further research to clarify the nature of the relationship between these variables. However, Paoli and Merllié's (2001) finding that 60% of respondents believe that their health is negatively impacted by their work is a serious cause for concern. In terms of absence from work due to work related health problems, Finland (18%) and the Netherlands (17%) suffer the highest levels while Portugal (4%) and Ireland (5%) report the lower levels (see figure 4).

Fig. 4 Absences due to work-related health problems in the EU by Country (%)

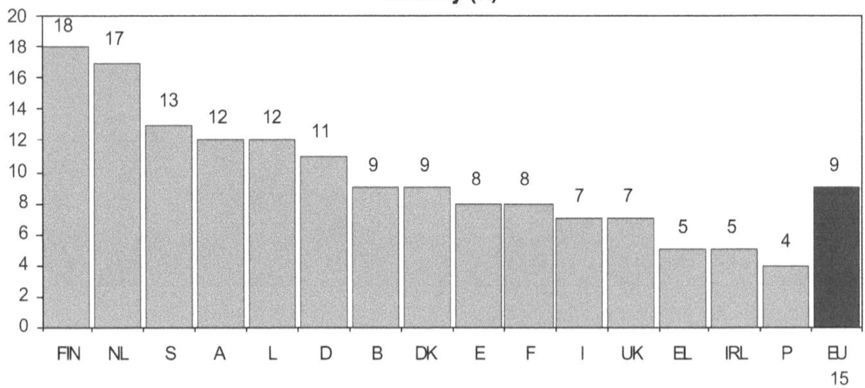

Source: *Third European Working Conditions Survey 2000*

A number of interesting implications arise when some of these metrics are analysed simultaneously. Firstly, The Netherlands report the lowest average weekly working hours of the 15 EU countries. Yet, it has the second highest level of absences due to work-related health problems (17%). Further research should explore if these factors are related and if number of hours worked actually has an effect on perceptions of health. Greece reports the highest levels of stress and also reports the highest number of working hours per week. These two variables may be related. Yet, contrary to expectations, Greece's level of employee absence due to work-related illness is well below the EU average and is in fact the second lowest figure. These somewhat contradictory trends pose interesting questions for some of the assumptions that are made about work-life balance, hours of work, and the impact on these factors on stress and health.

In a recent publication evaluating the impact of the European Employment Strategy in Ireland[3], it is reported that "rates of flexibilisation of work continue to be lower in Ireland than elsewhere in the European Union". The report goes on to underline the scarcity of empirical investigation into flexible working practices in Ireland. Notwithstanding, some studies have explored work-life balance in Ireland and the following section discusses some of the key findings emanating from this research, focussing specifically on the Irish public sector.

Work-Life Balance in Ireland and the Irish Public Sector

Mahon (1998) argues that until recently, there has been little emphasis on work-life or family friendly work arrangements in Ireland. A number of developments have occurred over the past decade which have resulted in significant change in public sector management in Ireland. Humphreys and Worth-Butler (1999) argue that the vibrant national labour market, rising consumer expectations for improved quality of service provision, and reorganisation and restructuring of public service bodies has changed human resource recruitment, management, and retention practices.

In the past, the Irish public sector was the employer of choice as it offered prospective employees job security in the form of a 'pensionable, permanent' job. In a country that operated in a poor economic climate for much of the 1970's, 1980's and early 1990's, and where unemployment hit a high of 17% in 1986, the promise of job security was a significant

[3] Impact Evaluation of the European Employment Strategy in Ireland, (2002: 4) DETE, Dublin: Stationary Office.

attraction to many job-seekers. However, in the Ireland of the new millennium, where unemployment rates are under 5%, the country is experiencing greater immigration than emigration, and a tight labour market, the public sector is faced with new challenges in terms of employee recruitment and retention (Humphreys *et al.*, 2000).

Moreover, private sector wage rates have tended to grow at a significantly faster rate than public sector pay. The Government undertook a comprehensive benchmarking exercise to redress the imbalance in pay between the public and private sectors in 2000. However, the Government has not relied on pay alone to ensure they attract and recruit high skilled employees but have focused on work-life and family-friendly work practices as a means of motivating staff (Humprheys & Worth-Butler, 1999). The significant increase in female participation rates, from 28% in 1971 to just over 48.1% in 2002 (The Central Statistics Office, 2002), has also acted as a catalyst in the development of more family-friendly working arrangements (Houston, 1999; Bates *et al.,* 2002).

Recent research carried out by Butler and Connolly (2002), on behalf of the Irish Congress of Trade Unions (ICTU), has found that, in general, it appears family-friendly policies are most accessible to union members within the civil service, followed by those in the public service who, in general, have more access than those in the private sector. In the private sector, it is mainly only statutory provisions that are available. Furthermore, in the private sector, family-friendly arrangements tend to be informal and individually based. The Irish civil service is to the fore in offering a wide range of initiatives to their employees but within the wider public service, and particularly in the private sector, a mixed and complex picture is emerging.

Fynes *et al.* (1996) conducted an extensive survey of flexible working practices in Ireland in both the public and private sector. Unfortunately, a more up-to-date study has not been replicated but some of the data and trends are most likely still relevant. They report that the average hours worked per week in the private sector for managers/professionals is 44.4 while the corresponding average for the public sector is 36.9. This difference is quite high. Fynes *et al.*'s. (1996) study indicates that there is a significant gender difference in terms of employees preferring more time off even if it meant a reduction in pay. Females were more disposed to taking more time off than males, regardless of its impact on their salary.

At an institutional level in Ireland, policy makers have increasingly noted the importance of work-life balance. The reconciliation of work and family life was a central objective in the national wage agreement, the Programme for Prosperity and Fairness (PPF), signed in March 2000. To advance the work-life balance objective, the programme established the National Framework Committee for Family Friendly Policies. This agreement specifically provides for "supporting and facilitating family-friendly policies through the development of a package of practical measures that can be applied at the level of the enterprise" (Programme for Prosperity and Fairness, 2000: Annex 5). The new agreement that was signed in 2003, Sustaining Progress, also has provisions for enhancing employees' work-life balance.

Recently the Equality Authority commissioned research to investigate the provision, range and benefits of work-life balance initiatives amongst 133 SMEs. 53% of respondents stated that they provided one or more family-friendly policies. The most common initiatives being, emergency and special leave, part-time working, and flexible hours. These initiatives were more prevalent in medium sized organisations (50-249 employees) than in small firms (1-49 employees). However, the overall numbers of employees availing of such initiatives is small (Fisher, 2000).

The legislative framework has also impacted work-life balance. There are a number of acts, which have passed through the Irish legislature aimed at providing legal entitlements for employees, and specifically working parents. These include the Maternity Protection Act, the Carer's Leave Act, the Adoptive Leave Act, the Parental Leave Act and the Worker Protection (Regular Part-Time Employees) Act. The maternity leave act provides for 18 weeks paid leave and an optional four to eight weeks unpaid leave can be taken. There are a numbers of changes to the maternity entitlements in Ireland resulting from the Maternity Protection (Amendment) Bill, 2003. The Bill implements the recommendations made by the Working Group on the Review and Improvement of the Maternity Protection Legislation. It is specifically stated in the explanatory memorandum for the act that the implementation of the Working Group's recommendations is aimed to fulfil a statutory component of the Work/Life Balance Programmes to which the Government is committed under the Sustaining Progress agreement.

The Adoptive Leave Act, 1995 was amended by Order in February 2001. It provides for fourteen weeks paid adoptive leave, previously ten weeks, for an adopting mother or sole adopting father. There is also provision for an additional eight weeks unpaid leave. The Carer's Leave Act (2001) allows employees to leave their employment temporarily to provide full-time care for a period of 65 weeks. Employers are not required to pay employees on Care Leave but are required to provide employees with the same job on their return. Parental Leave provides an opportunity for employees to take up to 14 weeks unpaid leave to care for each child, up to the time the child is 5 years old. The Worker Protection (Regular Part-Time Employees) Act the purpose of this Act was to bring part-time/atypical employees who are in regular employment and work in excess of eight hours per week within the scope of legislation providing employment protection rights. Most of these statutory entitlements have an inherent work-life balance objective.

The following section reviews the main work-life balance schemes in operation in the Irish public sector and where provision is at the discretion of management. Where possible, statistics are presented to demonstrate the popularity of these arrangements among workers.

Job Sharing

Job sharing enables two or more workers to share one job. Fynes *et al.* (1996: 121) define job-sharing as "dividing one former full-time position into two or more positions while retaining all the rights and privileges attached to the full-time position". There are a number of forms that job-sharing can take. Table 2 sets out the proportion of employees in the public sector availing of the various job sharing forms. Spilt week and week on/week off are the most popular means of sharing jobs. The table also sets out the comparative figures for the Irish private sector.

Table 2 Public and Private Sector Job Sharing Arrangements and Employee Uptake

Basis of Job Sharing	**Public Sector %**	**Private Sector %**
Split week	53.5	67.2
Week on/week off	40.2	4.4
Mornings/afternoons	5.6	13.8
Other	0.7	14.6

Source: Fynes et al. (1996)

Fynes *et al.* (1996) report interesting differences in perceptions of the benefit of job-sharing between the public and private sector in Ireland. A resounding 75% of respondent managers in the private sector believe that there were no benefits to job-sharing. The corresponding figure for the public sector was 39%. Among the most often cited advantages referred to by public sector management include the retention of key staff and expertise which might otherwise be lost, more productive employees and an improvement in motivation. Among the disadvantages highlighted by public sector management include the lack of continuity and the high cost incurred.

From the participating employees' perspective, time off for family was cited by 82% of respondents as a key benefit that is accrued from job-sharing. Other benefits mentioned include creating jobs and time off for leisure. Not surprisingly, the key disadvantage reported by public sector employees who job-share is lower pay. Other disadvantages include poor career development and problems encountered with their job-share partner. These benefits and problems are not unlike those documented elsewhere in the job-sharing literature (Armstrong, 2001; Bevan, 1996; Humphreys *et al.*, 2000).

Fine-Davis *et al.* (2002) studied the perceptions of work-life balance across four EU countries. They report that, in Ireland, job-sharing is available to 60% of male respondents and 54% of female respondents. Of these, only 4% of males use this arrangement and 12% of females job-share. These figures relate to both the public and private sector.

Part-Time Working

From an Irish perspective, part-time employment as a percentage of total employment rose from 6.7% in 1983 to 16.7% by 1999 (Coughlan, 2000). Part-time work is more prevalent among women than men. Women's increased labour market participation is cited as the explanation for much of the growth in part-time employment in Ireland (mainly within the services sector) (Coughlan, 2000). Fisher's (2000) research for the Equality Authority found the incidence of part time working within small to medium sized enterprises (SMEs) to be 49%.

Fine-Davis *et al.* (2002) report that part-time working is available to 66% of males respondents and 83.7% of female respondents in Ireland. Of these, the take-up rate among males is 12% for males and 42% for females.

Term-Time

Term-time is a form of flexibility which allows parents time off to care for school-going children over the summer holidays. A parent can take either

10 or 13 weeks unpaid leave from June until the end of August to match their working arrangements to their children's summer holidays (Humphreys *et al.*, 2000). To be eligible, a member of staff must have a child or children up to 18 years of age or be acting in *loco parentis.* Humphreys *et al.* (2000) report that there are inconsistencies in terms of granting term-time to employees within and across Government functions and recommend that clearer criteria be set for evaluating applications.

Fine-Davis *et al.* (2002) report that only 24% of male and 4% of females respondents indicate that term-time working is available in their workplaces. The take-up rate for males was 10.2% and for females, it was 2%. However, these figures relate to all workers and data are not presented for public versus private sector employees. The availability of term-time working is essentially a public sector phenomenon. However, this does not necessarily account for low levels of availability of term-time reported, as the balance of respondents was quite even between the two sectors (52% of respondents worked in the private sector and 48% in the public sector). The highest instance of availability and use of term-time is in France.

Flexitime

Flexitime schemes allow employees to vary their starting and finishing times and must be present during a compulsory core hours period. In the Civil Service, for example, a person may start work between 8.30a.m. and 10a.m. and finish between 4p.m. and 6.30p.m. A person may build up hours during a four-week flexi period, which can be taken as leave in a later period and this is termed 'flexi-leave'.

Many advantages have been cited regarding flexitime arrangements. From the employee perspective, they allow for the closer alignment of working hours with commitments outside work such as dropping children to school. Flexitime also helps alleviate commuting traffic problems during rush hours. From the employer's perspective, increased employee motivation, reduced absenteeism, and increased commitment are among the advantages of flexitime. However, flexitime can pose problems for management. Humphreys *et al.* (2000) report that managers felt employees were engaging in a 'clock-watching' approach to the workday. Many organisations have also reported that flexitime has adverse consequences for customer service quality when employees are not guaranteed to be at work during the flexi-hours. Humpreheys *et al.* (2000) go on to argue that flexitime is not enjoyed by all Irish public sector employees but is limited, in the majority of departments, to non-management grades.

Fine-Davis *et al.* (2002) reported that 21% of respondents in Ireland had a formal flexitime arrangement at work and 60% reported that an informal agreements existed. Flexi-time is available to 48% of the males respondents and 50% of the females. Of these, 36% of males take up the scheme and the corresponding figure for females is 38%. Again, these figures related to both the private and public sector but the sectors are quite evenly represented so one would not expect big differences between the sectors.

Career Breaks

Career breaks are another form of flexibility which allow employees to take time off according to their needs and responsibilities in their private lives. A career break is a period of unpaid leave from work usually ranging from six months to ten years (Humphreys *et al.*, 2000). In the Civil Service, staff may take two career breaks during their career. In 1995, it was estimated that a total of 5,500 staff were on career breaks in the Irish public sector (Humphreys *et al.*, 2000). Humphreys *et al.* go on to report that women are more likely to take career breaks for caring reasons and men take career breaks more often for travel and study.

Teleworking/e-working

In a teleworking arrangement, the employee works from a home office for some or all of the week. He or she maintains a presence in the office electronically via computer, telephone, fax and e-mail. Ireland has often been presented as a country with strong drivers towards high levels of e-working, including a young workforce, a large ICT sector, a proactive government that promotes e-working, high business property prices and urban traffic congestion. However, results of surveys indicate that compared with the rest of Europe, the existence of e-work is modest in Ireland (Bates *et al.*, 2002). According to Butler and Connolly, (2002), teleworking/e-working is the least common non-statutory family-friendly policy.

Within the Irish civil service teleworking is available in some departments. As it is quite a new initiative, there is no official agreement about it yet (Butler & Connolly, 2002). There is little evidence of the existence and uptake of teleworking in the Irish public sector. However, Fine-Davis *et al.*'s (2002) study gives a general indication for employees in both the public and private sectors. They report that teleworking is available to 34.7% of male respondents and 20% of females. Only 10% of males engage in some form of teleworking and the corresponding figure for females is 8.2%.

Conclusions & Recommendations

Governments play a critical role in shaping the policy context in which men and women make choices concerning balancing their work, family and community responsibilities. Policies that are well designed can make it easier for parents to participate in the workforce and can support them in their choices in how they want to do so. Governments must lead by example and provide the focus for community debate (Campbell *et al*, 2002).

Within the political framework discussed in section three above, the Joint Employment Report (2002) sets out the principal measures each member State has undertaken to comply with EU Employment Guidelines. This report states that across the member States, "efforts to reconcile work and family life have been intensified, but adequate, high quality and affordable childcare services are still not sufficiently accessible to reach the targets set by the Barcelona European Council" (Joint Employment Report, 2002: 8). This finding indicates that countries need to invest more resources in family friendly working arrangements. If the EU aspire to have a harmonised level of work-life balance across its member States, the harmonisation of other factors will have to precede this achievement. For example, the provision of childcare facilities varies greatly across countries. There are also considerable difference in tax systems.

Fine-Davis *et al.*'s (2002) study concludes that Ireland offers the most family friendly policies among the four countries investigated (the others being France, Italy, and Denmark). This would appear to contradict the assertion made in the European Employment Strategy in Ireland Report[4] that Ireland has the lowest rates of flexibilisation. Fine-Davis *et al.* (2002) also report that participants in higher socio-economic status occupations have a greater availability of the policies than those in lower socio-economic occupations. This finding has implications for policy-makers who must further consider the issues that differentiate social class. Is work-life balance yet another discriminating factor depending on social class? This area needs further investigation.

---

[4] Impact Evaluation of the European Employment Strategy in Ireland, (2002: 4) DETE, Dublin: Stationary Office.

The most popular form of work-life balance is flexi-time. This offers a convenient option for employers and employees since terms of work, salary, and benefits essentially remain the same as traditional arrangements. This might account for the increased uptake of this form of flexibility over others such as part-time work and job-sharing where salary and terms of employment are significantly altered. The findings of the Fine-Davis *et al.* (2002) study indicate that there are significant differences between rates of availability of particular schemes and their up-take. Research needs to explore why this is the case.

As Humphreys *et al.* (2000) argue, there are key learning points from the experience to-date of family friendly and flexible work arrangements in the public sector. Most importantly, the uptake of these schemes appears to be different across departments and organisations. Humphreys *et al.* (2000) suggest that training and education of public sector managers regarding the management, benefits, and challenges of work-life balance initiatives need investment. Furthermore, the division which presently exists regarding who is eligible to participate in such schemes also needs to be revised. Humphreys *et al.* (2000) warn that the provision of these schemes for certain grades and not others may have serious implications for perceptions of discrimination.

Further research also needs to consider how work-life balance is conceptualised and measured. The Quality of Women's Work and Employment – Tools for Change report identifies some key future research directions for quality of females' working lives. It particularly points to the need for developing gender-sensitive indicators of quality of work and employment, including work-life balance. The report also suggests that further research should investigate the balance of working and non-working time with a life-course perspective.

It has been suggested earlier that there are varying interpretations and perceptions of what the term work-life balance actually means. Furthermore, varying terminology is often used interchangeably, for example family-friendly work arrangements and work-life balance. However, it is argued here that these terms do connote different things and the former can discriminate against those who do not have dependent family. More work needs to be done in terms of adequately theorising what is meant by these terms and arriving at a common understanding of them.

There are a number of propositions put forward in the paper regarding the impact of number of working hours, work related stress, and long hours culture on work-life balance and employee health. There is clearly a paucity of empirical research, at an international level as well as in Ireland and Europe, investigating the effect of these variables on work-life balance. To progress the debate in this field, much work needs to be done to redress this gap in the literature.

References

Armstrong, M. (2001) *A Handbook of Human Resource Management Practice*, London: Kogan Page.

Bates, P., Bertin, I. and Huws, U. (2002) *E-Work in Ireland,* Report No. 394. Dublin: The Institute for Employment Studies.

Bernas, K.H., and Major, D.A. (2003) *Time-based work-family conflcit: An assessment of underlying assumptions*, Paper presented at the 18th Annual Conference of the Society for Industrial and Organizational Psychology, Orlando, Florida, April.

Bevan, S. (1996) *Who Cares? Benefits of Career-Friendly Employment Policies*, Brighton: Institute for Employment Studies.

Bielenski, H., Bosch, G. and Wager, A. (2002) *European Foundation for the Improvement of Living and Working Conditions, Working Time Preferences in Sixteen EU Countries*, Office for Official Publication of the European Communities.

Brockwood, K.J., Hammer, L.B. and Neal, M.B. (2003) *An examination of positive work-family spillover among dual-earner couples in the sandwiched generation*, Paper presented at the 18th Annual Conference of the Society for Industrial and Organizational Psychology, Orlando, Florida, April.

Butler, I. and Connolly, G. (2002) *Initiating Change: Unions Developing Work-Life Balance*, Dublin: The Irish Congress of Trade Unions.

Campbell, I., Charlesworth, S., Probert, B., Allan, J. and Morgan, L. (2002) *Balancing Work and Family Responsibilities : Policy Implementation Options Report*, Australia: Centre for Applied Social Research, School of Social Science and Planning, RMIT University.

Clark, S.C. (2000) "*Work/family border theory: A new theory of work/life balance*", *Human Relations*, 53(6), pp. 747-770.

Coughlan, A. (2000) *Family-Friendly/Work-Life Balance Policies*, Dublin: IBEC Publishing.

DFEE (Department for Education and Employment) (2000) *Changing Patterns in a Changing World: A Discussion Document*, London.

Drew, E., Murphy, C. and Humphreys. P. (in press) *Off the Treadmill: Achieving Work/Life Balance*, Dublin: Stationary Office.

Drew, E., Emerek, R. and Mahon, E. (1998) (Eds.) *Women, Work and the Family in Europe*, London: Routledge.

Duxbury, C. and Higgins, C. (2001) *The 2001 National Work-life Conflict Study. Canada: The Healthy Communities Division*, Health Canada Report.

European Foundation for the Improvement of living and Working Conditions (2002) *Quality of Work and Employment in Europe Issues and Challenges* Foundation Paper No.1. Dublin.

Fagan, C. and Burchell, B. (2002) *European Foundation for the Improvement of Living and Working Conditions, Gender, Employment and Working Times Preferences in Europe*, Office for Official Publication of the European Communities.

Felstead, A., Jewson, N., Phizacklea, A. and Walters, S. (2002) *"Opportunities to Work at Home in the Context of Work-Life Balance", Human Resource Management*, 12(1), pp. 54-76.

Fine-Davis, M., Fangani, J., Giovannini, D., Højgaard, L., and Clarke, H. (2002) *Fathers and Mothers: Dilemmas of the Work-Life Balance*, Dublin: Centre for Gender and Women's Studies, TCD.

Fisher, H. (2000) *Investing in People, Family Friendly work arrangements in small and medium sized enterprise*, Dublin: The Equality Authority Publication.

Frone, M.R., Russell, J.K. and Cooper, K.S. (1997) "*Developing and testing an integrative model of the work-family interface*", *Journal of Vocational Behavior*, 50, pp. 145-167.

Fynes, B., Morrisey, T., Roche, W.K., Whelan, B.J., Whelan and Williams, J. (1996) *Flexible Working Lives - The Changing Nature of Working Time Arrangements in Ireland*, Dublin: Oak Tree Press.

Greenblatt, E. (2002) *"Work-life Balance: Wisdom or Whining", Organizational Dynamics*, 31 (2), pp. 177-193.

Greenhaus, J.H. and Parasuraman, S. (2002) *"Towards Reducing Some Critical Gaps in Work-Family Research"*, Human Resource Management Review 12(3), pp. 299-312.

Guest, D. (2001) "*Perspectives on the Study of Work-life Balance*" European Network of Organisational Psychology Symposium, Paris.

Handy, C. (1993) *Understanding Organizations: How understanding the ways organizations actually work can be used to manage them better*, New York: Oxford University Press.

Houston, E. (1999) *Work and Family Issues* in P. Gunnigle (Ed.) *The Irish Employee Recruitment Handbook*, Dublin: Oak Tree Press.

Humphreys, P.C., Fleming, S. and O'Donnell, O. (2000) *Flexible Working in the Public Service*, CPMR Research Report 3, Dublin: IPA.

Humphreys, P.C. and Worth-Butler, M. (1999) *Key HRM in the Irish Public Service*, CPMR Discussion Paper no. 10, Dublin: IPA.

Joint Employment Report (2002), Brussels, Commission of the European Communities.

Joshi, S., Leichne, J., Melanson, K., Pruna, C., Sager, N., Story, C.J. and Williams, K. (2002) *Work-Life Balance... A case of Social Responsibility or Competitive Advantage?* United States: The Georgia Institute of Technology.

Kopelman, R.E., Greenhaus, J.H. and Connolly, T.F. (1983) "*A model of work, family, and interrole conflict: A construct validation study*", *Organizational Behavior and Human Performance*, 32: 2, pp. 198-215.

Mahon, E. (1998) *Changing gender roles, state, work and family lives*, in E. Drew, R. Emerek & E. Mahon (eds.) *Women, Work and the Family in Europe*, London and New York: Routledge.

OECD (Organisation for Economic Co-operation and Development) (2001) *Balancing Work and Family Life: Helping Parents into Paid Employment*. OECD Employment Outlook, Paris: pp129-166.

Pahl, R. (1995) *After Success: Fin-de Siecle, Anxiety and Identity*, Cambridge: Polity Press.

Paoli, P. & Merllié (2001) *Third European Survey on Working Conditions 2000*, European Foundation for the Improvement of Living and Working Conditions, Dublin.

Stoeva, A.Z., Chiu, R.. and Greenhaus, J.H. (2002) "*Negative affectivity, role stress, and work-family conflict*", *Journal of Vocational Behavior*, 60(1), pp. 1-16.

Williams, A. (2002) "*For The Sake of The Children*", People Management 8(3), pp. 20-21.

Zemke, R., Raines, C. and Filipczak, B. (2000) "*Generations at Work: Managing the Clash of Veterans, Boomers, Xers, and Nexters in Your Workplace*", *Training & Development*, 54(1), pp. 60-71.

Passing from Low-Road to High Road Competition Strategies in CEE Countries with a View to Working Relations

BÉLA GALGÓCZI

Introduction

Enterprises with dominant foreign ownership play a key role in the in the most advanced CEE economies. In some countries these provide 40-45% of GDP, give the majority of exports and private investments. Within total working capital imports, about one third was used for privatisation. The majority of foreign working capital was put into green-field investments or into joint ventures with local partners. Even if scattered negative experiences were seen, there is a broad consensus among economic analysts that FDI was the main vehicle of structural change of the economies of the region.

With the establishing of the institutions of democracy and market economy by the early nineties the risks of foreign investments were reduced substantially. By this time the geographical vicinity, the relatively well skilled labour force together with the factor of low labour costs made the region an attractive target of foreign investments.

However, foreign involvement in the nineties was primarily capitalising on low labour costs in CEE, that made up on average one tenth of those in the advanced market economies. The basic pattern of investments in the manufacturing industry was low added value assembly and job processing. The involvement of CEE countries in the share of labour with Western developed market economies often showed similar characteristics to what Western countries have with third world countries. Low labour and environmental standards of some of the operations underlined these similarities.

Experiences showed however that multinationals in general had a positive impact on enterprise development, they brought technology, management skills, renewed work organisation and developed work culture. It is a question however, if they had a role in the transformation of enterprise cultures and industrial relations.

From the late nineties on a certain shift started to evolve with regard to the structure of foreign investments in the most advanced CEE countries. The profile of FDI was gradually shifting from labour intensive, mass production facilities, low value added assembly and wage processing towards high quality and value added knowledge intensive activities. Parallelly, previous production facilities that were only based on cheap labour, have started to move further to the East, mostly to China.

The acceleration of the integration process of CEE countries to the EU brought the speeding up of the harmonisation process among others in labour legislation and in the development of wages. Dynamic wage increases were more due a changing government policy, than to a bottom up pressure. Increasing wage levels and the realistic perspective of the EU accession has started to modify the investment environment.

In order that the early signs of this process could become an enduring and sustainable trend, the industrial relations systems of these countries need substantial consolidation. Up till now, the improving labour standards and wage conditions were mostly a result of external pressure. It is only well established social dialogue based on strong social partners that can guarantee the continuation of this trend.

We have to see also that industrial relations and corporate cultures are still in the process of transformation in CEE countries. There is an interrelation between domestic and foreign patterns.

Multinationals companies (especially those with an EU headquarter) would also have a crucial role in the process, as potential transmitters of European social values and co-operative management patterns. Some of the EU directives promoting workers participation (EWC, Information/Consultation and on the European Company) could also consolidate this process.

The main topic of this study is to investigate, if the chances of a high road competition strategy for CEE countries could be a realistic scenario for the future.

Signs of Change from "Low Road" towards "High Road" Strategies of Competition in Certain CEE Countries

Changing Wage Policies in CEE

The development of real wages still showed a pattern when real wages were lagging substantially behind labour productivity developments and also behind GDP growth in the period between 1992 and 2000 in most of the countries of the CEE region.

To some extent, Lithuania, Latvia and Estonia were exceptions, where wages have increased close to productivity and much more than GDP in the 8 year period. In these latter countries wage increases in the eight year period seemed to be somewhat beyond economic performance.

It is the Czech Republic, Slovenia, Slovakia and Poland, where wage increases followed productivity developments to some extent and corresponded or even surpassed GDP growth. In the Czech Republic, productivity in the eight-year period grew by 10 % faster than wages. Beside Baltic states, the Czech republic was the only candidate country, where wages grew faster than GDP.

The productivity/wage discrepancy in the case of Poland was 34%, but wage increases were still somewhat higher than GDP growth. The situation in Slovenia was similar to that of Poland. These two countries seemed to manage a rather proportional development of wages and economic performance.

This could by no means be said about Romania, Bulgaria and especially about Hungary. In these countries wages were lagging much behind economic performance. In Romania the relative level of productivity is twice as high than that of wages regarding the period of 1992-2000. Wage dynamics were lagging behind GDP developments, as well. The situation was most dramatic in Bulgaria, as wages are a mere 60% of the 1992 level, while the level of GDP almost reaches the 1992 level and productivity exceeds the value of 1992 by almost 50%.

Wages, by the year 2000, were the most depressed compared to economic performance in Hungary however, as the level of productivity was almost 2,5 fold higher, than that of wages, if the level of 1992 is taken as basis. Wages were also roughly 20% behind GDP growth.

It must be emphasised that the situation was most concerning in Romania and Bulgaria, as there not only the relative position of wages was very low, but wages were very low on absolute levels, as well. In Hungary the very depressed level of wages according to economic performance still meant a wage level, which belonged to the upper range of candidate countries. In

Hungary a very strong development of productivity stood against a very moderate (almost stagnating) wage increase. In Romania and Bulgaria however a substantial productivity growth faced a substantial drop of real wages.
The trends of the first decade of transformation can well be followed on the graphs below.

Figure 1: Development of industrial labour productivity, real wages and real GDP in candidate countries in the period 1992-2000 (cumulative index; 1992=100)

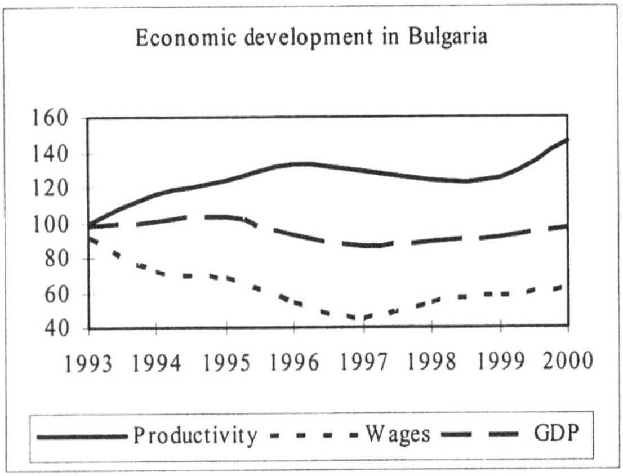

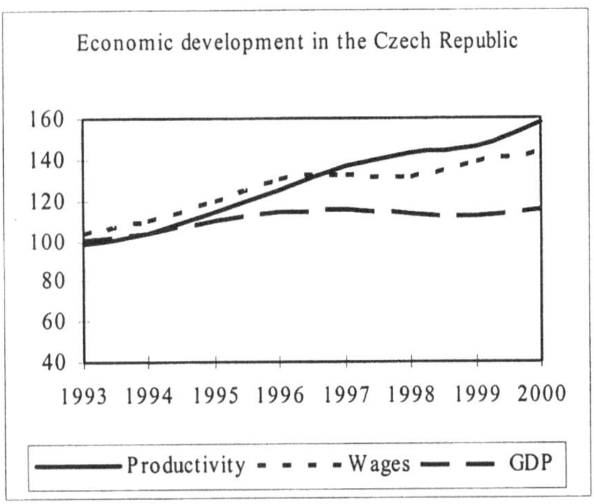

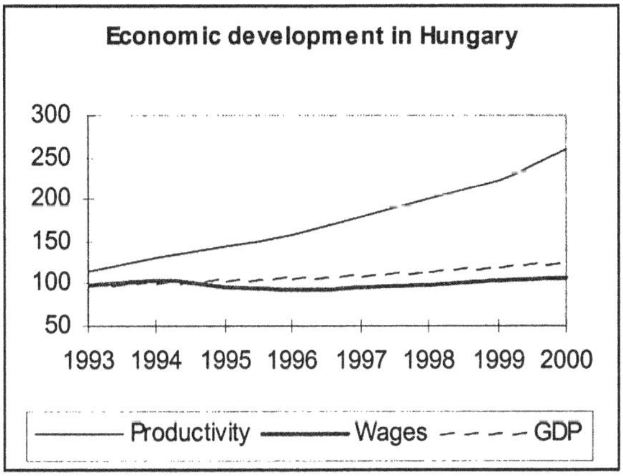
Economic development in Hungary
300
250
200
150
100
50
1993 1994 1995 1996 1997 1998 1999 2000
Productivity
Wages
GDP

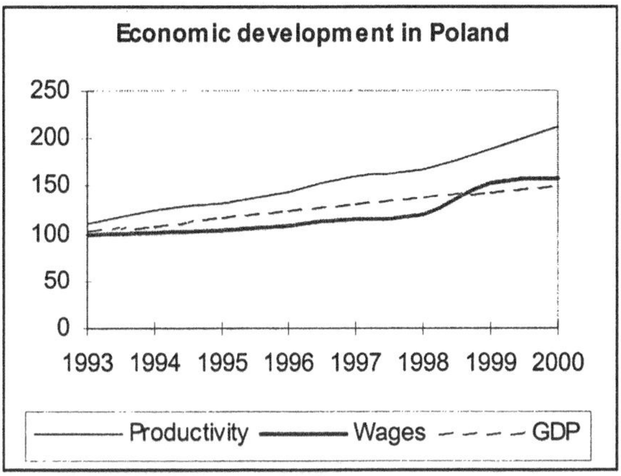
Economic development in Poland
250
200
150
100
50
0
1993 1994 1995 1996 1997 1998 1999 2000
Productivity
Wages
GDP

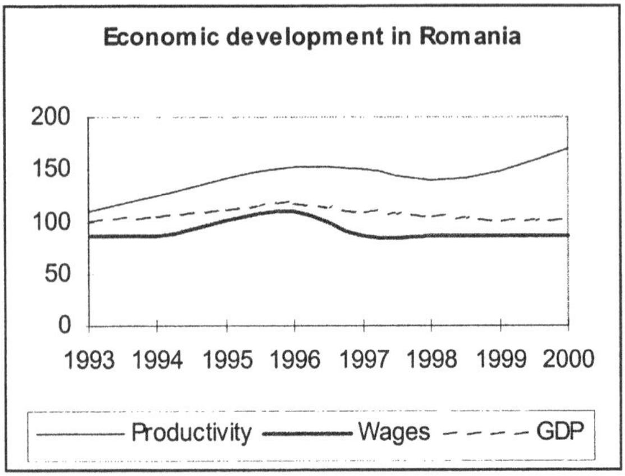

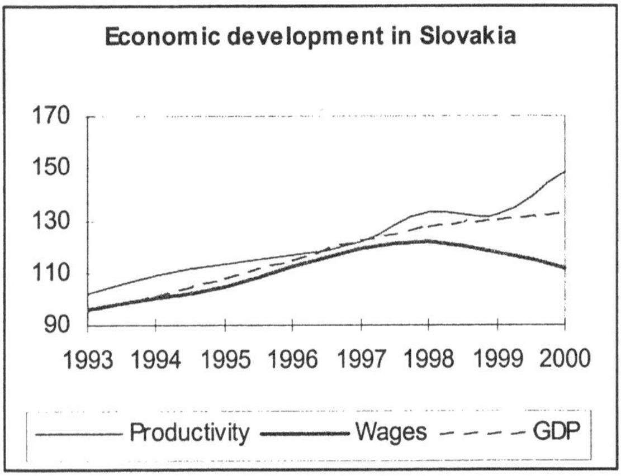

From 2001 on a new trend has been unfolded in certain countries, which was marked by dynamic wage increases under the notion of „catching up to European levels". The process was accompanied by an appreciation of several CEE currencies in the region resulting double digit wage increases in Euro levels. The process was most radical in Hungary, where wages in Euro increased by 50% in the period of 2000-2002.

Disproportional wage increases during 2001 and 2002, especially in Hungary, have substantially departed from the rate of GDP and productivity growth, having been one reason behind aggravating equilibrium positions of the economy.

Wage increases would not be a problem in themselves, because Hungary (for example) disposes of a substantial productivity reserve and this can also be seen as a late-coming compensation for former losses. The timing

and the extent of the discrepancy is however posing a threat to future growth prospects.
As a result, average wage levels in the three reform countries of the CEE region in 2002 (Poland, Czech Republic and Hungary) were around 550 Euro at exchange rate, meaning a level between 1000 and 1100 Euro at purchasing power parity (this latter is 50% of the EU average).
These figures indicate clearly that a competitive strategy based on low wages does not work anymore. The real question is, how these countries manage to remain competitive under the new conditions,

Productivity Gains in CEE Countries

Massive structural change of the last decade has led to a structure of manufacturing industry in most candidate countries that is quite close to European patterns with the exception of Bulgaria, Romania and the Baltic states. Productivity growth was substantial in candidate countries, especially from the second half of the nineties, although in an uneven distribution among individual countries. Hungary is the productivity leader among Eastern European candidate countries, slightly surpassing the 50% of the EU average. On the other hand Bulgarian and Romanian labour productivity is just around one fourth of the Hungarian level. According to a study of WIIW on industrial competitiveness of candidate countries, their exports are generally still more specialised on labour intensive industries, than EU member states. However, the Czech Republic, Slovakia, Slovenia and especially Hungary focus less on labour intensive industries in their exports to the EU than Greece and Portugal. Hungary's representation of labour intensive exports to the EU is comparable to that of Austria, Denmark and Italy. As regards the representation of technology driven exports to the EU, Hungary has the greatest share among candidate countries (similar to that of the UK and Ireland), followed by Slovakia, the Czech Republic and Estonia, while Bulgaria, Romania, Latvia and Lithuania have the lowest share.

Table 1. Labour productivity in manufacturing industry at PPP in candidate countries, 1999 (Austria=100,0)

CZ	SK	HU	Pl	Sl	RO	BG	EE	LV	LT
45,5	39,6	66,4	48,0	43,4	25,5	24,0	28,7	25,1	28,6

Source: WIIW Competitiveness of Industry in candidate Countries, 2001

Labour productivity in candidate countries shows substantial differences across candidate countries. Hungary has the highest productivity level, roughly two-third of that of Austria, followed by Poland, which has slightly less than the half of the Austrian level. Romania, Bulgaria and the three Baltic states only have one fourth of the Austrian productivity level.
As regards the relation between real wage and labour productivity developments in industry, data for all candidate countries are available from 1993, thus a full overview can be given for this period only. Nevertheless productivity figures for most CEE countries were available from 1990 as well, thus a full scope of changes can be followed for the whole transition period. If we only notice the index of labour productivity of industry in 2000 with a basis of the 1989 level taken for 100, we get the following results.

Table 2 - Index of industrial labour productivity in 2000, level of 1989=100,0

CZ	SK	HU	Pl	Sl	RO	BG
131,2	122,2	220,2	187,5	151,5	101,2	118,9

Source: WIIW Competitiveness of Industry in candidate Countries, 2001

Most candidate countries show a substantial productivity development in the ten years of transition, although differences among individual countries are great. Hungarian labour productivity grew spectacularly reaching in 2000 more than twice the level of 1989. Poland follows by almost doubling its pre-transition level productivity. Bulgaria, the Czech Republic, Slovakia and Slovenia reached productivity improvements between 18 and 51% in the eleven-year period. The level of Romanian productivity in 2000 was not significantly higher, than it was in 1989.

Second Wave of Structural Change

Since the end of the nineties we are witnessing a process, that is often called "second wave of structural change" in certain CEE countries. The profile of FDI is gradually shifting from labour intensive, mass production facilities, low value added assembly and wage processing towards high quality and value added knowledge intensive activities. Parallelly, previous production facilities that were based on cheap labour have started to move further to the East, mostly to China. Mannesmann, IBM, Philips have closed low skill assembly plants in CEE countries and moved their activities to China.

It is quite clear that the future of the CEE industry can not rely on the comparative advantage of low wages. Higher added value, than loan work based assembly is required in order to have a chance of integration into a higher level of European industrial co-operations.

There are signs already that this development has started, since the importance of the quality of human resources plays an increasing role in investment decisions. It is a positive tendency, as well that more and more multinationals decide to move research & development facilities to Hungary, to the Czech Republic and in certain cases to Poland (Audi, GE, Pharmaceutical industry, IT industry).

It can be stated that some 50.000 workplaces were lost in the low skill mass production sector during 2001 and 2002 in Hungary, but this was counterbalanced by new employment by jobs demanding higher skills and competencies.

Even IBM, which in 2002 closed its plant assembling computer hard discs in Western-Hungary having employed 3500 relatively low skilled employees, opened a new software development facility with couple of hundred high skilled people. Similar moves were done by Siemens, Flextronics and Nokia.

Philips, which seemed to follow the traditional pattern by moving a part of its display & monitor production from Germany to the Czech Republic, while keeping the knowledge intensive prototype manufacturing at the German plant, now considers to relocate this activity to the Czech Republic in the coming years, as well.

There is another trend unfolding in the last couple of years that shows the extending of the previous logic of FDI in emerging economies. The deployment of business administration and services centres of transnational companies is getting more and more widespread.

A US consultancy firm, AT Kearney published a list of classifying 11 countries according to what extent they are attractive for the deployment of business administration, financial and computing activities (according to their measurement, costs have a 40% weight, the environment has 30% and the human factor 30%).

India is on top of the list, with attracting business administration functions of the GE Capital, American Express, Citibank, Conseco, British Airways, Dell Computer. CEE countries are also ahead on the list. Hungary had the highest score (see some examples above), followed by the Czech Republic.

The most spectacular move was however that of General Electric, which moved its business administration and financial centre for Europe, Middle East and Africa from London to Budapest with an investment of 4.6 million USD in 2002, employing several hundred new employees (GE is otherwise present already for 12 years in Hungary with a total number of 13000 employees).
The US firm, Alcoa has deployed two of its European regional centres to Hungary in 2002. The one is a business administration and financial centre with 150 high skill employees. The other is a regional computer centre with 60 software specialists in 2003 with an investment of 5.5 million USD.

A Critical Review of Industrial Relations in CEE Countries

The Nature of Industrial Relations in CEE Countries

Although most of the legal preconditions and institutional framework conditions of a European based industrial relations system are given in most CEE countries, several problems appear in its functioning. It is no question about a European or American model of industrial relations, since both the traditions and the targeted pattern is European. This does not mean however that the adaptation of the basic framework of the European industrial relations means that it has set its foot in an organic way. It must be acknowledged that the discreditedness of institutional interest representation under state socialism still has its impact in the behaviour of most acteurs. As a result, social atomisation and growing individualism with informal bargaining became the major way of survival. This together with the low legitimacy of interest representation bodies and the scepticism towards institutional solutions has generated such individual bargaining strategies among employees, which survived the change of the political climate.
Decentralised bargaining and the lack of effective social regulation above the company level still enables a variety of management strategies, including the relentless pursuit of a low wage - low skill - low commitment strategy in certain companies.
Apart from sheer competition, there is no solid institutional force or societal pressure to push employers to a higher wage/higher skill production strategy and thus to promote the continuous upgrading of production, productivity and human resources.
There are various forms of workplace level bargaining strategies however that emerged at companies of major importance in the manufacturing

sector. The majority of unionised companies, which inherited strong union organisation from the past, are covered by local collective agreement and usually have a high level of enterprise culture (examples are GE-Tungsram and Matáv Telecommunication Company). At newly organised green-field facilities, however, unions are not always able to conclude an agreement to regulate terms and conditions of employment. In these companies collective bargaining has been supplemented by consultation, information exchange and ad-hoc problem solving.

Most of the unionised companies are pursuing a high wage/high commitment management strategies. There emerged a kind of quasi bargaining in the form of consultation and information. However, the agent on behalf of employees in this quasi bargaining is not always the union, but sometimes it has to share this role with the works' council. It even might occur that in lack of union, the works' council which is really entering into bargaining over terms and conditions of employment. The parallel existence of local union organisation and works' council in some countries at the same venue resulted that, in fact, there are two organisations which are entitled to represent employees. These doubling of employee representation resulted in a situation, when local factors decide whether unions and works councils are co-operating together, or have a rather competitive relationship, and which organisation became the main partner of management.

At company level, the ethos of quasi bargaining seeks the common interest of both management and workers in the maintenance of continuous, problem-free production. In the pursuit of this common goal the role of the employee representatives is to stress the importance of the maintenance of human resources. In other words a kind of productivity coalition has been established between management and the employees' representatives, within which the employees' representatives see their role as being to raise the complaints and the demands of the workers. Within the scope of the productivity coalition, the problems raised by employees' representatives can be grouped into three major categories:

1) those which are directly related to production, that relate to the maintenance of problem-free continuous work, 2) the kinds of working conditions necessary to the completion of high quality work, and 3) those based on the achieving a high commitment high wage/high quality workplace.

Above company level, most problems arise from the weakness of the branch level social dialogue. Neither unions, nor employer federations have acknowledged the importance of this level, although some improvement has been made in the last couple of years (this was primarily an impact of the European influence).

Tripartism as the Major Terrain of Industrial Relations

In the first ten years of transformation, tripartite bodies provided the institutional framework for trade union participation in preparing labour-related legislation and practicing collective bargaining at the national level.
It is certainly true that tripartism yielded great benefits for its participants in reinforcing their legitimacy in critical periods. They were the tripartite organisations, which paved the way for trade unions and also for employer federations to become national players with an influence on the processes of transformation. Sometimes it was a good occasion for government officials to pass on responsibility for critical decisions to the tripartite body, which in this way also served their public acceptance.
From a critical point of view, it was often raised that agreements on the tripartite level could endanger the sovereignty of Parliament. It is certainly true that the authority of the tripartite body has never been clearly defined. Its agreements were not compulsory for the Parliament, although it never happened that decisions were brought in contrary to a reached agreement at the tripartite talks.
We have to see however that the disproportional weight of the tripartite structures in the industrial relations is itself the result of the transformation period. There are already signs in many CEE countries that the central importance of these structures will decrease in the future.

Shortcomings of Collective Bargaining

In the area of collective agreements Hungary confirms the general tendency that characterises CEE countries, i.e. that such agreements tend to be concluded at company level and that the practice of sectoral collective agreements is particularly weak.
The major question in this regard relates to why sectoral bargaining practice is so weak in most CEE countries.
Generally, it is considered that the legislative rules on labour relations are so detailed that they leave little room for free negotiations. There is a dilemma if not a contradiction between the trade unions' claim that they want to negotiate pay increases in the framework of the national labour council (tripartism) and also promotion of sectoral bargaining practice. If account is taken of the rules contained in the labour code, and if the

possibility of tripartite concertation on pay is added, little is left for negotiation between the social partners acting at sectoral level.
The weakness of collective bargaining comes partially from the attitude of social partners. Trade unions have a weak presence in private companies, which by now constitute the central pillar of CEE economies. Second, in several cases trade union pluralism has proved to be a serious obstacle to conclusion of collective agreements, at both company and sectoral level. Often, the trade unions do not manage to arrive at common positions in negotiations, which makes it impossible to conclude agreements for formal reasons, independent of the willingness of employers in this regard.
Employers sometimes lack adequate political will. Employer organisations are sometimes not authorised to conclude collective agreements. They are sometimes too heterogeneous in terms of the interests they claim to defend and too weak institutionally to be able to act with competence in the area of collective agreements. Last, the very notion of an economic sector does not mean much to most employers. From their viewpoint, it is very difficult if not impossible to use the category of sector or branch because businesses performing similar activities often differ greatly from one another in terms of their financial and social condition.

Industrial Relation Systems and Enterprise Culture at Foreign Enterprises

Multinationals in general have positive impact on enterprise cultures in CEE countries. They bring technology, management skill, renew work organisation and develop work culture. In general they have well maintained industrial relations (in the rule at larger organisations) and most have collective agreements. Multinationals adapt to the local conditions also, especially if it is more easy-going to fit local patterns.
It would be a populist approach to say that multinationals do not let trade unions work, and that they block the expansion social dialogue.
There are of course problematic cases, especially with Japanese and Korean enterprises, since they usually force their own models in a totally different environment, and say for example that trade unions are not necessary. It is not true however that American companies do not care for industrial relations and co-operative management styles.
It is more so that German enterprises are more keen on that, although not without exception, even for Audi it took several years in Hungary to establish a collective agreement. Siemens is not a good example either, as

several of their factories are union free and they do not delegate an EWR member from Hungary.
It is generally characteristic that industrial relations work much smoother at privatised enterprises, where trade union presence has a tradition, than at green-field investments, where the establishment of a union is sometimes difficult.
At privatised enterprises, massive reorganisation of the company is necessary in most cases, which is often accompanied with substantial staff reductions. It is an elementary interest of the employer also to implement these measures through negotiations with labour representations in a co-operative manner.
At green-field investments on the other hand, when the starting position is not affected by conflict solution, but on the contrary foreign employers offer higher wages, than usual in the given labour market environment, the necessity of interest representation does not seem to be evident at the beginning.
Multinationals pay on average 30% higher wages than their Hungarian counterparts, as a consequence of which there is not much terrain for military unions.
Experiences show two major kinds of approaches of industrial relations by foreign enterprises.
The first one could be characterised as "adaptive", since the management adapts its relation to the traditions and legal framework of the host country in forming its attitude to the employees and the interest representation bodies. Changes in this case are mostly limited to "fine tuning" and reforms.
The second one is the "innovative" approach, where the management wants to transfer the enterprise culture of its home country. In this case not only the company organisation, the management style and the organisation of production will be fundamentally transformed, but also the industrial relations. For example, if works councils at the mother firm are dominant, they try to favour works councils and weaken trade unions. In certain cases the presence of trade unions is not requested at all.
It is rather difficult to classify individual countries along these categories. Experiences are not that simple. It is true however, what we mentioned at the introduction. Rigid transfer of domestic cultures is more characteristic for Asian enterprises. Americans prefer efficiency above all, and if it is a co-operative enterprise culture that promotes this goal, they do not object, on the other hand they are not making much effort to establish such systems. Corporate identity and loyalty is much more important for them.

As regards European, especially German enterprises, they have an innovative approach of enterprise culture, but in most cases they adapt their models to the local conditions also.
Usually they do not force their models on the local enterprise, they easily adapt however, if it means a looser, more flexible structure, than what they are used to at home.
It happens however in certain cases that they force the development of a German model, including the dominance of works councils vis-a-vis trade unions, but this strategy is not deemed for success in the local environment. Without strong enterprise union representation industrial relations would not function efficiently in CEE countries.
It is also true that human resource policies of enterprises have also great importance in enterprise culture and can also have an impact on industrial relations. In this regard the influence of foreign enterprises is generally positive. The most important mission of such a creative HR strategy is the development of a learning organisation.
In this regard it is a rather frustrating experience that Audi, the flagship of German enterprises in Hungary, follows a rather defensive HR policy. The attitude of Audi is to exploit the reservoir of qualified labour to be found on the local (regional) labour market, but not to invest extensively in qualification programmes in order to raise the skill potential in the region, which would be essential for the further development of the enterprise. Instead of this, after the local sources have been squeezed, they rely on guest workers from Slovakia and match the scope of future investments to the available labour resources.
This attitude is quite characteristic for most foreign enterprises (and is rather natural for medium size firms), but some of the large enterprises are more keen on strategic HR development (e.g. GE Tungsram, and Matáv).

The Impact of IR Systems of Foreign Enterprises on the National IR Systems

It is rather difficult to identify concrete trends in this regard. On the one hand it is clear that the present pattern of industrial relations in CEE countries was formed in close interaction with the practices of foreign enterprises, that make up a substantial part of industrial production.
On the other hand the direct influence of foreign enterprises is a controversial issue, as we saw at the above examples. It is much better to say that there is a strong interrelation between national and foreign

enterprise cultures with the clear dominance of the European model. This can not be forced out however, as some of the bad examples indicate.
Most of the experiences show that the bulk of foreign enterprises do not feel the necessity of a missionary role and do not force the transmission of their models mechanically. The main goal is to achieve a system, which works efficiently and in a co-operative way among local conditions. This is an elementary interest of the company management, as well.
There is no empirical evidence of any sort of transfer of co-operative management styles or industrial relations through the activities of multinationals. In this regard they do not play a missionary role. The are optimising resources and adapt policies to the local conditions, as a result of which they apply as much co-operative enterprise culture and participatory practices, they find necessary under the given environment. In this regard, both local legislation and the pressure of local interest representation bodies have a key importance.

Positive Examples and Conditions for Their Broader Dissemination

As we saw above, positive examples for industrial relation systems and for co-operative enterprise cultures are mostly found at large enterprises. The expansion of these patterns to other spheres of the economy runs through several channels. Good practices expand spontaneously on the one hand, as the success of those companies motivates other organisations to follow. Through a wide range of subcontractor networks large enterprises exert a positive impact on their co-operation partners. In case of certain companies it is a conscious policy to disseminate some elements of their corporate culture and enterprise ethos. This is a strong effort in the case of General Electric for example, which imposes strong standards on its subcontractors not only relating to technical standards and quality requirements. There are of course limits in the direct transmission of these good practices.
Much more than that is needed in order that the deficits of co-operative enterprise culture in the SME sector could be handled.
Decentralised bargaining and the lack of effective social regulation above the company level enables the management to pursue low wage/low skill/low commitment strategies in several companies. This tendency would be a dangerous scenario for enterprises.

Perspectives of Co-operative Enterprise Cultures and Industrial Relation Systems in CEE Countries

Major Obstacles of a Sound and Stable IR System in CEE

The greatest obstacles of a well working industrial system in the CEE region can be grouped, as follows:

- Relatively weak positions of trade unions, within which the following factors play a role:
  - Legitimacy problems,
  - Conflicts arising from trade union pluralism,
  - Shrinking organisation grade,
  - Lack of new strategies to expand towards the SME and services sectors,
  - Over-politicised approach, which is counter-productive on the national level in the long-run.
- Fragmented employer organisations, that are not always devoted supporters of social dialogue
- Distorted structure of social dialogue
  - Over-dimensioned national level
  - Weak branch level structures
- Dual channel model of IR not having developed in an organic way
- Functional disturbances between trade unions and works councils on the enterprise level.

Some shortcomings of the CEE IR systems were demonstrated in the above sections. To approach the problem in a more general manner, it must be emphasised, that the whole system has developed at the impact of external impulses, and not through an organic development. On the one hand, the underlying legislation was introduced from above, often reflecting daily interests of acteurs. Enterprise level structures on the other hand developed under the influence of foreign patterns. The time was not enough maybe to have a system integrated into national traditions in an organic way.

As emphasised before, the heritage of state-socialism on human attitudes still plays an important role. Individualism, the general lack of solidarity and surviving paternalistic attitudes are all obstacles for having a genuine system of interest representation. Some people have still fears to express their opinions and interests openly.

It must be emphasised however that lots of progress has been made in the last decade and the industrial relation systems in most CEE countries have gained a profoundly European character. As regards enterprise cultures in a broader sense, some progress can be observed, as well. Co-operative management patterns at company level are rather wide-spread nowadays, especially in the case of larger enterprises.

Apart from sheer competition, there was no institutional force or societal pressure up till most recent times to push employers to promote the continuous upgrading of performance, productivity and human resources.

Above company level, most problems arise from the weakness of the branch level social dialogue. Neither unions, nor employer federations have acknowledged the importance of this level.

It is therefore of extraordinary importance to develop an environment, including strong branch level interest representation structures in order to exert pressure towards a higher wage/higher skill/higher productivity strategy.

The recent examples of high road competition in CEE countries could then well prove to be scattered examples.

Economic Integration and Transnational Social Regulation: a Comparison between the European Union and NAFTA"

ISABEL DA COSTA, UDO REHFELDT

The link between international trade and social rights is a central issue in the ongoing debate about economic globalization. For years, international trade union organizations have been fighting for the introduction of social clauses into international trade agreements[1]. Until recently the defenders of strict liberal policies opposed these clauses considering any form of social regulation as tantamount to "trade barriers". The dominant position of the European Union (EU) in international trade, however, proves that there is no necessary contradiction between high levels of social regulation and strong economic competitiveness. Since 1994, North America has also linked labor standards to an international trade agreement, the North American Free Trade Agreement (NAFTA), by signing a labor side agreement called the North American Agreement on Labor Cooperation (NAALC). Europe and North America are the two most important zones of economic and financial exchanges in the planet. These exchanges take place both inside each region of economic integration and between the two regions through transatlantic exchanges[2]. They therefore represent a crucial piece of economic globalization. This article will compare the transnational social dimensions in these two zones of regional economic integration. This analysis of Europe's and North America's specific responses to the challenges of economic integration should contribute to the discussion of the need for a social regulation in the process of globalization as well as to

---

[1] See for example, International Confederation of Free Trade Unions, *Building Workers' Human Rights into the Global Trading System,* Brussels, 1999.

[2] See for example, Joseph P. Quinlan, *Drifting Apart or Growing Together ? The Primacy of the Transatlantic Economy*, Washington DC (Center for Transatlantic Relations) 2003.

the identification of a "high road" of development which raises social standards rather than trigger a race to the bottom by eroding the existing ones.

The institutional mechanisms and the density of the economic integration process differs between the EU and the NAFTA zones. The European zone of economic integration is more homogeneous both economically and socially. Development differences persist between the central European countries and the peripheral ones, such as Spain, Portugal or Greece, but these differences have decreased partly thanks to the European structural funds. The development gap is much wider between Mexico the United States. Moreover, in North America, there is an asymmetrical economic and political relationship between the United States and the two other countries which creates a dominance problem[3]. NAFTA is a free trade zone with only ten years experience and a weak form of institutionalization, whereas the EU now has half a century of existence and includes supranational institutions and a multidimensional integration – economic, monetary, political and social. Our article will focus on the social aspects of this institutionalization not on the economic impact of economic integration in terms of jobs, incomes, etc. It will present and compare the institutional mechanisms set up for the protection of labor standards in NAFTA and the EU. It will also outline the role of labor unions and governments in the functioning of these mechanisms. Finally, it will show that the European zone has a more developed form of social regulation than NAFTA and that the transnational action of labor unions is also more developed in Europe.

The North American Agreement on Labor Cooperation

The North American Free Trade Agreement (NAFTA) between the United States, Canada and Mexico was originally negotiated, at the request of President Carlos Salinas of Mexico, by the Bush administration, in the period 1990-92. NAFTA is essentially a trade agreement. It ensures that multinational companies and investors have free access to the markets of the three counties, but it does not give migrant workers freedom of

[3] Rainer Dombois, Erhard Hornberger, Jens Winter, "Transnational labor regulation in the NAFTA –a Problem of Institution Design ? The case of the North American Agreement on Labor Cooperation between the USA, Mexico and Canada", paper presented at the 13th World Congress of the International Industrial Relations Association (IIRA) in Berlin in September 2003, p.18.

movement and establishes no structural funds for development, for example. In the United States, NAFTA was strongly criticized by different sections of the public, including labor and environment groups but also Congress Democrats and even populist presidential candidate Ross Perrot. During the presidential campaign of 1992, candidate Bill Clinton declared he would approve the treaty under the condition that side agreements dealing with labor and the environment be negotiated to supplement it. After the election, the new Clinton administration proposed to Canadian and Mexican negotiators the creation of independent commissions with the power to ensure that the three countries enforce their own labor and environment laws. But with business, Republicans, and the Mexican and Canadian governments opposing the proposals and U.S. unions taking no part in the negotiating process, the Clinton administration backed away and agreed to a much weaker set of enforcement procedures, especially with respect to labor standards[4]. NAFTA and the two side agreements, the North American Agreement on Labor Cooperation (NAALC) and the North American Agreement on Environmental Cooperation (NAAEC), were approved by Congress by a small margin in November 1993[5] and went into effect on the 1st of January 1994.

The NAALC represents the first time labor standards were linked to an international trade agreement in North America. But the NAALC is just a side agreement, which means that labor principles are not directly included in NAFTA. Furthermore, labor principles do not get in NAALC the same enforcement mechanisms and sanctions economic rights are granted in NAFTA.

Institutional Framework

- Objectives and obligations

The first objective of the NAALC is to improve working conditions and living standards in the United States, Mexico and Canada. The second is to promote the following 11 basic Labor Principles (Annex 1):

1. Freedom of association and protection of the right to organize
2. The right to bargain collectively

---

4 James Shoch, "Organized Labor versus Globalization: NAFTA, Fast Track, and PNTR with China" in Lowell Turner, Harry Katz and Richard Hurd, *Rekindling the Movement: Labor's Quest for Relevance in the Twenty-First Century*, ILR Press, Ithaca, 2001, p.283.

5 idem, p.284. NAFTA was approved by the House of Representatives by votes of 234 to 200 and by the Senate by votes of 61 to 38. Three-quarters of House Republicans but only 40 percent of House Democrats were in favor of the treaty. Over three-quarters of Senate Republicans and half of Senate Democrats backed it.

3. The right to strike
4. Prohibition of forced labor
5. Labor protections for children and young persons
6. Minimum employment standards
7. Elimination of employment discrimination
8. Equal pay for women and men
9. Prevention of occupational injuries and illnesses
10. Compensation in cases of occupational injuries and illnesses
11. Protection of migrant workers

Other objectives include promoting international cooperation in the labor arena and ensuring the effective enforcement and transparent administration of labor law.
Following these objectives, in the second part of the NAALC, the three countries agree to a set of six obligations concerning labor law and its enforcement[6]. While the obligations reaffirm national sovereignty over labor legislation contents and procedures, the countries commit themselves to enforce domestic labor law through accessible, fair and transparent procedures.

The NAALC's eleven Labor Principles and six Obligations define the scope of the agreement and cover a wide range of labor rights. However, the Agreement stipulates that the Principles do not constitute common laws

[6] Briefly summarized, the NAALC obligations are the following :

- Levels of Protection: Affirming full respect for each Party's constitution, and recognizing the right of each Party to establish its own domestic labor standards, and to adopt or modify its labor laws and regulations, each Party shall ensure that its labor laws and regulations provide for high labor standards, consistent with high quality and productivity workplaces, and shall continue to strive to improve those standards in that light.
- Government Enforcement Action: Each Party shall promote compliance with and effectively enforce its labor laws through appropriate government action.
- Private Action: Each Party shall ensure that persons with a recognized interest under its laws have appropriate access to administrative, quasi-judicial or labor tribunals for the enforcement of the Party's labor law.
- Procedural Guarantees: Each Party shall ensure that its administrative, quasi-judicial, judicial and labor tribunal proceedings for the enforcement of its labor law are fair, equitable and transparent.
- Publication: Each Party shall ensure that its laws, regulations, procedures and administrative rulings of general application respecting any matter covered by this Agreement are promptly published or otherwise made available.
- Public Information and Awareness: Each party shall promote public awareness of its labor law.

or standards. The Parties have not committed themselves to harmonize labor laws across North America but rather to effectively enforce their own domestic labor laws (art.3). The content and the procedures for enforcement of labor laws remain matters of national sovereignty. The NAALC does not create a supranational tribunal in charge of enforcing labor rights in the three countries, but it does provide some oversight mechanisms concerning labor law enforcement: consultations, evaluations and dispute resolution. The goal of the Agreement is to resolve issues in a cooperative manner but, theoretically, dispute resolution can go as far as fines or trade sanctions in case of persistent failure to enforce labor law in three areas: occupational safety and health, child labor and minimum wage technical standards.

- Institutional structure

The NAALC creates both international and national institutions. The international institution is the Commission for Labor Cooperation. The Commission consists of a Ministerial Council and a Secretariat. The national institutions are the National Administrative Offices (NAOs) and National and Governmental Advisory Committees.

The Council of Ministers is composed of the three Ministries of Labor (called Secretaries in Mexico and the United States). The Council is the governing body of the Commission. It oversees the implementation of the NAALC; directs the activities of the Secretariat; and promotes tri-national cooperative activities in 15 non-exhaustive areas of labor law, labor standards, labor markets and labor relations (art.11). The Council meets at least once a year.

The Secretariat is headed by an Executive Director appointed by consensus of the three Parties for a term of three years renewable once and the position rotates between each country. Staff positions were initially set at 15 with equitable proportions coming from each country and include labor economists, labor lawyers and other professionals with experience in labor affairs. They work in the three official languages of the Commission: English, French and Spanish. The Secretariat provides technical support to the Council and provides information through research and public reports on a wide range of labor issues including labor law and administrative procedures, trends and administrative strategies related to the implementation and enforcement of labor law, labor market conditions, and human resources development issues such as training and adjustment programs.

The three National Administrative Offices (NAOs), located in each country's Ministry or Department of Labor, serve as points of contact between Commission entities and national governments. They can consult with each other and exchange information on labor matters. They coordinate the cooperative activities of the Commission, which include seminars and joint research projects, and can also engage in direct bilateral cooperative activities. NAOs receive and respond to complaints (called "public communications" or "submissions") regarding labor law issues arising in another NAFTA country. Each country determines the functions and procedures of its own NAO and how it will be staffed.
The Agreement also allows each country to establish Governmental and National Advisory Committees to their NAOs. All three countries have done so. The Governmental Committees comprise representatives of federal and state or provincial governments. The National Advisory Committees comprise members representing the labor community, the business community, academia and the public at large. Advisory committees have a consultative role, they provide advice on issues arising under the NAALC. They are not compulsory under the treaty and are the only NAALC institution in which the social partners are represented.

- Four levels of treatment of "labor law matters"

The NAALC creates four levels of treatment of "labor law matters" as defined in the Agreement:

1. NAO Review and Consultation

Individuals, unions, employers, non-governmental organizations or other private parties may file submissions regarding labor law matters arising in the territory of another Party and seek NAO reviews in accordance with each country's NAO procedures. The definition of "labor law matters" covers the 11 Labor Principles. NAOs can recommend Ministerial Consultations at the Council level on any of these 11 Labor Principles. There are variations in the procedures. For instance, the Mexican review process must be carried out "within a reasonable period of time", whereas the U.S. and Canadian procedures specify fixed time frames – 60 days to accept or decline a communication and 120 days to issue a public report. There are also differences in how information is gathered: the U.S. process calls for a public hearing, the Canadian process may involve a "public meeting or consultation", and the Mexican process may involve "information sessions".

2. Ministerial Consultations

Ministerial Consultations can be demanded by the labor minister of any NAALC Party concerning any matter within the scope of the Agreement. Consultation can be bilateral or trilateral, if the invitation to participate in the Consultation is extended to the minister of the third country. Article 22 encourages the Parties to solve issues through consultation. For the first three Labor Principles – freedom of association and protection of the right to organize; the right to bargain collectively; and the right to strike -- this is the final step of the procedure.

3. Evaluation Committee of Experts (ECE)

If a matter has not been solved after Ministerial Consultations, a country can initiate the establishment of an ECE composed of independent experts. ECEs examine patterns of practice in the enforcement of technical labor standards (defined as labor matters related to Labor Principles 4 to 11). They will undertake a comparative study and make recommendations on the matter as it is treated in each of the countries. Matters subject to Evaluation and Dispute Resolution must be trade-related and covered by mutually recognized labor laws.

4. Dispute Resolution by an Arbitral Panel

Following consideration by the Council of an ECE report and subsequent required consultations, a party involved in the consultations may request the establishment of an Arbitral Panel for the purpose of addressing "alleged persistent patterns of failure to effectively enforce occupational safety and health, child labor or minimum wage technical labor standards". The establishment of a Panel requires a two-thirds vote of the Council. Composed of five members, Arbitral Panels are empowered to develop an "action plan" to remedy a persistent pattern of failure to enforce the laws in question. Failure to implement the plan may result in fines (of a maximum of 0,007 percent of the total trade in goods between the Parties during the most recent year for which data are available) that will be used to improve the environment or labor conditions or the enforcement of labor laws in the territory of the Party complained against, consistent with the law of that Party. Failure to pay a fine within 180 days can result in a suspension of NATFA trade benefits until the amount of the monetary assessment has

been reached. Dispute Resolution applies to only three Labor Principles and also introduces the notion of "persistent patterns of failure to effectively enforce" which further reduces the cases to which it could apply.
These four levels of treatment of "labor law matters" are not judicial steps but depend on the political good-will of the Parties to examine labor law matters which fall into three categories according to the levels of treatment they can undergo. So far no submission has reached the third and fourth levels.

The NAALC Experience

During its first ten years of existence, the NAALC has been the basis for an important cooperative work program, the development of the research activities of the Secretariat and a series of submissions concerning the three countries.

- *Cooperative and research activities*
The Secretariat has undertaken a substantial program of research whose results have largely been published, providing new comparative information on labor markets and labor law in the three NAALC countries[7]. The Secretariat also has, at the request of the Council, organized a seminar series on incomes and productivity within the labor markets of NAFTA countries whose proceedings have been published; and provided support for a working group on Workers' compensation in North America. The publications and reports of the Secretariat constitute a valuable source of information on labor matters and a positive outcome of the NAALC[8].

---

[7] Such as: the study on North American labor markets published in 1997; the comparative labor law study published in 2000; the study on plant closings and labor rights" following Mexican NAO Submission 9501; the study on the practices in the North American apparel industry; as well as short reports on specific labor market topics such as the employment of women in North America published in 1998, or the rights of workers in non-conventional sectors published in 2003. See the NAALC site: www.naalc.org.
[8] As Graciela Bensusan outlines: "For the first time in many decades, the federal jurisdiction Mexican labor authorities have made data on union affiliation rates publicly available (...) the studies prepared by the National Secretariat of the NAALC (...) show the importance of cooperative activities oriented towards providing rigorous labor information that enables comparisons and identifies tendencies." Graciela Bensusan, "Integracion regional y cambio institutional: la reforma laboral en el norte del continente", in Graciela Bensusan (compiladora), *Estandares laborales despues del TLCAN*, Plaza y Valdés Editores, México, DF, 1999, p.189.

The majority of cooperative activities have been organized by the NAOs, others have been assigned to the Secretariat by the Council. The activities have addressed three broad areas: workplace safety and health; employment and training; and labor legislation and workers' rights. The early cooperative activities concentrated primarily on occupational safety and health, and ranged from public conferences on topics such as high-hazard industries, to smaller meetings of government officials, exchanges of technical information and training for inspectors[9]. The cooperative activities have contributed to a greater mutual understanding among labor officials who had no previous experience of working together as well as to the identification of "best practices" for some issues.

Some activities also have emerged from the submission and review process, such as the tri-national conference on "Protecting the Labor rights of Working Women" in 1999, the seminar on "Freedom of Association in Mexico" in 2000, or the public forum on "Promoting Dialogue among Migrant Agricultural Workers, Growers and Government Officials" in 2001[10]. These activities are representative of the aim of the treaty to deal with issues in a cooperative manner. This kind of end result, however, though it fosters public awareness of the issues, does not provide individual remedies and often leaves the plaintiffs disappointed. For example, it cannot order the reinstatement with back pay of women proved to have been fired for being pregnant in the Mexico's *maquiladora* industry, it cannot order the recognition of unions denied freedom of association, nor eliminate the health hazards and labor market discrimination suffered by Mexican migrant workers in the US. The NAALC establishes a mechanism for the political and public acknowledgment that there is a problem with the enforcement of a labor principle which in itself can be seen as an advance, but it does not establish an institutional mechanism such as the European Court of Justice with power to enforce labor law. This is one of the reasons why its critics say it has "no teeth".

- *Submissions or public communications*

---

[9] Between 1994 and 2000, out of a total 46 activities, 24 were related to occupational safety and health, 13 to employment and training, 8 to labor law and worker rights and one was a conference on "The Role of the New NAFTA Institutions. See U.S. Trade Deficit Review Commission, "The North American Agreement on Labor Cooperation – An Overview of the Institutions, Activity and Accomplishments", Washington, U.S. GPO, 2000, pp-7-10.

[10] See National Administrative Office, U.S. Department of Labor, « Cooperative Activities, 1994-2001 », www.dol.gov.

The NAALC offers only a minimal role to representatives of business or labor in its institutional structure on the advisory boards. However, it creates the possibility for direct public participation through the submission of public communications on labor law matters arising in a different country. Representatives of business or labor play no specific role in the treatment of the matters but, as any other group or even individual, can bring submissions to the NAOs on matters that correspond to the 11 Labor Principles.

Between 1994 and 2003, the three NAOs have received a total of 26 submissions, with 7 submissions being filed between 1994 and 1996; 13 between 1997 and 1998; 3 between 1999 and 2000; 2 in 2001, and 1 in 2003. Of the total 26 submissions filed, 15 were against Mexico, 9 were against the U.S., and 2 were against Canada. All the submissions in the first three years dealt with the first labor principle (freedom of association and protection of the right to organize). Overall, 21 submissions address the three first principles; 10 submissions address principles which can be submitted to ECEs, and 16 submissions address principles which can theoretically reach the Arbitral panel level (numbers exceed 26 because a submission can address multiple labor principles). No submission went further than the first two levels of treatment.

A short summary of two cases dealing with plant closures to avoid unionization and pregnancy testing in the *maquiladoras* will give an idea of the issues at stake. The most recent submissions have dealt mostly with health and safety ant the protection of migrant workers.

Mexico NAO Submission 9501 (Sprint) was filed in 1995 by the Mexican Telephone Workers Union (Sindicato de Telefonistas de la Republica Mexicana, STRM) and concerned the closure of a subsidiary of the Sprint corporation in San Francisco just before a union representation election was to take place. The Mexican NAO issued a public report and requested ministerial consultations. A Ministerial Consultations Agreement resulted in a public forum in San Francisco and a study by the Secretariat on the effects of plant closings on the principle of freedom of association. The study found that plant closures to avoid unionization or threats to that effect were widespread in the U.S. This case is interesting for several reasons. First, one of the arguments in favor of a labor side agreement was to reduce the potential US job loss due to plants moving to Mexico by ensuring that Mexico enforced its labor law and improved its labor standards but, in this case, it was a Mexican union which helped its US counterpart to defend its freedom of association. It resulted in the acknowledgment of the particular problem at Sprint and also in a study that showed US employers used "unfair" labor practices, to avoid unionization. But despite the public display of the problem and the international level of support for the application of the law, no remedy was provided. At the national level, US employers continue to threaten to close down or move to Mexico during unionization campaigns, in order to pressure the workers not to vote for the unions. Concerning the Sprint workers, the Communications Workers of America (CWA) also filed an unfair labor practice case with the National Labor Relations Board (NLRB). The NLRB ordered Sprint to reinstate the dismissed workers with back pay. But the company appealed the decision to the Federal Courts and, in 1997, the U.S. Court of Appeals for the District of Columbia reversed the NLRB, ruling that Sprint had closed the facility for financial reasons. The workers were not reinstated and the union was not recognized. Although the NAALC procedure acknowledged the problem and led to a Ministerial Agreement, a public forum and a study, and although the NLRB, the national institution in charge of the administration of labor legislation, ruled against the company, in the end the workers and the union lost their case before the US Court of Appeals. Thus, despite the political willingness to acknowledge the problem with freedom of association in the United States, labor law enforcement in that matter still leaves plenty of room for improvement.

U.S. NAO Submission N°9701 (Gender) was filed in 1997 by Human Rights Watch, the International Labor Rights Fund, and the National Association of Democratic Lawyers of Mexico. The submission raised issues of gender-based discrimination in the Mexican *maquiladora* industry, where companies, such as General Motors, Zenith, Siemens, Thompson, Samsung, Sanyo and other subsidiaries of multinationals, tested female job applicants for pregnancy and denied employment, and even went as far as discharging, pregnant employees in order to avoid paying maternity benefits. The U.S. NAO accepted the submission for review, conducted a public hearing and issued a report confirming widespread pregnancy testing and recommending ministerial level consultations. A Ministerial Consultations Implementation Agreement was signed in October 1998 and the parties agreed to coordinate a conference and to conduct outreach sessions to educate workers close to the U.S.-Mexico border. The Secretariat is compiling a public report on the issues raised at the conference and the outreach sessions. Many of the U.S. firms announced they would stop the practice although according to Human Rights Watch they haven't quite done so. However, as Lance Compa points out, "the NAALC complaint made an international affair of what had been a decades-long, hidden, entrenched, accepted practice in Mexico's burgeoning maquiladora sector. It set in motion a dynamic for changing the practice."[11]

Public communications generate public attention and media coverage as well as debate over the issues and cross-border labor solidarity. But this positive aspect has its limits. The NAALC does not create a mechanism for individuals to pursue private rights and seek individual remedies. Individual remedies must be found at the national level. In fact, in some cases, after international attention was drawn to a labor principle by a NAALC submission and hearing, the national institutions, labor boards or others, have found remedies for the situation, such as when Han Young was fined by the Mexican government for health and safety violations[12], or when the province of Quebec reached an agreement with the plaintiffs in order to avoid a hearings on a case concerning a McDonald's restaurant[13]. In other cases, however, despite Ministerial consultations concluding to the repetition of the same problems, particularly, for example, the enforcement of Mexican laws dealing with the first three labor principles, no real change seems to have taken place which, as Pierre Verge notes, leads to a certain disillusion as to NAALC's efficiency concerning these labor issues[14].

- A limited social dimension

The procedures of the NAALC are government to government and relate strictly to the terms of the Agreement. What is under international

[11] Lance Compa, "Free Trade, Fair Trade, and the Battle for Labor Rights" in Lowell Turner, Harry Katz, and Richard Hurd, *Rekindling the Movement: Labor's Quest for Relevance in the Twenty-First Century*, ILR Press, Ithaca, 2001, p.326.

[12] *U.S. NAO Submission N°9702 (Han Young)* was filed in October 1997 by a coalition of Mexican, U.S. and Canadian unions and NGOs. It raised freedom of association issues as well as health and safety issues and was the first NAALC case susceptible to arbitration and possible fines. After a public hearing in San Diego on the health and safety conditions at Han Young (a supplier of Hyundai Motors Corp.), the Mexican government gave the company the largest fine for safety violations in Mexican history.

[13] *U.S. NAO Submission N°9803 (McDonald's)* was filed in October 1998 by the International Brotherhood of Teamsters, Teamsters Canada, the Quebec Federation of Labor, Teamsters Local 973 (Montreal) and the International Labor Rights Fund. It raised different issues and particularly that of an anti-union motivated plant closing during efforts to organize employees of a McDonald's restaurant in Quebec (Saint-Hubert). The labor organizations dropped the submission after reaching an agreement with the government of Quebec to have the issues of sudden and anti-union motivated plant-closings studied at the provincial council in the context of an overall review of the Quebec Labor Code.

[14] Pierre Verge, *Présentation Analytique de l'Accord Nord-Américain de Coopération dans le Domaine du Travail* (ANACT), BIT, Bureau Régional pour L'Amérique Latine et les Caraibes, Lima, 2002, p.42.

consideration is the national administration of labor law. Nevertheless, as Lance Compa[15] outlines, the significance of accepting external scrutiny into labor law enforcement should not be underestimated, especially in a context where defenders of labor rights in both Canada and Mexico consider their labor laws as more protective and fear that harmonization might lead to the deregulation of industrial relations as the United States dominates the economic relation between the three countries.

However, for the groups, namely labor and NGOs, who invest considerable time and resources in the public communications, the results were often deceiving contributing to the perception of NAALC as being "toothless". Different resolutions and cooperative activities might with time contribute to the evolution of labor law, but the procedure is basically dependent on the political willingness of the parties to solve the problem. As Compa and Turner point out: "the governments shrank from any real enforcement in these cases. Ministerial consultations led to conferences and research reports, but no discernible improvement in labor law enforcement."[16]

The experience of the NAALC has required cooperation and network building across North America among unions, NGOs, lawyers, labor official, researchers and other groups involved in its activities. Because submissions about labor principles in one country must be filed in a different country, the unions, NGOs or lawyers that file them must have links with their counterparts in the other country. New forms of cross-border solidarity and cooperation among unions and NGOs have thus emerged in the three countries[17] not only to file complaints and support them through collective action but also to promote exchanges at the workplace level[18]. While these efforts are noteworthy, the role of the social partners in the institutional framework of the NAALC is very limited: they

---

15 Lance Compa, "El ACLAN: un recuento de tres anos", in Graciela Bensusan (compiladora), *Estandares laborales despues del TLCAN*, Plaza y Valdés Editores, México, DF, 1999, p.75.

16 Lance Compa and Lowell Turner, "Paths to Global Social Regulation – What Can Americans Learn from the European Union?", in Reiner Hoffmann, Otto Jacobi, Berndt Keller, Manfred Weiss (eds.), *European Integration as a Social Experiment in a Globalized World*, Hans-Böckler-Stiftung, Düsseldorf, 2003, p.153.

17 See Graciela Bensusan, op.cit., and Lance Compa, "NAFTA's Labor Side Agreement and International Labor Solidarity", in Peter Waterman and Jane Wills, eds., *Place, Space and the New Labour Internationalisms*, Oxford, Blackwell Publishers, 1994.

18 These efforts have had the support of the ORIT, the IMF, the Friedrich Ebert Stiftung, the AFL-CIO Solidarity Center, the RMALC (Red Mexicana de Accion Frente al Libre Comercio), the IRNAA (International Research Network on Autowork in the Americas) and many other groups and individual unions.

file submissions and sit on advisory boards (when and if these boards meet). The NAALC does not provide for anything approaching social partner recognition as representative bodies at the transnational or sector levels, let alone a possible evolution towards collective bargaining at the North American regional level. The social dimension of North American economic integration remains therefore quite thin or embryonic especially when compared with what exists in the European Union.

The European Union

European integration begun during the 1950s and is still an on-going process. Its most important achievement is the European Economic Community created by the Treaties of Rome in 1957. A series of amending treaties (Single European Act 1985, Treaties of Maastricht 1993, Amsterdam 1999 and Nice 2000) have introduced substantial and nominal changes from which the European Union (EU) emerged.
The original driving force behind the process of European integration was economic. According to the functionalist approach that guided its inception, political and social integration would emerge as spill-over effects. To this day, the economic dimension is still far ahead of the social and political ones. Yet, since the 1970s, a framework of transnational social regulation has gradually been implemented[19].

[19] For a detailed overview cf. the two reports by the Directorate-General for Employment and Social Affairs of the European Commission, *Industrial Relations in Europe*, Luxembourg (Office for Official Publications of the European Communities) 2000 and 2002. There are two annual update reviews of collective bargaining and social legislation. The first is established by the European Foundation for the Improvement of Living and Working Conditions, based on data provided by the European Industrial Relations Observatory EIRO (www.eiro.eurofound.eu.int). The latest edition has been published jointly with the Directorate-General for Employment and Social Affairs of the European Commission under the title *Industrial Relations Developments in Europe 2002*, Luxembourg (Office for Official Publications of the European Communities) 2003. The second is the annual report by the European Social Observatory in Brussels (www.ose.be.), established upon request by the European Trade Union Institute (ETUI) and the ETUC, with the support of the the SALTSA program of the Swedish National Institute for Working Life ant the Swedish Trade Unions. Cf.: Christophe Degryse and Philippe Pochet, *Social Developments in the European Union 2002, Fourth Annual Report*, (Brussels (ETUI) 2003.

The Procedures of Transnational Social Regulation

- Legislation and social policies

Generally speaking, social regulation can take the form of legislation, government policies or collective bargaining. At the European level, it mainly takes the form of intergovernmental legislation. It is prepared by a supranational body, the European Commission, and adopted by the Council of Ministers. According to the Treaties, the Commission, the executive branch of the European institutions, has the monopoly of legislative initiative. In case of interpretation disputes, the European Commission as well as the member states, but also citizens, groups or companies can appeal to the European Court as the highest judicial body of the EU. Member states can be fined for failure to comply with the obligations resulting from the Treaties and European law.

The directive is the main form of social legislation in Europe. Directives do not apply directly as national law, but oblige the member states to conform their legislation to the newly created European standards. About a hundred directives have been adopted on social matters since the 1960s, most of them during the 1990s. Initially, a unanimous vote was required for the adoption of a social directive by the Council of Ministers. Since the Single European Act of 1986, however, directives concerning health and safety can be adopted by a "qualified majority". Majority voting has been further extended since the Maastricht treaty of 1991. But, upon the request of the British government, three issues have been excluded from European legislation. Social matters thus fall into three categories according to the type of vote they require in order to be adopted.

1. Issues that require a majority vote:

- health and safety,
- working conditions,
- information and consultation,
- gender equality,
- social integration.

2. Issues that require unanimity:

- financial contributions for employment creation,
- social protection,
- workers' representation and co-determination,
- the employment conditions of non-EU immigrants.

3. Issues that are definitely excluded from European legislation:
- pay,
- the right of association,
- the rights of strike and lockout.

The European Economic and Social Committee, where national social partners and organizations are represented, has a consultative role in the legislation process, as does the European Parliament. The Maastricht and Amsterdam Treaties have reinforced the role of the European Parliament in the legislative process. It now has a "co-decision" power about social matters covered by the majority vote. This means that it can amend what the Commission proposes and eventually veto a decision by the Council of Ministers which would not include these amendments.
In 1989, an attempt was made by 11 out of 12 member states to proclaim a European "Charter of Fundamental Social Rights"[20]. The Charter had numerous shortcomings, particularly that of being a mere declaration of principles and thus not enforceable. In order to compensate for the weakness of the 1989 Charter, the European Commission decided that same year to translate it into a "Social action program" which intended to implement the proclaimed rights by appropriate legislation. A series of directives have been adopted on the basis of this action program. Not all of these directives were "hard" regulations with detailed uniform rules. For instance, the most important of them, the directive on the European works council of 1994, simply contains an obligation for multinational companies to accept negotiations about the institutionalization of an information and consultation procedure. If no agreement is reached, however, a works council must be set up that respects a set of minimum standards.
Since the mid 1990s, whereas the competence of the European Union in social matters has been considerably enlarged by the treaties, the number of social legislation proposals by the European Commission has paradoxically been reduced. In its new social action program 2001-2005, the Commission announces only a few legislative initiatives[21]. This is apparently the result of a change in the general political climate, several national governments

[20] The conservative government of the United Kingdom had refused to sign this Charter but, in 1991, the New Labour government agreed to do it. A reference to the Charter was thus integrated into the Amsterdam Treaty (in the preamble and art. 136), alongside with a reference to the earlier European Social Charter adopted in 1961 by the members of the Council of Europe.
[21] "Agenda for Social Policy", COM(2000)379 final.

and employers organization demanding less central regulation and more decentralization and experimentation.

Following the inclusion of a chapter on employment into the Amsterdam Treaty in 1997, at the Lisbon summit of 2000, a "European employment strategy" was adopted and a new form of intergovernmental social regulation, called the "open method of co-ordination", was introduced to implement it. The "open method of co-ordination" fosters voluntary co-ordination of action by the governments through the definition of common objectives and a system of benchmarking, monitoring and common evaluation of national performances and policies[22].

At the Nice summit, in December 2000, the European governments adopted an EU "Charter of Fundamental Rights" which contains a series of individual and collective social rights, including collective bargaining and industrial action. The status of this Charter is still unsettled. It is intended to be integrated into the future European Constitution[23].

- *Collective bargaining*

Social regulation can be implemented at the European level not only through intergovernmental legislation and co-ordination, but also through collective bargaining. This possibility has emerged only recently and is still undergoing a difficult learning process[24]. The idea was first mentioned in the Single European Act of 1986 (art. 118 B) which invited the European commission to develop the "dialogue" between the "European social partners" as a basis for possible European-wide collective bargaining. This article gave a legal foundation to the "European Social Dialogue of Val Duchesse" which had been initiated in 1985 by the European Commission under the presidency of Jacques Delors. This dialogue produced a number of "joint opinions", between the European Trade Union Confederation (ETUC) and two employers' organizations: the Union of Industrial and

---

[22] Cf. Caroline de la Porte and Philippe Pochet (eds.), *Building Social Europe Through the Open Method of Coordination*, Brussels (P.I.E.-Peter Lang) 2002.

[23] For its legal consequences cf. Brian Percussion, European Labor Law and the EU Charter of Fundamental Rights, Brussels (European Trade Union Institute) 2002; Isabelle Schulman and Stefan Clauwaert, "The EU Charter of Fundamental Rights in case laws of the Courts of the European Union: towards recognition of the constitutional value of the EU Charter", in: Emilio Gabaglio and Reiner Hoffmann (eds.) *European Trade Union Yearbook 2002*, Brussels (European Trade Union Institute) 2003.

[24] For an overview, cf. Jürgen Hoffmann et al. (eds.), *The Europeanisation of Industrial Relations in a Global Perspective: A literature review*, Dublin (European Foundation for the Improvement of Living and Working Conditions) 2002. For a critical appraisal by a labor lax specialist of cf. Antonio Lo Faro, *Regulating Social Europe, Reality and Myth of Collective Bargaining in the EC Legal Order*, Oxford-Portland, Oregon (Hart) 2000.

Employers' Confederations of Europe (UNICE) and the European Centre of Public Enterprises (CEEP). These agreements were of little legal relevance, because the UNICE strongly opposed the transformation of this kind of dialogue into collective bargaining. The negotiation of the Treaty of Maastricht in 1991-92, however, brought about a decisive break-through in this matter. A "Social Protocol", which initially was supposed to constitute the "social chapter" of this treaty, was finally adopted by 11 out of 12 governments (again without the UK). It is worth noting that this Social Protocol reproduced the text of a collective agreement signed 31 October 1991 between the ETUC, the UNICE and the CEEP. In 1997, after the removal of the British opting out, this Social Protocol was integrated into the Amsterdam Treaty, of which it constitutes the social chapter, so that it now has a binding character for all member states.

Formally, art. 138 of the social chapter has introduced a corporatist element into the social legislation procedure, by assigning a public status and a pre-emptive legislative power to the European social partners. The European Commission now has the obligation to consult them prior to any initiative on social legislation. If the Commission formulates a proposal for a directive, the European social partners can decide to deal with the matter through collective bargaining. In case they reach a negotiated agreement, the Council of Ministers must extend this agreement as the basis for European legislation. Whether the Council is allowed to amend the agreement at the margin or not, is still matter of controversy among experts.

In fact, legislation through collective bargaining under art. 138 has been very limited. The main reason for this is the attitude of some employers organizations which are, notwithstanding the October 1992 agreement, still opposed to collective bargaining on controversial subjects such as information-consultation. Their refusal has restricted European social dialogue to negotiations on "soft" subjects. At the European level, the trade unions have not developed a bargaining power sufficient to force the employers to negotiate on controversial subjects. They strongly depended on the initiatives by the European Commission. Transnational industrial action is still limited to rather symbolic forms as demonstrations or one-hour strikes. As a consequence, ten years after the Maastricht protocol, only four agreements have been signed at the cross-industry level: parental leave (1995), part-time work (1997), fixed-term work (1999), and tele-work (2002). This last agreement was the first one to be negotiated on an autonomous basis (without prior proposal of the European Commission). Under pressure from the European Commission, who wanted to be relieved from the burden of initiative taking, the social partners have agreed in November 2002 on a work program for autonomous negotiations in 2003-2005. Most of the subjects are to be treated by methods such as the organization of common seminars, the exchange of good practices, etc. As far as real negotiations are concerned, they have begun with some difficulty on the subject of restructuring.

At the industry or sector level, there are now a number of agreements, most of them on "soft" subjects[25]. They mostly occur in sectors, where there are common European policies (agriculture, transportation etc.). In these sectors, the representation of unions and employers had been institutionalized through “sectoral consultative committees”. These have recently been transformed into "sectoral social dialogue committees", the main difference being that the national organizations have been replaced by the European federations of unions and employers. At the sector level, unions are better organized than employers. In some important industrial sectors like the metal or the chemical industries, the employers have up to now refused to set up appropriate organizations, which explains the absence of collective bargaining and agreements in these sectors.

At the company level, there is a potential actor for collective bargaining: the European Works Council (EWC). Out of more than 1800 companies falling under the scope of the EWC directive (companies employing more than 1000 workers with over 150 in more than two member states), more than 600 have established an EWC. They are amongst the largest companies and employ 11 million workers out of 17 million workers virtually concerned[26]. The European Directive neither fosters nor precludes an evolution from consultation to collective bargaining. Up to now, in most companies, management was opposed to such an evolution. Nevertheless, a dozen agreement have been signed by EWCs. Most of them are framework agreements on procedural issues but, more recently, a couple of agreements with binding substantial rules have been signed concerning industrial restructuring in European subsidiaries of US automobile manufacturers[27]. The legal status of such agreements is still uncertain.

---

[25] Cf. the review by the Directorate-General for Employment and Social Affairs of the European Commission, *The Sectoral Social Dialogue in Europe*, Luxembourg (Office for Official Publications of the European Communities) 2003.

[26] Peter Kerckhofs, *European Workscouncils. Facts and Figures*, Brussels (European Trade Union Institute) 2002.

[27] Cf. Udo Rehfeldt, "European Works Councils and International Restructuring: A Perspective for European Collective Bargaining", in Elsie Charon and Paul Stuart (eds.), *Work and Employment. Relations in the Automobile Industry, London*, Palgrave MacMillan, 2003.

The Social Partners

The European social partners have now gained a high degree of recognition, as the legislator has assigned them a central role in social regulation. The treaties do not define who is a "European social partner" and therefore empowered to participate in the consultation and negotiation process. In two communications in 1993 and 1998[28], the European Commission has defined a series of criteria for the representativeness of unions and employers' organizations and their rights to be consulted under the terms of art. 138.

Representative organizations should:

- be organized at the European level;
- consist of national organizations that are a "recognised part of Member States' social partner structures", with the capacity to negotiate agreements;
- be representative in all Member States ("as far as possible");
- "have adequate structures to ensure their effective participation in the consultation process".

In order to check these criteria, the Commission has asked an independent expert network to elaborate a study on the representativeness of the different European union and employers organizations[29]. On the basis of this study, the Commission has established a list of organizations that meet the criteria for representativeness, which is annexed to the communication of 1998. As far as the cross-industry level is concerned, three organizations are considered as legitimate to participate in the consultation process: the ETUC on the union side, the UNICE and the CEEP on the employers' side, precisely those who had been invited to participate in the European social dialogue of Val Duchesse in 1985. All three organizations have already a long experience in lobbying and informal consultation in the European legislation process. UNICE has been created in the beginning of the European Community in 1958, the CEEP in 1961. The ETUC has officially been created only 1973, but has emerged out of other trade union organizations that existed at the European level since 1950[30].

---

[28] COM(93)600 final and COM(98)322 final.

[29] The study, co-ordinated by the Institute of Labour of the Catholic University of Louvain, is regularly updated (www.trav.ucl.ac.be).

[30] In this article, we had to leave out the issue of the development of a common strategy by the ETUC. For a first overview cf. Jon Erik Dolvik, *Redrawing Boundaries of solidarity? ETUC, Social Dialogue and the Europeanisation of Trade Unions in the 1990s*, Oslo

The history of organized European unionism begun in 1950, when the International Confederation of Free Trade Unions (ICFTU) created a European regional organization. In 1952, a secretariat for the European Coal and Steel Community was set up, and in 1958 the same type of secretariat was established for the European Economic Community. In 1969, it became the European Confederation of Free Trade Unions, which transformed itself into the ETUC in 1973, at the occasion of the first enlargement of the EC. The ETUC later admitted trade unions with other ideological and religious tendencies and from countries outside the European Community (but which were supposed to later integrate the EC). In 1974, it admitted unions affiliated the World Confederation of Labour (the former International Federation of Christian Trade Unions), as well as to the first communist trade union, the Italian CGIL. The integration of unions with communist tendencies was more difficult than that of those with Christian tendencies: the Spanish CCOO were admitted only in 1990, the Portuguese CGTP in 1995 and the French CGT as late as 1999. From 1996 on, the ETUC has also progressively integrated the new independent unions created in the Eastern European countries. Today, the main national union confederations in Europe are members of the ETUC.

At the cross-industry level, other social partner organizations have made claims to participate in the European Social Dialogue, namely, on the employers' side, the European Association of Craft and Small and Medium-sized Enterprises (UEAPME) and, on the union side, the European Confederation of Executives and Managerial Staff (CEC). Their claims have not been granted by the European Commission. In 1999, the CEC and the ETUC-linked Council of European Professional and Managerial Staff (EUROCADRES) established a "liaison committee", which allows the CEC to participate in cross-industry negotiations within the delegation of

---

(Arena) 1997, and an abridged version under the title "An emerging island?", Brussels (ETUI) 1999. For a more critical appraisal of the history of the ETUC, cf. Corinne Gobin, *L'Europe syndicale. Entre désir et réalité*, Brussels (Labor) 1997; id., "La difficile construction d'un syndicalisme transnational: la Confédération européenne des syndicats", in: Tania Régin and Serge Wolikow (eds.), *Les Syndicalismes en Europe. A l'épreuve de l'international*, Paris (Syllepse) 2002. We also had to leave out the issue of the relationship between the strategies of the ETUC, its industry federations and their national member organizations. For a first overview, cf. Jacques Freyssinet et al.: Les acteurs sociaux nationaux face à la construction européenne, *Chronique International de l'IRES*, special issue, Noisy-le-Grand October 1998.

the ETUC. The same type of arrangement was established to allow the UEAPME to be represented within the UNICE delegation[31].
The social partners recognized as representative organizations at the European level, and particularly the ETUC, have also tried to reinforce their intrinsic legitimacy by getting an explicit mandate from their member organizations in order to bargain at the European level and they have established internal mechanisms to validate the agreements. The ETUC, for instance, requires a qualified majority vote in order to adopt a European agreement.

Comparative analysis and conclusion

After having presented the institutional forms of social regulation in the two regions of economic integration, we can now outline their main differences.

1. NAFTA has no common labor or social norms. The objective of the NAALC is to promote 11 basic labor principles and ensure the enforcement of national labor laws. The European Union, on the other hand, not only has several charters of Social rights but also a social legislation that sets common minimal labor norms.
2. Social regulation is very dimly institutionalized by the NAALC. It is limited to a system of mutual monitoring (observation) with complaint reviews. The system is strictly intergovernmental and based upon the respect of national sovereignty. The EU has a complex legislative system in which the European Commission plays an important role of initiative and monitoring and which has broadened the role of the European Parliament and the possibility of a majority vote of the Council of Ministers to a wide range of labor or social issues.
3. Labor unions have a very weak role in NAFTA's social regulation. They are not represented in NAALC's Secretariat, the transnational institution set up by the labor side agreement; they are only represented in the non compulsory national institutions, the national advisory committees. They also have the possibility to file complaints or submissions, but that's a possibility they share with other groups and individual citizens. In the EU, there is a mechanism to recognize and

[31] The UEAPME has even made an appeal to the European Court of Justice to invalidate the directive on parental leave based upon the social partner agreement of 1995, on the grounds that the UEAPME had not been allowed to participate in the negotiation. The First Instance Court has rejected this appeal.

ensure the representativeness of the "social partners" and recognized labor unions play an official and important role in the supranational institutions: not only are they necessarily consulted during the legislative process on matters dealing with labor, but they also have the possibility to negotiate collective bargaining agreements that will be imposed upon the member states.

4. In North America, unions act mainly through cross-border cooperation and solidarity when filing submissions and following up the complaint mechanisms. In the EU, national unions have transferred a part of their sovereignty to the ETUC. The ETUC and its sector federations do more than just lobbying in Brussels, they have become strategic actors that coordinate collective bargaining and even industrial action.

Considering these four points, the EU is far ahead of NAFTA in labor or social regulation matters. This assessment, however, needs to be balanced by taking into account the national levels in each of the regions of economic integration. When the comparison at the transnational level is supplemented by the national configurations, the picture becomes more ambiguous concerning the same four points.

1. The European Charters of social rights remain for the moment a mere declaration. It does not entail directly enforceable rights. This can change, however, if the Nice Charter is integrated into the European Constitution. Nevertheless, so far, despite the large number of social directives enacted, the workers' level of protection for several issues remains very unequal from one country to the next. The continuous social improvement the EU treaties promise has not yet come about. On the contrary, attempts at eroding or reducing worker rights have even taken place in some member states.
2. The adoption of new common social rules has slowed down in the EU despite the possibility of majority vote. One can even fear that this trend might continue after the enlargement to Eastern Europe. Of course, this does not result from a particular flaw in the European institutions but rather from the evolution of political majorities in the member states towards neoliberal governments bent on social deregulation.
3. The strong role of labor unions in the EU institutional framework did not prevent the adoption of neoliberal economic and monetary policies and transnational collective bargaining has made little progress. Here again, one should not necessarily blame European institutions since labor union have the same type of difficulties opposing the same type of

policies at the national level. The current political cycle does not favor unions, whose power relations are further weakened by the economic situation and the continuous high level of unemployment, both at the national and European levels.

4. Despite considerable progress in terms of organization, the labor movement remains relatively weak at the European level when compared to the national level. One of the shortcomings of European unionism is its distance from local and national union life and the related danger of political and financial dependency on the European Commission. This danger can only be avoided if the national organizations decide to intensify transnational communications and debates and increase the resources they grant the European organization. There have been some promising efforts but, overall, European unionism has yet to prove a real capacity to swing the pendulum of power in its direction.

Our comparative analysis of the social dimensions of NAFTA and the EU is closely akin to that of Lance Compa and Lowell Turner. For these two authors, there is room for mutual learning between Europe and North America. While labor unions in the US strongly oppose a Free Trade Agreement of the Americas (FTAA), Compa and Turner recommend "preserving and strengthening positive elements of the NAALC while overcoming its main flaws."[32]. Drawing lessons from the NAALC, the EU, and Mercosur, they list a series of elements of a social dimension for future hemispheric integration in America. For them, such a progress would depend on the revitalization, coalition building and political influence of the unions. Revitalization, coalition building and political influence are also valid recommendations to overcome some of the weaknesses of the European labor movement despite its institutional advantages. Of course, such recommendations are easier to make than to put into practice and Compa and Turner might be a bit too optimistic as to their possible results in North America. Our provisional conclusion will thus be that in a difficult period for unionism, the good usage of institutional mechanisms, at the national and transnational level, is an important element in order to avoid a larger deterioration of the power relations of labor unions. From this perspective European unionism still benefits from a comparatively more comfortable situation than North American unionism.

[32] Lance Compa and Lowell Turner, "Paths to Global Social Regulation – What Can Americans Learn from the European Union?", in Reiner Hoffmann, Otto Jacobi, Berndt Keller, Manfred Weiss (eds.), *European Integration as a Social Experiment in a Globalized World*, Hans-Böckler-Stiftung, Düsseldorf, 2003, p.156.

Which European Social Model? A Challenged Balance between Regulation and Deregulation[1]

ALAIN CHOURAQUI, KEVIN P O'KELLY

Introduction

The vision of Jacques Delors in building a social dimension into the project for a single, common, market for goods and services leaves open the question as to whether the social dimension is a distinct entity, in its own right, a support mechanism for the free market aspects of the European adventure, or are both the social and economic objectives complementary and mutually inclusive?

Furthermore, there is the growing challenge to the European social model from the creeping influence of the Anglo-American business culture which places an emphasis on maximising shareholder returns to the detriment of social values and rights at work, the increased use of workplace flexibilities and minimising the importance of the quality of working life.

It is clear from the evolution of social policy over the past two decades that the political imperative of finding agreement has resulted, on many occasions, in compromise, in reaching the lowest common denominator between the, very often, conflicting demands of the social partners, on the one hand, and the extent to which governments are politically prepared to go, on the other. Consequently, it might be argued that the European Social Model still is, at present, the sum total of the national social systems and priorities of the Member States and is moving towards a convergence. A dynamic approach is now needed to better understand the on-going evolution of this emerging Model.

During the 1990s European Social Policy changed significantly with employment becoming a policy priority. The debate on how to achieve

[1] An introduction to the aix-en-provence european seminar held by the European Foundation and the LEST, in partnership with Le Monde, (10/11 Sept, 2001)

higher levels of employment within the EU economy focuses on what the degree of balance should be between the acquired rights of workers and the competitiveness of the enterprise. This is evident in the contrasting arguments for greater workplace flexibility, on the one hand and the proponents of regulating the employment relationship, on the other.

A consequence of this change has been the shift in emphasis, within the EU, from legislation and regulation, to finding solutions through consensus and 'joint-regulation', on issues that are considered to impact on the efficient operation of the European labour market. These changes are influencing the relationship between the social partners and between them and the EU institutions. Much of this change in approach is in response to the pressure to 'de-regulate' the labour market, by encouraging greater flexibility in the organisation of work and employment contracts, which is emerging at a national level in the Member States, and, through the implementation of the European Employment Strategy, at EU level.

Part of this shift to this 'soft policy' is to be found in the approach to employment in the Amsterdam Treaty where the emphasis is on co-operation between Member States and on 'peer pressure' to follow active employment policies at national level. The Employment Strategy is implemented through a series of National Action Plans (NAPs) submitted through the European Commission for consideration and scrutiny by the governments of the other Member States. There is no mechanism for compulsion, apart from the treaty obligation, if a Member State does not deem it necessary to co-operate.

The promotion of better quality employment is also a key transversal theme of the European Foundation's Four-year Rolling Programme, 2001 to 2004[2].

---

[2] This paper was elaborated within a joint research project of the European Foundation (Dublin) and the Laboratoire d'Economie et de Sociologie du Travail (CNRS/Universities, Aix-en-Provence) on "An evaluation of the European Social Model". A European Conference on this topic will be held in Aix-en-Provence (10th/11th September 2001)

Methodology

Three methodological remarks can be made about this paper. First, for the purpose of the paper we consider that employment policy is part of European Social Policy, which is itself part of the European Social Model. What is this Model? It covers a wide range of both living and working issues, such as social protection, health, education and environmental issues, public services, as well as all aspects of employment rights, social dialogue, direct participation, training and equal opportunities/non-discrimination issues. Central to the European Social Model is the achievement of social inclusion in all aspects of life and this can be realised by establishing a culture of partnership between governments, voluntary organisations in the civil society and NGOs, social partners, citizens and workers.

Second, our hypothesis is that the formal rules and policies are producing social effects, but they are, at the same time, produced by social factors. This is not only related to the balance of power, but it includes cultural and ideological values which historically are the common features of European society. In order to understand the European Social Model better, it should not be seen only as a formal or political model, it includes societal aspects also, which often are its main, but neglected, dimensions. For example, our assumption is that European society has tried to keep a balance between two significant and complementary ideas: "Entre le pauvre et le riche, entre le faible et le fort, c'est la liberté qui opprime et c'est la loi qui libère" (Lacordaire); and "Trop de droit tue le droit"(legal aphorism). This approach leads us to say that the European Social Model might be considered as based on a wider European Societal Model.

Third, in order to contribute to a present debate about the main trends of and challenges to the European Social Model, the purpose of this paper is to focus on issues beyond the normal rhetoric and formal statements about the detailed contents of this Model. The paper, therefore, will be placed within a short historical overview of how the European Social Model developed. The common view of what constitutes the European Social Model is challenged with a few theoretical remarks and, in that way, the paper focuses on the evolution towards a European industrial relations system, which can be seen as the institutional backbone of the model.

Towards a Multi-Level European Social Model of Regulated Autonomy?

The economic crisis of the 1970s and early 1980s is considered to have produced, or reinforced, in most industrial countries, a process of deregulation designed to bring about a more flexible economic and social environment, as well as greater flexibility in the industrial relations systems and this has been the focus of social unrest and academic debate. However, the regulatory process has, in fact, been more diverse, mixing forms of regulation, of deregulation and of what might be called 're-regulation'.

This complex situation in the various national industrial relations systems converge into a multi-level European Social Model of 'regulated autonomy' which would also include regulation at the EU-level. This seems to be a possible third way, falling somewhere between regulation and deregulation. This can be illustrated by the main steps in the building of the Model.

Social Dialogue and Social Rights

The European Communities were originally founded as an economic and market union. Social and political cohesion, where these existed, were subjected to and intended to support the reduction and eventual elimination of trading barriers and the introduction of a 'level playing field' for business, so that it could achieve the objective of economic growth, greater prosperity and higher standards of living for European citizens.

Social policy in general and employment policies, in particular, moved centre stage through the determination of Jacques Delors, during his presidency of the European Commission (1985-94). In the first weeks of his presidency, in January, 1985, he initiated a process of meetings, or 'social dialogue', between the European employers organisation, UNICE, its public sector equivalent, CEEP, and the European trade unions, ETUC, to discuss joint action, to negotiate and to assist the Commission in the development of social policy. These discussions resulted in a number of Joint Opinions on, for example, the economic situation of the European Communities, on training, motivation, information and consultation of employees and on the freedom of association and collective bargaining. The Single European Act, which was agreed by the Member States in 1987, formally recognised this role for the social partners.

Parallel to this social dialogue, the Commission also followed the legislative approach. A Charter of the Fundamental Social Rights of

Workers was published and was agreed by eleven heads of governments at their meeting in Strasbourg, December, 1989, (the UK Government did not sign up to what became known as the Social Charter). The Social Charter was drafted by the Economic and Social Committee and set out a number of basic social values, such as democracy and individual rights; the right to free collective bargaining; the importance of the market economy; equality of opportunity for all; and social welfare and solidarity. It also stated, for the first time, that economic and social progress must go hand-in-hand[3]. The action programme for the implementation of the Social Charter set out the need for some forty-seven measures covering both health and safety and labour law issues, such as working time, maternity leave and information and consultation. Delors wanted agreement on this document, as he was concerned that the European trade union movement might not continue to support the project to achieve an open and single market by 1992.[4] He saw these measures as justified for two reasons, first to prevent social dumping in a single market (the movement of jobs to regions which have a less restrictive, more flexible workplace regime) and second as an expression of common European social democratic values, based on a common cultural history, from Antiquity to modern revolutions and reforms:

> *Europeans have always had a kind of balance between the individual and society. That goes back to the base of their civilization, to Christianity, Roman law, to the Greek civitas and, in the more recent period, to the influence of social democracy.*[5]

This increased emphasis on social rights was the basis for much dissention between the Commission, the Socialist dominated European Parliament and the trade unions, on the one hand, and UNICE and the Council of Ministers, in particular the UK Government, on the other. This disagreement on the direction of social policy came to a head in 1992, when there was an attempt to formalise the social dialogue process as a treaty obligation in the Treaty on European Union (the Maastricht Treaty).

---

[3] *Charter on Fundamental Social Rights for Workers*

[4] *Delors: Inside the house that Jacques built* by Charles Grant, Nicholas Brealey Publishing (London), 1994, page 84.

[5] Ibid. page 87

The Commission wanted to extend qualified majority voting to directives on workplace issues. The proposed Social Chapter would also extend European Community competence to
equal opportunities, information and consultation of workers and working conditions. It also proposed that, if employers and employee representatives reached agreements on an issue, then this would be transposed into European-wide legislation. However, faced with the implacable opposition of the UK Prime Minister, John Major, even to a watered-down Social Chapter, the other eleven heads of governments agreed a protocol to the treaty which allowed them to 'opt-in' to an agreement on social policy.
With the adoption of the Maastricht Treaty, the eleven Member States, through the Agreement attached to the Social Protocol, affirmed

> *their objectives of promoting of employment, improving living and working conditions, proper social protection, dialogue between management and labour, the development of human resources with a view to lasting high employment and the combating of exclusion.* [6]

The Agreement also formally allowed for the social partners to be more involved in EU-level decision-making and it set up procedures for the negotiations and adoption of legislation, while recognising the need to avoid imposing any impediment on job creation or the development of small and medium sized enterprises.

"Social Policy at the Heart of the Union"

Following the adoption of the Maastricht Treaty, there were two further developments which contributed to the evolution of the European Social Model. First, the Commission published a white paper on Growth, Competitiveness, Employment: The Challenges and Way Forward into the 21st Century. This marked a turning point in the development of joint action by the Member States in addressing the problem of employment as a central issue in the wider economic strategy. It raised a number of key issues, such as the central role of competitiveness and growth in job creation and the need for labour market policies to be re-oriented to support

---

[6] Article 1 of the Agreement on Social Policy, Treaty on European Union, Office for Official Publications of the European Communities, (Luxembourg), 1992, ISBN 92-824-0959-7

this position through 'a remodelled, rational and simplified system of regulation and incentives'. [7]

Second, the Commission published a further white paper, European Social Policy – A way forward for the Union[8], after extensive consultation on a discussion (green) paper[9] during 1993-94. The paper, making the point that European social policy was at a watershed, sought to point the direction of social policy developments in the second half of the 1990s, to set out how the EU should build a link between the existing body a legislation and rights, acquis, and an agenda for the future, ensuring that social policy 'is put where it belongs, at the heart of the Union'.

Picking up the theme of the first white paper, the Social Policy white paper viewed competitiveness and social progress as 'two sides of the same coin':

> *While wealth creation is essential for social progress, the social environment is also an essential factor in determining economic growth. Progress cannot be founded simply on the basis of the competitiveness of economies, but also on the efficiency of European society as a whole.* [10]

Arguing that Europe had, for too long, focused on the management of unemployment, jobs were now considered central to the objectives of economic and social progress. So as to increase employment, investment in new technologies, greater workplace flexibility, training, new forms of work organisation and building a genuine European labour market were considered essential, and the white paper set out in detail a number of objectives, including the roles which could be played by the trade unions, employers' organisations and voluntary organisations in achieving these objectives.

Following on from the two white papers, the Essen European Council (1994) identified five priority areas for action to promote employment:

---

[7] Office for Official Publications of the European Communities, (Luxembourg), 1993, ISBN 92-826-7000-7, page 123.

[8] Office for Official Publications of the European Communities, (Luxembourg), 1994, COM(94) 333, ISBN 92-826-8526-8

[9] *European Social Policy – Options for the Union* Office for Official Publications of the European Communities, (Luxembourg), 1993, COM(93) 551, ISBN 92-826-6897-5

[10] ibid. page 12

- improving employment opportunities by promoting investment in vocational training;
- increasing the employment-intensiveness of growth;
- reducing non-wage labour costs;
- increasing the effectiveness of labour-market policies;
- improving help for groups that are particularly hard hit by unemployment.

The new Commission President, Jacques Santer, presented a 'Confidence Pact for Employment' to the heads of government in 1996, which sought to mobilise all the actors concerned in a genuine strategy to make employment a matter of common interest at European level and incorporate the fight against unemployment in a medium and long-term vision of society.
An extraordinary summit on employment was held in Luxembourg (1997), which agreed an Employment Strategy, consisting of four pillars - employability, entrepreneurship, adaptability and equal opportunities. The Member States then decided to bring forward to 1998 the application of the provisions on co-ordinating their employment policies.
Following from this, the next major development in the evolution of the European social model was the inclusion of an Employment Title (Title VIII) and articles on social provisions, vocational training and economic and social cohesion in the Amsterdam Treaty, in 1997.

Article 136 of the Treaty sets out the main aims of European social policy:

> *...the promotion of employment, improving living and working conditions, so as to make possible their harmonisation while the improvement is being maintained, proper social protection, dialogue between management and labour, the development of human resources with a view to lasting employment and combating of exclusion.*

With the entry into force of the treaty, the Commission, working with the Member States, was assigned the responsibility of co-ordinating the Employment Strategy. The Member States still retain responsibility for employment policies, but must now have regard for the fact that it is a matter of common concern. The new Title also requires that:
- employment be taken into consideration in other EU policies;
- co-ordination mechanisms are to be established at EU-level (for example, adoption by the Council of guidelines for employment and surveillance of their implementation in the Member States);

- a new permanent advisory body, the Employment Committee, be set up to provide a forum for debate on employment issues at EU-level.

Under the Employment Strategy, the Member States are now required to draw up national action plans for employment (NAPs) and provide the Commission with reports on their implementation. These reports describe the main measures taken by the governments to apply their annual programmes over the last twelve months, assess the impact of these measures on employment - in certain cases - and announce major changes or new initiatives for the coming year. In practical terms, in implementing this procedure, there are two main innovations:

- the Council draws up guidelines for employment each year that are compatible with the broad lines of economic policy. It does so acting by a qualified majority on a proposal from the Commission and after consulting the European Parliament, the Economic and Social Committee, the Committee of the Regions and the Employment Committee;
- the Council can also make recommendations to the Member States in the light of its annual review of their employment policies, acting by a qualified majority on a recommendation from the Commission.

This process, including guidelines from the Council, national plans and monitoring by the Commission and the Council, is a good example of the implementation of a multi-level model of "regulated autonomy" within European Social Policy.

The Social Policy Agreement (of the Maastricht Treaty) was also incorporated into the Amsterdam Treaty, thus putting an end to the complex situation where, from 1993 to 1999, there were two distinct legal bases for social policy measures: the treaty itself and a separate agreement from which the UK had opted out. Now all social policy measures can be adopted on the basis of a new Title XI.

Employment at the Top of the EU Agenda

Since 1995 the Commission has adopted a series of Social Action Programmes to implement agreed policies. The first, from 1995 to 1997, sought to develop a more broadly-based and innovative approach to European social policy. [11] As a result, the debate on social policy was expanded to include such issues as demographic trends, social protection and the fight against racism. There was also a move to link social policy to

---

[11] *Social Action Programme, 1995-1998* Office for Official Publications of the European Communities (Luxembourg)

other EU policies, such as the mainstreaming of equal opportunities between men and women, the integration of health protection into other EU policies and the publication of a Communication on the environment and employment.

Other topics that became the focus of this expanding social policy were:

- Dealing with the problem of social inclusion of vulnerable groups in society, such as ethnic minorities, people with disabilities, and young and old workers;
- The expansion of training to a wider focus on vocational education, life-long-learning and non-formal education, to ensure that skills and qualifications remain relevant to the requirements of the current labour market and workers remain employable;
- The shift in the policies of the governments from passive labour market policies to the application of social benefits and social protection to a pro-active and interventionist approach to these policies, through training, job placement and work experience programmes.

The second Social Action Programme (1998-2000)[12] put employment at the top of the EU agenda making it a matter of common concern for the Member States, reflecting the commitments set out in the Amsterdam Treaty. In this context it promoted the creation of conditions for sound and sustainable growth, encouraging entrepreneurship and promoting active policies to improve the employability of school leavers, workers and the unemployed, so as to meet current and future job and skill demands and provide the opportunities for work. The programme recognised the need for European workplaces to modernise work organisation and to adapt to the change business environment. The achievement of an inclusive society, dealing with the problems of discrimination, inequalities and poverty were also included in the objectives of this second programme. It also brought into the social policy debate, for the first time, the challenges of enlargement and monetary union.

The latest programme, (Social Policy Agenda 2000-2005), which was adopted at the Nice European Council (2000), sets as its objective a programme of action for the implementation of the aspirations in the Amsterdam Treaty. The Social Policy Agenda 'seeks to work towards

[12] *Social Action Programme, 1998-2000* Office for Official Publications of the European Communities (Luxembourg), COM(98) 259 final, ISBN 92-78-35517-8.

common European objectives and increased co-ordination of social policies in the context of the internal market and the single currency'. [13]

The Lisbon European Council meeting (March, 2000) stimulated a debate on the substance and process of European economic policymaking, proposed a 'new strategic goal for the Union in order to strengthen employment, economic reform and social cohesion as part of a knowledge-based economy'. The Council agreed a system of open co-ordination which involves the establishment of common social policy guidelines, indicators and benchmarks which are intended to have greater co-ordination of national policies and peer evaluation by the Member States.

This process lead to the adoption of a number of initiatives for the modernisation of social protection and new approaches to social policy, such as 'fixed guidelines for social policy with specific timetables for achieving short, medium and long-term goals; setting quantitative and qualitative benchmarks designed to meet the needs of the Member States and different sectors; translating European guidelines into national and regional policies by setting specific targets and measures; periodic monitoring, evaluation and peer review as mutual learning processes; and benchmarking 'best practices' on managing change to be devised by the Commission, networking with companies, social partners and NGOs'[14].

The progress of implementing and operating this new co-ordination process was reviewed by the European Council meeting in Göteborg (15-16 June, 2001).

While the agenda and range of topics which are included in the European Social Model have been expanding, either as areas of EU competence or as issues for greater co-ordination, increasingly, during the past decade, European Social Policy has come more and more to place employment at the centre of its objectives and activities.

A Principle - Participation and Social Partnership

Central to these developments is the employment relationship or industrial relations system emerging within the EU which is based on the principle of social partnership. This principle of participation found expression in the employment rights directives going back to the 1970s – on the right to

---

[13] *Social Policy Agenda* Office for Official Publications of the European Communities (Luxembourg), COM (2000) 379 final, ISBN 92-894-0049-8, page 8.

[14] *Lisbon: Europe's 'Maastricht for Welfare?'* Prof M Rhodes, ECSA Review, Summer, 2000.

consultation, for example, in the event of collective redundancies, the transfer of undertakings - and in the occupational health and safety framework directive. It also was the basis for the establishment of the social dialogue process in 1985 and the subsequent adoption of the directive on information and consultation in transnational enterprises (the European Works Council directive).

This latter directive is the first piece of legislation, which has a direct impact on the employment relationship in enterprises operating within the EU, and the format used is now the blueprint for information, consultation and participation of employees within a European company registered under the Statute for a European Company (SE) or the extension of the right to information and consultation to all firms with more than 50 employees.[15] This is a further example of the multi-level model of "regulated autonomy", with common European norms for adaptation at national and enterprise levels.

The principle of social partnership comes easily to employers and workers, and their representatives, in many Member States but in other countries where an adversarial system has been the norm it is not as readily incorporated into the culture or ethos of employee/ management relations. In general, this process of trying to find a common denominator on EU policies and action has resulted in an 'à la carte' Union and this is also identified in the development of the social model – for example, the UK opt-out at Maastricht or the more recent derogation for Spain from aspects of the employee information, consultation and participation European Company Statute directive.

The EU directives or regulations reflect agreement on general principles at EU-level, but the detailed implementation at national levels more often takes into consideration the traditions, culture and history of the particular industrial relations system or a common system found in groups of countries (for example, the Nordic Member States or Germany and the Netherlands).

This balance between common principles at central (EU) level and specific requirements at lower levels is the aim of the model of "regulated autonomy" which is being implemented within the regulatory system of the European Social Model.

---

[15] Political agreement reached on 11 June, 2001.

'Regulated Autonomy' as a Third Way between Regulation and Deregulation?

Converging with, and sometimes leading to, the above institutional developments, there has been a rapid development of interactivity between individuals, groups and organisations, which is based, on the one hand, on the growing autonomy of better trained and better informed actors and, on the other, on the expansion and wide availability of information, greater communication, transport and media. This development underlines the development towards two strong and closely linked trends - the increase in social complexity and diversity and a continuous acceleration in the pace of change [16].

This might lead to a hypothesis on an emerging societal system which could be called a 'permanent dynamic complexity'. This system destabilises the traditional ways of regulation, particularly those which are centralised, as it exposes their lack of adaptability when confronted with more complex social situations which are becoming much more diverse and are changing more than ever before.

In the national systems of industrial relations formal and legal rules are an essential part and when these traditional systems began to be faced with "permanent dynamic complexity" and social destabilisation, the first reaction was deregulation, that is the rescinding of legal regulation, and a reliance on non-legal forms of regulation. There were also attempts for legislation to "follow" the social changes, thus finally "giving the power to the force, not to the law", as deregulation does. [17]

However, more recently, another approach has emerged, which allows for adaptability at the local level within common rules set at regional or national levels. This model, which has been called 'regulated autonomy', based on the participation of the actors, deals more efficiently with the long-term trends and challenges of "permanent dynamic complexity", and, therefore, it could be considered a third way of re-regulation, laying somewhere between regulation and deregulation.

---

[16] See A. Chouraqui, *Towards a European model of regulated autonomy: a third way for re-regulation between regulation and deregulation?*, IREC 1999 Conference on Employment Relations: Regulation and Deregulation in Europe, LEST-CNRS, Aix-en-Provence, May 20-22nd 1999.

[17] SUPIOT A, Critique du droit du travail, Collection « les Voies du droit », 1994, P.UF., Paris, 288 pages.

Within this model, various topics outside and inside industrial relations systems (working time, training, direct participation itself, computer and privacy, bioethics...), are regulated through 'regulatory complexes'.
A "regulatory complex" is a socio-legal system that links rules and actors at various levels, and organises these levels of regulation so that they are complementary to each other. It combines at the central level general but substantive rules, and rules of procedure, which entrusts the details of the regulation to decentralised levels, agreed through negotiated and/or participative arrangements. At each level of such a "regulatory complex", actors become regulators.
As an example, the recent French "Aubry law" on reducing working time implemented such a regulatory complex which illustrates this "model" of regulated autonomy. It establishes a new compulsory connection between, on the one hand, a central regulatory framework, which sets out the general principles governing the substantive rules, and the rules of procedure governing the lower levels -through collective bargaining at sectoral or enterprise levels- and, on the other hand, the detailed substantive rules agreed at and applied to these lower levels. This ensures that these rules can be continuously adapted to the specific context and constraints of each individual sector, or establishment.
It might be argued that this model of "regulated autonomy" is an alternative to other regulatory systems, because it can combine, instead of hindering, deregulation and regulation, local and central regulation, autonomy and heteronomy systems. In a "regulatory complex", central and local regulations are formally interlinked in an integrated system aimed at providing adaptability, by requiring the autonomy of the actors and, at the same time, at providing common norms and controls from the central levels. Therefore, it can be said that "regulatory complexes" fits perfectly with the requirements of dynamic complexity, economic efficiency and social cohesion.

Within this context, a few key points can be stressed:

- These regulatory complexes no longer follow the old legal rule of top-down within which people have to obey. On the contrary, it gives the actors certain autonomy to produce or co-produce the substantive regulation, within a very general and limited central framework - a regulated autonomy within a limited heteronomy. It allows for links to exist between rules and actors; between 'micro' and 'macro' levels; between legal and social regulations; legal coherence and social cohesion. This can also contribute to a renewal of the democratic process, as the legitimacy of law can be reinforced by workers' participation in the processes of producing socio-legal regulations. It also provides the actors with a legitimacy that is strengthened by the recognition of their new roles and powers in legal regulation.

- The development of different arrangements of workers' participation, based on negotiation, decentralisation and direct participation, is in the heart of the regulatory complexes. The process comes full circle as the systems are built in reaction to a situation of "permanent dynamic complexity" which is itself largely produced by the actors - social partners, individuals, micro-collectives, firms, etc. - whose aspirations are a major factor in the destabilisation of the old regulatory systems and institutions. However, while the autonomy of the actors and their roles in the regulatory process is important, frequent problems can occur when some of the actors are too weak, when the balance of power in co-producing rules is too unbalanced or when the process of learning their new regulators' roles takes too long. For the success of the system, it is crucial that all the actors are able to participate on an equal basis. Therefore consciousness raising and day-to-day participation in regulation processes should be supported as much at workplace level as at upper levels.
- In such a model, direct and representative forms of employee participation can clearly be interlinked and complementary. The ideal form of a regulatory complex involves direct participation at the lower levels, and negotiation by representatives at the upper levels. Representatives take into account the concerns of the workers, which ensures their legitimacy, and workers participate inside the framework which is agreed through collective bargaining at the upper level(s). Workers are then clearly part of the process which produces the regulations and even become regulators themselves.
- Time and change dimensions are taken into account in these systems. Regulatory complexes are aimed at a continuous adjustment between substantial rules and social diversity and change. The central framework can be stable, expressing the basic values on the topic, while the decentralised complementary rules can be adjusted to respond to change. This adaptability is possible because central rules are more procedural, establishing the different levels and actors, and are aimed at ensuring common conditions within which the substantive rules can be continuously adapted at the lower levels.

A Balanced System of European Regulation: the Example of Direct Participation.

Regulated autonomy and regulatory complexes can be observed in the systems of organisations and even geographically. Traditionally, most examples are at a national level, with legislation or national agreements, within which firms or workplace reach agreements at the micro, lower, level. Similarly a European system of regulated autonomy can also be detected through multi-level regulatory complexes, working through the national transposition and implementation system down to the enterprise level. With this system there would be no more difficult choices between the European, national or micro levels – all are involved and interlinked in the regulatory processes.

The question, therefore, is no longer to choose at which level regulation should be introduced, as it happens with the principle of subsidiarity, but how a balance between the powers and issues, at the various levels, and between the actors, can be achieved.

The different national systems of industrial relations in Europe are faced with the same challenges and effects of the 'permanent dynamic complexity'. All these systems are searching for new ways to formulate regulation that will ensure both the necessary economic flexibility and social cohesion, and will avoid the negative effects of deregulation, as much as those of central regulation. New formal regulation, or re-regulation, are now often based on a re-distribution and a 're-linking' of the roles of the various levels and actors' in the formulation of rules.

This development has then resulted in common approaches to meet this new challenge for regulation by improving the internal balance in each national system. Therefore the theoretical model of "regulated autonomy" and its regulatory complexes are now being implemented, in various but converging ways. For example, the centralised industrial relations systems (in terms of legal or negotiated norms) are endeavouring to achieve flexibility through decentralised negotiation, while, in contrast, there is a tendency in the traditionally decentralised systems towards the establishment of complementary central standards which are aimed at dealing with common problems.

One question arising out of this theoretical approach is whether there are any indications of a 'convergence' in the evolution of the various national industrial relations systems within an EU-wide system. If this is the case, such an evolution could strongly reinforce the possibilities for a strong and

flexible European multi-level system of regulation through European regulatory complexes.
In that way, one precise indication of such a trend can be found in the results of the European Foundation's EPOC workplace survey about employee direct participation. [18] This topic of participation is a major one within the European Social Model, because of its values as much as its system of regulation. The recent debate about the right of information and consultation confirmed that, on this topic, the issue of regulation/deregulation was always very sensitive.
In fact, the findings of this survey of 5800 European workplace managers confirmed that employee involvement, and particularly of employee representatives, is important in the regulation of direct employee participation in order to improve both the quality of the participation itself and its economic and social effects. The survey showed that the greater the involvement, in terms both of form and extent (and this applies particularly to negotiation and joint decision-making), the more the economic and social indicators were positive.
The high degree of actual convergence shown by the various results on the regulation of direct participation indicate that the differences between European countries are less significant than it was expected on such a sensitive topic, despite the marked differences between the various national industrial relations systems. Therefore, the findings of the EPOC survey clearly reveal a few common conditions for a European regulation of direct participation, combining central regulation and local autonomy. This is a good example of a possible directive or collective agreement introducing, at European level, a balanced "regulatory complex", which might include [19]:

• Negotiation (and preferably joint decision-making) between management and employee representatives on the introduction, monitoring and evaluation of direct participation;
• Consultation with (and at least the extensive provision of information to) the employees concerned;

---

[18] *New Forms of Work Organisation: Can Europe realise its potential?* The EPOC Research Group, European Foundation for the Improvement of Living and Working Conditions, Dublin, and Office of Official Publications, Luxembourg, 1997, EF/97/46/EN; ISBN 92-828-1888-8

[19] Chouraqui A., Towards a European model of regulation of direct participation?/Vers un "modèle européen" de régulation de la participation directe? Conference on employee direct participation in Europe, Dutch Ministry of Social Affairs/European Foundation, Amsterdam, 10-11th April, 1997.

• The establishment of lasting arrangements (direct participation is a lengthy learning process);
• Training for employees and management in the operation of direct participation (team-working, assessment of information, joint decision-making etc.);
• Dual objective of efficiency on the economic and technological level (productivity, quality, flexibility), as well as in the social aspects of work (working conditions, employment security, motivation);
• Financial and / or symbolic compensation for this new form of involvement;
• Individuals' right to participate in and the real involvement of the greatest possible number of employees in stable groups;

• Integration of direct participation into a wider process of work organisation and the modernising of the workplace.

Incorporating these into the European Social Model would illustrate the system of regulated autonomy which would be based, on the one hand, on a convergence of the national industrial relations systems and, on the other hand, on the emergence of a European industrial relations system. The European level of regulation is in fact the upper part of this emerging European multi-level system of regulation.

As seen, there are two changes which should be stressed. First, the levels are changing - Europe is emerging as a new level of regulation/re-regulation of industrial relations. Without the model of regulated autonomy which combines regulation and deregulation, this implementation of a new level of regulation could have been paradoxical when deregulation still remains a major trend. Second, the role of the actors in regulation is growing, along with their regulated autonomy; and, indeed, new actors are appearing on the scene through the powers conferred on the social partners in the Social Chapter of the Amsterdam Treaty.

Conclusions and Prospects

Following this overall analysis of the history and major changes in the European Social Model, it may be argued that the basic elements to build a strong and efficient model already exists, both methodologically and in content.

Despite this a central challenge in analysis is to get beyond the much-used rhetoric and beyond formalised statements and decisions. When reviewing

the history and the characteristics of the European Social Model, a complex evolution can be observed. Because of the economic crisis beginning in the 1970's, then of the global challenge of competitiveness and of the ideological background of the "pensée unique", the historical balance in Europe between economic and social goals was destabilised. There is a tension between two objectives, the first is flexibility/free market/deregulation, and the second, social cohesion/common landmarks/regulation on the other hand. These objectives are as much practical as ideological. They were sometimes managed in a complementary way, sometimes in a contradictory way, sharpening tension and tending towards conflict. Many compromises between flexibility and regulation have been reached on a range of topics at EU-level.
When reviewing the last decade, a contradictory shift can be observed. On the one hand, the concept of a social dimension in the EU was strengthened, and its contents have been improved, step-by-step. On the other hand, in many aspects of EU policies, the actual "compromises" have put the emphasis more and more on the pole of flexibility, forgetting the historical European view that the economy is not a goal in itself but a means for social development.
In order to go further in this analysis of the present and of the challenges of the European Social Model, the Aix Seminar will propose a brain-storming around three sets of questions, on the system; on the values; and on the perspectives of this Model.
The first set of questions is about the institutional system itself and the evolution of the emerging multi-level system. The models of centralised regulation and of neo-liberal deregulation often failed to address both the issues of preserving social cohesion and of managing economic efficiency in a context of diversity and change. The emerging model of multilevel "regulated autonomy" is more relevant to this challenge, in integrating on the one hand, a common central regulation preferably produced by social dialogue, with on the other hand, local actors producing various regulations adapted to each economic context. This multilevel system also fits with the fact that enlargement, as much as globalisation, are processes that need a strong but decentralised European social model.
How will it be possible to strengthen this emerging model, aimed both at economic adaptability and at common social common norms? What may become the political and ideological balance between flexibility and regulation? Will they work as complementary or conflicting tools? How is the regulatory balance between heteronomy and autonomy to be achieved? What will be the ability of the actors to play their necessary roles in the

growing regulatory model? How long will their learning process be? How can acceptable balance and connections between the various levels of regulation be found?

Second, what are the societal values that support the model? The contents of the European Social Model are based on common European values and rights which are set out and formally agreed, for example, in the new Charter of Fundamental Rights - justice, freedom, equity, dignity, democratic participation (in political, economic and social affairs), quality of work and employment, social protection and inclusion, quality of working and living conditions. It is generally agreed that economic and financial developments are also essential tools to achieve these human and social goals. Furthermore, it is believed that the focus of European history and culture has been on finding an acceptable social balance between the economic means and human and social goals. Beyond the official rhetoric about this balance, is it happening in practice or is there a slow but dramatic change leading to a focus which is mainly on the economic dimension and which considers the social dimension only as 'human capital', in support of the economic goals? As has happened in the past, will this balance become much more a balance of conflicting powers, rather than a fair balance of values and interests? This question can also be applied to the historical balance between the roles of the public and private sectors. When compared to the United States or Japan, the answers to these fundamental questions might indicate that the European Social Model is based, in fact, on a European Societal Model.

The last set of questions is about the challenges for the future. Two complementary and/or contradictory processes - enlargement and globalisation - will influence the future direction of the EU and its Social Model. There has been a rapid process of change in the candidate countries. Is it possible for the social actors in the candidate countries to quickly contribute to the emerging European system of regulated autonomy? Will enlargement lead to a greater focus on free trade, financial and economic dimensions and less so on social and human issues? Will it bring more wealth and prosperity to Europe? Will it strengthen, or weaken, the European Social Model which, at the same time, will have to face the challenge of continued globalisation and its clear focus on trade and financial dimensions? Will Europe be able to stand as a strong regional centre of regulation within an emerging multi-level global regulatory system? Consequently, to what degree will Europe be able to play its role in the process of regulation of increasingly integrated global markets?

In short, the key question is will European actors, building on their common historical and cultural values, learn how to use the emerging multi-level model of participatory regulation in order to strengthen the still fragile Social Model and to achieve its goals? Will the EU be able to keep a balanced and efficient social model, to resist the pressures from other traditions and cultures and to contribute to the building of a socially balanced global economy?

References

These references were used in the paper, notably referring to the research programmes PAROLES and EPOC

CHOURAQUI A. (2001), Towards a European model of Direct Participation, A few lessons from the French experience; in European Labour Relations, ed. by G. Széll,,vol.2, Ashgate publ. (U.K.)

CHOURAQUI A. (1999) Towards a European model of regulated autonomy: a third way for re-regulation between regulation and deregulation? IREC Conference, first plenary session Aix-en-Provence, 20-22nd May.

CHOURAQUI A. (1997), Towards a European model of regulation of direct participation/Vers un "modèle européen" de régulation de la participation directe? Conférence sur la participation directe des salariés, Ministère Néerlandais des Affaires Sociales / Fondation Européenne pour l'Amélioration des Conditions de Vie et de Travail, Amsterdam, 10-11 avril

CHOURAQUI A. (1996), Entre hétéronomie et anomie, l'autonomie régulée: de nouveaux "ensembles régulatoires" face à une complexité dynamique durable. Vème Congrès de l'Association française de science politique - Aix-en Provence, 23-26 avril

EPOC Research Group (1997), New Forms of Work Organisation: Can Europe realise its potential?, European Foundation for the Improvement of Living and Working Conditions, Dublin, and Office of Official Publications, Luxembourg

GEARY J. and SISSON K. (1997), Conceptualising Direct Participation in Organisational Change - The EPOC Project, European Foundation for the Improvement of Living and Working Conditions, Dublin, and Office of Official Publications, Luxembourg

PINAUD H., LE TRON H. et CHOURAQUI A., (1999) Syndicalisme et démocratie dans l'entreprise/Trade-unions and democracy in companies, Paris, Editions L'Harmattan.

REGALIA I. (1995) , Humanise Work and Increase Profitability? Direct - Participation in Organisational Change Viewed by the Social Partners in Europe, EPOC project, European Foundation for the Improvement of Living and Working Conditions, Dublin, and Office of Official Publications, Luxembourg

SISSON K., (2001), Direct Participation and the Modernisation of Work Organisation, EPOC project, European Foundation for the Improvement of Living and Working Conditions, Dublin, and Office of Official Publications, Luxembourg

SUPIOT A. (1994) Critique du droit du travail, Collection « les Voies du droit », PUF., Paris.

SZELL G. ed. (2001) European Labour Relations, 2 vol., Ashgate (U.K.)

The Role and Prospects of RLDWL Europe

GYÖRGY SZÉLL

Since its inception four years ago during its first conference in Ravello in September 1999, the international network Regional and Local Development of Work and Labour has developed quite well. We have organised in the meantime two other international conferences, one in Rio de Janeiro in November 2002,[1] and another one Osnabrück in May 2002,[2] each time with more than one hundred participants. The fourth conference will take place in February 2004 in Durban, South Africa under the title "Trans-national co-operation on social regulation".

The founding document "*The role of intermediate institutions: The case of Research Institutes Concerned with Work and Labour" was edited by* Francesco Garibaldo and Voler Telljohann und published in Italian and English in 2000. The conferences in Ravello and Rio de Janeiro were documented in the volume "The Injustice at Work: an international view on the world of labour and society", edited by György Széll and Gian Primo Cella in 2002, the Osnabrück proceedings will be published in English and German under the title "*Labour, Globalisation and the New Economy"* by myself, Carl-Heinrich Bösling and Johannes Hartkemeyer in 2004.

Certainly the network is somehow European biased, as its headquarters are in Bologna, Italy, and its two chair-persons as well as most officers are Euroepan based. This is largely due to the organisational facilities, and in even in times of financial restrictions to the possibilities of fundings. So, we are grateful namely to the European Commission, Directorate General Employment and Social Affairs (DG V), to the European Foundation for the Improvement of Living and Working Conditions in Dublin, the European Trade Union Institute (ETUI) in Brussels, the Hans Böckler Foundation of the German Trade Union Confederation (HBS) Düsseldorf,

---

[1] For a short report cf. Széll/Jacobi in Transfer 1/2001: 158-161.

[2] For a short report cf. Széll in Transfer 2/2001: 158-161

and the German Friedrich Ebert Foundation (FES) in Bonn for their generous and ongoing support from the very beginning.

But this makes it also that European issues stood at the forefront of many discussions, and led us to the decision to create a European network during our first European Conference from 18 to 21 June 2003 in Bologna, which is documented in this volume. A second conference will already follow soon under the title "New Forms of Work Organisation and Industrial Relations – Where does Italy stand?" from 1 to 3 April 2004 in Rome. For sure we hope that as outcomes of further conferences there will be African, Asian, and American networks as well. Because for sure – even in a world of largely deregulated air travel – travelling between the continents is still expensive, especially for participants from the Third World.

Already in our founding documents the reference to Europe was strong. I am arguing now that this is for some good reasons. In today's process of globalisation different models of labour relations are at stake. After the break-down of the Soviet system of really existing socialism in most parts of the world there are mainly three models for choice:

- The dominant US-American model of shareholder-value, weak workers' and union rights and participation (Deutsch 2001);
- the Japanese model with company based unions, which realise some form of participation, however, neglect participation and union rights on the macro and meso level (Széll 2001b);
- the European model, although with many national and cultural variants, based on the stakeholder principle and strong unions but also strong employers associations for good, longterm relations (Széll 2001a, 2002a; Busch et al. 2000).

So the issue on the global level as well as on the European level is not only to reach Minimum Labour Standards, but Decent Work, as the new programme and campaign by the International Labour Office (ILO) is named. Corporate Governance and Corporate Responsibility Standards are certainly topics, which are also broadly discussed on the other side of the Atlantic, and after the recent scandals around ENRO and Worldcom there are very good reasons to do so. However, Good governance and industrial democracy go much further than these strategies (Széll 2002b).

Today‘s Challenges

Europe's challenges are manifold today also in the field of local and regional development of work and labour. First of all the European Union will be enlarged in May 2004 by ten new members, most of the them were formerly part of the COMECON and the Soviet Empire. The transition period, which started already in the mid-eighties of the last century, will certainly take another 15 to 20 years (Széll 1995; Thirkell et al. 1995; Schienstock et al. 1997; Martin et al. 1998). The main problem for a proper regional and local development and with it good labour relations is the weakness and diversity of labour unions and employers associations. Some experiments in tripartite regulations as in Hungary encountered great difficulties. But also the national state to replace collective agreements is weak. For creating a Social Dialogue on all levels and in all sectors, as preconised by the European Union and the International Labour Office, the well-functioning of social partnership is an absolute prerequisite.

RLDWL is nearly not implemented at all in these countries, so special efforts have to be developed in this direction. A special case is the Russian Federation. Europe is not ending at the new borders of the enlarged EU, but they end geographically at the Ural mountains. Russia has such a size and is confronted with such huge problems to the other European countries and the EU with its organisations demands special relationships and special attention. Unfortunately there is no counterpart organisation to be seen in Russia so far.

But also within the EU itself problems have accumulated over the last 45 years of its existence, the subsidies for the agriculture, which consume still half of the whole EU-budget, are not the minor ones, and which by the way prevent a fair economic world systems, because the Third World has no chance to sell their own products on our markets, and which are destroyed by the subsidised agr-products and agro-business of the rich countries. Regional and local development of work and labour in the Third World are heavily hampered by this system of unequal distribution. Perhaps the failure of the WTO Cancun summit in September 2003 is a sign of hope for awareness and a new kind of more equal relations. This leads us back to the issue of globalisation vs. world regions, i.e. Europe. Our relationship to Africa will be one of the topics and workshops of our 4th Conference in Durban, SA, next year. But also the co-operation with Mercosur, the Latin-American free trade zone, – including Brazil, Argentina, Uruguay and Paraguay, Chile is associated – designed according to the model of the European Economic Community, is another point of reference. There exist

other regional associations in Asia, like ASEAN, SARC, APEC too. And also not to forget the North American Free Trade Association, including the USA, Canada and Mexico (cf. Rehfeldt/Da Costa in this book).
The negotiations and agreements within the World Trade Organisation affect the different world regions quite differently, as it can be seen into regard of the already above mentioned agricultural issues, but also the General Agreement for Trade on Services, which may be treated as a trade-off for the agricultural negotiation package.
The European Social Model is characterised by its divergent welfare systems – Esping-Andersen differentiates between three (1990) –, a dynamic process over the last 150 years. In so far it is certainly better in this context to speak of the different Europe**s**, than just of one Europe, as the harmonising and restructuring process is in full swing. Already some twenty years ago the research group Industrial Democracy in Europe (IDE 1981a, b) arrived at distinguishing at least four variants:

- the Nordic
- the Anglo-Saxon
- the Central European
- the Mediterranean, and at the time of publication also
- the Yugoslav.

In how far these differentiations still hold, could be, should be part of our research agenda.
But coming back to the challenges for promoting good work in Europe reference should be made to the draft for a Europoean Constitution, as it is has been proposed by the Convent under the leadership of Former French President Valérie Giscard d'Estaing in 2003. All efforts had been in vein to include into this draft elements for the promotion of a real European Social Union – besides the Economic and Monetary Union. This is still on the agenda for further research and action.

What to Do?

So that old Leninist question what to do under these conditions. The Work Research Institutes and individuals united in our network have different background and possibilities of action. Some are part within larger organisations (universities, research centres, academies), some are independent entities. Some are acting on the national, others on the regional or local level. So far, as mentioned we have some privileged partners as already mentioned before – the European Foundation and the European

Trade Union Confederation (ETUC), however, for sure we have still to improve our co-operation with European Employers Associations, as well in the private (UNICE) as in the public sector (CEEP) to improve our capacity to intervene into the Social Dialogue on the regional and local level.

As in the past we have a good relationship with the International Labour Organization (ILO), and namely the International Industrial Relations Association (IIRA), which has its secretariat at the ILO headquarters in Geneva. We took part at their 11th World Congress in Bologna in 1998, where actually the idea to create this network was born. We had own sessions at its 12th World Congress in Tokyo in May 2000, as well as recently at its 13th World Congress in Berlin in September 2003. We were present at the VIth European IIRA Conference in 2000 in Oslo, and we will organise sessions during the forthcoming VIIth European IIRA Conference in September 2004 in Lisboa.

In regard to the co-operation on the European level we should consider "Euroscience", an association of European scientists, founded in 1997 in Strasbourg. Although there are mainly natural scientists involved so far, the focus is similar as it is to become a privileged partner with the different European institutions, i.e. the European Commission as well as the European Parliament. Another valuable partner is the European Centre for Work & Society (ECWS) in Maastricht and Brussels, its Director Dany Wijgaerts took actually part in the founding of RLDWL.

Networking is the notion of today, and social scientists like Manuel Castells even speaks of the Network Society. Many people, especially young ones are reluctant to join formal organisations, after the bad experiences during the 20th century. So even non-governmental organisations have problems to integrate people. Modern social movements like attac flourish so far, however, the limits of this kind of action become already evident. By the way this an age-old debate within the workers' movement, i.e. the relationship between spontaneity and organisation. (Mattick 1975) Our network is something in between: it has statutes, a secretariat, a board, membership fees. So, we could speak of an "organised network".

The Next Tasks

As decided during the first business meeting of the European network the focus of activities will be directed to the following on fields:

1. *Direct and indirect participation.* About this subject it has been proposed to adopt a research method based on case studies right to find out some empirical evidences at the European level. There is also the intention to involve the candidate countries in this typology of research.
2. *Government and Governance.* The research projects of the European Network may focus on the importance of a clear definition of what falls under the competence of government and under the competence of governance also trough a redefinition of the concept of networking: it should be an opportunity for everybody and not only for few actors endowed with power. A comparison at the European level may be a fit research method.
3. *Learning Organisations.* In a dynamic context it is necessary to develop a common learning framework for all the organisations. The best manner to pursue this aim it could be the analysis of some cases at the European level.
4. *The new role of the trade unions and the employer associations at the national and at the European level.* [3]

The Organisation

Not only in capitalism but every where You need funds to realise a project and research. The main partner shall be the European Union, mainly the already mentioned Directorate General for Employment, and the one for Research, especially within the 6th Framework Programme. However, also those responsible for innovation, for education, for regional development shall be addressed. In so far our network has only organised conferences and meetings, as an exchange forum.

The question stands, if we are able to organise common research projects. On the other hand there are also many other possibilities and necessities. Within the European Research Area Thematic Networks (TN) play an increasing role. Within these TNs the exchange of scholars, especially of

---

[3] Minutes of the constituting Assembly of RLDWL Europe in Bologna on 21 June 2003.

young ones, amongst the institutes shall be one main activity. Also the Marie Curie Fellowships of the EU will be useful tool for our network. They are designed for Ph.D. students, post-docs and experienced researchers. Two new programmes within FP6 seem to be especially appropriate for our network:

- Early Stage Training Fellowship
- Transfer of Knowledge.

On the other hand there are also research funds within the European Regional Funds and the European Social Funds. They have to be applied to directly on the regional and/or local level.
The Euro-regions, i.e. the transborder co-operation between Member States is also especially encouraged by the EU. Special funds are available for these activities, including research.

Research Questions

The European integration process raises many new research questions, which may lead to new strategies. Especially the role of research and development on the regional and local level is by itself already an important issue. If Europe will really become a knowledge-based society and a world leader in the economy by this strategy, research is as the very heart of this development.
Within the European integration process new forms of labour relations have developed. First of all the European Works Councils, as instituted from 1994 on, are a major field of transnational, European co-operation for labour. In principle about 1,500 should have been implemented already, but there are at the moment not more than 500. However, some – as in the case of Volkswagen e.g. – of these European Works Councils already extend to Global Works Councils. Another – more recent institution, dating only back to 2001 – is the European Company (SE) with also codetermination rights, though differentiated according to national regulations, and by that circumventing the very idea of a European company as such.
Another already classical field is the issue of Quality of life and working life, but enlarged since the Rio-Conference on the question of sustainability. As catastrophes like the disaster of oil tankers on the sea demonstrate, these catastrophes are first of all local and regional disasters – though they may be linked to global systems and issues. The Local Agenda 21 has been picked up as a new orientation for the development of work

and labour. This link should be one of the main focuses of our work – in co-operation with the Dublin Foundation, which has already chosen since a number of years this topic as one of its main fields of activity.
Demography has been neglected in our research so far, although the ageing of population includes apparently also the workforce. This affects the future of the social security systems, including health, old-age care, pensions. Closely linked to this is the issue of migration, which first of all is still labour migration. Nearly all European nations are affected by a low fertility rate, which does not guarantee anymore the stability of population and its workforce. However, the situation is quite different according to regions and cities. Differences between the country-side and the urban centres are still quite remarkable.
The main issue for work and labour is the issue of unemployment, especially for young, older, sometimes women and immigrants. This problems leads us to the employment policy. The EU has decided four pillars, which are:

- Employability
- Flexibility
- Entrepreneurship
- Gender mainstreaming.

The EU-national governments have to deliver every year for benchmarking purposes the accomplishments in their National Action Plan. We should assess them on the basis of the differences in regard to the local, regional and sectoral levels, i.e. micro and meso levels. The following table could be helpful for this purpose:

Table 1: Sectoral and horizontal levels

	Sectoral	**level**
horizontal	Meso	regional
level	Micro	local

New forms of work organisation have developed over the last couple of years. They are mainly linked to IT, like tele-work, call centres, etc. These forms are often part of outsourcing schemes, even to far-away regions or countries in Asia and elsewhere. Somehow this may be regarded as a kind late justice to former de-industrialisation and transfer processes. In a certain way also self-employment can be regarded as a new form of work organisation. The employment risk is completely transferred to the

individual, this again is an issue for the social security systems, as these individuals are not covered and do not contribute to these systems. Part of the financial problems of these institutions are definitely due to this new phenomenon.
To overcome these problems of flexibility against social security the term of 'flexicurity' has been coined.[4] The challenge for unions and works councils, but also for local, regional and national governments is to find a solution in a social dialogue. Unfortunately the strategy to find solutions via a round-table, as it has been the case for The Netherlands with its Wassenaar agreement in 1982, are not supported by the employers. The *Bündnis für Arbeit*-initiative (Federation for Work) in Germany has failed on the national level due to this resistance, however, on the regional or even the company level some of these initiatives are still pursued.
Research was centred in the eighties around issues of industrial districts or clusters. The Emilia Romagna, where our headquarters are there – certainly no hazard – was regarded as a prototype of the kind of regional development. (Piore/Sabel 1984) The International Institute of Labour Studies of the ILO promoted a great number of surveys in this area. (Telljohann 1996) However, – perhaps since Werner Sengenberger retired – it has become rather quiet on this front. This is an area of research, which could and should be revived as well.
Also the topic of the social economy, including co-operatives, has been neglected as well during the last couple of years. This may be a result of the crisis of this sector, but still in a perspective of the new Member States of the EU this is a very important of their past, and hopefully of their future as well.
Finally, work and labour are not just economic, political and social issues, but include the cultural and societal dimension as well. So we find differences in work culture not only on the level of nations or regions, but also in regard to clusters, e.g. Mediterranean vs. Scandinavian countries,[5] or Anglo-Saxon vs. Central European ones. The Industrial Democracy in Europe research group has done interesting cross-country comparisons in the eighties of the last century, which after the end of the East-West conflict in Europe and with the enlargement of the EU should be redone.
So, one of the questions is: Do we have more convergence in labour relations since the eighties in Europe in general? Or in specific areas or

---

[4] The Hans Böckler Foundation has made this issue to one of its core research area from 2003 on.
[5] e.g. our Rome Conference in April 2004 will focus on these dimensions.

sectors, or regions? Does size matter – of the nation, of the region, of the company? How are regional and local specificities on the one hand and generalities, e.g. of global influences, are coped with? (cf. Széll 2001)
This brings us to another issue, with which we will treat during a special seminar after the Second European RLDWL Conference in Rome in 2004, the question of an appropriate methodology for our studies and comparisons, resp. common strategies: e.g. the relation between case studies and the overall picture.

Implementation

The question of the implementation of research results into the praxis is always a great problem. E.g. only 10 % of companies have implemented so far the results in regard to the positive effects of participation on the productivity, although this is well documented since at least 20 years. (Cf. Brödner and Latniak in this volume)
Therefore the dissemination of our results is one of the main tasks of our network. We do it so far through conferences and publications like this one. But this is definitely not enough. We have to think of new outlets and new forms of co-operation. The close co-operation with the review *Transfer* of the European Trade Union Institute and with its South East European Review are good bases to build on. However, we should also think of being more engaged in consultation activities, which may give our young members also professional perspectives.
Concerning globalisation the EU is definitely not only an object but also a subject of this process, as has already been mentioned above. We have to take our responsibilities in the social division of labour on the global level, as it is the target of our global network. The Global Social Forum started in Porto Alegre in January 2003 with the slogan "Another World is Possible!". The Second European Social Forum was organised in November 2003 in Paris. So these global issues are brought down again onto the European level.
In the good old times – i.e. before the George W. Bush and Rumsfeld era – one used to speak of 'Good Old Europe' on the other side of the Atlantic Ocean: But since this Good Old Europe tries with its Union, its own currency and its foreign policy to become more independent from Big Brother it is regarded with mistrust and even hampered, and the US-Administration to divide Europe in the 'Good New Europe' and the 'Bad Old Europe'. Solidarity vs. Shareholder Value is one of the specificities of

the European work cultures in the triad competition (cf. the contribution by Rainer Zoll in this book and also Busch/Széll et al. 2000).

Actually we may be proud of this accomplishment, as it indicates that we have something else to offer than main-stream economics, labour relations and development. The European Network for Regional and Local Development of Work and Labour will hopefully play a positive role in this process.

References:

Busch, Klaus; Széll, György et al. (eds.) (2000): *Ways to Social Peace in Europe.* Osnabrück, Secolo.

Castells, Manuel (2000): *The Rise of the Network Society.* Oxford, Blackwell.

Clarke, Linda; de Gijsel, Peter & Jörn Janssen (eds.) (2000): *The Dynamics of Wage Relations in the New Europe.* Amsterdam: Kluwer.

Deutsch, Steven (2001): 'An Economic Leader Seeks Answers for the Future', in György Széll (ed.), *European Labour Relations.* Aldershot, Gower/Ashgate, vol. 2: 206-219.

Ehlert, Wiking; Russell, Raymond & György Széll (eds.) (1994): *Return of Work, Production, and Administration to Capitalism.* Frankfurt a.M. et al.: Peter Lang.

Esping-Andersen, Gøsta (1990): *The Three Worlds of Welfare Capitalism.* Cambridge: Polity Press.

Feldman, Jonathan Michael & Jessica Gordon Nembhard (eds.): *From Community Economic Development and Ethnic Entrepreneurship to Economic Democracy: The Cooperative Alternative*, Stockholm, PfMI, 2002, 1/02.

Garibaldo, Francesco & Volker Telljohann (eds.) (2000): *The role of intermediate institutions: The case of Research Institutes Concerned with Work and Labour*, Milano, Franco Angeli.

Hoffmann, Jürgen (ed.) (2002): *The solidarity dilemma: globalisation, Europeanisation and trade unions*. Brussels: ETUI.

Hoffmann, Reiner; Jacobi, Otto, Keller; Berndt & Manfred Weiss (eds.) (2003): *European Integration as a Social Experiment in a Globalized World*. Düsseldorf: Hans Böckler Stiftung.

Industrial Democracy in Europe (IDE) International Research Group (1981a): *Industrial Democracy in Europe*. Oxford: Oxford University Press.

Industrial Democracy in Europe (IDE) International Research Group (1981b) *European Industrial Relations*. Oxford: Oxford University Press.

Kaisergruber, Danielle et al. (2001): *Les villes et l'emploi en Europe.* Paris, éditions de l'aube.

Kester, Gérad & Henri Pinaud (eds.), *Trade unions and democratic participation in Europe. A scenario for the 21st Century.* Aldershot etc., Avebury, 1996.

Kocar, Lydia (2003): Globale Ökonomie und nationale Politik. Die Forschungs- und Technologiepolitik der EU. Frankfurt/Bern/New York, Peter Lang..

Kuruvilah, Sarosh (2003): *Social dialogue for Decent Work.* Geneva, International Institute for Labour Studies (Discussion Paper DP/149/2003).

Martin, Roderick; Ishikawa, Akihiro; Makó, Csaba & Francesco Consoli (eds.) (1998): *Workers, Firms and Unions – Industrial Relations in Transition.* Frankfurt a.M. et al.: Peter Lang.

Mattick, Paul (1975): *Spontaneität und Organisation: vier Versuche über praktische und theoretische Probleme der Arbeiterbewegung.* Frankfurt a.M., Suhrkamp (es 735).

Piore, Michael J. & Charles F. Sabel (1984): The Second Industrial Divide. New York, Basic Books,.

Schienstock, Gerd; Thompson, Paul & Franz Traxler (eds.) (1997): *Industrial Relations between Command and Market. A Comparative Analysis of Eastern Europe and China.* New York: Nova Science Publishers.

Széll, György (ed.) (1992): *Labour Relations in Transition in Eastern Europe.* Berlin/New York: de Gruyter (Studies in Organization 33).

Széll, György (ed.) (2001a): *European Labour Relations.* 2 vols. Aldershot, Gower/Ashgate.

Széll, György (2001b): 'To learn from Japan?', in György Széll (ed.), *European Labour Relations.* Aldershot, Gower/Ashgate, vol. 2: 191-205.

Széll, György (2002a): 'Fifteen Challenges for a European Social Model', in György Széll & Gian Primo Cella (eds.) (2002), *The injustice at Work: an international view on the world of Labour and Society.* Frankfurt/Bern/New York, Peter M. Lang: 588-606.

Széll, György (2002b): ‚Sociology and Industrial Democracy', in Nikolai Genov (ed.), *Advances in Sociological Knowledge*, Paris: ISSC: 396-418.

Széll, György (2002c): 'Third international congress of the Work & Labour Network 'Labour, globalisation and the new economy', 22-25 May 2002, Osnabrück, *Transfer* 8/2, Summer 2002: 331-333.

Széll, György; Bösling, Carl-Heinrich & Johannes Hartkemeyer (eds.) (2004): *Labour, Globalisation and the New Economy.* Frankfurt/Bern/New York, Peter Lang.

Széll, György & Gian Primo Cella (eds.) (2002): *The injustice at Work: an international view on the world of Labour and Society.* Frankfurt/Bern/New York, Peter Lang.

Széll, György & Wiking Ehlert (eds.) (2001): *New Democracies and Old Societies in Europe.* Frankfurt/Bern/New York, Peter M. Lang.

Széll, György & Otto Jacobi (2001): ‚2nd international conference of the international network "Regional and Local Development of Work and Labour": Regional development, employment and the role of intermediate institutions, Rio de Janeiro, Brazil, 22-24 November 2000', *Transfer* 7/1, Spring 2001: 158-161.

Széll, György & Heiko Schlatermund (eds.): *Arbeitsorientierte Wissenschaft und Forschung in den Neunziger Jahren in Europa – Labour Oriented Science and Research in Europe in the Nineties.* Osnabrück, Secolo, 1993.

Telljohann, Volker (1996): Globaler Wettbewerb – lokale Entwicklung. Gewerkschaftliche Konzepte. Frankfurt/Bern/New York, Peter Lang.

Thirkell, John; Scase, Richard & Sarah Vickerstaff (1995): *Labour Relations & Political Change in Eastern Europe. A comparative perspective.* London: UCL Press.

Winkelmann, Olaf (2002): Entwicklung in der Mitbestimmung: Industrial Relations, Industrial Districts und Netzwerke. Das Beispiel „Betriebsräte-Netzwerk" im Industrial District Ostwestfalen-Lippe. Frankfurt/Bern/New York, Peter Lang.

Authors

Giovanna **Altieri,** Institute for Economic and Social Research, Rome, Italy

Palle **Banke**, Danish Technological Institute, Taastrup, Denmark

Peter **Brödner**, Institute Work and Technology, Gelsenkirchen, Germany

Alain **Chouraqui,** CNRS LEST, Aix-en-Provence, France

Isabel **Da Costa,** Centre d'Etudes de l'Emploi, Noisy-Le-Grand, France

Andy **Danford,** University of the West of England, Bristol, United Kingdom

Michiel **Drucker,** University of Twente, Netherlands

Rosemary **Exton**, The Work Institute, Nottingham Trent University, United Kingdom

Béla **Galgóczi,** European Trade Union Institute, Brussels, Belgium

Francesco **Garibaldo**, Institute for Labour Foundation, Bologna, Italy

Anja **Gerlmaier**, Institute Work and Technology, Gelsenkirchen, Germany

Rainer **Greca**, University of Eichstätt-Ingolstadt, Germany

Annemarie **Holsbo**, Danish Technological Institute, Taastrup, Denmark

Erich **Latniak,** Institute Work and Technology, Gelsenkirchen, Germany

Jan Kees **Looise,** University of Twente, Netherlands

Alma **Mc Carthy,** National University of Ireland, Galway

Juan **Monreal,** University of Murcia, Spain

Kevin P **O'Kelly,** University of Limerick, Ireland

Carmina **Pérez,** University of Murcia, Spain

Ulrich **Pekruhl,** University of Applied Sciences, Solothurn, Switzerland

Wolfgang **Potratz**, Institute Work and Technology, Gelsenkirchen, Germany

Lauge Baungaard **Rasmussen,** Technical University of Denmark, Lyngby, Denmark

Udo **Rehfeldt,** Institut de Recherches Economiques et Sociales, Noisy-Le-Grand, France

Mike **Richardson,** University of the West of England, Bristol, United Kingdom

Giuseppe **Strina,** Institute for Enterprise Cybernetics, Mülheim, Germany

György **Széll,** University of Osnabrück, Germany

Volker **Telljohann**, Institute for Labour Foundation, Bologna, Italy

Peter **Totterdill**, The Work Institute, Nottingham Trent University, United Kingdom

Martin **Upchurch,** University of the West of England, Bristol, United Kingdom

Rainer **Zoll,** University of Bremen, Germany

WORK – TECHNOLOGY – ORGANIZATION – SOCIETY
ARBEIT – TECHNIK – ORGANISATION – SOZIALES

Edited by Wiking Ehlert, György Széll and Heinz Sünker
Herausgegeben von Wiking Ehlert, György Széll und Heinz Sünker

Band 1 György Széll/Wiking Ehlert (eds.): New Democracies and Old Societies in Europe. 2001.

Band 2 Norbert H. Pieper: Arbeitsmarktpolitik in Deutschland und Japan im Vergleich. 1996.

Band 3 Volker Telljohann: Globaler Wettbewerb – lokale Entwicklung. Gewerkschaftliche Konzepte innovativer Industriepolitik zur Nutzung endogener regionaler Entwicklungspotentiale am Beispiel der Erfahrungen im Bereich der Maschinenbauindustrie Bolognas. 1997.

Band 4 Roderick Martin/Akihiro Ishikawa/Csaba Makó/Francesco Consoli (eds.): Workers, Firms and Unions, Part 1. Industrial Relations in Transition. 1998.

Band 5 Martin Schwanholz: Informationstechnologien im Wandel. Marktstrukturen – Aufholprozesse – Wettbewerbschancen. 1998.

Band 6 Klaus Tischler: Betriebliches Umweltmanagement als Lernprozess. Theorie und Praxis organisationsorientierter Umweltbildung als Beitrag zur Steigerung der Fortschrittsfähigkeit der Unternehmung. 1998.

Band 7 Maria Deuling: Qualifikationsanforderungen in den kaufmännischen Berufen. Regionale Arbeitskräftebedarfsanalyse. 1999.

Band 8 Kotaro Oshige: Konvergenz der Interessenvertretungen durch Globalisierung? Ein Vergleich der Funktionsmechanismen der Arbeitnehmerinteressenvertretungssysteme in Deutschland und Japan am Beispiel der Elektroindustrie. 1999.

Band 9 Khaleda Akter Siddiqui: Urban Working Women in the Formal Sector in Bangladesh. 2000.

Band 10 Akihiro Ishikawa/Roderick Martin/Witold Morawski/Veljko Rus (eds.): Workers, Firms and Unions, Part 2. The Development of Dual Commitment. 2000.

Band 11 Karl Bruckmeier/Wiking Ehlert (eds.): The Agri-Environmental Policy of the European Union. The Implementation of the Agri-environmental Measures within the Common Agricultural Policy in France, Germany, and Portugal. 2002.

Band 12 Désirée M. Nana: L'éducation environnementale des enfants et jeunes au Sahel. L'exemple du Burkina Faso. 2001.

Band 13 Wiking Ehlert: Unternehmen und betriebliche Umweltschutzverbände. 2002.

Band 14 György Széll, Dasarath Chetty, Alain Chouraqui (eds.): Participation, Globalisation & Culture. International and South African Perspectives. 2002.

Band 15 Olaf Winkelmann: Entwicklung in der Mitbestimmung - Industrial Relations, Industrial Districts und Netzwerke. Das Beispiel *Betriebsräte-Netzwerk* im Industrial District Ostwestfalen-Lippe. 2002.

Band 16 Thomas Volkening: Ansätze zu organisatorischen Reformstrategien in einem Krankenhaus in kommunaler Trägerschaft. Eine Bestandsaufnahme. 2004.

Band 17 György Széll / Gian Primo Cella (eds.): The Injustice at Work. An International View on the World of Labour and Society. 2002.

Band 18 Lydia Kocar: Globale Ökonomie und nationale Politik. Die Forschungs- und Technologiepolitik der EU. 2003.

Band 19 Heinz Sünker: Politik, Bildung und soziale Gerechtigkeit. Perspektiven für eine demokratische Gesellschaft. 2003.

Band 20 Nicola Bücker: Historische Aspekte und Entwicklungstendenzen des japanischen Beschäftigungssystems. 2003.

Band 21 Faping He: Struktur und Funktionsweise des chinesischen Arbeitsmarktes. Der Gestaltungsprozess des Arbeitsmarktes unter dem wirtschaftlich-sozialen Strukturwandel in der VR China seit 1978. 2003.

Band 22 Thomas Swiderek: Kinderpolitik und Partizipation von Kindern. Im Spannungsfeld von Vergesellschaftung und der Möglichkeit größerer Selbstbestimmtheit, Mündigkeit und dem Erlernen von Demokratie. 2003.

Band 23 Heinz Sünker / Russell Farnen / György Széll (eds.): Political Socialisation, Participation and Education. Change of Epoch – Processes of Democratisation. 2003.

Band 24 Birgit Riße: Mündigkeit in der Postmoderne. Ansatzpunkte und Zielperspektiven von Erwachsenenbildung als Identitätsbildung im Rahmen der gegenwärtigen gesellschaftlichen Wandlungsprozesse. 2004.

Band 25 Francesco Garibaldo / Volker Telljohann (eds.): Globalisation, Company Strategies and Quality of Working Life in Europe. 2004.

www.peterlang.de

FSC
www.fsc.org
MIX
Papier | Fördert
gute Waldnutzung
FSC® C083411

Kolibri 360 GmbH
Ferdinand-Jühlke-Straße 7
99095 Erfurt, Deutschland
produktsicherheit@kolibri360.de

Druck:
CPI Druckdienstleistungen GmbH
im Auftrag der
Kolibri 360 GmbH
Ferdinand-Jühlke-Str. 7
99095 Erfurt